Robotics: Current Advances and Future Prospects

Robotics: Current Advances and Future Prospects

Edited by **Rowland Wilson**

LANRYE INTERNATIONAL

New Jersey

Published by Clanrye International,
55 Van Reypen Street,
Jersey City, NJ 07306, USA
www.clanryeinternational.com

Robotics: Current Advances and Future Prospects
Edited by Rowland Wilson

© 2015 Clanrye International

International Standard Book Number: 978-1-63240-456-5 (Hardback)

Contents

Preface

Technology that deals with the intricacies of designing, constructing, operating and other applications of robots is popularly known as Robotics. Save for the futuristic name that seems to point towards a fictional field, Robotics is largely a field which has been around for quite a few years. Recently grabbing a foothold in the technological industry, the unexplored possibilities are vast. Most ideas about Robotics do seem to revolve around the idea of bio-inspired autonomous machines, the concepts for which hark back to classical times. Much development is still in its rudimentary stages but a field which combines various others like mechanics, metalworking and electronics is bound to be lucrative. Another reason for this rapidly growing field is the possibility of using robots in situations which might be hazardous to human life. Though possibilities are ripe, the market in the present scenario is not really mature enough for the more advanced ideas. The concept of using robots within highly specialized fields like medicine is clear and some machines are already doing work that might not be possible for a human or is too menial, but only in rare occasions. More exposure as well as development is required in Robotics before it inserts itself in our daily lives completely

The book is an attempt to understand the various developmental researches and studies being done in the field of Robotics. I would like to thank those whose works have gone into the making of this book as well as my family and friends for their support.

Editor

Contextual Awareness in a WSN/RFID Fusion Navigation System

Guillermo Enriquez,[1] **Sunhong Park,**[2] **and Shuji Hashimoto**[1]

[1] *Department of Advanced Science and Engineering, Waseda University, 3-4-1 Okubo, Shinjuku, Tokyo 169-8555, Japan*
[2] *Korea Automotive Technology Institute, 303 Pungse-ro, 303 Pungse-ro, Pungse-Myeon, Dongnam-gu, Cheonan-si, Chungnam 330-912, Republic of Korea*

Correspondence should be addressed to Guillermo Enriquez; enriquez@shalab.phys.waseda.ac.jp

Academic Editors: J.-S. Liu and K. Watanabe

We present insight into how contextual awareness can be derived from, and improve, a fusion algorithm combing a WSN and a passive RFID for autonomous mobile robot navigation. Contextual awareness of not where the robot is, but rather the context in which it exists in relation to the environment and human user serves to improve accuracy in navigation, alters the speed of the robot, and modifies its behavior. The WSN system, using a virtual potential field, provides fast general navigation in open areas and the RFID provides precision navigation near static obstacles and in narrow areas. We verified the effectiveness of our approaches through navigational and guidance experiments.

1. Introduction

As robots become more common in our everyday lives, the need for an awareness beyond what simple sensors can detect also grows. While navigation of a mobile robot can be performed with only such data, a behavior that allows it to seamlessly integrate with humans is desirable. In this paper, we present contextual awareness concepts as derived from a wireless sensor network (WSN) and radio frequency identification (RFID) fusion approach to indoor, mobile robot navigation. A WSN-based navigation system allows a robot to move at faster speeds than an RFID-only approach, albeit with reduced accuracy. Conversely, RFID is a well known and utilized technology that can provide high levels of precision, but it requires the robot to move at a slower speed in order to ensure that all tags are read. By combining the two, we have developed a system capable of moving at relatively high speeds when precision is not a priority and slower speeds when the robot is moving in critical areas or higher accuracy is needed. Experiments were conducted with our fusion approach, as well as with an omnivision camera included, to show not only the method's efficacy, but also how the system can be simply further augmented.

1.1. Previous and Related Works. The use of radio-based systems for navigation is a well-developed field, and a WSN can be used in a similar fashion. In [1], a virtual potential field was created by combining information from nodes deployed around the navigable area for an indoor mobile robot. The radio signal strength intensities (RSSI) were combined with that field in order to allow the robot to navigate. In that same system, a servo-mounted camera combined with a CamShift algorithm-based method, [2], allowed the robot to estimate the human's distance and angle relative to the robot. RFID technology is well known in robotic applications involving localization and navigation. A passive RFID-only method was presented in [3] for mobile robot navigation. The locations of previously read tags were combined with those of currently read tags to estimate not only the location, but also the pose of the robot, thereby navigating towards the goal.

Service robotics in general is a growing field, and to increase navigational accuracy, techniques combining image processing systems, laser range finders, sonar sensors, and inertial sensors have typically been proposed [4–7]. These approaches are not without their drawbacks, however. In the case of image processing, computational complexity is always a concern, as is image degradation due to obstacles and ambient light. Distance measuring sensors such as sonar and lasers can also suffer from instability due to anomalies or nonreflective surfaces in the external environment. In order to increase performance, low level sensors such as encoders can also be used. However, they often suffer from some compounding errors, which can lead to poor navigation when the system runs for extended periods of time. Another problem that can arise is that of growing costs. Laser range finders and cameras in particular can be expensive, and when several robots working in the same area are considered, the expense can grow quickly. Instead, creating an infrastructure to which other systems can be added or used in has been proposed [8–10]. By incorporating sensors into the building itself, the robots can be freed to use smaller, less expensive sensors while still performing the same tasks.

Additionally, these aforementioned sensors can of course be used to provide location awareness, or in other words, they provide the robot with a position estimate from which it can make decisions on which action it should take. Contextual awareness, which can of course to a certain extent include location information, goes further by determining how the robot should behave in certain situations, often creating a more natural behavior in terms of integration into environments where humans are living and working. For example, in [11], this concept of a more seamless integration is achieved by allowing the robot to determine contexts based on objects and their affordances through a Bayesian intent recognition system. We do not require such an algorithm to determine context, as at our current stage, we only focused on impacting the navigational behavior based on the context, and so the modifications in behavior are a result of the navigational algorithms. In [12], we see a tour guide robot that develops a context-based map in order to improve the tours provided. Our system does not perform SLAM, and again, it relies on the context to be determined based on the fusion algorithms. Contextual awareness is also useful in applications when a mobile robot is not involved. The system in [13] monitors energy usage in a home to develop certain "Energy-Prone" contexts. This shows how monitoring the human can provide clues on how a system, in our case a guidance robot, can modify its behavior to improve the quality and efficiency of the tasks being performed.

2. Wireless Sensor Network

Originally used in applications involving the collection of data from sensors spread over a large area and still used for various commercial and industrial purposes, wireless sensor network (WSN) technology also provides abilities useful to a mobile robot navigation system, as well as the capabilities for acquisition and monitoring of the surrounding environment. Moreover, being ad-hoc and scalable means that the navigable area for the robot can be simply extended by adding more nodes into the field. For the WSN nodes used in these researches, we utilized Crossbow Technology MICAz MPR2400 Motes, with a Chipcon CC2420, IEEE 802.15.4 compliant transceiver, operating in the 2400 MHz

to 2483.5 MHz band, and an integrated Atmega128L microcontroller.

Much as in [14, 15], we utilize a WSN field to serve as the core of the navigation system, with WSN nodes placed throughout the field in a prescribed way, as determined based on our experience using the system. Nodes are, in general, placed at critical areas such as both concave and convex corners and long straight areas. The location of these nodes is stored in a map, which represents the navigable area of the robot. The map is created before run time and is accessed statically. It is not used in order to perform localization, but rather to determine the direction each node will "suggest" to the robot. The direction the nth node suggests is calculated as a unit vector, $\vec{d}_n$. The direction of $\vec{d}_n$ is first calculated as the direction from the nth sensor to the goal. If an obstacle, such a wall, is detected on the map between the said node and goal along that direction, then the direction is next calculated towards a "safety point", a subgoal which is precoded into the map. These safety points are also determined by the user, but they are generally placed where paths would intersect, such as the center of where two hallways cross. Ideally, the safety points are decided such that there is at least one visible from any node, ensuring a path can be calculated regardless of the goal and the robot's initial position. The nature of the map's encoding allows these checks to be performed using ray tracing, a technique commonly used in graphics programming to determine, for example, the ambient light in a 3D rendered scene. It should be noted that this map is not used to determine the path of the robot expressly; that is, no offline path planning is performed. At run time, the robot only accesses the map in the form of a table, with the nodes listing their suggested directions.

With these directions calculated for each node, the system performs navigation by combining them with weights in a summation. The weights are calculated based on a running average of the radio signal strength intensities (RSSI) of each node. The running average is a set of ten viable RSSI values, as read from messages received by the node mounted on the robot. Here, viable means a signal strength that is determined to be reliable, based on its similarity to the existing values in the set. A running average is maintained for all nodes, and each time the system recalculates the direction the robot should move in, it sorts these values from largest to smallest. Then, the direction the robot will move in, $\vec{V}_{\text{wsn}}$, is calculated by performing vector addition with the nodes having the two largest RSSI averages, as described in (1). While the nature of WSN-based systems and radiowaves in general can make it difficult to accurately estimate a distance based on instantaneously perceived RSSI, there is an analogue to be made between RSSI and relative distance; that is, a shorter distance will result in a stronger RSSI. As such, and by using the running averages, we can assume that in general the two nodes with the highest RSSI averages will be the two closest nodes to the robot. Using (1), we can then create a virtual potential field that will have a trend toward the goal. In the event the goal is set to a node, which is recommended as it results in a more reliable navigation, (2) is used, as the goal's direction cannot point to itself. As we are at this point concerned only with incoming RSSI values, the message content of the WSN is inconsequential. They are programmed to transmit a counter at a rate of twice per second:

$$\vec{V}_{\text{wsn}} = \sum_{n=1}^{2} s_n \vec{d}_n, \tag{1}$$

$$\vec{V}_{\text{wsn}} = \sum_{n=1}^{3} s_n \vec{d}_n. \tag{2}$$

3. RFID System

Often used in robotics applications, radio frequency identification (RFID) systems are a well-developed and widely used technology. Their properties lend themselves well to tasks such as object recognition and tracking as well as navigation. Though there are many permutations, a passive RFID system generally consists of a reader, one or more antennas, a number of tags. For our research we selected the relatively compact and inexpensive Midrange Reader Module made by Texas Instruments which operates in the 13.5 MHz frequency. It also features an anticollision function, which makes it capable of reading multiple RFID tags simultaneously. As we intended to mount our antenna to the underside of the robot, we constructed a circular antenna capable of reading tags within 5 cm, vertically, and 10 cm, horizontally, of the center of the antenna. This was an ideal range for the RFID tags we deployed on the floor of our navigable area. As the robot passes over RFID tags, they are automatically read, and their serial numbers are checked against a table which holds their suggested direction, similarly to how WSN directions are stored. Conversely, RFID tag directions are goal independent, and so their directions are calculated only based on their deployment.

These deployments, presented initially in [14], can be thought of as variations on two basic types, strips and radials. For the researches presented here, we focused on the radial layout, for its versatility. We laid out tags in three concentric arcs, spanning 90° or 270°. The tags are spaced such that they are at most 15 cm apart, in order to ensure the robot will read at least one tag when it is over a deployment. As was said, the direction of each node is determined not by the position of the goal, but rather by the shape of their deployment. This is due to the conceptual difference in the contextual awareness derived from the WSN and RFID systems. The WSN is conceptually pushing the robot toward the goal; however, the RFID system is conceptually pushing the robot away from obstacles. As such, the direction of tags is calculated as vectors emanating away from the center of the circle their arc is from. This means that the calculation is simple once they tag deployments are placed.

4. Approaches to Contextual Awareness

4.1. Contextual Awareness from Relational Position. The main facet of WSN/RFID fusion is how the two incoming signals should be merged to determine the direction the robot should ultimately move in. In general, the system always moves in the direction provided by the WSN; however, when an RFID is read, its direction should be incorporated in order to avoid some obstacles or otherwise to increase precision. When a tag becomes readable, it can be inferred that the robot is near such an obstacle. However, the context of which direction the robot is moving in relation to the said obstacles can be used to improve how the two signals are merged. By comparing the suggested directions of WSN and the RFID, we can determine if the robot is inbound or outbound, to or from the obstacle.

The robot is deemed outbound from an obstacle if the suggested direction of the RFID tag, $\vec{V}_{\text{tag}}$, is within ±90° of $\vec{V}_{\text{wsn}}$, the direction suggested by the WSN. Contextually, we can infer the robot is moving away from an obstacle. As such, the robot is most likely not in immediate danger of colliding with the obstacle, and so the slight modification of the WSN suggestion can be accomplished by performing vector addition with the two suggestions, as described in (3). However, if $\vec{V}_{\text{tag}}$ is not within ±90° of $\vec{V}_{\text{wsn}}$, contextually we can infer the robot is inbound or is approaching an obstacle. In this case, the likelihood of colliding with the obstacle is larger, and so a larger course correction is preferable. To do this, we calculate the two directions perpendicular to the tag's suggested direction and choose the direction that is the closest to the WSN's suggestion. This is more readily understood by considering the suggested directions as numerical angles instead of vectors A_{tag} and A_{wsn}, respectively. These perpendicular angles are compared as in (4). If the comparison in (4) evaluates to true, (5) is used to calculate A_{fusion}. If instead the values are evaluated as true for (6), then (7) is used:

$$\vec{V}_{\text{fusion}} = \vec{V}_{\text{wsn}} + \vec{V}_{\text{tag}}, \tag{3}$$

$$A_{\text{tag}} < A_{\text{wsn}} \le A_{\text{tag}} + 90°, \tag{4}$$

$$A_{\text{fusion}} = A_{\text{tag}} + 90°, \tag{5}$$

$$A_{\text{tag}} \ge A_{\text{wsn}} > A_{\text{tag}} - 90°, \tag{6}$$

$$A_{\text{fusion}} = A_{\text{tag}} - 90°. \tag{7}$$

4.2. Contextually Aware Speed Adjustment. The next form of contextual awareness that can be derived from the WSN/RFID fusion system is an awareness of how quickly the robot should move in relation to critical areas in the field. As has been said, nodes and tags are placed in critical areas, such as corners or near large, static obstacles. As such, when even the closest WSN nodes are deemed to be fairly distant, that is, their RSSI are low, the robot can assume that it is relatively distant from walls and other obstacles. This means the robot can increase its speed, based on the context. By modifying its speed using (8), not only will the robot approach its maximum speed in open areas, but it will also slow down as the RSSI increase, as the context implies that the robot is nearing a critical area and may need to perform some higher precision navigation. The slowing also ensures

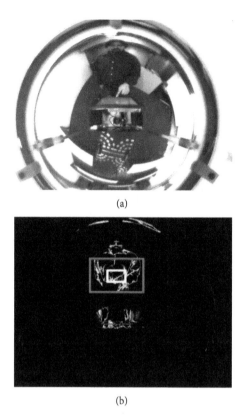

(a)

(b)

FIGURE 1: (a) Raw input image from camera. (b) Image after processing.

RFID tags will not be missed, a common problem with RFID tags if the antenna moves over them too quickly:

$$\text{spd}_{\text{final}} = \text{spd}_{\text{max}} - \left(\text{rssi}_{\text{current}} \frac{\text{spd}_{\text{max}} - \text{spd}_{\text{min}}}{\text{rssi}_{\text{max}}} \right). \quad (8)$$

In (8), $\text{rssi}_{\text{current}}$ represents the highest RSSI of field nodes, spd_{max} and spd_{min} represent the maximum and minimum speeds the robot should move at, rssi_{max} is the maximum value for signal strength expected from the field nodes, and $\text{spd}_{\text{final}}$ is the speed the robot will be set to move at. Although it is rare, it is possible for the RSSI of a node to temporarily spike beyond what the field has displayed previously. The values of spd_{max} and spd_{min} are therefore used to restrict the robot from performing in a manner that could potentially damage it. In the event a tag is read, the robot is set to move at spd_{min}, regardless of what speed the evaluation of $\text{spd}_{\text{final}}$ results in.

The ideal values for spd_{max} and spd_{min}, of course, will depend on the RFID reader, and to some extent the robot platform, used in the system. In order to determine the correct values for our setup, we performed experiments running the robot in a straight line, approaching a WSN node. Along this path, it passed over an RFID tag. We ran the robot at various speeds and tested at which speeds the tag was readable. Based on these experiments, our robot was able to read messages from the WSN at speeds of approximately 42 cm/s, the maximum speed of the robot with its current payload. Predictably, RFID tags became unreadable at this speed. The maximum speed at which a tag was readable was

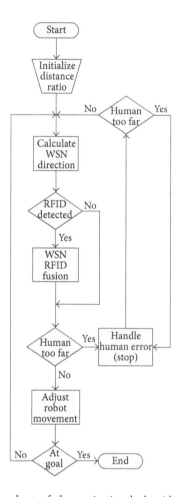

FIGURE 2: Flowchart of the navigational algorithm with WSN/RFID/Cam handling.

FIGURE 3: Chamuko: the robot used in both experiments.

(a)

(b)

FIGURE 4: Experimental space in existing building.

FIGURE 5: WSN node and RFID tag mat inside elevator.

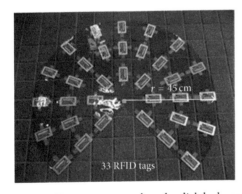

FIGURE 6: RFID tag mat: prepackaged radial deployment.

approximately 17 cm/s. At this speed, however, the tags were only readable about 25% of the time, and we determined this was insufficient as the RFID tags are used to prevent the robot from colliding with large obstacles. In the interest of safety, we set spd_{min} to 8 cm/s.

4.3. Contextual Awareness through Vision Subsystem. When robots are introduced into working and living spaces of humans, their need for contextual awareness becomes more critical. This increasing need for flexibility was one of the aspects we considered in developing this WSN/RFID fusion system, in the form of the ease with which other subsystems could be incorporated into it. For example, in order to extend our navigation robot to the task of a guide robot, we can add a vision system to provide a new level of contextual awareness to the robot. By using an Artray 200MI CMOS camera mounted vertically under a hemispherical mirror, we created an omnicamera capable of viewing the entire 360° area around the robot. Running a modified version of the well-known CamShift algorithm, [2], we could not only track a human user's relative angular position to the robot, but also gain some estimation of the robot's relative distance. As shown in the top portion of Figure 1, the omnivision camera provides a circular view around the robot. The human can be seen interacting with the robot via the touch screen. In the bottom portion, we see the above image after processing. The red, outer frame is the bounding box around the user, in this case, the user's clothes. The yellow, inner frame is the sampling region for the CamShift algorithm. The most basic implementation of the CamShift algorithm works by first selecting a section of a frame, often selected by color, and then creating a bounding box around it which is used to minimize the search area of subsequent frames. This allows tracking to be processed more efficiently, as we are not expecting the human to jump from one side of the robot to the other in an instant. To further improve the performance, we use only the color within the yellow box of the previous frame to search the new area. This allows changes in ambient lighting to occur without the system losing the tracking of the human. As this experiment was conducted in a closed environment with only one user, the color of the user's shirt was sufficient for tracking. As the guidance proceeds and the human's relative distance changes, the size of the outer bounding box will also change; the inner box however remains constant. Continual sampling of the inner frame allows the vision system to continue tracking despite changes in ambient lighting. Based on the ratio, (9), between the current box size, size, and when the human was interfacing with the screen, $size_{init}$, we can also make some contextual inference about how far the human is from the robot and by extension how the human is behaving in relation to, the robot within the context of a guidance task. In this case, we set the robot's speed, spd_{cam}, to zero when the ratio is below some limit, which we determined based on the size of our experimental space.

FIGURE 7: Screen captures of experimental results.

Otherwise, the robot's speed is calculated as described in (8):

$$\text{spd}_{\text{cam}} = \begin{cases} \text{spd}_{\text{final}}, & \dfrac{\text{size}}{\text{size}_{\text{init}}} \geq \text{limit}, \\ 0, & \text{otherwise}. \end{cases} \quad (9)$$

In Figure 2, we see an overview of how the navigation takes place. In practice, the WSN, RFID, and camera subsystems run in concurrent processes on the robot, but their values are evaluated in the order as shown. First,

the navigation begins with the initial ratio being set when the user interacts with the robot to set a goal. Then the navigation proceeds by first calculating the suggested direction of the WSN subsystem after which the presence of RFID tags is checked. If one or more tags are detected, the robot adds the directions of each via the fusion algorithm explained above; otherwise, it skips this step. Finally, before using the new suggested direction to adjust the robot's speed and heading, the relative distance between the robot and human is checked by the vision subsystem. If the human is deemed to be too far as described above, then the process enters a loop until this distance is brought under the threshold. In this simplified example, the robot stops and waits for the human to return, but other behaviors could be performed at this step. After the robot's speed and heading are adjusted, the robot checks if it has reached the goal, in which case it stops and navigation ends; otherwise, it again calculates the direction to the goal and so on.

5. Experimental Validation

In order to demonstrate the efficacy of the proposed methods, we developed two tests: one for the vision and positional context and the other for positional context and speed adjustment. For both experiments, we used a prototype robot platform called Chamuko, Figure 3, which is built upon the MobileRobots Pioneer 3 DX differential drive base. The P3-DX is equipped with sonar and bumper sensors, but neither of them was used. Instead the system relied solely on the system we have presented in this paper. The P3-DX used internal sensors to determine its pose, and a WSN node was mounted to the front bumper to interface with the WSN field. As described above, the RFID antenna was mounted to the underside of the robot chassis. For the first experiment, the omnivision camera was installed on top of the robot, behind the display.

5.1. Experimental Conditions: Speed and Positional Contexts. In this iteration of experiments, we set up our navigation infrastructure in an actual hallway of an existing building. The robot is set at a far end from an elevator, with a relatively wide open area in between, Figure 4. The open area before the elevator was chosen in order to highlight the speed changes as the robot approaches critical areas. Once the robot successfully navigates to the elevator, a tag mat placed in front of the elevator notifies it that it must wait for the doors to open. Once the elevator doors have opened, a WSN node inside the elevator, Figure 5, is sensed by the robot. The signal from the node inside the elevator is blocked completely by the doors, and so is only detectable when the doors are open. This alerts the robot to move forward into the elevator, where the RSSI of the node inside is used to stop the robot. In the second experiment, RFID tags were deployed in 90° arcs. However, as this experiment was not conducted in a controlled environment but rather in a real world setting, we mounted the RFID tags to easily installed vinyl mats, Figure 6.

5.2. Results. In Figure 7, we can see screen captures of an exemplar run of the system. The robot successfully crosses from the hallway to the elevator and then is able to enter once the doors are opened. Figure 8 shows the path taken in the same run. It can be seen that initially the robot moves toward the elevator door, nearly colliding with the wall. However, this is easily corrected by the RFID tag mat that

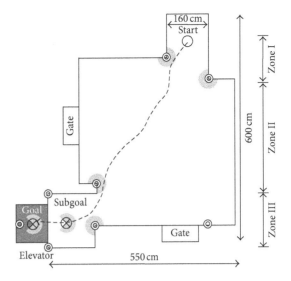

◎ WSN mote
⬚ RFID tag mat

FIGURE 8: Path taken by the robot.

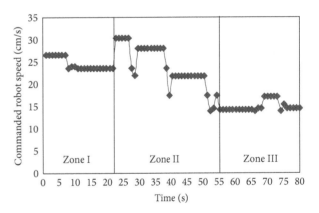

FIGURE 9: Speed adjustment algorithm results over time.

is placed there and the robot smoothly navigates around it to line up with the elevator. After waiting for the doors to open, it then successfully enters and stops inside the elevator. Along the right side of the image, we can three "zones" marked. These relate to the zones marked in Figure 9, a graph showing the robot's rate of speed that was commanded to the robot throughout the navigation. In reality, the robot speed fluctuates when the robot turns, resulting in temporarily slightly lower values than those depicted in the graph. Additionally, the robot comes to a full stop in front of and inside the elevator, which is detected by RFID tags. These are not included into the speed calculation and as such are not reflected in the graph.

5.3. Experimental Conditions: Vision and Positional Contexts. In this experiment, we tested two conditions: could the robot detect when the human stopped following correctly and could the robot use its positional awareness to smoothly

FIGURE 10: Vision and positional context experiment environment.

navigate through a tight space. In a controlled space, we arranged six tables, Figure 10, in staggered sets of two, such that a path between them requires consecutive sharp turns. The gap between a pair of tables was 90 cm, a width that would not be navigable using the WSN alone. Radial deployments of tags were arranged as described above, with an entrance and exit set for each obstacle, resulting in a total of 156 RFID tags being used. Also placed on either side of the entrance to a gap and at the start and goal were 8 WSN nodes. In this experiment, the robot's speed was kept at 12.2 cm/s, in order to ensure all tags were read. To test the contextual awareness of the human's behavior in relation to guidance, the human user intentionally erred in following the robot, failing to turn after passing between the first set of obstacles.

5.4. Results. In the environment described above, we tested the system with both cases; the human following correctly and making an error. In both cases, the robot was able to successfully navigate to goal. It also correctly stopped to wait when the human user did not initially make the turn into the second set of obstacles. In Figure 11, screen captures can be seen of an exemplary run of the system when the human has erred. Figure 12 shows the corresponding path taken by the robot. The curved line represents the path of the robot, and the dashed line shows the error the human makes in following the robot. When the human walked too far, the robot initially continued on, until the distance between them exceeded the threshold and the robot stopped at the point marked by the "X." Once the human returned to a prescribed distance from the robot, it resumed navigation until arriving at the goal. In Figure 13, we can see values estimated from a video recording of the exemplar run. The estimated distance between the human and the robot, blue line, from the same run is depicted. When the human walks straight instead of turning, the distance exceeds the threshold, red line, and the robot comes to a stop, to wait. We can see that once the human's distance comes under the threshold again, the robot proceeds. The green line represents the robot's estimated speed.

6. Discussion on Experimental Results

The focus of this paper was to show the contextual awareness that can be produced from the WSN/RFID fusion navigation approach. Additionally, it was desirable that the system be easily augmented with other systems, as a navigation system is often only one aspect of a robot's task.

The contextual awareness of not precisely how far the robot is from a wall, but rather its approaching of a critical area was also used to adjust the robot's speed. This means that it is not simple location awareness. Looking at Figure 9, we can see a clear pattern as the navigation proceeds. The robot's speed gradually decreases over time, with it mostly moving at its minimum speed in front of the elevator. This is expected, as the area in front of the elevator is a critical area and highly populated with RFID tags. The instantaneous drops in speed visible are caused either by tags being read or the robot slowing itself in order to turn. Using the RSSI of the WSN node inside the elevator, we also showed how the presence of signal, as opposed to the signal itself, can be used to determine a context. In this case, the presence or absence of signal from the WSN node can be used to determine the state of the elevator doors.

In the second experiment, we showed how such an addition of an omnivision subsystem could be used to modify the navigational behavior of the robot. As the robot moved through a series of obstacles, it was capable of integrating the tracking information from the camera, thereby performing actual guidance. That is to say, the robot was able to ensure the human was correctly following it. In Figure 12, the overall smoothness of the robot's path shows that the video system has no effect on the navigation other than to provide a contextual awareness of whether or not the human is following. This seamless integration shows the flexibility of the WSN/RFID system to be combined with other types of sensors or inputs, such as laser range finders or speech recognition systems. Additionally, the contextual awareness of the robots position in relation to obstacles was also shown to be useful in processing the fusion of the respective WSN and RFID signals. While some would argue that this is location awareness, we consider this not to be the case, as the actual location of the tag is inconsequential, but rather the conceptual state of whether it is moving toward or away from an obstacle is what we can derive by comparing the WSN and RFID signals.

7. Conclusion and Future Work

In this paper, we presented contextual awareness as displayed in a WSN/RFID fusion approach to indoor, mobile robot navigation. Capable of providing fast, general navigation in open areas, it can slow down for more precise navigation in narrow spaces. The inclusion of contextual awareness to the WSN/RFID fusion navigational scheme improves the reliability of the system and its ability to incorporate a behavioral pattern into its task. In

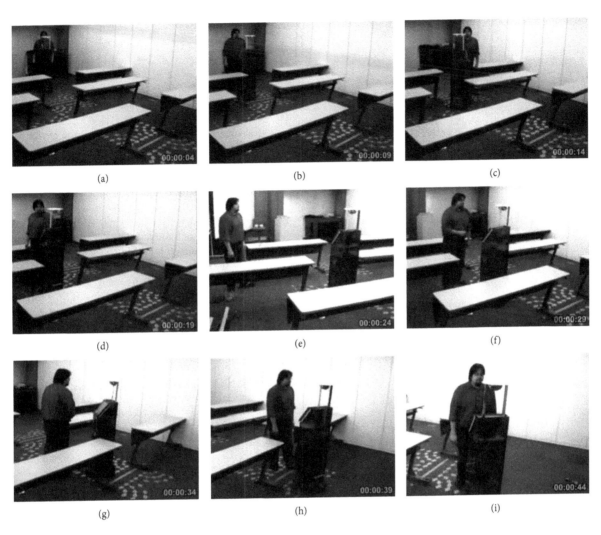

FIGURE 11: Video of experiment when human makes an error.

the experimental evidence, we showed how contextual aware-ness from a new subsystem can easily be incorporated in the form of an omnivision camera subsystem. A 360° area around the robot is monitored using an omnivision camera, and the human user is detected and tracked, allowing the system to be aware of the human's relative distance. With this contextual awareness, the system was able to perform not only navigation, but also true guid-ance, as the robot stopped and waited when the human strayed too far away. In both experiments, the relation between WSN and RFID inputs was used to determine the robot's positional relation to obstacles in the environ-ment. This contextual awareness is used to determine how the inputs should be fused. When a robot is deter-mined to be moving away from an obstacle, it can be assumed that it is not in immediate danger of a colli-sion, and so only a small modification of the WSN's sug-gested direction is sufficient. Conversely, when the robot is approaching an obstacle, a larger modification is nec-essary in order to ensure no collision occurs. The final

contextual awareness presented in this paper is that of adjusting the robot's speed in relation to its distance from nodes. When nodes are relatively far away, it can be assumed that no static obstacles exist near the robot, and so the speed can be increased. Of course, as the robot approaches the nodes, and by extension obstacles, then the system reduces its speed, not only improving handling, but also ensuring that any RFID tags that may exist in the area will be reliably read. These last two capabili-ties are displayed in a second experiment, in which a robot autonomously approaches and then enters an eleva-tor.

The future plans for this system involve the furthering of the system's contextual awareness and its overall usefulness in a number of applications. By including a higher awareness of where the robot is conceptually, we hope to develop methods to further modify the navigation behavior in relation to external stimulus, from not only humans in and around the navigable area, but also from other robots and the environment itself. We also plan to incorporate a method

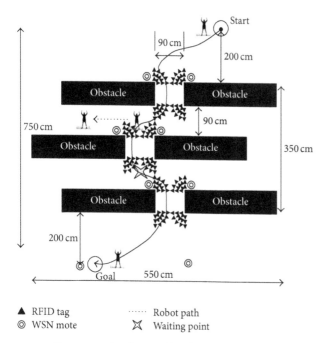

RFID tag — ▲
WSN mote — ◎
Robot path — ·····
Waiting point — ✕

FIGURE 12: Resulting paths of human and robot.

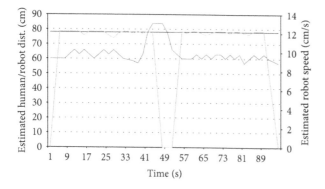

FIGURE 13: Estimated human/robot distance and robot speed over time.

by which WSN and RFID layouts can be automatically determined by software, further simplifying the installation process into existing environments.

Conflict of Interests

The authors declare that there is no conflict of interests regarding the publication of this paper.

References

[1] G. Enriquez, S. Park, and S. Hashimoto, "Wireless sensor network and RFID sensor fusion for mobile robots navigation," in *Proceedings of the IEEE International Conference on Robotics and Biomimetics (ROBIO '10)*, pp. 1752–1756, December 2010.

[2] J. G. Allen, R. Y. D. Xu, and J. S. Jin, "Object tracking using CamShift algorithm and multiple quantized feature spaces," in *Proceeding of the Pan-Sydney area workshop on Visual information processing*, pp. 3–7, 2003.

[3] S. Park and S. Hashimoto, "Autonomous mobile robot navigation using passive RFID in indoor environment," *IEEE Transactions on Industrial Electronics*, vol. 56, no. 7, pp. 2366–2373, 2009.

[4] A. Kelly, "General solution for linearized systematic error propagation in vehicle odometry," in *Proceedings of the IEEE/RSJ International Conference on Intelligent Robots and Systems (IROS '01)*, pp. 1938–1945, November 2001.

[5] A. Motomura, T. Matsuoka, T. Hasegawa, and R. Kurazume, "Real-time self-localization method by using measurements of directions of two landmarks and dead reckoning," *Journal of the Robotics Society of Japan*, vol. 23, no. 3, pp. 39–48, 2005.

[6] J. Hightower and G. Borriello, "A Survey and Taxonomy of Location Systems for Ubiquitous Computing," Technical Report UW CSE, 2001.

[7] J. Minguez, "The Obstacle-Restriction Method (ORM) for robot obstacle avoidance in difficult environments," in *Proceedings of the IEEE IRS/RSJ International Conference on Intelligent Robots and Systems (IROS '05)*, pp. 2284–2290, August 2005.

[8] W. Gueaieb and S. Miah, "An intelligent mobile robot navigation technique using RFID technology," *IEEE Transactions on Instrumentation and Measurement*, vol. 57, no. 9, pp. 1908–1917, 2008.

[9] M. N. Lionel, Y. Liu, Y. C. Lau, and A. P. Patil, "LANDMARC: indoor location sensing using active RFID," *Wireless Networks*, vol. 10, no. 6, pp. 701–710, 2004.

[10] S. Park and S. Hashimoto, "Autonomous mobile robot navigation using passive RFID in indoor environment," *IEEE Transactions on Industrial Electronics*, vol. 56, no. 7, pp. 2366–2373, 2009.

[11] R. Kelley, A. Tavakkoli, C. King, A. Ambardekar, M. Nicolescu, and M. Nicolescu, "Context-based Bayesian intent recognition," *IEEE Transactions on Autonomous Mental Development*, vol. 4, no. 3, pp. 215–225, 2012.

[12] C. V. Smith III, M. V. Doran, R. J. Daigle, and T. G. Thomas Jr., "Enhanced situational awareness in autonomous mobile robots using context-based mapping," in *Proceedings of the International Multi-Disciplinary Conference on Cognitive Methods in Situational Awareness and Decision Support (CogSIMA '13)*, pp. 134–138, 2013.

[13] M. Weng, C. Wu, C. Lu, H. Yeh, and L. Fu, "Context-aware home energy saving based on energy-prone context," in *Proceedings of the IEEE/RSJ International Conference on Intelligent Robots and Systems*, pp. 5233–5238, 2012.

[14] G. Enriquez and S. Hashimoto, "Wireless sensor network-based mobile robot navigation with RFID path refinement," in *Proceedings of the 27th Annual Conference of the Robotics Society of Japan*, pp. 2034–2039, February 2009.

[15] G. Enriquez, S. Park, and S. Hashimoto, "Wireless sensor network and RFID fusion approach for mobile robot navigation," *ISRN Sensor Networks*, vol. 2013, Article ID 157409, 10 pages, 2013.

2

An Improved ZMP-Based CPG Model of Bipedal Robot Walking Searched by SaDE

H. F. Yu, E. H. K. Fung, and X. J. Jing

Department of Mechanical Engineering, Hong Kong Polytechnic University, Hung Hom, Kowloon, Hong Kong

Correspondence should be addressed to H. F. Yu; fai5121988@yahoo.com.hk

Academic Editors: D. K. Pratihar and K. Terashima

This paper proposed a method to improve the walking behavior of bipedal robot with adjustable step length. Objectives of this paper are threefold. (1) Genetic Algorithm Optimized Fourier Series Formulation (GAOFSF) is modified to improve its performance. (2) Self-adaptive Differential Evolutionary Algorithm (SaDE) is applied to search feasible walking gait. (3) An efficient method is proposed for adjusting step length based on the modified central pattern generator (CPG) model. The GAOFSF is modified to ensure that trajectories generated are continuous in angular position, velocity, and acceleration. After formulation of the modified CPG model, SaDE is chosen to optimize walking gait (CPG model) due to its superior performance. Through simulation results, dynamic balance of the robot with modified CPG model is better than the original one. In this paper, four adjustable factors ($R_{\text{hs,support}}$, $R_{\text{hs,swing}}$, $R_{\text{ks,support}}$, and $R_{\text{ks,swing}}$) are added to the joint trajectories. Through adjusting these four factors, joint trajectories are changed and hence the step length achieved by the robot. Finally, the relationship between (1) the desired step length and (2) an appropriate set of $R_{\text{hs,support}}$, $R_{\text{hs,swing}}$, $R_{\text{ks,support}}$, and $R_{\text{ks,swing}}$ searched by SaDE is learnt by Fuzzy Inference System (FIS). Desired joint angles can be found without the aid of inverse kinematic model.

1. Introduction

Recently, many approaches have been adopted for generation of bipedal walking gait. Some researches [1–3] adopted a simplified dynamic model to generate walking gait calculated through inverse kinematic model which is complex and hence the computation load is high.

Inspired by neural science, some researchers investigated central pattern generator (CPG). The prime reason for arousing their interest is that CPG models provide several parameters for modulation of locomotion, such as step stride and rhythm, and are suitable to integrate feedback sensors. Hence, a good interaction between the robot and the environment can be achieved [4]. According to Ijspeert [4], CPG becomes more and more popular in robot community. Taga et al. [5] integrated feedbacks with neural oscillators for unpredicted environment. Yang et al. [6], Shafii et al. [7], and Yazdi et al. [8] utilized TFS to formulate ZMP-based CPG model as the basic walking pattern of bipedal robot. Or [9] presented a hybrid CPG-ZMP control system for flexible spine

humanoid robot. Aoi and Tsuchiya [10] proposed a locomotion control system based on CPG model for straight and curved walking. Farzenah et al. [11] noted that many researches on CPG model are designed for specific motion only and thus cannot generate arbitrary walking gait, such as changing step length and proposed 31 TS-Fuzzy systems for adjusting speed and step length.

Ijspeert [4] and Gong et al. [12] stated that stochastic population-based optimization algorithms have been chosen to optimize parameters of CPG model in many studies. Genetic Algorithm (GA) [6, 13], Genetic Programming (GP) [14], Particle Swarm Optimization (PSO) [7], and Bee Algorithm [8] are adopted in searching the parameters of CPG model. Besides the above-mentioned techniques, there are still other gradient-free optimization techniques. Storn and Price [15] proposed Differential Evolution (DE) and conducted comparisons with some prominent algorithms, such as Adaptive Simulated Annealing (ASA) and the Breeder Genetic Algorithm (BGA). DE outperforms the above-mentioned prominent algorithms in terms of least number of generations for finding global minimum [15]. Similar results are reported in the following studies [16–18]. Hegery et al. [16] carried out comparisons between DE and GA on N-Queen and travelling salesman problem and concluded that the performance of DE is better. Tušar and Filipič [17] carried out comparisons between DE-based variants DEMO and basic GA on multiobjective optimization problem and their result showed that DEMO outperforms basic GA. Vesterstrøm and Thomsen [18] noted that DE outperforms PSO and Evolutionary Algorithms (EAs) on majority of numerical benchmark problems. DE consists of population size (NP), scaling factor (F), and crossover rate (CR) which significantly affect the performance of DE [19–22]. Different problems require different parameters and strategies for effective optimization. Even in the same problem, different regions of search space may require different strategies and parameters for better performance [20]. It is time consuming to search the most appropriate strategy and parameters by trial and error. Hence, Omran et al. [21] and Brest et al. [22] have proposed different methods to adjust CR and F. However, appropriate mechanism for choosing suitable strategies is not considered in [21, 22]. Qin et al. [20] proposed Self-adaptive Differential Evolution Algorithm (SaDE) which can adjust CR, F and choose strategy automatically during optimization. SaDE outperforms conventional DE variants and the other adaptive DE, such as SDE [21] and jDE [22], in terms of higher successful rate.

Based on the above-mentioned findings, this paper focuses on (1) CPG model for trajectory generation and (2) providing an efficient method to adjust step length. In this paper, original CPG model proposed by Yang et al. [6] is adopted since it provides a good foundation for the goal stated in this paper. The angular velocity of trajectories generated by GAOFSF [6] is usually discontinuous which has an adverse effect on ZMP. As a result, GAOFSF is modified to ensure that the trajectory generated is continuous in angular position and its first and second derivatives. After formulation of modified CPG model, parameters of CPG model are searched based on kinematic and dynamic constraints. It shows that the problem can be formulated as a multiobjectives and multiconstraints optimization. Gradient-free optimization technique is chosen since a set of parameters is searched in a highly irregular and multidimensional space which cannot be handled by standard gradient-based search method [12]. SaDE is chosen as the method for optimizing the walking gait of robot in this paper because (1) its performance is superior and (2) appropriate strategies and parameters are not chosen manually. Based on [6, 23], step length can be varied by simply changing several adjustable factors of GAOFSF. Look-up table proposed by Yang et al. [6] is not adopted in this paper because (1) a lot of memory is occupied if tremendous data is stored and (2) arbitrary step length within specific range cannot be commanded to the robot. To deal with this problem, four parameters ($R_{hs,support}$, $R_{hs,swing}$, $R_{ks,support}$, and $R_{ks,swing}$) are added to the modified CPG model and searched by SaD. Four FIS systems are used to learn the relationship between (1) desired step lengths and $R_{hs,support}$, $R_{hs,swing}$, $R_{ks,support}$, and $R_{ks,swing}$. Then, desired joint angles can be found without the aid of inverse kinematics.

TABLE 1: Joint number of support leg and swing leg corresponds to different joints.

Joints of leg	Support leg	Swing leg
Ankle joints	1-2	5-6
Knee joint	3	4
Hip joints	4–6	1–3

TABLE 2: Height of each link in support leg and swing leg.

Link number	Support leg	Swing leg
0	0.026 m	N/A
1	0.04 m	0.028 m
2	0.0645 m	0.0385 m
3	0.0645 m	0.0645 m
4	0.0385 m	0.064 m
5	0.028 m	0.04 m
6	0.096 m	0.026 m

2. Kinematic Model and Dynamic Model of Bipedal Robot

In Figure 1, it shows that the bipedal robot consists of 12 DoF. Each leg has 6 DoF. RL and LL represent right and left legs respectively, while $1, 2, 3, \ldots, 6$ represent joint number. Figure 1 assumes that right leg is the support leg while the left leg is the swing leg. Joint number n of support leg and swing leg corresponds to different joint shown in Table 1. Also, z-axis of local coordinates attached on different joints acts as rotation axis and the direction of rotation is determined by right-hand rule.

Information of physical dimension of bipedal robot is measured and simplified based on a modified Kondo-3HV. The total mass of the bipedal robot is about 1.4 kg. The mass of upper trunk and lower body is about 0.4 kg and 1 kg, respectively. Since the mass of each link in lower body is almost the same, then their masses are simply obtained by $1 \text{ kg}/12 = 0.083 \text{ kg}$. The height of each link is shown in Table 2.

Since Denavit-Hartenberg notation [24, 25] and iterative Newton-Euler dynamic algorithm [26, 27] are maturely developed and commonly used in many studies of bipedal robot, these two methods are adopted to formulate forward kinematic model and inverse dynamic model, respectively, in this paper. Since this paper focuses on bipedal walking on horizontal flat plane in sagittal plane (parallel to the $Y_G - Z_G$ plane of global coordinate), only ZMP_y shown in (1) is considered and acts as an indicator to evaluate the dynamic equilibrium of the bipedal robot. In Figure 2, a local coordinate is attached to the center of support foot to observe the variation of ZMP_y with time.

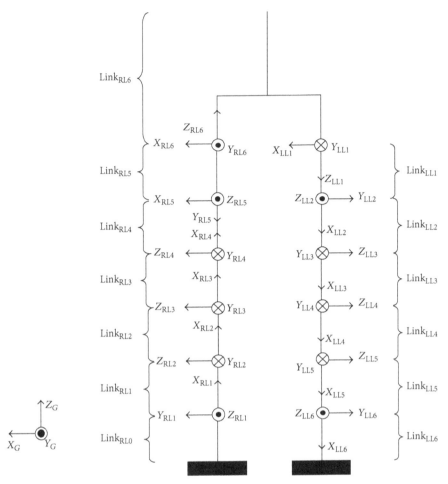

FIGURE 1: Schematic diagram of bipedal robot.

Consider

$$\text{ZMP}_y = \left(\sum_{i=1}^{6} m_{i,RL} \left(\ddot{z}_{i,RL} + g \right) y_{i,RL} + \sum_{i=1}^{6} m_{i,LL} \left(\ddot{z}_{i,LL} + g \right) y_{i,LL} \right.$$

$$\left. - \sum_{i=1}^{6} m_{i,RL} \ddot{y} z_{i,RL} - \sum_{i=1}^{6} m_{i,LL} \ddot{y} z_{i,LL} \right)$$

$$\times \left(\sum_{i=1}^{6} \left(\ddot{z}_{i,RL} + g \right) m_{i,RL} + \sum_{i=1}^{6} \left(\ddot{z}_{i,LL} + g \right) m_{i,LL} \right)^{-1} .$$

$$(1)$$

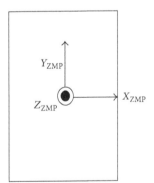

FIGURE 2: Local coordinate system attached on the foot sole (top view).

3. Formulation of Modified ZMP-Based CPG Model

Hip and knee trajectories of GAOFSF [6] consist of two different sections. For hip joint, two different Truncated Fourier Series (TFS) are used to formulate the upper portion (θ_h^+) and lower portion (θ_h^-) of trajectory. For knee joint, TFS and lock phase are joined together to formulate the whole trajectory. Based on Figure 3, the angular position is observed to be continuous. However, angular velocity of searched trajectory generated by GAOFSF is usually discontinuous (1) at the transition between θ_h^+ and θ_h^- (t_3 and t_6 or t_0) and

(2) at the beginning (t_1 or t_4) and the end of lock phase (t_2 or t_5). Abrupt change in angular velocity has an adverse effect on ZMP and hence the dynamic equilibrium of bipedal robot. In this paper, the GAOFSF is modified to ensure that the trajectories generated are continuous in angular position and its first derivative and second derivative. $[t_5, t_2]$ and $[t_2, t_5]$ are regarded as the period of left support phase and right support phase, respectively. Then, t_2 and t_5 are the

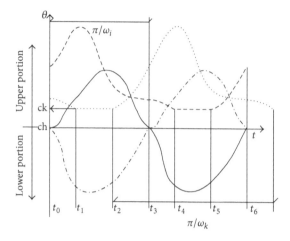

FIGURE 3: General shape of GAOFSF [6].

landing time of left support phase and right support phase, respectively [6]. The time duration $(t_5 - t_2)$ of one step is set as 1 s to ensure a reasonable walking speed. t_2 and t_5 are set as 0.7 s and 1.7 s while t_3 and t_6 are set as 1 s and 2 s. Four different parameters ($R_{\text{hs,support}}$, $R_{\text{hs,swing}}$, $R_{\text{ks,support}}$, and $R_{\text{ks,swing}}$) are added for adjustment of step length. Details of finding the values of these four parameters are discussed in Section 5. In this section, investigation is mainly focused on the formulation of modified CPG model.

3.1. Hip Trajectory in Sagittal Plane.

Since the peaks of θ_h^+ and θ_h^- are different, two different TFS are required to formulate the hip trajectory. Yang et al. [6] have proposed 5th order TFS and showed that the amplitudes of 4th and 5th orders are too small which can be neglected. 3rd order TFS is adopted. In (2)-(3), angular velocity of $\dot{\theta}_h^-$ and $\dot{\theta}_h^+$ at t_3 and t_6 is set as equal to ensure angular velocity is continuous. Thus, two more orders are added to θ_h^- to satisfy this constraint and are calculated by (4)-(5).

Consider

$$\dot{\theta}_h^-(t_6) = \dot{\theta}_h^+(t_6), \tag{2}$$

$$\dot{\theta}_h^-(t_3) = \dot{\theta}_h^+(t_3), \tag{3}$$

$$B_5 = \frac{-(2A_1 + 6A_3 + 2B_1 + 6B_3)}{10}, \tag{4}$$

$$B_4 = \frac{(-A_1 + 2A_2 - 3A_3 - B_1 - 2B_2 - 3B_3 - 5B_5)}{4}, \tag{5}$$

$$t \in [t_0, t_3] \quad \theta_{\text{rhs}} = \theta_h^-(t) \quad \theta_{\text{rhs}} = \theta_h^+(t),$$
$$\tag{6}$$

$$\theta_h^- = \sum_{n=1}^{5} R_{\text{hs,swing/support}} B_n \sin(n\omega_h t) + ch,$$

$$\theta_h^+ = \sum_{n=1}^{3} R_{\text{hs,swing/support}} A_n \sin(n\omega_h t) + ch,$$
$$\tag{7}$$

$$t \in [t_3, t_6] \quad \theta_{\text{rhs}} = \theta_h^+(t - t_3) \quad \theta_{\text{lhs}} = \theta_h^-(t - t_3),$$

$$\theta_h^- = \sum_{n=1}^{5} R_{\text{hs,swing/support}} B_n \sin(n\omega_h(t - t_3)) + ch, \tag{8}$$

$$\theta_h^+ = \sum_{n=1}^{3} R_{\text{hs,swing/support}} A_n \sin(n\omega_h(t - t_3)) + ch, \tag{9}$$

$$\omega_h = \frac{\pi}{t_3 - t_0}. \tag{10}$$

3.2. Knee Trajectory in Sagittal Plane.

In the knee trajectory, Yang et al. [6] proposed a lock phase ($[t_1, t_2]$ and $[t_4, t_5]$) in knee trajectory which assumes constant joint angle and zero angular velocity and acceleration. This introduces abrupt change in angular velocity. The main goals to be achieved in the modified knee trajectory are (1) continuity in angular position, velocity, and acceleration and (2) the advantage proposed in GAOFSF that can be maintained. Then, a new formulation is proposed in the following equation:

$$t \in [t_0, t_2],$$

$$\theta_{\text{lks}} = \sum_{n=1}^{3} R_{\text{ks,swing/support}} C_n \sin(n\omega_k(t + (t_6 - t_5)))$$
$$+ \sum_{n=1}^{N=3} R_{\text{ks,swing/support}} C_n + ck$$

$$t \in [t_2, t_6],$$

$$\theta_{\text{lks}} = \sum_{n=1}^{3} R_{\text{ks,swing/support}} C_n \sin(n\omega_k(t - t_2))$$
$$+ \sum_{n=1}^{N=3} R_{\text{ks,swing/support}} C_n + ck$$

$$t \in [t_0, t_5],$$
$$\tag{11}$$

$$\theta_{\text{rks}} = \sum_{n=1}^{3} R_{\text{ks,swing/support}} C_n \sin(n\omega_k(t + (t_6 - t_5)))$$
$$+ \sum_{n=1}^{N=3} R_{\text{ks,swing/support}} C_n + ck$$

$$t \in [t_5, t_6],$$

$$\theta_{\text{rks}} = \sum_{n=1}^{3} R_{\text{ks,swing/support}} C_n \sin(n\omega_k(t - t_5))$$
$$+ \sum_{n=1}^{N=3} R_{\text{ks,swing/support}} C_n + ck$$

$$\omega_k = \frac{2\pi}{t_6 - t_0}.$$

In (11), lock phase is canceled to ensure continuous angular velocity. By adjusting ck [6], GAOFSF can achieve energy efficient and stable "bent knee" walking gait. This advantage is still remained in the proposed modified model. The general shape of the hip and knee trajectories generated by modified CPG model is shown in Section 6.

3.3. Ankle Trajectory in Sagittal Plane. Right and left ankle joint trajectories are simply formulated as (12) to ensure that the trunk is upright and swing foot is parallel to the horizontal flat plane.

Consider

$$\theta_{as} = -\theta_{hs} - \theta_{ks}. \tag{12}$$

4. Optimization of Basic Walking Pattern by SaDE

This section focuses on how to search the basic walking pattern of bipedal robot by SaDE [19, 20]. To simplify the whole process in this section, $R_{hs,support}$, $R_{hs,swing}$, $R_{ks,support}$, and $R_{ks,swing}$ are set as 1. The following are the main objectives of basic walking pattern to be achieved through using SaDE.

(1) The desired step length is set as 0.05 m.

(2) Upper bound and lower bound of swing height are set as 0.02 m and 0.01 m, respectively.

(3) Premature landing should not occur throughout the walking cycle.

(4) ZMP is within the area of support polygon throughout the walking cycle.

The procedure of SaDE takes the following steps. Also, a flow chart of SaDE is shown in Figure 30 of the Appendix to facilitate the understanding of readers. Details of the procedure are discussed in Sections 4.1–4.7.

(1) Select fitness functions (f_i) and constraints (S_i).

(2) Code the parameters to be searched to form target vector ($X_{i,G}$).

(3) Initialize the first generation (G_1) of population (i).

(4) Initialize crossover rate ($CR_{u_{i,j}}$), scaling factor ($F_{u_{i,j}}$), and probability (P_j) for each mutation strategies (j) based on $\overline{CR}_j$ and $\overline{F}_j$.

(5) Select mutation strategies (j) based on probability (P_j) through MATLAB function rand() and perform mutation operation to generate mutant vectors (v_i).

(6) Perform crossover operation to generate trial vectors (u_i).

(7) Perform selection operation to select next generation of target vectors ($X_{i,G+1}$).

(8) During learning period (LP), record the successful time (ST_j) and failure time (FT_j) of each strategy (j).

(9) During learning period (LP), record values of $CR_{u_{i,j}}$ and $F_{u_{i,j}}$ for each strategy (j) that successfully help the trial vectors (u_i) enter the next generation G_{i+1}.

(10) Upon completion of LP, probability (P_j) for choosing suitable strategies (j) is adjusted based on successful rate of strategy j (SR_j) calculated through ST_j and FT_j.

(11) Upon completion of LP, $\overline{CR}_j$ and $\overline{F}_j$ are adjusted based on the mean values of stored $CR_{u_{i,j}}$ and $F_{u_{i,j}}$, respectively.

(12) Repeat procedures (4)–(11) until maximum generation is completed

4.1. Fitness Functions and Constraints (Step 1). Fitness functions (f_n) and constraints (S_n) are designed or modified based on [6]. Since trunk occupies a large proportion of the whole body mass, abrupt change in trunk velocity can lead to abrupt change in ZMP_y. f_1 is formulated as follows:

$$\overline{V}_{trunk} = \sum_{n=1}^{N} \frac{V_{trunk,n}}{N},$$

$$f_1 = \sqrt{\sum_{n=1}^{N} \frac{\left(V_{trunk,n} - \overline{V}_{trunk}\right)^2}{N}}, \tag{13}$$

where N is number of data.

Strike velocity during landing should be as small as possible since impact between landing foot and the ground can cause mechanical wear of parts and unstable walking. f_2 is stated as follows [6]:

$$f_2 = \sqrt{V_{strike,x}^2 + V_{strike,y}^2 + V_{strike,z}^2}. \tag{14}$$

If ZMP_y is within the area of support polygon [0.061, −0.061] throughout the walking cycle, dynamic equilibrium of the robot is satisfactory. To deal with the discrepancies between simulation model and physical test bed, a safety factor (0.01 m) is added to ensure good performance during experiment. S_1 is formulated as follows:

$$S_1 = \sum_{n=1}^{N} \max\left(\left|ZMP_{y,n}\right| - \left(L_y - \text{safty factor}\right), 0\right), \tag{15}$$

where L_y is length (0.121 m) of foot sole/2.

The robot is assigned to walk forward along positive y-axis. To ensure correct direction, S_2 and S_3 are designed as follows:

$$S_2 = \max\left(-\overline{V}_{trunk,y}, 0\right),$$

$$S_3 = \max\left(-\overline{V}_{swing foot,y}, 0\right), \tag{16}$$

where $\overline{V}_{trunk,y}$ is mean trunk velocity in y-direction and $\overline{V}_{swing foot,y}$ is mean swing foot velocity in y-direction.

To achieve natural human-like walking gait, S_4 and S_5 are designed based on the modified CPG model.

If $t \geq t_0$ && $t \leq t_3$,

$$S_4 = S_4 + \max\left(\theta_{\mathrm{rhs},n} - ch, 0\right)$$
$$+ \max\left(-\left(\theta_{\mathrm{lhs},n} - ch\right), 0\right).$$

Else if $t \geq t_3$ && $t \leq t_6$, $\qquad$ (17)

$$S_4 = S_4 + \max\left(\theta_{\mathrm{lhs},n} - ch, 0\right)$$
$$+ \max\left(-\left(\theta_{\mathrm{rhs},n} - ch\right), 0\right).$$

End

$$S_5 = \sum_{n=1}^{N} \max\left(-\theta_{\mathrm{lks},n}, 0\right). \qquad (18)$$

S_6 is designed to ensure that the robot can achieve desired step length:

$$S_6 = |\text{desired step length} - \text{step length}|. \qquad (19)$$

To ensure reasonable swing height, S_7 is designed to ensure that the swing height is within the $[0.01, 0.02]$ m.

If $\max\left(H_{\text{swing foot}}\right) \qquad (20)$

$\geq H_{\text{lower}}$ && $\max\left(H_{\text{swing foot}}\right) \leq H_{\text{upper}}$,

$$S_7 = 0.$$

Else $\qquad (21)$

$$S_7 = \sum_{n=1}^{N} |H_{\text{desired}} - H_{\text{swing Foot},n}|.$$

End.

S_8 is designed to prevent the swing foot from penetrating through the ground and hence reduce the chance of premature landing while S_9 is designed to ensure swing foot lands on the ground ($H_{\text{ground}} = 0$ m) at landing time which is t_2 and t_5:

$$S_8 = \sum_{n=1}^{N} \max\left(H_{\text{support foot},n} - H_{\text{swing foot},n}, 0\right), \qquad (22)$$

$$S_9 = \left|H_{\text{swing foot},t_2}\right| + \left|H_{\text{swing foot},t_5}\right|.$$

The total scores used for evaluating each target vector ($X_{i,G}$) are formulated as follows:

$$\text{scores} = -1200 + \sum_{i=1}^{N} \omega_{o,n} f_n + \sum_{i=1}^{N} \omega_{p,n} S_n. \qquad (23)$$

These weightings are set by trial and error to ensure their importance is almost the same and walking gait with satisfactory performance can be obtained:

$$\omega_o = [1000, 500],$$

$$\omega_p = [2500, 285, 265, 100, 2200, 12000, 300, 960, 25000],$$
$$\qquad (24)$$

where $\omega_{o,n}$ is weighting of fitness functions and $\omega_{p,n}$ is weighting of constraints.

4.2. Initialization of Parameters of Target Vectors ($X_{i,G}$) (Steps 2 and 3). The target vector ($X_{i,G}$) is formulated as follows:

$$X_{i,G} = [A_1, A_2, A_3, B_1, B_2, B_3, C_1, C_2, C_3, ch, ck]. \qquad (25)$$

Then, the parameters of population (i) are initialized by MATLAB function rand() which generates $[0, 1]$ randomly.

4.3. Initialization of Parameters of SaDE (Step 4). Since the range $[-1, 1]$ of parameters to be searched is small, then population (i) of one generation (G) is set as 30 to balance between good diversity of population and low computation load. Four mutation strategies ($j = 1, 2, 3, 4$) are adopted. For strategy j, MATLAB function *normrnd* (mean value, σ) is used to generate $\mathrm{CR}_{u_{i,j}}$ and $F_{u_{i,j}}$ for each trial vector (u_i). In the initial phase, the crossover rate ($\mathrm{CR}_{u_{i,j}}$) should not be too high to prevent premature convergence while the scaling factor ($F_{u_{i,j}}$) should not be too small to affect the exploration ability. Hence, a moderate value (0.5) is assigned to $\overline{\mathrm{CR}}_j$ and $\overline{F}_j$ (mean value) and σ is set as 0.1. This function can generate random numbers from the normal distribution through mean value ($\overline{\mathrm{CR}}_j, \overline{F}_j$) and standard deviation (σ). P_j is set as 0.25 for strategy j so that each strategy has the equal chance to be chosen during the first learning period:

$$\mathrm{CR}_{u_{i,j}} = normrnd\left(\overline{\mathrm{CR}}_j, \sigma\right),$$
$$F_{u_{i,j}} = normrnd\left(\overline{F}_j, \sigma,\right). \qquad (26)$$

4.4. Mutation Operation of SaDE (Step 5). DE/rand/1, DE/rand/2 and DE/current-to-rand/2 provide good exploration ability while DE/current-to-best/2 demonstrates good convergence speed. To balance between exploration ability and convergence speed, these four strategies are adopted. These four mutation strategies are stated in (27)–(30) as follows:

(1) DE/rand/1,

$$v_{i,G} = X_{r1,G} + F_{i,j}\left(X_{r2,G} - X_{r3,G}\right), \qquad (27)$$

(2) DE/rand/2,

$$v_{i,G} = X_{r1,G} + F_{i,j}\left(X_{r2,G} - X_{r3,G}\right) + F_{i,j}\left(X_{r4,G} - X_{r5,G}\right), \qquad (28)$$

(3) DE/rand-to-best/2,

$$v_{i,G} = X_{i,G} + F_{i,j}\left(X_{\text{best},G} - X_{i,G}\right) + F_{i,j}\left(X_{r1,G} - x_{r2,G}\right)$$
$$+ F_{i,j}\left(X_{r3,G} - X_{r4,G}\right), \tag{29}$$

(4) DE/current-to-rand/2,

$$v_{i,G} = X_{i,G} + F_{i,j}\left(X_{r1,G} - X_{i,G}\right) + F_{i,j}\left(X_{r2,G} - X_{r3,G}\right). \tag{30}$$

4.5. Crossover Operation of SaDE (Step 6). Because of its popularity, binomial crossover operator [20] is utilized in all mutation strategies.

If $\left(\text{rand}() \leq \text{CR}_{i,j}\right) || \left(q == q_{\text{rand}}\right)$,

$$u_{q,i,G} = v_{q,i,G}.$$

Else if $\left(\text{rand}() > \text{CR}_{i,j}\right)$, $\qquad\qquad$ (31)

$$u_{q,i,G} = x_{q,i,G}.$$

End,

where q is the parameter number $(1, 2, 3, 4, \ldots, 11)$ in the target $(X_{i,G})$ and mutant $(v_{i,G})$ vector. Arbitrary parameter number is assigned to q_{rand} to ensure that trial vector $(u_{i,G})$ is different from target vector $(X_{i,G})$. If values of $u_{q,i,G}$ exceed the desired range $[-1, 1]$ of parameters to be searched, $u_{q,i,G}$ is reset by MATLAB function rand ().

4.6. Selection Operation of SaDE (Step 7). If score of trial vector $(u_{i,G})$ is lower than that of target vector $(x_{i,G})$, then trial vector enters the next generation. Otherwise, target vector enters the next generation.

If $\text{scores}_{u_{i,G}} \leq \text{scores}_{x_{i,G}}$,

$$x_{i,G+1} = u_{i,G}.$$

Else $\qquad\qquad$ (32)

$$x_{i,G+1} = x_{i,G}.$$

End.

4.7. Adjustment of P_j, $\overline{CR}_j$ and $\overline{F}_j$ (Steps 8–11). Initially, a learning period (LP = 5 *generations*) is assigned to balance between good sample size of data and update frequency. During learning period, successful times (ST_j) and failure times (FT_j) of each mutation strategy $(j = 1, 2, 3, 4)$ in each generation are recorded. For example, if strategy j is chosen and helps one trial vector $(u_{i,G})$ to enter next generation, then ST_j is added by 1. Otherwise, FT_j is added by 1. Once learning period is completed, P_j is adjusted by the successful

TABLE 3: Lower bound of desired swing height corresponding to different step lengths.

Step length (m)	Lower bound of maximum desired swing height (m)
0.05 m	0.01 m
0.04 m	0.009 m
0.03 m	0.008 m
0.02 m	0.007 m
0.01 m	0.006 m

rate (SR_j). Then, ST_j and FT_j are reset to zero for the next learning period to eliminate effect of the past data:

$$\text{SR}_j = \frac{\text{ST}_j}{\text{FT}_{j,G} + \text{ST}_{j,G}}$$
$$P_j = \frac{\text{SR}_j}{\sum_{j=1}^{N=4} \text{SR}_j}. \tag{33}$$

Similar approach is applied to adjust $\overline{\text{CR}}_j$ and $\overline{F}_j$. During learning period (LP = 5 generations), for strategy j, $\text{CR}_{u_{i,j}}$ and $F_{u_{i,j}}$ corresponding to the trial vectors $(u_{i,G})$ that successfully enters next generation are stored in database. Once learning period is completed, mean value $(\overline{\text{CR}}_j$ and $\overline{F}_j)$ of the stored value corresponding to strategy j is calculated and is used to generate a new set of $\text{CR}_{u_{i,j}}$ and $F_{u_{i,j}}$. Then, storage data of $\text{CR}_{u_{i,j}}$ and $F_{u_{i,j}}$ are removed for the next learning period to eliminate the effects of past data.

5. Optimization of Factors ($R_{\text{hs,support}}$, $R_{\text{hs,swing}}$, $R_{\text{ks,support}}$, and $R_{\text{ks,swing}}$) for Step Length Adjustment

5.1. Objective Functions and Constraints of SaDE. The objective functions and constraints mentioned in Section 4 are adopted to search appropriate value of $R_{\text{hs,support}}$, $R_{\text{hs,swing}}$, $R_{\text{ks,support}}$, and $R_{\text{ks,swing}}$ final corresponding to different desired step length (0.04 m, 0.03 m, 0.02 m, and 0.01 m).

5.2. Lower Bound of Maximum Desired Swing Height. It is natural that the maximum swing height becomes lower to consume less energy if step length is smaller. Lower bound of swing height is reset as lower value for different step lengths (Table 3) while the upper bound (0.02 m) remains the same.

5.3. Smooth Transition of $R_{\text{joint,support/swing}}$. Values of $R_{\text{joint,support/swing}}$ (joint = rhs, lhs, rks, and lks) of support leg and swing leg are different. At the moment of landing time, $R_{\text{joint,support}}$ is changed to $R_{\text{joint,swing}}$ since the support leg is changed to swing leg in the next step. In order to have a smooth transition, fifth order polynomial shown in equation (34) is utilized. The period of transition time $(t_f - t_0)$ is set as 0.4 s which is 40% of time duration (1 s) of one step to balance between rapid transition time and good dynamic equilibrium.

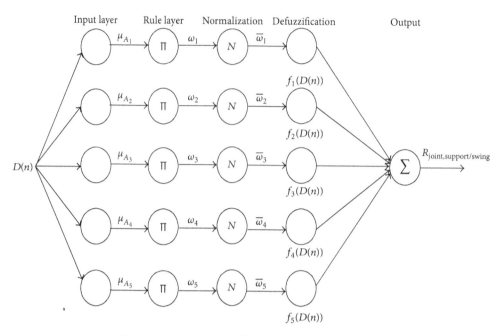

FIGURE 4: Architecture of Fuzzy Inference System (FIS).

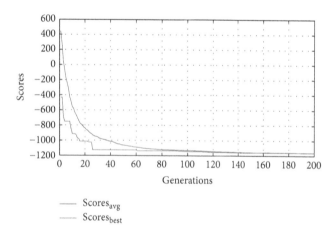

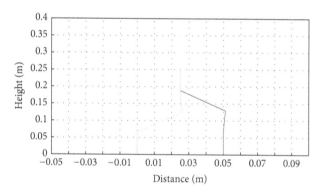

FIGURE 7: The Landing instant of right swing leg (modified CPG Model).

FIGURE 5: Average scores and scores of best target vector of modified CPG model.

TABLE 4: $R_{\text{hs,support}}$, $R_{\text{ks,support}}$, $R_{\text{hs,swing}}$, and $R_{\text{ks,swing}}$ searched by SaDE.

Desired step length (cm)	$R_{\text{hs,support}}$	$R_{\text{ks,support}}$	$R_{\text{hs,swing}}$	$R_{\text{ks,swing}}$
5	1	1	1	1
4	0.8391	0.9419	0.7923	0.9714
3	0.7915	0.8469	0.5576	0.9672
2	0.6090	0.7861	0.3165	0.8709
1	0.4885	0.7157	0.0494	0.7779
0	0	0	0	0

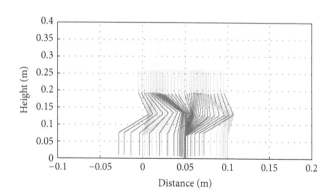

FIGURE 6: Walking gait of modified CPG model searched by SaDE.

Consider

$$R_{\text{joint,support/swing}} = c_0 + c_1 t + c_2 t^2 + c_3 t^3 + c_4 t^4 + c_5 t^5.$$

(34)

TABLE 5: Parameters of FLS tuned by LSE.

	$f_1(D)$	$f_2(D)$	$f_3(D)$	$f_4(D)$	$f_5(D)$
$\text{FLS}_{\text{hs,support}}$	$k_{11} = 6.6435$ $k_{12} = 25.6113$	$k_{21} = -15.4254$ $k_{22} = -17.4962$	$k_{31} = 7.3103$ $k_{32} = 22.3738$	$k_{41} = 7.3103$ $k_{42} = 7.3103$	$k_{51} = -8.2392$ $k_{52} = 13.8564$
$\text{FLS}_{\text{ks,support}}$	$k_{11} = 4.3824$ $k_{12} = 24.6557$	$k_{21} = -9.6047$ $k_{22} = -14.8921$	$k_{31} = 2.6114$ $k_{32} = 15.1129$	$k_{41} = 3.7569$ $k_{42} = -9.1219$	$k_{51} = -5.5025$ $k_{52} = 7.3744$
$\text{FLS}_{\text{hs,swing}}$	$k_{11} = -2.7274$ $k_{12} = -9.6848$	$k_{21} = 5.7349$ $k_{22} = 7.1272$	$k_{31} = -1.2563$ $k_{32} = -7.2583$	$k_{41} = -0.6222$ $k_{42} = 5.9490$	$k_{51} = 3.6331$ $k_{52} = -3.4074$
$\text{FLS}_{\text{ks,swing}}$	$k_{11} = 7.1051$ $k_{12} = 32.6818$	$k_{21} = -16.0968$ $k_{22} = -21.0042$	$k_{31} = 6.2666$ $k_{32} = 24.1201$	$k_{41} = 4.0344$ $k_{42} = -17.0796$	$k_{51} = -9.0802$ $k_{52} = 13.2950$

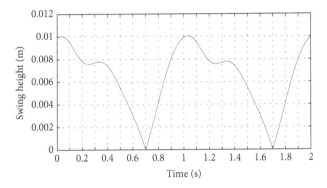

FIGURE 8: Variation of height of swing foot with time (modified CPG model).

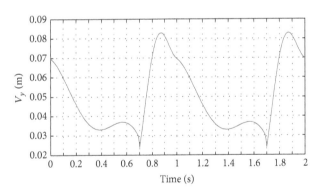

FIGURE 11: $\dot{\theta}_{\text{ks}}$ versus θ_{ks} of modified CPG model.

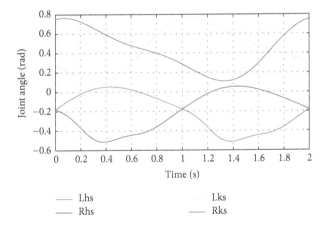

Lhs   Lks
Rhs   Rks

FIGURE 9: Joint trajectories of modified CPG model searched by SaDE.

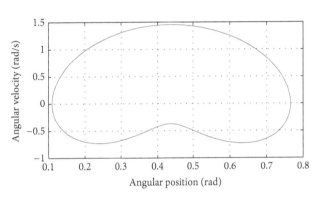

FIGURE 12: Variation of $V_{\text{trunk},y}$ with time (modified CPG model).

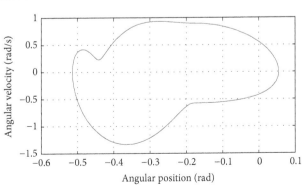

FIGURE 10: $\dot{\theta}_{\text{hs}}$ versus θ_{hs} of modified CPG model.

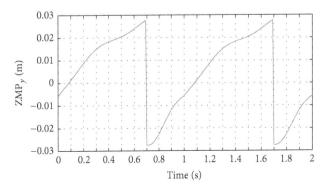

FIGURE 13: Variation of ZMP_y with time (modified CPG model).

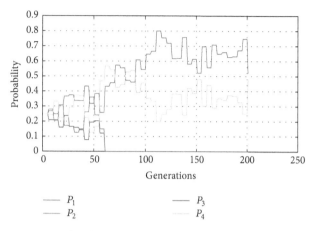

FIGURE 14: Probability of mutation strategy j to be chosen (modified CPG model).

The coefficients of $R_{\text{joint,support/swing}}$ are solved by the following constraints:

$$
\begin{aligned}
R_{\text{joint,support/swing}}\left(t_0\right) &= R_{\text{joint,support/swing,initial}}, \\
R_{\text{joint,support/swing}}\left(t_f\right) &= R_{\text{joint,support/swing,final}}, \\
\dot{R}_{\text{joint,support/swing}}\left(t_0\right) &= 0, \\
\dot{R}_{\text{joint,support/swing}}\left(t_f\right) &= 0, \\
\ddot{R}_{\text{joint,support/swing}}\left(t_0\right) &= 0, \\
\ddot{R}_{\text{joint,support/swing}}\left(t_f\right) &= 0.
\end{aligned}
\tag{35}
$$

5.4. Fuzzy Inference System (FIS). Four FISs are adopted to learn the relationship between (1) $R_{\text{hs,support}}$, $R_{\text{hs,swing}}$, $R_{\text{ks,support}}$, and $R_{\text{ks,swing}}$ and (2) desired step length (5 cm, 4 cm, 3 cm, 2 cm, 1 cm, and 0 cm). The architecture of FIS proposed by [28] is shown in Figure 4. The desired step length $(D(n))$ is the input of FIS while $R_{\text{joint,support/swing}}$ is the output of FIS which is obtained through the summation of $f_m(D(n))$. Based on [24], $f_m(D(n))$ is a function of desired step and can be represented as a first order polynomial stated in (40).

In this section, the membership function (M_m) is set as Gaussian function as follows:

$$
\mu_{A_m} = e^{-0.5((x-c_m)/\sigma_m)^2},
\tag{36}
$$

$$
\omega_m = \mu_{A_m},
\tag{37}
$$

$$
\overline{\omega}_m = \frac{\omega_m}{\sum_{m=1}^{5} \omega_m},
\tag{38}
$$

$$
f_m\left(D\left(n\right)\right) = k_{m,1} + k_{m,2} D\left(n\right),
\tag{39}
$$

$$
R_{\text{joint,support/swing}} = \sum_{m=1}^{5} \overline{\omega}_m f_m\left(D\left(n\right)\right),
\tag{40}
$$

where μ_{A_m} is degree of membership function of M_m, σ_m is parameter that affects the width of Gaussian function of M_m, c_m is parameter that affects the center of Gaussian function of M_m, ω_m is firing strength of rule m, and $\overline{\omega}_m$ is normalized firing strength.

This section focuses on adjusting the consequent parameters $(k_{m,1}, k_{m,2})$ of $f_m(X)$ by least square estimation (LSE) [28] stated in (41). Gradient descent algorithm is not adopted to adjust premise parameters since the size of training data $(N = 6)$ is relatively small. Hence, premise parameters are fixed during the training process. In this paper, c_{1-5} are set as 0.2, 0.4, 0.6, 0.8, and 1, respectively, while σ_{1-5} are set as 0.3. After 50 training cycles, an appropriate set of consequent parameters is found. Details of result in this section are stated in Section 6.

Consider

$$
K^* = \left(U^T U\right)^{-1} U^T Y,
\tag{41}
$$

$$
K^* = \left[k_{1,1};\; k_{1,2};\; k_{2,1};\; k_{2,2};\; \ldots\; k_{5,1};\; k_{5,2}\right],
\tag{42}
$$

$$
U = \begin{bmatrix} \overline{\omega}_1(1) & \overline{\omega}_1(1)D(1) & \overline{\omega}_2(1) & \overline{\omega}_2(1)D(1) & \ldots & \overline{\omega}_5(1) & \overline{\omega}_5(1)D(1) \\ & & & \vdots & & & \\ \overline{\omega}_1(N) & \overline{\omega}_1(N)D(N) & \overline{\omega}_2(N) & \overline{\omega}_2(N)D(N) & \ldots & \overline{\omega}_5(N) & \overline{\omega}_5(N)D(N) \end{bmatrix},
\tag{43}
$$

where D is vector of desired step length and Y is vector of desired output.

6. Results and Discussions

6.1. Scores and Searched Parameters of Modified CPG Model. According to Figure 5, the maximum generation is set as 200. The scores of the best target vector is −1163.5. The values of fitness functions and constraints are [0.018 ms⁻¹,

0.0369 ms⁻¹] and [0 m, 0 ms⁻¹, 0 ms⁻¹, 0 rad, 0 rad, 0 m, 0 m, 0 m, and 0 m], respectively. The searched parameters are [0.2290 0.0257 0.0016 −0.3161 −0.0199 −0.0001 0.2892 0.0861 0.0004 −0.1786 0.0619]. The results show that the modified CPG model can achieve a satisfactory performance.

6.2. Kinematic Aspects of Modified CPG Model. The walking gait searched by SaDE is visualized in Figure 6. Figure 7

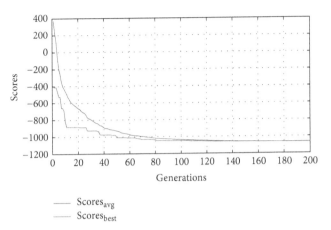

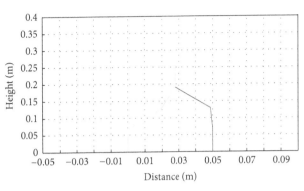

Figure 17: The landing instant of right swing leg (original CPG model).

Figure 15: Average scores and scores of best target vector of original CPG model.

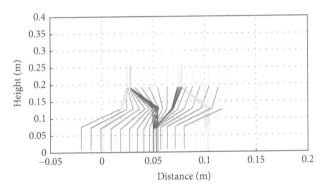

Figure 16: Walking gait of original CPG model searched by SaDE.

shows that step achieved by bipedal robot is the same as the desired step length (0.05 m). In Figure 8, maximum height of swing foot is satisfactory based on Table 3. Swing foot lands on the ground at desired landing time ($t_2 = 0.7$ s and $t_5 = 1.7$ s). The joint trajectories of modified CPG model are shown in Figure 9. Based on Figures 10 and 11, angular position and velocity of each joint trajectory is observed to be continuous and smooth. Because of the heavy trunk mass, abrupt change in $V_{\text{trunk},y}$ should be prevented. From Figure 12, it shows that $V_{\text{trunk},y}$ is continuous and smooth except the landing time.

6.3. Dynamic Aspects of Modified CPG Model.
Figure 13 shows that dynamic equilibrium of the robot is satisfactory since ZMP_y is within the area of support polygon $[-0.061, 0.061]$ m. The length of foot sole is 0.122 m while ZMP_y margin is defined to be (length of foot sole/2) − $\max(|ZMP_y|)$. Based on Figure 13, ZMP_y margin is observed to be at least 0.03 m which is large enough to allow larger step. ZMP_y is smooth and the only abrupt change happens at the landing time ($t_2 = 0.7$ s and $t_5 = 1.7$ s) since ZMP_y shifts to the support foot of the next step at these two moments.

6.4. Observations on Mutation Strategies of SaDE.
During searching parameters of modified CPG model, it shows

that mutation strategy 2 and strategy 3 do not favor for searching feasible walking gait since they are suppressed completely after 60 generations (Figure 14). Figure 5 shows that scores of target vectors tend to converge in the range of generation 100 to 200. Strategy 1 can help trial vector converge faster since it involves the best trial vector in the mutation operation. Hence, from generation 100 to 200, the probability for choosing strategy 1 is always higher than that of strategy 4.

6.5. Results of Original CPG Model.
Except constraint 1, the original CPG model [6] is searched by SaDE under the same setting. Safety factor is set as 0 m since it becomes difficult to search a feasible walking gait for original CPG model if safety factor is set as 0.01 m. Based on Figure 15, the scores of the best trial vector is −1105.9. Also, the searched parameters are [0.0519 0.0012 0.0070 −0.5237 −0.0053 −0.0068 0.3579 0.1459 0.0025 0.0891 0.1736]. The values of fitness functions and constraints are [0.0694 ms^{-1}, 0.0484 ms^{-1}] and [0.0002 m, 0 ms^{-1}, 0 ms^{-1}, 0 rad, 0 rad, 0 m, 0 m, 0 m, 0 m], respectively. Compared with the performance of modified CPG model, the original CPG model is less satisfactory. The walking gait of original CPG model searched by SaDE is visualized in Figure 16. Also, in Figure 17, desired step length (0.05 m) is successfully achieved. In Figure 18, maximum height of swing foot is satisfactory based on Table 3. Also, swing foot lands on the ground at desired landing time ($t_2 = 0.7$ s and $t_5 = 1.7$ s).

The joint trajectories of modified CPG model are shown in Figure 19. Based on Figures 20 and 21, angular velocity of each joint trajectory is observed to be discontinuous. The standard deviation ($\sigma_{\text{original}} = 0.0694$ ms^{-1}) of $V_{\text{Trunk},y}$ is larger than that ($\sigma_{\text{modified}} = 0.018$ ms^{-1}) of modified CPG model. The prime reason is that, in Figure 22, $V_{\text{Trunk},y}$ is observed to be discontinuous because of discontinuity in angular velocity. In Figure 23, obvious abrupt change in ZMP_y is observed. Also, ZMP_y exceeds the area of support polygon ($S_1 = 0.0002$ m). This shows that dynamic equilibrium of bipedal robot is affected by discontinuous angular velocity. Although the area of foot sole can be made larger to tolerate the abrupt change of ZMP_y, the agility of the robot is sacrificed. For the original CPG model, a larger step is not allowed since ZMP_y has exceeded the support polygon when the robot walks with 5 cm step length.

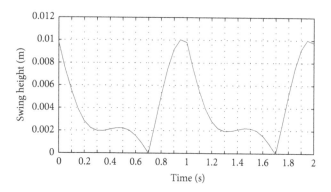

FIGURE 18: Variation of height of swing foot with time (original CPG model).

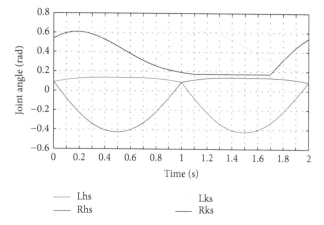

— Lhs   — Lks
— Rhs   — Rks

FIGURE 19: Joint trajectories of original CPG model searched by SaDE.

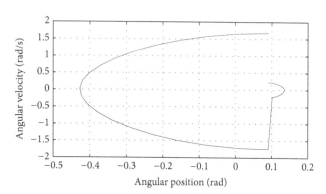

FIGURE 20: $\dot{\theta}_{hs}$ versus θ_{hs} of original CPG model.

6.6. Results of $R_{hs,support}$, $R_{ks,support}$, $R_{hs,swing}$, and $R_{ks,swing}$ Searched by SaDE.

$R_{hs,support}$, $R_{ks,support}$, $R_{hs,swing}$, and $R_{ks,swing}$ searched by SaDE are shown in Table 4. In Figure 24, it shows that the bipedal robot can achieve desired step length (4 cm, 3 cm, 2 cm, and 1 cm). Also, in Figure 25, the maximum swing height corresponding to different desired step length reaches reasonable swing height based on Table 3 and no premature landing occurs during walking.

In Figure 26, ZMP_y is always within the area of support polygon [0.061, −0.061]. Hence, the dynamic equilibrium of

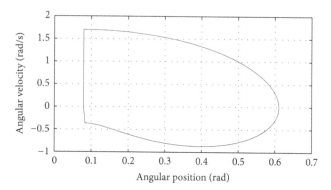

FIGURE 21: $\dot{\theta}_{ks}$ versus θ_{ks} of original CPG model.

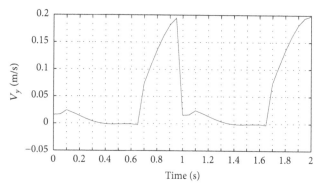

FIGURE 22: Variation of $V_{Trunk,y}$ with time (original CPG model).

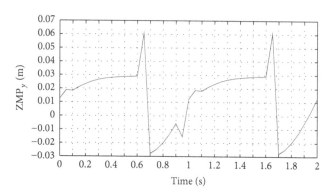

FIGURE 23: Variation of ZMP_y with time (original CPG model).

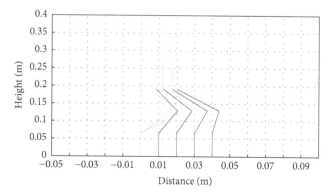

FIGURE 24: Different step length achieved by bipedal robot.

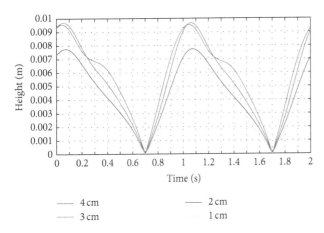

FIGURE 25: Variation of height of swing foot with time (different desired step length).

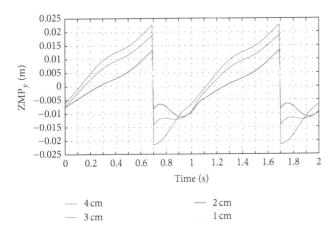

FIGURE 26: Variation of ZMP$_y$ with time (different desired step length).

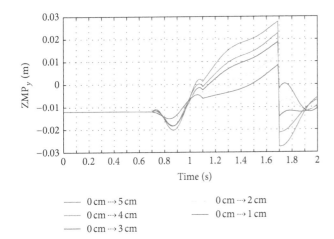

FIGURE 27: Variation of ZMP$_y$ corresponding to different desired step length change.

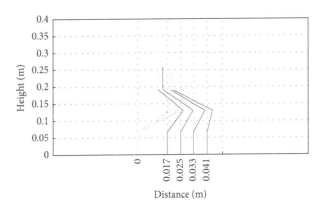

FIGURE 28: Step length achieved by bipedal robot (arbitrary desired step length command).

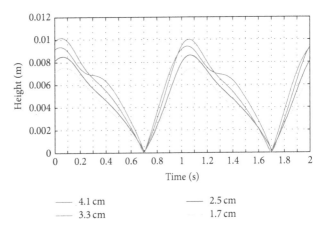

FIGURE 29: Height of swing foot (arbitrary desired step length command).

the robot for different desired step length is satisfactory. Then, an attempt is made to show that when desired step length is adjusted in the next step, ZMP$_y$ can still be maintained within the area of support polygon $[-0.061, 0.061]$. The bipedal robot is at rest initially and is commanded to change its step length at $t_2 = 0.7$ s. In Figure 27, it shows that if change in step length is larger, then change in ZMP$_y$ is larger. It also shows that, in the case of the largest change in step length (0 cm to 5 cm), ZMP$_y$ is still within area of support polygon. Hence, robot can keep its dynamic balance well when desired step length is changed in the next step.

6.7. Relationship between $R_{hs,support}$, $R_{ks,support}$, $R_{hs,swing}$, and $R_{ks,swing}$ and Desired Step Length Learnt by FIS. The parameters of FLS tuned by LSE are shown in Table 5. Arbitrary desired step lengths (0.041 cm, 0.033 cm, 0.025 cm, and 0.017 cm) within a specific range (0 cm–5 cm) are commanded to the robot. In Figure 28, it shows that the robot can achieve arbitrary desired step length successfully. In Figure 29, premature landing does not occur throughout the whole walking cycle. Hence, the relationship between (1) $R_{hs,support}$, $R_{ks,support}$, $R_{hs,swing}$ and $R_{ks,swing}$, and (2) desired step length is learnt successfully.

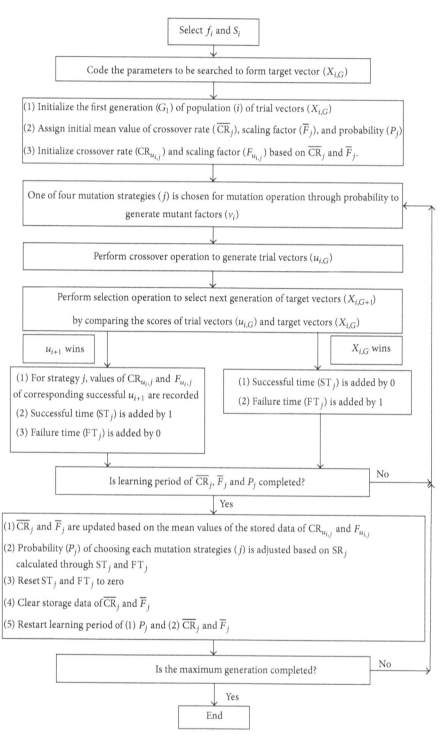

FIGURE 30: Flow chart of SaDE.

7. Conclusions

In this paper, GAOFSF [6] is modified to ensure that trajectories generated are continuous in angular position and its first and second derivatives. Through simulations, bipedal robot with modified CPG model yields better dynamic balance. SaDE is firstly applied to search the parameters of CPG model of bipedal walking. Performance of modified CPG model

searched by SaDE is found to be satisfactory. Four adjustable parameters ($R_{hs,support}$, $R_{ks,support}$, $R_{hs,swing}$, and $R_{ks,swing}$) are added to modified CPG model and searched by SaDE. The robot is able to adjust its step length by simply changing these four factors. Instead of using look-up table [6], the relationship between (1) $R_{hs,support}$, $R_{ks,support}$, $R_{hs,swing}$, and $R_{ks,swing}$ and (2) desired step length is successfully learnt. Simulation results show that the robot is able to walk with arbitrary desired step length within specific range (0 cm–5 cm). The desired joint angles can be obtained without the aid of inverse kinematics.

Appendix

For more details see Figure 30.

Symbols

A, B, C:	Coefficients of truncated Fourier series
CR:	Crossover rate
$\overline{\text{CR}}$:	Mean crossover rate
f:	Fitness functions
F:	Mutation rate
$\overline{F}$:	Mean mutation rate
g:	Gravity
$H_{\text{swing foot}}$:	Height of swing foot
H_{desired}:	Desired height of swing foot
H_{ground}:	Height of ground
m_i:	Mass of link i
M:	Membership function
q:	Gene number $= 1, 2, 3, 4, \ldots, 11$
S:	Constraints
u:	Trial vector
v:	Mutant vector
V_{trunk}:	Velocity of trunk
$\overline{V}_{\text{trunk}}$:	Mean velocity of trunk
V_{strike}:	Velocity of swing foot at landing time
ω_h, ω_k:	Natural frequency of hip and knee trajectory
$\omega_{o/p}$:	Weighting factor of fitness functions/constraints
X:	Target vector
y:	y-Coordinate of CoM of link i
z:	z-Coordinate of CoM of link i
$\ddot{y}$:	Linear acceleration in y-direction at CoM of link i
$\ddot{z}$:	Linear acceleration in z-direction at CoM of link i
R:	Scaling factor of truncated Fourier series
$\theta_{\text{hs/ks}}$:	Hip/knee joint angle in sagittal plane
μ_{A_m}:	Degree of membership function
σ:	Standard deviation.

Conflict of Interests

The authors declare that there is no conflict of interests regarding the publication of this paper.

Acknowledgment

The authors would like to thank the Department of Mechanical Engineering of The Hong Kong Polytechnic University for providing the research studentship.

References

[1] S. Kajita, F. Kanehiro, K. Kaneko et al., "Biped walking pattern generation by using preview control of zero-moment point," in *Proceedings of the IEEE International Conference on Robotics and Automation*, pp. 1620–1626, September 2003.

[2] J.-Y. Kim, I.-W. Park, and J.-H. Oh, "Walking control algorithm of biped humanoid robot on uneven and inclined floor," *Journal of Intelligent and Robotic Systems*, vol. 48, no. 4, pp. 457–484, 2007.

[3] K. Erbatur, O. Koca, E. Taşkiran, M. Yilmaz, and U. Seven, "ZMP based reference generation for biped walking robots," *World Academy of Science, Engineering and Technology*, vol. 58, pp. 943–950, 2009.

[4] A. J. Ijspeert, "Central pattern generators for locomotion control in animals and robots: a review," *Neural Networks*, vol. 21, no. 4, pp. 642–653, 2008.

[5] G. Taga, Y. Yamaguchi, and H. Shimizu, "Self-organized control of bipedal locomotion by neural oscillators in unpredictable environment," *Biological Cybernetics*, vol. 65, no. 3, pp. 147–159, 1991.

[6] L. Yang, C.-M. Chew, T. Zielinska, and A.-N. Poo, "A uniform biped gait generator with offline optimization and online adjustable parameters," *Robotica*, vol. 25, no. 5, pp. 549–565, 2007.

[7] N. Shafii, L. P. Reis, and N. Lau, "Biped walking using coronal and sagittal movements based on truncated Fourier series," in *Proceedings of 14th Annual Robo Cup International Symposium*, pp. 324–335, 2010.

[8] E. Yazdi, V. Azizi, and A. T. Haghighat, "Evolution of biped locomotion using bees algorithm, based on truncated Fourier series," in *Proceedings of the World Congress on Engineering and Computer Science*, pp. 378–382, 2010.

[9] J. Or, "A hybrid CPG-ZMP control system for stable walking of a simulated flexible spine humanoid robot," *Neural Networks*, vol. 23, no. 3, pp. 452–460, 2010.

[10] S. Aoi and K. Tsuchiya, "Adaptive behavior in turning of an oscillator-driven biped robot," *Autonomous Robots*, vol. 23, no. 1, pp. 37–57, 2007.

[11] Y. Farzaneh, A. Akbarzadeh, and A. A. Akbaria, "Online bio-inspired trajectory generation of seven-link biped robot based on T-S fuzzy system," *Applied Soft Computing*, 2013.

[12] D. Gong, J. Yan, and G. Zuo, "A review of gait optimization based on evolutionary computation," *Applied Computational Intelligence and Soft Computing*, vol. 2010, Article ID 413179, 12 pages, 2010.

[13] H. Inada and K. Ishii, "Bipedal walk using a central pattern generator," in *Proceedings of International Congress Series*, pp. 185–188, 2004.

[14] K. Miyashita, S. Ok, and K. Hase, "Evolutionary generation of human-like bipedal locomotion," *Mechatronics*, vol. 13, no. 8-9, pp. 791–807, 2003.

[15] R. Storn and K. Price, "Differential evolution—a simple and efficient heuristic for global optimization over continuous spaces," *Journal of Global Optimization*, vol. 11, no. 4, pp. 341–359, 1997.

[16] B. Hegery, C. C. Hung, and K. Kasprak, "A comparative study on differential evolution and genetic algorithms for some combinatorial problems," in *Proceedings of 8th Mexican International Conference on Artificial Intelligence*, 2009.

[17] T. Tušar and B. Filipič, "Differential evolution versus genetic algorithms in multi-objective optimization," in *Proceedings of*

4th International Conference on Evolutionary Multi-Criterion Optimization, 2007.

[18] J. Vesterstrøm and R. Thomsen, "A comparative study of differential evolution, particle swarm optimization, and evolutionary algorithms on numerical benchmark problems," in *Proceedings of the Congress on Evolutionary Computation (CEC '04)*, pp. 1980–1987, June 2004.

[19] A. K. Qin and P. N. Suganthan, "Self-adaptive differential evolution algorithm for numerical optimization," in *Proceedings of the IEEE Congress on Evolutionary Computation (IEEE CEC '05)*, pp. 1785–1791, September 2005.

[20] A. K. Qin, V. L. Huang, and P. N. Suganthan, "Differential evolution algorithm with strategy adaptation for global numerical optimization," *IEEE Transactions on Evolutionary Computation*, vol. 13, no. 2, pp. 398–417, 2009.

[21] M. G. H. Omran, A. Salman, and A. P. Engelbrecht, "Self-adaptive differential evolution," in *Proceedings of International Conference on Computational Intelligence and Security*, pp. 192–199, 2005.

[22] J. Brest, S. Greiner, B. Bošković, M. Mernik, and V. Zumer, "Self-adapting control parameters in differential evolution: a comparative study on numerical benchmark problems," *IEEE Transactions on Evolutionary Computation*, vol. 10, no. 6, pp. 646–657, 2006.

[23] L. Yang, C.-M. Chew, and A.-N. Poo, "Real-time bipedal walking adjustment modes using truncated fourier series formulation," in *Proceedings of the 7th IEEE-RAS International Conference on Humanoid Robots (HUMANOIDS '07)*, pp. 379–384, December 2007.

[24] C. Hern ndez-Santos, E. Rodriguez-Leal, R. Soto, and J. L. Gordillo, "Kinematics and dynamics of a new 16DOF Humanoid biped robot with active toe joint," *International Journal of Advanced Robotic Systems*, vol. 9, no. 190, 2012.

[25] K.-C. Choi, H.-J. Lee, and M. C. Lee, "Fuzzy posture control for biped walking robot based on force sensor for ZMP," in *Proceedings of the SICE-ICASE International Joint Conference*, pp. 1185–1189, October 2006.

[26] D. Tlalolini, Y. Aoustin, and C. Chevallereau, "Design of a walking cyclic gait with single support phases and impacts for the locomotor system of a thirteen-link 3D biped using the parametric optimization," *Multibody System Dynamics*, vol. 23, no. 1, pp. 33–56, 2010.

[27] A. P. Sudheer, R. Vijayakumar, and K. P. Mohanda, "Stable gait synthesis and analysis of a 12-degree of freedom biped robot in sagittal and frontal planes," *Journal of Automation, Mobile Robotics and Intelligent System*, vol. 6, no. 4, pp. 36–44, 2012.

[28] J.-S. R. Jang, "ANFIS: adaptive-network-based fuzzy inference system," *IEEE Transactions on Systems, Man and Cybernetics*, vol. 23, no. 3, pp. 665–685, 1993.

3

Comparative Study between Robust Control of Robotic Manipulators by Static and Dynamic Neural Networks

Nadya Ghrab[1] and Hichem Kallel[2]

[1] *National Institute of Applied Science and Technology (INSAT), Northern Urban Center Mailbox 676, 1080 Tunis, Tunisia*
[2] *Department of Physics and Electrical Engineering, National Institute of Applied Science and Technology (INSAT), Tunisia*

Correspondence should be addressed to Hichem Kallel; golden.k@gnet.tn

Academic Editors: A. Bechar, A. Sabanovic, R. Safaric, K. Terashima, and C.-C. Tsai

A comparative study between static and dynamic neural networks for robotic systems control is considered. So, two approaches of neural robot control were selected, exposed, and compared. One uses a static neural network; the other uses a dynamic neural network. Both compensate the nonlinear modeling and uncertainties of robotic systems. The first approach is direct; it approximates the nonlinearities and uncertainties by a static neural network. The second approach is indirect; it uses a dynamic neural network for the identification of the robot state. The neural network weight tuning algorithms, for the two approaches, are developed based on Lyapunov theory. Simulation results show that the system response, equipped by dynamic neural network controller, has better tracking performance, has faster response time, and is more reliable to face disturbances and robotic uncertainties.

1. Introduction

Several orders of neural robot control approaches have been proposed in the literature. These approaches are classified into two main classes: direct and indirect neural controls. If it requires prior identification of the controlled process model, it is called indirect control; otherwise it is called direct control. For the direct one, many architectures of control are mentioned in the literature [1–5]. For the second class, we cite neural control via dynamic neural network [6, 7], Model Reference Adaptive Control (MRAC) [8–10], Internal Model Control (IMC) [11–13], and predictive neural control [14, 15]. Both of these control classes are robust thanks to their ability to overcome the nonlinearities and uncertainties in the robot dynamics.

In this paper, the aim is to compare the performance of static neural networks to dynamic neural networks in robotic systems control. For this, two types of control, from the already mentioned, are selected, presented, and tested for a two-link robot. One uses a static neural network; the other uses a dynamic neural network. The first approach is a direct neural control for improvement of a classic controller proportional derivative (PD), proposed by Lewis [1]; it manages to approximate the nonlinearities and uncertainties in the robot dynamics by a static neural network. The second approach is an indirect neural control via a high-order dynamic neural network, proposed by Sanchez et al. [7], which manages to use a dynamic neural network for a dynamic identification of the robot state. Based on simulation results, a comparative study between these two approaches is presented using different performance criteria.

The rest of this paper is organized as follows. Section 2 presents the dynamic model of the robot manipulator. Section 3 describes the direct neural control proposed by Lewis [1]. Section 4 describes the indirect neural control proposed by Sanchez et al. [7]. Section 5 is intended for the simulation results, and a comparative study between the two approaches is mentioned in Sections 3 and 4. And finally, Section 6 draws conclusion and sums up the whole paper.

2. Dynamic Model of the Robot Manipulator

In this section, the dynamic model of the robot manipulator is presented. The equation of the robot dynamics is

$$J(\theta)\ddot{\theta} + h(\theta, \dot{\theta})\dot{\theta} + G(\theta) + F(\dot{\theta}) + \tau_d = \tau. \tag{1}$$

$\theta, \dot{\theta}, \ddot{\theta} \in \mathbb{R}^n$ denote the joint angle, the joint velocity, and the joint acceleration; $J(\theta) \in \mathbb{R}^{n \times n}$ denote the inertia matrix; $h(\theta, \dot{\theta}) \in \mathbb{R}^{n \times n}$ denote the Centrifugal and Coriolis force matrix; $G(\theta) \in \mathbb{R}^n$ denote the gravitational force vector; $F(\dot{\theta}) \in \mathbb{R}^n$ the friction term such as $F(\dot{\theta}) = F_v \dot{\theta} + F_c(\dot{\theta})$ where $F_c(\dot{\theta}) \in \mathbb{R}^n$ is the coulomb parameter; $F_v \in \mathbb{R}^{n \times n}$ the viscous parameter; $\tau_d(t) \in \mathbb{R}^n$ represents disturbances; and $\tau(t) \in \mathbb{R}^n$ is the torque vector.

3. Direct Neural Controller via Static Neural Network

In this section, the approach of direct neural control for improvement of a classic controller proportional-derivative (PD), proposed by Lewis [1], is briefly presented. This approach manages to approximate the nonlinearities and uncertainties, in the robot dynamics, by a static neural network.

To make the dynamic of the robot manipulator, defined in (1), follow a prescribed desired trajectory $\theta_d(t) \in \mathbb{R}^n$; the tracking error $e(t)$ and the filtered tracking error $r(t)$ are defined as follows:

$$e = \theta_d - \theta, \tag{2}$$

$$r = \dot{e} + \Lambda e. \tag{3}$$

$\Lambda > 0$ is a symmetric positive definite design parameter matrix. The dynamic of the robot (1), in terms of the filtered error (3), is as follows:

$$J(\theta)\dot{r}(t) = -h(\theta, \dot{\theta})r(t) - \tau(t) + f(x) + \tau_d(t), \tag{4}$$

where the unknown nonlinear robot function is defined as

$$f(x) = J(\theta)(\ddot{\theta}_d + \Lambda\dot{e}) + h(\theta, \dot{\theta})(\dot{\theta}_d + \Lambda e) + G(\theta) + F(\dot{\theta}), \tag{5}$$

with

$$x = \begin{bmatrix} e^T & \dot{e}^T & \theta_d^T & \dot{\theta}_d^T & \ddot{\theta}_d^T \end{bmatrix}^T. \tag{6}$$

3.1. Approximation of Nonlinearities and Uncertainties by a Static Neural Network. The universal *Function Approximation Property* [16]. Let $f(x)$ be a general smooth function from $\mathbb{R}^n$ to $\mathbb{R}^m$. Then, it can be shown that, as long as x is restricted to a compact set S of $\mathbb{R}^n$, there exist weights and thresholds such that one has

$$f(x) = W^T \sigma(M^T x) + \varepsilon. \tag{7}$$

It is difficult to determine the ideal neural network weights, in matrices W and M that are required to best approximate a given nonlinear function $f(x)$. However, all one needs to know for controls purposes that, for a specified value of Neural Network, some ideal approximating weights exist. Then, an estimate of $f(x)$ can be given by

$$\hat{f}(x) = \hat{W}^T \sigma(\hat{M}^T x). \tag{8}$$

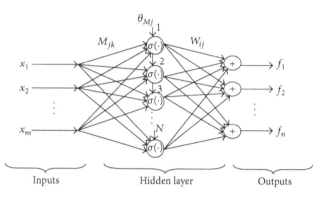

FIGURE 1: The static feed forward neural network architecture.

The neural network architecture, proposed for the approximation of nonlinearities and uncertainties in the robot dynamics, is shown in Figure 1, where $\sigma(\cdot) : \mathbb{R} \to \mathbb{R}$ is the activation functions and N is the number of hidden-layer neurons. The first-layer interconnection weights are denoted by M_{jk} and the second-layer interconnection weights by W_{ij}. The threshold offsets are denoted by θ_{Mj}.

3.2. Synthesis of the Control Law. A general sort of approximation-based controller is derived by setting:

$$\tau(t) = \hat{f}(x) + k_v r(t) - v(t) \tag{9}$$

with $\hat{f}(x)$ being the approximation of $f(x)$ by the neural network, k_v. $r(t)$ an outer PD tracking loop, and $v(t)$ an auxiliary signal to provide robustness. The proposed neural network control structure is shown in Figure 2.

Substituting the control law (9) in (4), the closed-loop error dynamics become as follows:

$$J(\theta)\dot{r}(t) = -(k_v + h(\theta, \dot{\theta}))r(t) + \tilde{f}(x) + \tau_d(t) + v(t). \tag{10}$$

Let us define the functional approximation error are

$$\tilde{f} = f - \hat{f}. \tag{11}$$

The weight approximation errors

$$\widetilde{W} = W - \hat{W}, \qquad \widetilde{M} = M - \hat{M}. \tag{12}$$

The Lyapunov function proposed for the stabilization of the error dynamic is

$$V(r, \widetilde{W}, \widetilde{M}) = \frac{1}{2} r^T J(\theta) r + \frac{1}{2} \text{tr}\{\widetilde{W}^T F^{-1} \widetilde{W}\} + \frac{1}{2} \text{tr}\{\widetilde{M}^T G^{-1} \widetilde{M}\}, \tag{13}$$

with any constant matrices being $F = F^T > 0$ and $G = G^T > 0$.

The robotic system is asymptotically stable if the following conditions, which guarantee $\dot{V}(r, \widetilde{W}, \widetilde{M}) < 0$, are satisfied.

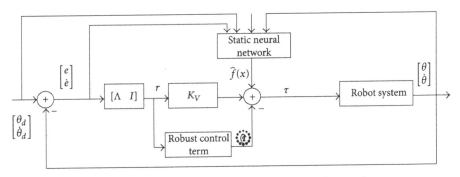

FIGURE 2: Direct neural controller via static neural network.

(i) The neural network weight tuning algorithms are

$$\dot{\widehat{W}} = F\hat{\sigma}r^T - F\hat{\sigma}'\widehat{M}^T x r^T - kF \|r\| \widehat{W},$$

$$\dot{\widehat{M}} = Gx\left(\hat{\sigma}'^T \widehat{W}r\right)^T - kG \|r\| \widehat{M}. \tag{14}$$

With $k > 0$ being a small scalar design parameter and σ' the Jacobian of σ.

(ii) The robustifying term is

$$v(t) = -k_Z \left(Z_B + \|\widehat{Z}\|_F\right) r. \tag{15}$$

With $Z = \begin{bmatrix} W & 0 \\ 0 & M \end{bmatrix}$, $\|Z\|_F < Z_B$ such that Z_B is the bound of ideal weights, $k_Z > 0$ is positive scalar parameter.

(iii) PD controller gain is

$$k_{V\min} > \frac{C_0 + k\left(C_3^2/4\right)}{\|r\|}. \tag{16}$$

In practice, the tracking error can be kept as small as desired by increasing the gain k_v.

4. Indirect Neural Control via High-Order Dynamic Neural Network

In this section, the second approach, an indirect neural control via a high-order dynamic neural network proposed by Sanchez et al. [7], is briefly presented. This approach manages to use a dynamic neural network for the online identification of the robot state.

The proposed neural network control structure is shown in Figure 3.

The equation of the robot dynamics, defined in (1), under state representation is

$$\dot{X} = f(x) + g(X)\tau(t), \tag{17}$$

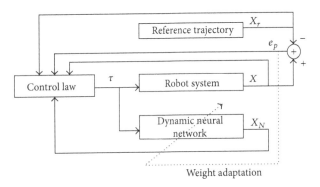

FIGURE 3: Indirect neural control via a high-order dynamic neural network.

with

$$f(X) = \begin{bmatrix} 0 & I \\ 0 & 0 \end{bmatrix} \begin{bmatrix} \theta \\ \dot{\theta} \end{bmatrix}$$

$$+ \begin{bmatrix} 0 \\ -J(\theta)^{-1} \left(h(\theta,\dot{\theta})\dot{\theta} + G(\theta) + F(\dot{\theta}) + \tau_d(t)\right) \end{bmatrix},$$

$$g(X) = \begin{bmatrix} 0 \\ J(\theta)^{-1} \end{bmatrix},$$

$$X = \begin{bmatrix} \theta & \dot{\theta} \end{bmatrix}^T. \tag{18}$$

4.1. Identification of the Robot State by the High-Order Dynamic Neural Network. The proposed neural network structure, for the identification of the robot state, is shown in Figure 4.

$A_N = -\lambda_i I_{2n \times 2n}$ is the state matrix of the neural network with $\lambda_i > 0$ for $i = 1, \ldots, 2n$, $X_N = [x_{N1} \cdots x_{N2n}] \in \mathbb{R}^{2n}$ is the state vector of the neural network, and $\tau(t) \in \mathbb{R}^n$ is the torque vector.

The dynamics of this neural network are resulted by the state feedback X_N around a neural structure formed by two static neural networks RN1 and RN2 shown in Figure 5 [7, 17]:

$$RN1(X_N) = W_f Z(X_N). \tag{19}$$

$W_f = [w_{f1} \cdots w_{f2n}]^T \in \mathbb{R}^{2n \times L}$ is weights matrix of RN1.

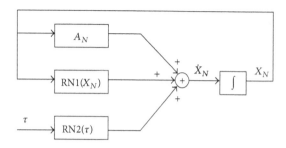

FIGURE 4: The high-order dynamic neural network architecture.

$Z(X_N) = [z_1 \cdots z_L]^T \in \mathbb{R}^L$ is nonlinear operator which defines the high-order connections, z_i are called high-order connections, and L is the number of high order connections.

$z_i = \prod_{j \in I_i} y_j^{d_j^{(i)}}$, $j = 1, \ldots, 2n$; $i = 1, \ldots, L$ and $d_j^{(i)}$ are positive integers, $y_j = \varphi(x_{Ni})$, $i = 1, \ldots, 2n$, $\varphi(\cdot) : \mathbb{R} \to \mathbb{R}$ is the activation function of RN1, here selected as the hyperbolic tangent.

The outputs of RN1 are denoted by $C = [c_1 \cdots c_{2n}]^T$

$$RN2(\tau) = W_g \phi(\tau(t)) = W_g \tau(t). \tag{20}$$

$\phi(\cdot) : \mathbb{R} \to \mathbb{R}$ is the activation function of RN2, here selected as the linear one.

$W_g = [w_{g1} \cdots w_{g2n}]^T \in \mathbb{R}^{2n \times n}$ is weights matrix of RN2. The outputs of RN2 are denoted by $D = [d_1 \cdots d_{2n}]^T$. Let us denote $\widehat{W}_f$ and $\widehat{W}_g$ to be the estimated value, respectively, for the unknown weight matrices W_f and W_g.

The weight estimation errors are

$$\widetilde{W}_f = W_f - \widehat{W}_f, \qquad \widetilde{W}_g = W_g - \widehat{W}_g. \tag{21}$$

The equation of this neural network dynamics is defined by

$$\dot{X}_N = A_N X_N + W_f Z(X_N) + W_g \tau(t). \tag{22}$$

The identification of the robot dynamics by the neural network is ensured by the following pole placement:

$$\dot{X}_N - \dot{X} = -(X_N - X). \tag{23}$$

Equation (23) is equivalent to the following equation:

$$\dot{X} = A_N X_N + W_f Z(X_N) + W_g \tau(t) + (X_N - X). \tag{24}$$

4.2. Synthesis of the Control Law. It is desired to design a robust controller which enforces asymptotic stability of the tracking error between the system and the reference signal. The equation of the reference signal dynamic is

$$\dot{X}_r = f_r(X_r, \tau_r(t)). \tag{25}$$

X_r is the reference signal state vector, $\tau_r(t)$ is the desired torque vector, and $f_r(\cdot)$ is the vector field for reference dynamics.

Let us denote the tracking error between the system and the reference signal to be

$$e_p = X - X_r. \tag{26}$$

To ensure the desired dynamic, the asymptotic stability of the tracking error must be ensured.

The time derivative of (26) is

$$\dot{e}_p = A_N X_N + W_f Z(X_N) + W_g \tau(t) + (X_N - X) - \dot{X}_r. \tag{27}$$

Now, it is proceeded to add and subtract in (27) the terms $\widehat{W}_f Z(X_r)$, $A_N e_p$, $A_N X_r$, and X_r so that

$$\begin{aligned} \dot{e}_p = {} & A_N e_p + W_f Z(X_N) + W_g \tau(t) \\ & + \left(-\dot{X}_r + A_N X_r + \widehat{W}_f Z(X_r) + X_r - X \right) \\ & - A_N e_p - \widehat{W}_f Z(X_r) - A_N X_r - X_r + X_N + A_N X_N. \end{aligned} \tag{28}$$

It is assumed that there exists a function $\alpha_r(t, \widehat{W}_f, \widehat{W}_g)$ such that:

$$\begin{aligned} & \alpha_r\left(t, \widehat{W}_f, \widehat{W}_g\right) \\ & = -\left(\widehat{W}_g\right)^+ \left(-\dot{X}_r + A_N X_r + \widehat{W}_f Z(X_r) + X_r - X \right). \end{aligned} \tag{29}$$

$\left(\widehat{W}_g\right)^+$ is the pseudo inverse of $\widehat{W}_g$ calculated as follows: $\left(\widehat{W}_g\right)^+ = \left(\widehat{W}_g^T \widehat{W}_g\right)^{-1} \widehat{W}_g^T$.

Then, it is proceeded to add and subtract the term $\widehat{W}_g \alpha_r(t, \widehat{W}_f, \widehat{W}_g)$ in (28) so that we obtain:

$$\begin{aligned} \dot{e}_p = {} & A_N e_p + W_f Z(X_N) + W_g \tau(t) - \widehat{W}_g \alpha_r\left(t, \widehat{W}_f, \widehat{W}_g\right) \\ & - A_N(X - X_r) - \widehat{W}_f Z(X_r) + (A_N + I)(X_N - X_r). \end{aligned} \tag{30}$$

Let us define

$$\widetilde{\tau} = \tau - \alpha_r\left(t, \widehat{W}_f, \widehat{W}_g\right) = \tau_1 + \tau_2, \tag{31}$$

so that (30) is reduced to

$$\begin{aligned} \dot{e}_p = {} & A_N e_p + \widetilde{W}_f Z(X_N) + \widehat{W}_f \left(Z(X_N) - Z(X_r) \right) \\ & + \widetilde{W}_g \tau(t) + \widehat{W}_g \widetilde{\tau}(t) - A_N(X - X_r) \\ & + (A_N + I)(X_N - X_r). \end{aligned} \tag{32}$$

Then, it is proceeded to add and subtract the term $Z(X)$ and X in (32) so that we obtain:

$$\begin{aligned} \dot{e}_p = {} & A_N e_p + \widetilde{W}_f Z(X_N) \\ & + \widehat{W}_f \left(Z(X_N) - Z(X) + Z(X) - Z(X_r) \right) \\ & + \widetilde{W}_g \tau(t) + \widehat{W}_g \widetilde{\tau}(t) - A_N(X - X_r) \\ & + (A_N + I)(X_N - X + X - X_r). \end{aligned} \tag{33}$$

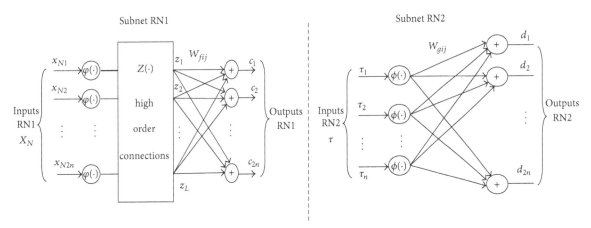

FIGURE 5: The two subnets RN1 and RN2 included in the dynamic neural network.

Then by defining

$$\tau_1 = \left(\widehat{W}_g\right)^+$$
$$\times \left(-\widehat{W}_f\left(Z\left(X_N\right) - Z\left(X\right)\right) - \left(A_N + I\right)\left(X_N - X\right)\right). \tag{34}$$

Equation (33) is reduced to

$$\dot{e}_p = \left(A_N + I\right)e_p + \widehat{W}_f Z\left(X_N\right) + \widehat{W}_f\left(Z\left(X\right) - Z\left(X_r\right)\right)$$
$$+ \widetilde{W}_g \tau\left(t\right) + \widetilde{W}_g \tau_2\left(t\right). \tag{35}$$

Then, the tracking problem is reduced to a stabilization problem of the error dynamics defined in (35).

The Control Lyapunov Function (CLF) proposed for the stabilization of the error dynamics is

$$V\left(e_p, \widetilde{W}_f, \widetilde{W}_g\right) = \frac{1}{2}\left\|e_p\right\|^2 + \frac{1}{2}\operatorname{tr}\left\{\widetilde{W}_f^T \Gamma^{-1} \widetilde{W}_f\right\}$$
$$+ \frac{1}{2}\operatorname{tr}\left\{\widetilde{W}_g^T \Gamma_g^{-1} \widetilde{W}_g\right\}. \tag{36}$$

$\Gamma = \operatorname{diag}\{\gamma_1, \ldots, \gamma_L\}$ and $\Gamma_g = \operatorname{diag}\{\gamma_{g1}, \ldots, \gamma_{gn}\}$ are symmetric positive definite diagonal matrices.

Let us define the function $\phi_Z = Z(X) - Z(X_r)$ and L_{ϕ_Z} to be its Lipschitz constant.

The robotic system is asymptotically stable if the following conditions, which guarantee $\dot{V}(e_p, \widetilde{W}_f, \widetilde{W}_g) < 0$, are satisfied.

(i) The control law τ_2 is

$$\tau_2 = -\mu\left(\widehat{W}_g\right)^+ \left(1 + L_{\phi_Z}^2 \left\|\widehat{W}_f\right\|^2\right) e_p. \tag{37}$$

Optimal with respect to the following cost [18]:

$$J\left(\overline{\tau}\right)$$
$$= \lim_{t \to \infty}\left\{2\beta V + \int_0^t \left(l\left(e_p, \widehat{W}_f, \widehat{W}_g\right) + \tau_2^T R\left(e_p, \widehat{W}_f, \widehat{W}_g\right)\tau_2\right) dt\right\}. \tag{38}$$

(ii) The neural network weight tuning algorithms are

$$\dot{\widehat{w}}_{fij} = -e_{pi}\gamma_j Z\left(X_j\right), \quad \text{RN1 weights tuning algorithm,}$$

$$\dot{\widehat{w}}_{gij} = -e_{pi}\gamma_{gj} \tau_j\left(t\right), \quad \text{RN2 weights tuning algorithm.} \tag{39}$$

(iii) The parameter of the neural network state matrix is $\lambda_i > 1$.

(iv) The parameter which manages the control law τ_2 is $\mu > 1$.

5. Simulation Results and Comparative Study on a Two-Link Robot

In order to test the applicability and compare the performance of the two proposed neural control types, the trajectory tracking problem for a robot manipulators model is considered. The dynamics of a 2-link rigid robot arm on 2D environment, with friction and disturbance terms, can be written as

$$J\left(\theta\right)\ddot{\theta} + H\left(\theta, \dot{\theta}\right) + G\left(\theta\right) + F\left(\dot{\theta}\right) + \tau_d\left(t\right) = D\tau\left(t\right), \tag{40}$$

with

$$J\left(\theta\right) = \begin{bmatrix} I_1 + m_1 k_1^2 + m_2 l_1^2 & m_2 l_1 k_2 \cos\left(\theta_1 - \theta_2\right) \\ m_2 l_1 k_2 \cos\left(\theta_1 - \theta_2\right) & I_2 + m_2 k_2^2 \end{bmatrix},$$

$$H\left(\theta, \dot{\theta}\right)$$
$$= h\left(\theta, \dot{\theta}\right)\dot{\theta}$$
$$= \begin{bmatrix} 0 & m_2 l_1 k_2 \sin\left(\theta_1 - \theta_2\right) \\ -m_2 l_1 k_2 \sin\left(\theta_1 - \theta_2\right) & 0 \end{bmatrix}\begin{bmatrix} \dot{\theta}_1^2 \\ \dot{\theta}_2^2 \end{bmatrix},$$

$$G\left(\theta\right) = g\begin{bmatrix} \left(m_2 l_1 + m_1 k_1\right)\cos\theta_1 \\ m_2 k_2 \cos\theta_2 \end{bmatrix},$$

$$D = \begin{bmatrix} 1 & -1 \\ 0 & 1 \end{bmatrix},$$

$$F\left(\dot{\theta}\right) = \operatorname{diag}\left(2, 2\right)\dot{\theta} + 1.5\operatorname{sign}\left(\dot{\theta}\right). \tag{41}$$

The robot model parameters are shown in Table 1.

The simulations of the variation of positions and torques, exerted at each of the two joints, as well as the weights of the neural network, were carried out over a period of 10 seconds.

The initial conditions are selected as follows:

$$\theta(0) = \begin{bmatrix} 20 & 20 \end{bmatrix}^T, \qquad \dot{\theta}(0) = \begin{bmatrix} 0 & 0 \end{bmatrix}^T. \qquad (42)$$

The reference signal is

$$\theta_d(t) = \begin{bmatrix} 45 & 45 \end{bmatrix}^T, \qquad \dot{\theta}_d(t) = \begin{bmatrix} 0 & 0 \end{bmatrix}^T. \qquad (43)$$

The external disturbances are

$$\begin{bmatrix} 0.1 & -0.1 \end{bmatrix} \quad \text{if } t \leq 1\text{sec},$$
$$\begin{bmatrix} -0.2 & 0.2 \end{bmatrix} \quad \text{if } t > 1\text{sec}. \qquad (44)$$

A variation in the coefficients of viscous friction by an error of 10% at time $t = 1$ sec.

A variation in the masses of the two bodies of the arm by an error of 10% at time $t = 2$ sec.

The neural network controller parameters are selected, for each of the two approaches, as follows.

(i) For the first approach: neural control for improvement of a classic controller proportional-derivative (PD), we have the following.

After several simulation tests, we have found suitable values for the initialization of the weights of the neural network and the various parameters as follows:

$$\mathbf{K_v} = 10 \times I_{2 \times 2}, \qquad \mathbf{K_z} = 0.1,$$
$$\mathbf{Z_B} = 5, \qquad \mathbf{F} = 10 \times I_{6 \times 6}, \qquad (45)$$
$$\mathbf{G} = 10 \times I_{10 \times 10}, \qquad \mathbf{K} = 0.1.$$

The number of neurons in the hidden layer of neural network is $\mathbf{N} = 6$. The activation function sigmoid is $\sigma(x) = 1/(1+e^{-x})$ and its Jacobian is $\sigma'(x) = \text{diag}\{\sigma(x)\} \times [I - \text{diag}\{\sigma(x)\}]$. No initial neural network training phase was needed. The neural network weights were arbitrarily initialized at zero in this simulation.

(ii) For the second approach: neural control via a high-order dynamic neural network, we have the following.

Initial state vector of the neural network is $X_N = [0 \cdots 0]^T$, and the number of high-order connections is $\mathbf{L} = 13$.

The activation function of the subnet RN1 is the hyperbolic tangent $\varphi(X_N) = (e^{2X_N} - 1)/(e^{2X_N} + 1)$.

Let us have: $X_N = [x_{N1} \cdots x_{N4}]^T$

$$N1 = \tanh(x_{N1}), \qquad N2 = \tanh(x_{N2}),$$
$$N3 = \tanh(x_{N3}), \qquad N4 = \tanh(x_{N4}). \qquad (46)$$

So that we define the high-order connections of the neural networks:

$$Z(X_N) = [N1, N2, N3, N4, N1 \times N2, N1 \times N3, N1 \times N4,$$
$$N2 \times N3, N2 \times N4, N3 \times N4, N1 \times N2 \times N3,$$
$$N1 \times N2 \times N4, N2 \times N3 \times N4]^T. \qquad (47)$$

TABLE 1: Parameters of 2-link rigid robot model.

Parameters	Designation	Value	Unit
Length of link 1	l_1	0.25	m
Length of link 2	l_2	0.16	m
Mass of link 1	m_1	9.5	Kg
Mass of link 2	m_2	5	Kg
Position of center of gravity of link 1	k_1	0.125	m
Position of center of gravity of link 2	k_2	0.08	m
Inertia of link 1	I_1	0.0043	Kg·m^2
Inertia of link 2	I_2	0.0061	Kg·m^2
Gravitational acceleration	g	9.8	N·Kg^{-1}

The activation function of the subnet RN2 is the linear function $\phi(\tau(t)) = \tau(t)$.

For this approach, the initialization of neural network weights is not arbitrary and a training phase is necessary.

After several simulation tests, we have found suitable values for the initialization of the weights of the neural network and the various parameters as follows:

$$\mathbf{\Gamma} = 0.01 \times I_{13 \times 13}, \qquad \mathbf{\Gamma_g} = 0.0001 \times I_{2 \times 2},$$
$$\mathbf{\lambda_i} = 300, \qquad \mathbf{A_N} = -300\, I_{4 \times 4}, \qquad (48)$$
$$\mathbf{L_{\phi_z}} = 0.02, \qquad \mathbf{\mu} = 1000.$$

The suitable values for the initialization of the weights are shown in Figure 11.

5.1. Simulation Results of the First Approach of Control: The Neural Control for Improvement of a Classic Controller Proportional Derivative. Each line, that appears in both diagrams of Figure 8, represents one variation of weight value $W_{i,j}$ in the update of weight matrix W or $M_{j,k}$ in the update of weight matrix M.

Analysis Results. The analysis of the simulation results of the response system equipped with NN controller for improvement of a classic controller PD, seen in Figure 6, shows that this control law can satisfy the stability of the system despite the presence of disturbances and robotic uncertainties.

However, due to disturbances and robotic uncertainties, the peak in the torques response makes this control strategy not reliable Figure 7.

5.2. Simulation Results of the Second Approach of Control: The Neural Control via a High-Order Dynamic Neural Network. For this approach, the initialization of neural network weights is not arbitrary and a training phase is necessary.

(i) *The Learning Step.* Each line, that appears in both diagrams of Figure 11, represents one variation of weight value $W_{fi,j}$

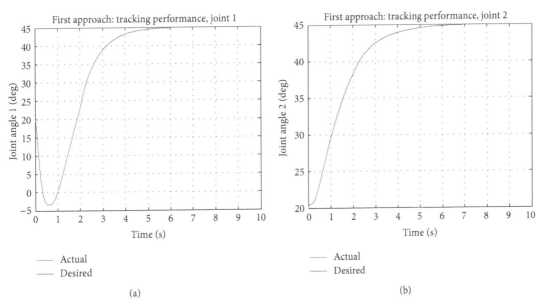

FIGURE 6: Response of joint angles: system equipped with NN controller for improvement of a classic controller PD.

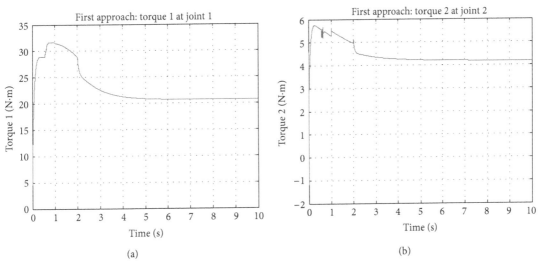

FIGURE 7: Response of torques in joint angles: system equipped with NN controller for improvement of a classic controller PD.

in the update of weight matrix W_f or $W_{gi,j}$ in the update of weight matrix W_g.

Analysis Results. The rigorous peak in the torques and joint angles response, due to disturbances and robotic uncertainties, seen in Figures 9 and 10, was able to be corrected thanks to the neural network adaptation.

At the end of this learning step, the best weight values, seen in Figure 11, are obtained.

(ii) *Final Simulation Results.* The best weights values, obtained in the end of the learning step, are used as initial values for this step.

Each line, that appears in both diagrams of Figure 14, represents one variation of weight value $W_{fi,j}$ in the update

of weight matrix W_f or $W_{gi,j}$ in the update of weight matrix W_g.

Analysis Results. The analysis of the simulation results of the response system equipped with NN controller via a high-order dynamic neural network, seen in Figure 12, shows that this control law can satisfy the stability of the system despite the presence of disturbances and robotic uncertainties.

The learning step is necessary to obtain the best weight values, seen in Figure 11, which represent the true initial weight values.

After the learning step and despite the presence of disturbances and robotic uncertainties, no malfunction was identified in the torques response, seen in Figure 13 (as the peak in the torques response, seen in Figure 7).

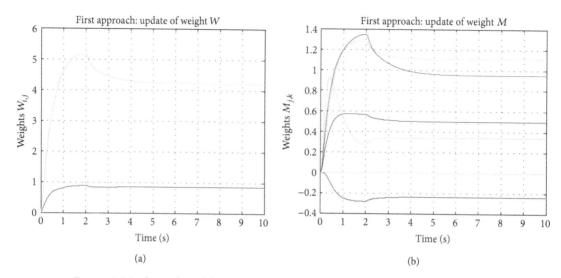

FIGURE 8: Weights update of the NN controller for improvement of a classic controller PD.

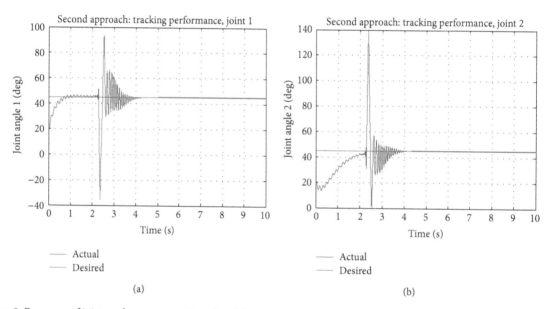

FIGURE 9: Response of joint angles: system equipped with NN controller via a high-order dynamic neural network (learning step).

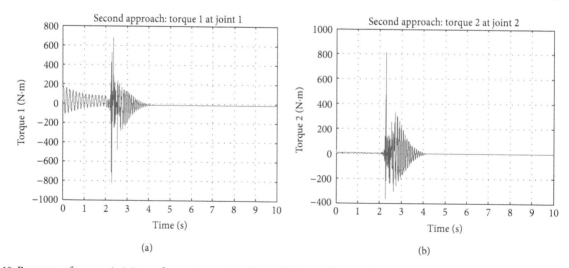

FIGURE 10: Response of torques in joint angles: system equipped with NN controller via a high-order dynamic neural network (learning step).

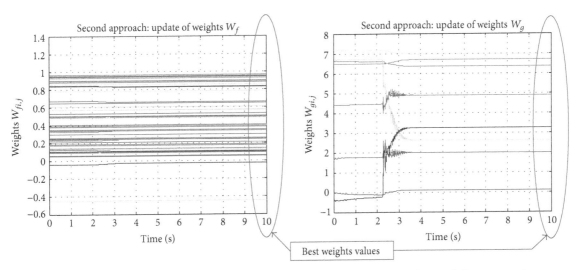

FIGURE 11: Weights update of the NN controller via a high-order dynamic neural network (learning step).

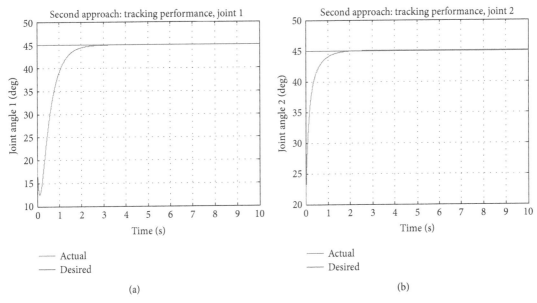

FIGURE 12: Response of joint angles: system equipped with NN controller via a high-order dynamic neural network.

In Figure 14, it is easy to see that weights have really achieved their best values in the learning step and they remain nearly constant.

5.3. Comparative Study. The advantages and limitations of each approach, of neural network control, are presented in Table 2.

The run-time performance of each approach is presented in Table 3.

6. Discussion and Conclusion

In this paper, two approaches of neural network robot control were selected, exposed, and compared. The aim of this comparative study is to find the performance differences between static and dynamic neural networks in robotic systems control. So, one of these two approaches uses a static neural network; the other uses a dynamic neural network. The first approach is a direct neural control for improvement of a classic controller proportional derivative (PD), proposed by Lewis [1]; it employs a static neural network to approximate the nonlinearities and uncertainties in the robot dynamics, so that the static neural network is used to compensate the nonlinearities and uncertainties; therefore it overcomes some limitation of the conventional controller PD and improves its accuracy. The second approach is an indirect neural control via a high-order dynamic neural network, proposed by Sanchez et al. [7]; it employs the dynamic neural network for an exact online identification of the robot state, and then

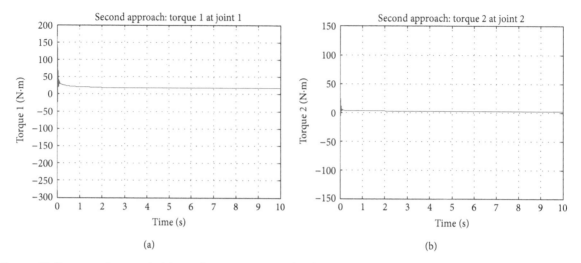

FIGURE 13: Response of torques in joint angles: system equipped with NN controller via a high-order dynamic neural network.

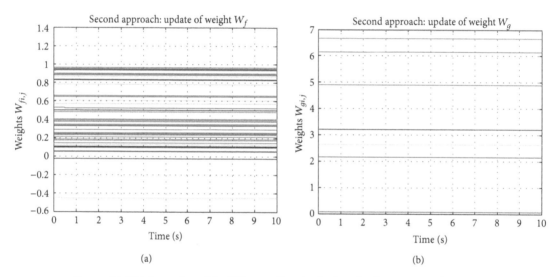

FIGURE 14: Weights update of the NN controller via a high-order dynamic neural network.

TABLE 2: Advantages and limitations of the neural network control approaches.

Control strategy	Advantages	Limitations
NN controller for improvement of a classic controller PD	(i) Initialization of the NN weights is arbitrary (ii) Online learning of the NN (iii) No offline training requirements (iv) Approximation, by the neural network, of the function which gathers the nonlinearities and uncertainties included in the robot dynamics (v) Overcoming some limitation of the conventional controller PD (vi) Guaranteed stability in presence of nonlinearities and uncertainties	No reliable response of the system, seen in Figure 7, due to the peak in the torques response, facesdisturbances and robotic uncertainties
NN controller via a high order dynamic neural network	(i) An exact online identification of the robot state thanks to the dynamic neural network (ii) Guaranteed stability in presence of nonlinearities and uncertainties (iii) Reliable response of the system faces disturbances and robotic uncertainties (Figures 12 and 13)	(i) Initialization of the NN weights is not arbitrary (ii) Offline training requirements to find the suitable initial NN weights values

TABLE 3: Run-time performance of the neural network control approaches (on a time-domain $t = [0-10]$ sec).

Control strategy	Elapsed time (in seconds)
NN controller for improvement of a classic controller PD	45.262542
NN controller via a high-order dynamic neural network	44.088512

it synthesizes the control law from this information recovered by this identification.

Simulation results under the framework MATLAB, of a two-link robot in 2D environment, showed the performance differences between the two neural network control approaches studied. Compared to the control with the static neural network, the neural control via dynamic neural network has significantly better tracking performance, has faster response time and is more reliable to face disturbances and robotic uncertainties. However, the indirect approach requires offline training to find the suitable initial neural network weights values, contrarily to the direct one in which the initialization of the neural network weights is arbitrary.

Although it is clear that further experimentation needs to take place, simulation results presented here indicate that dynamic neural networks have demonstrated a very good potential for applications in closed loop control of robot manipulators.

References

[1] F. L. Lewis, "Neural network control of robot manipulators," *IEEE Expert*, vol. 11, no. 3, pp. 64–75, 1996.

[2] W. Zhang, N. Qi, and H. Yin, "PD control of robot manipulators with uncertainties based on neural network," in *Proceedings of the International Conference on Intelligent Computation Technology and Automation (ICICTA '10)*, pp. 884–888, May 2010.

[3] Y. H. Kim, F. L. Lewis, and D. M. Dawson, "Intelligent optimal control of robotic manipulators using neural networks," *Automatica*, vol. 36, no. 9, pp. 1355–1364, 2000.

[4] Z. Tang, M. Yang, and Z. Pei, "Self-Adaptive PID control strategy based on RBF neural network for robot manipulator," in *Proceedings of the 1st International Conference on Pervasive Computing, Signal Processing and Applications (PCSPA '10)*, pp. 932–935, September 2010.

[5] D. Popescu, D. Selisteanu, and L. Popescu, "Neural and adaptive control of a rigid link manipulator," *WSEAS Transactions on Systems*, vol. 7, no. 6, pp. 632–641, 2008.

[6] M. A. Brdys and G. J. Kulawski, "Stable adaptive control with recurrent networks," *Automatica*, vol. 36, no. 1, pp. 5–22, 2000.

[7] E. N. Sanchez, L. J. Ricalde, R. Langari, and D. Shahmirzadi, "Rollover control in heavy vehicles via recurrent high order neural networks," in *Recurrent Neural Networks*, X. Hu and P. Balasubramaniam, Eds., Vienna, Austria, 2008.

[8] F. G. Rossomando, C. Soria, D. Patino, and R. Carelli, "Model reference adaptive control for mobile robots in trajectory tracking using radial basis function neural networks," *Latin American Applied Research*, vol. 41, no. 2, 2010.

[9] Z. Pei, Y. Zhang, and Z. Tang, "Model reference adaptive PID control of hydraulic parallel robot based on RBF neural network," in *Proceedings of the IEEE International Conference on Robotics and Biomimetics (ROBIO '07)*, pp. 1383–1387, December 2007.

[10] M. G. Zhang and W. H. Li, "Single neuron PID model reference adaptive control based on RBF neural network," in *Proceedings of the International Conference on Machine Learning and Cybernetics*, pp. 3021–3025, August 2006.

[11] H. X. Li and H. Deng, "An approximate internal model-based neural control for unknown nonlinear discrete processes," *IEEE Transactions on Neural Networks*, vol. 17, no. 3, pp. 659–670, 2006.

[12] I. Rivals and L. Personnaz, "Nonlinear internal model control using neural networks: application to processes with delay and design issues," *IEEE Transactions on Neural Networks*, vol. 11, no. 1, pp. 80–90, 2000.

[13] C. Kambhampati, R. J. Craddock, M. Tham, and K. Warwick, "Inverse model control using recurrent networks," *Mathematics and Computers in Simulation*, vol. 51, no. 3-4, pp. 181–199, 2000.

[14] M. Wang, J. Yu, M. Tan, and Q. Yang, "Back-propagation neural network based predictive control for biomimetic robotic fish," in *Proceedings of the 27th Chinese Control Conference (CCC '08)*, pp. 430–434, July 2008.

[15] K. Kara, T. E. Missoum, K. E. Hemsas, and M. L. Hadjili, "Control of a robotic manipulator using neural network based predictive control," in *Proceedings of the 17th IEEE International Conference on Electronics, Circuits, and Systems (ICECS '10)*, pp. 1104–1107, December 2010.

[16] S. Ferrari and R. F. Stengel, "Smooth function approximation using neural networks," *IEEE Transactions on Neural Networks*, vol. 16, no. 1, pp. 24–38, 2005.

[17] E. B. Kosmatopoulos, M. A. Christodoulou, and P. A. Ioannou, "Dynamical neural networks that ensure exponential identification error convergence," *Neural Networks*, vol. 10, no. 2, pp. 299–314, 1997.

[18] E. N. Sanchez, J. P. Perez, and L. Ricalde, "Recurrent neural control for robot trajectory tracking," in *Proceedings of the 15th World Congress International Federation of Automatic Control*, Barcelona, Spain, July 2002.

An Adaptive H^∞-Based Formation Control for Multirobot Systems

Faridoon Shabani, Bijan Ranjbar, and Ali Ghadamyari

School of Electrical Engineering, Shiraz University, Shiraz, Iran

Correspondence should be addressed to Faridoon Shabani; shabani@shirazu.ac.ir

Academic Editors: J. B. Koeneman and G. S. Virk

We describe a decentralized formation problem for multiple robots, where an H^∞ formation controller is proposed. The network of dynamic agents with external disturbances and uncertainties are discussed in formation problems. We first describe how to design social potential fields to obtain a formation with the shape of a polygon. Then, we provide a formal proof of the asymptotic stability of the system, based on the definition of a proper Lyapunov function and H^∞ technique. The advantages of the proposed controller can be listed as robustness to input nonlinearity, external disturbances, and model uncertainties, while applicability on a group of any autonomous systems with n-degrees of freedom. Finally, simulation results are demonstrated for a multiagent formation problem of a group of six robots, illustrating the effective attenuation of approximation error and external disturbances, even in the case of agent failure or leader tracking.

1. Introduction

All around the world, nature presents examples of collective behavior in groups of insects, birds, and fishes. This behavior has produced sophisticated functions of the group that cannot be achieved by individual members [1, 2]. Therefore, the research on the coordination of robotic swarms has attracted considerable attention. Taking the advantages of distributed sensing and actuation, a robotic swarm can perform some cooperative tasks such as moving a large object that is usually not executable by a single robot [3–7]. Applications about the analysis and design of robotic swarms included autonomous unmanned aerial vehicles, congestion control of communication networks, and distributed sensor networks autonomous, and so forth [1, 2, 8–10].

In general, a robotic formation problem is defined as the organization of a swarm of agents into a particular shape in a 2D or 3D space [8]. This kind of control strategy can be applied into several different fields. For example, in the industrial field, this formation control strategy can be applied to a group of Automated Guided Vehicles (AGVs) moving in a warehouse for goods delivery. The main idea is to make a group of AGVs cooperatively deliver a certain amount of goods, moving in a formation. The creation of a formation with the desired shape is useful to precisely constrain the action zone of the AGVs, thus reducing the chance of collisions with other entities (e.g., human guided vehicles).

In the literature, many different approaches to formation control can be found. The main existing approaches can be divided into two categories: centralized [11] and distributed [12]. Because of the intrinsic unreliability of centralized methods, we focus our attention to distributed ones: all the agents are equal, and if one of them stops working, the other ones can still complete their task. Several formation control strategies can be found as potential fields [8], behavior-based [13], leader-following [14–16], graph-theoretic [12], and virtual structure approaches [17, 18].

In recent years, some methods based on potential fields are integrated with some nonlinear control schemes such as feedback linearization method (e.g., Sliding Mode Control (SMC)), which concludes in more robust formation control designs of dynamic agents [15–18]. For example, Takahashi et al. [15] proposed an SMC-based formation control scheme for multiple mobile robots, using the leader-following strategy, in which they defined some performance indexes, so that robots can be controlled according to their ability. Defoort et al. [16] also developed a robust coordinated control scheme based on leader-follower approach to achieve formation maneuvers. They used first- and second-order SMC to address the formation problem of N mobile robots of unicycle type with two driving wheels. Moreover, Cheaha et al. [17] presented a region-based shape controller for a swarm of fully actuated robots, where a linear approximator was used to approximate the unknown dynamic model and an SMC controller integrated with artificial potential functions was used to satisfy a predetermined geometric 2D formation.

Recently, H^∞ optimal control techniques have been found to be an effective solution to treat robust stabilization and tracking problems, in presence of external disturbances and system uncertainties [19–24]. In an H^∞ control technique, the main design goal is to force the gain from unmodelled dynamics, external disturbances, and approximation errors to be equal or less than a prescribed disturbance attenuation level (H^∞ attenuation constraint) [19]. This goal is generally represented as a Linear Matrix Inequality (LMI) problem.

In the traditional H^∞ control the exact model of the system must be known. However, in order to propose a robust control method, an integration between this robust scheme with fuzzy logic approximators can propose effective controllers for uncertain dynamic models [25].

Since Zadeh [26] initiated the fuzzy set theory, fuzzy logic systems (FLS) have been widely applied to many real world applications [27–30]. However, fuzzy control has not been viewed as a rigorous science due to a lack of formal synthesis techniques which guarantee the very basic requirements of global stability and acceptable performance. In fact, if the mathematical model of a robot is known, then conventional linear and nonlinear approximation methods should be given higher priority. However, fuzzy control should be useful in situations where (1) there is no acceptable mathematical model for the robot and (2) there are experienced human operators who can satisfactorily approximate the plant and provide qualitative control rules in terms of vague and fuzzy sentences. There are many practical situations where both (1) and (2) are true. Besides, FLS schemes have been widely used in motion control of single robots [31, 32]. Using FLS integrated with H^∞ control technique can improve the robustness of controller and ensures the stability [25].

In this paper, a geometric formation is considered as the goal and an artificial potential is defined to guide the agents through this formation. A partially unknown nonlinear dynamic model is adopted to each n-degrees of freedom agent. Therefore, an adaptive interval type-2 fuzzy approximator is combined with H^∞ control technique to propose a novel decentralized adaptive fuzzy formation control methodology, with robust characteristics. The main advantage of this control strategy is insensitivity to robot dynamic uncertainties, external disturbances, and input nonlinearities.

Moreover, in existing adaptive nonlinear control methodologies which are based on SMC control (e.g., [17]), each agent approximator needs to know the position and velocity of all other robots to approximate the unknown model

dynamics; however, in the current proposed decentralized strategy, only the position and velocity of each robot are enough to be known to its approximator.

The rest of this paper is organized as follows: Section 2 presents the system description, problem formulation, and potential function evaluation. An introduction of interval type-2 fuzzy logics systems is described in Section 3. Design of the proposed controller and stability analysis are discussed in Sections 4 and 5, respectively. Simulation results are included in Section 6 and Section 7 provides the concluding remarks.

2. System Description and Problem Formulation

The major goal in this study is to solve a multiagent formation control problem (i.e., controlling the relative position and orientation of the agents to create a desirable formation). One of the effective solutions for this problem is using an electrostatic-like potential function design which guides the agents through continues smooth paths and avoids agent collisions. Such a potential function design has been discussed in various papers (e.g., [1, 2, 8, 18]). Therefore, in Section 2.1 we will explain a simple potential function design, in order to solve the formation control of a group of N point massless agents, where the kinematic of the ith agent is considered as

$$\dot{z}_i = u_i, \quad i \in \{1, 2, \ldots, n\}, \tag{1}$$

in which $z_i \in R^n$ is the coordinate matrix (for a robot with n-degrees of freedom) and $u_i \in R^n$ denotes the control inputs.

However, one of the main shortcomings of this kinematic model is that it does not correspond to the dynamics of realistic agents. To overcome this shortcoming more general dynamic models like unicycle models [33] or other wheeled vehicle models can be discussed.

In Section 2.2 one of the most general n-degrees of freedom dynamic models of real robots is considered to propose more realistic solutions for formation control of multiagent systems. The main feature of this model is that any agent (robot) with n-degrees of freedom (e.g., Autonomous Underwater Vehicles (AUVs) [34], Unmanned Aerial Vehicles (UAVs) [35, 36], etc.) can be adopted to this model.

2.1. Formation Control Massless Agents. To propose a control law, an artificial potential function is designed. This potential function can be comprised of interagent interactions, environmental effects (e.g., obstacles, goals, etc.), or other exceptional terms.

Consider the pairwise potential fields, which are defined between agents as

$$F_{ij} = L_{ij}\left(\left|z_i - z_j\right|\right), \quad \forall i, j \in \{1, 2, \ldots, n\}, \tag{2}$$

where L_{ij} is designed to define a proper interagent potential function. It is assumed that each agent senses the resultant potential of all other agents.

The overall potential function is proposed to be in the form of

$$F = \sum_{i=1}^{N-1} \sum_{j=i+1}^{N} L_{ij} \left(|z_i - z_j| \right) + \sum_{i=1}^{N} Q_i \left(|z_i| \right), \qquad (3)$$

where Q_i defines the global potential of each agent.

Finally, the following three assumptions for potential function are considered [17, 18].

Assumption 1. F is continuously differentiable.

Assumption 2. F is strictly convex.

Assumption 3. F is positive definite.

For example, the following potential function can be chosen for a desired polygonal formation in a 2D Space:

$$F = \sum_{i=1}^{N-1} \sum_{j=i+1}^{N} \left(|z_i - z_j|^2 - d_{ij} \right)^2 + \sum_{i=1}^{N} \left(|z_i|^2 - r_i \right)^2. \qquad (4)$$

At the first step, to propose a solution for multiagent formation control, the steepest descent direction [8, 17, 18] is chosen as

$$f_i = \frac{\partial F}{\partial z_i}, \qquad (5)$$

and the control law

$$u_i = -f_i, \quad \forall i \in \{1, 2, \ldots, n\} \qquad (6)$$

is proposed.

By substituting (6) in (1) the kinematic model is obtained as

$$\dot{z}_i = -f_i = -\frac{\partial F}{\partial z_i}, \quad \forall i \in \{1, 2, \ldots, n\}, \qquad (7)$$

which can be rewritten in the matrix form as $\dot{Z} = -\nabla F$ where $Z = [z_1, z_2, \ldots, z_n]$ is the overall generalized coordinate vector.

In the next subsection, it is proposed to assume the multiagent system with a general dynamic model. Furthermore, in Section 3 a robust adaptive fuzzy controller using an H^∞ approach is used to force the satisfaction of (7). In other words the proposed controller is designed to enforce the speed of each agent along the negative gradient of potential function in (7).

2.2. Formation Control of Robots with Dynamic Models. In this subsection a general dynamic model [37] is addressed to represent any kind of autonomous n-degrees of freedom system. This model has been previously used in some existing works (e.g., [17, 18]).

Consider a group of N fully autonomous agents. The dynamics of the ith simple agent is strongly nonlinear [37] and can be written in the general form

$$M(z_i) \ddot{z}_i + C(z_i, \dot{z}_i) \dot{z}_i + g(z_i) = u_i, \qquad (8)$$

where $z_i \in R^n$ is the coordinate matrix (for a robot with n-degrees of freedom); $M(z_i) \in R^{n \times n}$ is a symmetric positive definite matrix and represents the inertia coefficients. $C(z_i, \dot{z}_i) \in R^{n \times n}$ is the matrix of centripetal, Coriolis, damping, and rolling resistance forces; $g(z_i) \in R^n$ is an n-vector of gravitational forces and $u_i \in R^n$ denotes the control inputs.

In most practical control problems of multiagent systems the inertia matrix $M(z_i)$ is a known constant matrix independent of z_i. Therefore, the following assumption is considered.

Assumption 4. M is the inertia matrix of robots, which is assumed to be a known and constant matrix.

Let us rewrite (8) as

$$M\ddot{z}_i + C(z_i, \dot{z}_i) \dot{z}_i + g(z_i) = u_i. \qquad (9)$$

It is straightforward to rewrite (9) as

$$\ddot{z}_i = -M^{-1} C(z_i, \dot{z}_i) \dot{z}_i - M^{-1} g(z_i) + M^{-1} u_i. \qquad (10)$$

In the next sections, the dynamic of each single agent will be assumed to be in the form of (10).

3. Interval Type-2 Fuzzy Logic System

In this section, the interval type-2 fuzzy set and the inference of the type-2 fuzzy logic system will be presented. A type-2 fuzzy set in universal set X is denoted as $\widetilde{A}$ which is characterized by a type-2 membership function $u_{\widetilde{A}}(x)$ in (12). The $u_{\widetilde{A}}(x)$ can be referred to as a secondary membership function or referred to as a secondary set, which is a type-1 fuzzy set in $[0, 1]$. In (13), $f_x(u)$ is a secondary grade, which is the amplitude of a secondary membership function; that is, $0 \leq f_x(u) \leq 1$. The domain of a secondary membership function is called the primary membership of x. In (13), J_x is the primary membership of x, where $u \in J_x \subseteq [0, 1]$ for all $x \in X$; μ is a fuzzy set in $[0, 1]$, rather than a crisp point in $[0, 1]$,

$$\widetilde{A} = \int_{x \in X} \frac{u_{\widetilde{A}}(x)}{x} = \int_{x \in X} \frac{\left[\int_{u \in J_x} f_x(u)/u \right]}{x}, \quad J_x \subseteq [0, 1]. \qquad (11)$$

When $f_x(u) = 1$, for all $u \in J_x \subseteq [0, 1]$, then the secondary MFs are interval sets such that $u_{\widetilde{A}}(x)$ in (13) can be called an interval type-2 MF. Therefore, the type-2 fuzzy set can be rewritten as

$$\widetilde{A} = \int_{x \in X} \frac{u_{\widetilde{A}}(x)}{x} = \int_{x \in X} \frac{\left[\int_{u \in J_x} 1/u \right]}{x}, \quad J_x \subseteq [0, 1]. \qquad (12)$$

Also, a Gaussian primary MF with uncertain mean and fixed standard deviation having an interval type-2 secondary MF can be called an interval type-2 Gaussian MF (13). It can be expressed as

$$u_{\widetilde{A}}(x) = \exp\left[-\frac{1}{2} \left(\frac{x - m}{\sigma} \right)^2 \right], \quad m \in [m_1, m_2]. \qquad (13)$$

It is obvious that the type-2 fuzzy set is in a region, called a footprint of uncertainty (FOU) and is bounded by an upper MF and a lower MF, which are denoted as $\overline{u}_{\widetilde{A}}(x)$ and $\underline{u}_{\widetilde{A}}(x)$, respectively. Hence, (13) can be reexpressed as

$$\widetilde{A} = \int_{x \in X} \frac{\left[\int_{u \in [\underline{u}_{\widetilde{A}}(x), \overline{u}_{\widetilde{A}}(x)]} 1/u \right]}{x}. \tag{14}$$

A type-2 fuzzy logic system (FLS) is very similar to a type-1 FLS as shown in Figure 1; the major structure difference being that the defuzzifier block of a type-1 FLS is replaced by the output processing block in a type-2 FLS which consists of type-reduction followed by defuzzification.

There are five main parts in a type-2 FLS: fuzzifier, rule base, inference engine, type reducer, and defuzzifier. A type-2 FLS is a mapping $f : \mathbb{R}^P \to \mathbb{R}^1$. After defuzzification, fuzzy inference, type reduction, and defuzzification, a crisp output can be obtained.

Consider a type-2 FLS having p inputs $x_1 \in X_1, \ldots, x_1 \in X_p$ and one output $y \in Y$. The type-2 fuzzy rule base consists of a collection of IF-THEN rules, as in the type-1 case. We assume there are M rules and the rule of a type-2 relation between the input space $X_1 \times X_2 \times \cdots \times X_p$ and the output space Y can be expressed as

$$R^1 : \text{IF } x_1 \text{ is } \widetilde{F}_1^l \text{ and } \ldots \text{ and } x_p \text{ is } \widetilde{F}_p^l, \text{ THEN } y \text{ is } \widetilde{G}^l, \tag{15}$$
$$l = 1, 2, \ldots, M,$$

where $\widetilde{F}_j^l$ are antecedent type-2 sets ($j = 1, 2, \ldots, p$) and $\widetilde{G}^l$'s are consequent type-2 sets.

The inference engine combines rules and gives a mapping from input type-2 fuzzy sets to output type-2 fuzzy sets. To achieve this process, we have to compute unions and intersection of type-2 sets, as well as compositions of type-2 relations. The output of inference engine block is a type-2 set. By using the extension principle of type-1 defuzzification method, type-reduction takes us from type-2 output sets of the FLS to a type-1 set called the "type-reduced set." This set may then be defuzzified to obtain a single crisp value.

There are many kinds of type-reduction, such as centroid, height, modified weight, and center-of-sets. The center-of-sets type reduction will be used in this paper and can be expressed as:

$$Y_{\cos}\left(Y^1, \ldots, Y^M, F^1, \ldots, F^M\right) = [y_l, y_r]$$
$$= \int_{y^1} \cdots \int_{y^M} \int_{f^1} \cdots \int_{f^M} \frac{1}{\sum_{i=1}^M f^i y^i / \sum_{i=1}^M f^i}, \tag{16}$$

where $Y_{\cos}$ is the interval set determined by two end points y_l and y_r, and $f^i \in F^i = [\underline{f}^i, \overline{f}^i]$. In the meantime, an interval type-2 FLS with singleton fuzzification and meet under minimum or product t-norm $\underline{f}^i$ and $\overline{f}^i$ can be obtained as

$$\underline{f}^i = \underline{\mu}_{\widetilde{F}_1^i}(x_1) * \cdots * \underline{\mu}_{\widetilde{F}_p^i}(x_p), \tag{17}$$

$$\overline{f}^i = \overline{\mu}_{\widetilde{F}_1^i}(x_1) * \cdots * \overline{\mu}_{\widetilde{F}_p^i}(x_p). \tag{18}$$

Also, $y^i \in Y^i$ and $Y^i = [y_l^i, y_r^i]$ are the centroid of the type-2 interval consequent set $\widetilde{G}^i$. For any value $y \in Y_{\cos}$, y can be expressed as

$$y = \frac{\sum_{i=1}^M f^i y^i}{\sum_{i=1}^M f^i}, \tag{19}$$

where y is a monotonic increasing function with respect to y^i. Also, y_l is the minimum associated only with y_l^i, and y_r is the maximum associated only with y_r^i. Note that y_l and y_r depend only on mixture of $\underline{f}^i$ or $\overline{f}^i$ values. Therefore, the left-most point y_l and the right-most point y_r can be expressed as a fuzzy basis function (FBF) expansion, that is,

$$y_l = \frac{\sum_{i=1}^M f_l^i y_l^i}{\sum_{i=1}^M f_l^i} = \sum_{i=1}^M y_l^i \xi_l^i,$$
$$y_r = \frac{\sum_{i=1}^M f_r^i y_r^i}{\sum_{i=1}^M f_r^i} = \sum_{i=1}^M y_r^i \xi_r^i, \tag{20}$$

respectively, where $\xi_l^i = f_l^i / \sum_{i=1}^M f^i$ and $\xi_r^i = f_r^i / \sum_{i=1}^M f^i$.

If the FBF vector denoted as $\underline{\xi}_l = [\xi_l^1, \xi_l^2, \ldots, \xi_l^M]$ and $\underline{\xi}_r = [\xi_r^1, \xi_r^2, \ldots, \xi_r^M]$, and let $\underline{y}_l^T = [y_l^1, y_l^2, \ldots, y_l^M]$ and $\underline{y}_r^T = [y_r^1, y_r^2, \ldots, y_r^M]$, then (20) can be rewritten as

$$y_l = \frac{\sum_{i=1}^M f_l^i y_l^i}{\sum_{i=1}^M f_l^i} = \sum_{i=1}^M y_l^i \xi_l^i = \underline{y}_l^T \underline{\xi}_l, \tag{21}$$

$$y_r = \frac{\sum_{i=1}^M f_r^i y_r^i}{\sum_{i=1}^M f_r^i} = \sum_{i=1}^M y_r^i \xi_r^i = \underline{y}_r^T \underline{\xi}_r. \tag{22}$$

For illustrative purposes, we briefly provide the computation procedure for y_r. Without loss of generality, assume the y_r^is are arranged in ascending order, that is, $y_r^1 \leq y_r^2 \leq \cdots \leq y_r^M$.

Step 1. Compute y_r in (22) by initially setting $f_r^i = (\overline{f}^i + \underline{f}^i)/2$ for $i = 1, 2, \ldots, M$, where $\underline{f}^i$ and $\overline{f}^i$ have been precomputed by (18) and (19) and let $y_r' = y_r$.

Step 2. Find R ($1 \leq R \leq M - 1$) such that $y_r^R \leq y_r' \leq y_r^{R+1}$.

Step 3. Compute y_r in (22) with $f_r^i = \underline{f}^i$ for $i \leq R$ and $f_r^i = \overline{f}^i$ for $i > R$ and let $y_r'' = y_r$.

Step 4. If $y_r'' \neq y_r'$, then go to Step 5, If $y_r'' = y_r'$, then stop and set $y_r = y_r''$.

Step 5. Set y_r' equal to y_r'' and return to Step 2.

The point to separate two sides by number R can be decided from the above algorithm, one side using lower firing

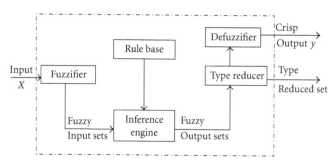

FIGURE 1: The structure of the type-2 fuzzy logic system.

strengths $\underline{f}^i$'s and another side using upper firing strengths $\overline{f}^i$'s. Therefore, the y_r in (22) can be rewritten as

$$y_r = \frac{\sum_{i=1}^{R} \underline{f}^i y_r^i + \sum_{i=R+1}^{M} \overline{f}^i y_r^i}{\sum_{i=1}^{R} \underline{f}^i + \sum_{i=R+1}^{M} \overline{f}^i} = \sum_{i=1}^{R} \underline{q}_r^i y_r^i + \sum_{i=R+1}^{M} \overline{q}_r^i y_r^i$$

$$= \begin{bmatrix} \underline{Q}_r & \overline{Q}^r \end{bmatrix} \begin{bmatrix} \underline{y}_r \\ \overline{y}^r \end{bmatrix} = \xi_r^T \underline{\Theta}_r,$$

(23)

where $\underline{q}_r^i = \underline{f}^i/D_r$, $\overline{q}_r^i = \overline{f}^i/D_r$ and $D_r = (\sum_{i=1}^{R} \underline{f}^i + \sum_{i=R+1}^{M} \overline{f}^i)$. In the meantime, we have $\underline{Q}_r = [\underline{q}_r^1, \underline{q}_r^2, \ldots, \underline{q}_r^R]$, $\overline{Q}^r = [\overline{q}_r^1, \overline{q}_r^2, \ldots, \overline{q}_r^R]$, $\xi_r^T = \begin{bmatrix} \underline{Q}_r & \overline{Q}^r \end{bmatrix}$, and $\underline{\Theta}_r^T = \begin{bmatrix} \underline{y}_r & \overline{y}^r \end{bmatrix}$.

The procedure to compute y_l is similar to compute y_r. Just in Step 2, we determine L ($1 \leq L \leq M-1$), such that $y_l^L \leq y_l' \leq y_l^{L+1}$ and in Step 3 let $f_l^i = \overline{f}^i$ for $i \leq L$ and $f_l^i = \underline{f}^i$ for $i > L$. Then y_l in (21) can also be rewritten as

$$y_l = \frac{\sum_{i=1}^{L} \overline{f}^i y_l^i + \sum_{i=L+1}^{M} \underline{f}^i y_l^i}{\sum_{i=1}^{L} \overline{f}^i + \sum_{i=L+1}^{M} \underline{f}^i} = \sum_{i=1}^{L} \overline{q}_l^i y_l^i + \sum_{i=L+1}^{M} \underline{q}_l^i y_l^i$$

$$= \begin{bmatrix} \overline{Q}_l & \underline{Q}^l \end{bmatrix} \begin{bmatrix} \overline{y}_l \\ \underline{y}^l \end{bmatrix} = \xi_l^T \underline{\Theta}_l,$$

(24)

where $\underline{q}_l^i = \underline{f}^i/D_l$, $\overline{q}_l^i = \overline{f}^i/D_l$ and $D_l = (\sum_{i=1}^{L} \overline{f}^i + \sum_{i=L+1}^{M} \underline{f}^i)$. In the meantime, we have $\underline{Q}_l = [\underline{q}_l^1, \underline{q}_l^2, \ldots, \underline{q}_l^R]$, $\overline{Q}^l = [\overline{q}_l^1, \overline{q}_l^2, \ldots, \overline{q}_l^R]$, $\xi_l^T = \begin{bmatrix} \overline{Q}_l & \underline{Q}^l \end{bmatrix}$, and $\underline{\Theta}_l^T = \begin{bmatrix} \overline{y}_l & \underline{y}^l \end{bmatrix}$.

The defuzzified crisp value from an interval type-2 FLS is obtained as

$$y(\underline{x}) = \frac{y_l + y_r}{2} = \frac{1}{2} \left(\xi_r^T \underline{\Theta}_r + \xi_l^T \underline{\Theta}_l \right)$$

$$= \frac{1}{2} \begin{bmatrix} \xi_r^T & \xi_l^T \end{bmatrix} \begin{bmatrix} \underline{\Theta}_r \\ \underline{\Theta}_l \end{bmatrix} = \xi^T \underline{\Theta},$$

(25)

where $(1/2) \begin{bmatrix} \xi_r^T & \xi_l^T \end{bmatrix} = \underline{\xi}^T$ and $\begin{bmatrix} \underline{\Theta}_r^T & \underline{\Theta}_l^T \end{bmatrix} = \underline{\Theta}^T$.

4. Controller Design Methodology

In this section a novel formation error based on the integral of formation gradient (5) will be proposed. Then, a robust H^{∞} controller will be designed and a fuzzy logic system will be utilized to approximate the unknown parts of dynamic models. The main feature of the proposed novel control scheme is its decentralized characteristic, robustness to external disturbances, input nonlinearities, and measurement noises. Besides, by using the proposed controller, the formation can be achieved from any initial conditions.

Consider, the novel formation error for the ith robot as

$$\underline{e}_i(t) = z_i(t) + \int_0^t f_i(\tau) \, d\tau,$$

(26)

where $\underline{e}_i \in R^n$, z_i represents the coordinate vector of ith robot in (10) and f_i is the gradient of potential function defined in (7). It is straightforward to write the first and second derivatives of (26) as

$$\dot{\underline{e}}_i(t) = \dot{z}_i(t) + f_i,$$

$$\ddot{\underline{e}}_i(t) = \ddot{z}_i(t) + \dot{f}_i.$$

(27)

Our design goal is to propose an adaptive fuzzy controller so that

$$\ddot{\underline{e}}_i + k_1 \dot{\underline{e}}_i + k_2 \underline{e}_i = 0$$

(28)

is achieved, where k_1 and k_2 are chosen to make (28) asymptotically stable.

To design the controller, consider the control law proposed as

$$u_i = M \left(H_i(z_i, \dot{z}_i) - \dot{f}_i - k_1 \dot{\underline{e}}_i - k_2 \underline{e}_i \right),$$

(29)

where

$$H_i(z_i, \dot{z}_i) = M^{-1} C_i(z_i, \dot{z}_i) \dot{z}_i + M^{-1} g(z_i).$$

(30)

In order to use this control law, which is designed based on the feedback linearization control method, the function $H_i(\cdot)$ (i.e., $C(\cdot)$ and $g(\cdot)$) must be known. However, in practice these matrices may be unknown for most of real dynamical robots. To overcome this, we make use of an adaptive fuzzy logic system $\widehat{H}_i(\cdot)$ to approximate $H_i(\cdot)$.

Therefore, using the singleton fuzzifier, product inference, and weighted average defuzzifier [38], the output of the fuzzy model can be expressed as

$$\widehat{H}_i\left(z_i,\dot{z}_i \mid \underline{\theta}_i\right) = \frac{1}{2}\left(\underline{\zeta}_{il}^T\left(z_i,\dot{z}_i\right)\underline{\theta}_{il} + \underline{\zeta}_{ir}^T\left(z_i,\dot{z}_i\right)\underline{\theta}_{ir}\right), \quad (31)$$

where

$$\underline{\zeta}_{il} = \begin{bmatrix} \underline{\zeta}_{1il}^T & 0 & \cdots & 0 \\ 0 & \underline{\zeta}_{2il}^T & \cdots & 0 \\ \vdots & \vdots & \ddots & \vdots \\ 0 & 0 & \cdots & \underline{\zeta}_{nil}^T \end{bmatrix}, \quad \underline{\theta}_{il} = \begin{bmatrix} \underline{\theta}_{1il} \\ \underline{\theta}_{2il} \\ \vdots \\ \underline{\theta}_{nil} \end{bmatrix},$$

$$\underline{\zeta}_{ir} = \begin{bmatrix} \underline{\zeta}_{1ir}^T & 0 & \cdots & 0 \\ 0 & \underline{\zeta}_{2ir}^T & \cdots & 0 \\ \vdots & \vdots & \ddots & \vdots \\ 0 & 0 & \cdots & \underline{\zeta}_{nir}^T \end{bmatrix}, \quad \underline{\theta}_{ir} = \begin{bmatrix} \underline{\theta}_{1ir} \\ \underline{\theta}_{2ir} \\ \vdots \\ \underline{\theta}_{nir} \end{bmatrix}. \quad (32)$$

Equation (31) suggests to us to rewrite the overall control law (29) as

$$u_i = M\left(\widehat{H}_i\left(z_i,\dot{z}_i \mid \underline{\theta}_i\right) - \dot{f}_i - k^T\underline{e}_i - \underline{u}_{ai}\right), \quad (33)$$

where u_{ai} is engaged to attenuate the fuzzy logic approximation error and external disturbances.

A block diagram of the proposed control methodology is shown in Figure 2.

Remark 1 (input nonlinearity). In what follows, another main property of the proposed H^∞ is introduced. It will be shown that the formation problem of multiagent system can be achieved even in the presence of dead-zone nonlinearities of the control actuators. Let us modify the dynamic model (9) as

$$M\ddot{z}_i + C\left(z_i,\dot{z}_i\right)\dot{z}_i + g\left(z_i\right) = \Phi\left(u_i\right) + d_i\left(t\right) \quad (34)$$

where

$$\Phi\left(u_i\right) = \begin{bmatrix} \phi\left(u_{i1}\right) \\ \phi\left(u_{i2}\right) \\ \vdots \\ \phi\left(u_{in}\right) \end{bmatrix} \quad (35)$$

and $\phi(\cdot) : R \rightarrow R$ represents the dead-zone function and can be expressed as

$$\phi\left(u\right) = \begin{cases} m\left(u - b\right) & u \geq b, \\ 0 & -b < u < b, \\ m\left(u + b\right) & u \leq -b, \end{cases} \quad (36)$$

where b is the width of the dead-zone and m is the slope of dead-zone line.

The dead-zone parameters b and m are assumed to be bounded and the bounds of m and b are known as $b \in [b_{\min}, b_{\max}]$ and $m \in [m_{\min}, m_{\max}]$. Therefore (36) can be rewritten as

$$\phi\left(u\right) = mu + v\left(u\right),$$

$$v\left(u\right) = \begin{cases} -mb & u \geq b, \\ -mu & -b < u < b, \\ mb & u \leq -b. \end{cases} \quad (37)$$

From the aforementioned assumption on bounds of m and b, $v(u)$ can be assumed bounded, (i.e., $v(u) \leq \rho$), where ρ is the known upper bound that can be chosen as $\rho = mb_{\max}$. By considering $\bar{d}_i(t) = d_i(t) + \Upsilon(u_i)$ and $\bar{u}_i = Mu_i$, where

$$\Upsilon\left(u_i\right) = \begin{bmatrix} v_1\left(u_{i1}\right) \\ v_2\left(u_{i2}\right) \\ \vdots \\ v_n\left(u_{in}\right) \end{bmatrix}, \quad M = mI_{n\times n} \quad (38)$$

then (34) can be rewritten as

$$M\ddot{z}_i + C\left(z_i,\dot{z}_i\right)\dot{z}_i + g\left(z_i\right) = \bar{u}_i + \bar{d}_i\left(t\right), \quad (39)$$

which is the same as (9). Therefore, we have proved that the proposed H^∞ feedback controller is also robust to dead-zone input nonlinearities (36).

5. Stability Analysis

This section presents the stability proof of the proposed novel adaptive fuzzy controller in (33). A Lyapunov candidate will be proposed and then an adaptation law and a robust compensator control input will be derived to satisfy the H^∞ tracking performance in (50).

To derive the adaptive law for adjusting $\underline{\theta}_i$, we first define the optimal parameter vector $\underline{\theta}_i^*$ as

$$\underline{\theta}_i^* = \arg \min_{\underline{\theta}_i \in \Omega}\left[\sup\left\|\widehat{H}_i\left(z,\dot{z} \mid \theta_i\right) - H_i\left(z,\dot{z}\right)\right\|\right], \quad (40)$$

and the minimum approximation error is defined as

$$\underline{w}_i = H_i\left(z_i,\dot{z}_i\right) - \widehat{H}_i\left(z_i,\dot{z}_i \mid \underline{\theta}_i^*\right), \quad (41)$$

where it can be assumed that $\underline{w}_i \in L_\infty$ [38].

By choosing the control input as [39] after some manipulations, (10) can be rewritten as

$$\ddot{z} + \dot{f}_i = \left(\widehat{H}_i\left(z_i,\dot{z}_i \mid \underline{\theta}_i\right) - H_i\left(z_i,\dot{z}_i\right)\right) + k_1\dot{e}_i + k_2e_i - \underline{u}_{ai}, \quad (42)$$

and the formation error dynamic can be expressed as

$$\ddot{\underline{e}}_i = \left(\widehat{H}_i\left(z_i,\dot{z}_i \mid \underline{\theta}_i\right) - H_i\left(z_i,\dot{z}_i\right)\right) + k_1\dot{e}_i + k_2e_i - \underline{u}_{ai}. \quad (43)$$

Moreover by defining $\underline{E}_i = [e_{1i},\dot{e}_{1i},e_{2i},\dot{e}_{2i},\ldots,e_{ni},\dot{e}_{ni}]$ it is straightforward to write

$$\dot{\underline{E}}_i = A\underline{E}_i + B\underline{u}_{ai} + B\left(H_i\left(z_i,\dot{z}_i\right) - \widehat{H}_i\left(z_i,\dot{z}_i \mid \underline{\theta}_i\right)\right), \quad (44)$$

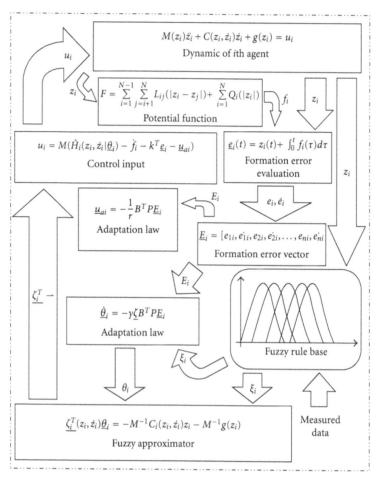

FIGURE 2: Block diagram of the proposed adaptive fuzzy H^∞ control scheme.

where

$$A = I_{n\times n} \otimes \begin{bmatrix} 0 & 1 \\ -k_2 & -k_1 \end{bmatrix}_{2\times 2}, \qquad B = I_{n\times n} \otimes \begin{bmatrix} 0 & 1 \end{bmatrix}^T. \quad (45)$$

Based on (31), (40), and (41), the matrix form of formation error in (44) can be rewritten as

$$\dot{\underline{E}}_i = A\underline{E}_i + B\underline{u}_{ai} + B\underline{\zeta}_i^T (z_i, \dot{z}_i) \, \widetilde{\underline{\theta}}_i + B\underline{w}_i, \quad (46)$$

where $\widetilde{\underline{\theta}}_i = \underline{\theta}_i - \underline{\theta}_i^*$.

In the following theorem, it will be shown that the proposed control law (33) guarantees the stability and robustness of formation problem.

Theorem 2. *Consider a group of N fully autonomous agents with the dynamic represented in (8) and with the control law in (33). The robust compensator of ith robot $\underline{u}_{ai}$ and the fuzzy adaptation law are chosen as*

$$\underline{u}_{ai} = -\frac{1}{r} B^T P\underline{E}_i, \quad (47)$$

$$\dot{\underline{\theta}}_{il} = -\gamma\underline{\zeta}_{il} (z_i, \dot{z}_i) \, B^T P\underline{E}_i, \qquad \dot{\underline{\theta}}_{ir} = -\gamma\underline{\zeta}_{ir} (z_i, \dot{z}_i) \, B^T P\underline{E}_i, \quad (48)$$

where r and γ are positive constants and P is the positive semidefinite solution of following Riccati-like equation:

$$PA + A^T P + Q - \frac{2}{r} PBB^T P + \frac{1}{\rho^2} PBB^T P = 0, \quad (49)$$

where Q is a positive semidefinite matrix and $2\rho^2 \geq r$.

Therefore, the H^∞ tracking performance

$$\sum_{i=1}^{N} \left[-\int_0^T \underline{E}_i^T Q\underline{E}_i \, dt \right]$$

$$\leq \sum_{i=1}^{N} \left[\underline{E}_i(0)^T P\underline{E}_i(0) + \frac{1}{2\gamma}\widetilde{\underline{\theta}}(0)_{il}^T\widetilde{\underline{\theta}}_{il}(0) + \frac{1}{2\gamma}\widetilde{\underline{\theta}}(0)_{ir}^T\widetilde{\underline{\theta}}_{ir}(0) \right]$$

$$+ \sum_{i=1}^{N} \left[\rho^2 \int_0^T \underline{w}_i^T \underline{w}_i \, dt \right]$$

$$(50)$$

can be achieved for a prescribed attenuation level ρ and all the variables of closed loop system are bounded.

In order to derive the adaptive law for adjusting $\underline{\theta}_i$, the Lyapunov candidate is chosen as

$$V = \sum_{i=1}^{N} \left[\frac{1}{2} \underline{E}_i^T P \underline{E}_i + \frac{1}{4\gamma} \tilde{\underline{\theta}}_{il}^T \tilde{\underline{\theta}}_{il} + \frac{1}{4\gamma} \tilde{\underline{\theta}}_{ir}^T \tilde{\underline{\theta}}_{ir} \right]. \quad (51)$$

Using (46), the time derivative of V is

$$\dot{V} = \frac{1}{2} \sum_{i=1}^{N} \left[\dot{\underline{E}}_i^T P \underline{E}_i + \underline{E}_i^T P \dot{\underline{E}}_i + \frac{1}{2\gamma} \dot{\tilde{\underline{\theta}}}_{il}^T \tilde{\underline{\theta}}_{il} + \frac{1}{2\gamma} \tilde{\underline{\theta}}_{il}^T \dot{\tilde{\underline{\theta}}}_{il} \right. $$
$$\left. + \frac{1}{2\gamma} \dot{\tilde{\underline{\theta}}}_{ir}^T \tilde{\underline{\theta}}_{ir} + \frac{1}{2\gamma} \tilde{\underline{\theta}}_{ir}^T \dot{\tilde{\underline{\theta}}}_{ir} \right]$$

$$= \frac{1}{2} \sum_{i=1}^{N} \left[\underline{E}_i^T A^T P \underline{E}_i + \underline{u}_{ai}^T B^T P \underline{E}_i + \frac{1}{2} \tilde{\underline{\theta}}_{il}^T \underline{\zeta}_{il}(z_i, \dot{z}_i) B^T P \underline{E}_i \right.$$

$$+ \frac{1}{2} \tilde{\underline{\theta}}_{ir}^T \underline{\zeta}_{ir}(z_i, \dot{z}_i) B^T P \underline{E}_i + \underline{w}_i^T B^T P \underline{E}_i + \underline{E}_i^T P A \underline{E}_i$$

$$+ \underline{E}_i^T P B \underline{u}_{ai} + \frac{1}{2} \underline{E}_i^T P B \underline{\zeta}_{il}^T(z_i, \dot{z}_i) \tilde{\underline{\theta}}_{il}$$

$$\left. + \underline{E}_i^T P B \underline{\zeta}_{ir}^T(z_i, \dot{z}_i) \tilde{\underline{\theta}}_{ir} + \underline{E}_i^T P B \underline{w}_i \right]$$

$$+ \frac{1}{4} \sum_{i=1}^{N} \left[\frac{1}{\gamma} \dot{\tilde{\underline{\theta}}}_{il}^T \tilde{\underline{\theta}}_{il} + \frac{1}{\gamma} \tilde{\underline{\theta}}_{il}^T \dot{\tilde{\underline{\theta}}}_{il} + \frac{1}{\gamma} \dot{\tilde{\underline{\theta}}}_{ir}^T \tilde{\underline{\theta}}_{ir} + \frac{1}{\gamma} \tilde{\underline{\theta}}_{ir}^T \dot{\tilde{\underline{\theta}}}_{ir} \right]. \quad (52)$$

Substituting (47) in (52) and using the fact that $\dot{\tilde{\underline{\theta}}}_{il} = \dot{\underline{\theta}}_{il}, \dot{\tilde{\underline{\theta}}}_{ir} = \dot{\underline{\theta}}_{ir}$, we get

$$\dot{V} = \frac{1}{2} \sum_{i=1}^{N} \left[\underline{E}_i^T A^T P \underline{E}_i - \frac{1}{r} \underline{E}_i^T P B B^T P \underline{E}_i + \frac{1}{2} \tilde{\underline{\theta}}_{il}^T \underline{\zeta}_{il}(z_i, \dot{z}_i) B^T P \underline{E}_i \right.$$

$$+ \frac{1}{2} \tilde{\underline{\theta}}_{ir}^T \underline{\zeta}_{ir}(z_i, \dot{z}_i) B^T P \underline{E}_i + \underline{w}_i^T B^T P \underline{E}_i$$

$$\left. + \underline{E}_i^T P A \underline{E}_i - \frac{1}{r} \underline{E}_i^T P B B^T P \underline{E}_i + \frac{1}{2} \underline{E}_i^T P B \underline{\zeta}_{il}^T(z_i, \dot{z}_i) \tilde{\underline{\theta}}_{il} \right.$$

$$\left. + \frac{1}{2} \underline{E}_i^T P B \underline{\zeta}_{ir}^T(z_i, \dot{z}_i) \tilde{\underline{\theta}}_{ir} + \underline{E}_i^T P B \underline{w}_i \right]$$

$$+ \frac{1}{4} \sum_{i=1}^{N} \left[\frac{1}{\gamma} \dot{\underline{\theta}}_{il}^T \tilde{\underline{\theta}}_{il} + \frac{1}{\gamma} \tilde{\underline{\theta}}_{il}^T \dot{\underline{\theta}}_{il} + \frac{1}{\gamma} \dot{\underline{\theta}}_{ir}^T \tilde{\underline{\theta}}_{ir} + \frac{1}{\gamma} \tilde{\underline{\theta}}_{ir}^T \dot{\underline{\theta}}_{ir} \right]$$

$$\times \frac{1}{2} \sum_{i=1}^{N} \left[\underline{E}_i^T \left(A^T P + P A - \frac{2}{r} P B B^T P \right) \underline{E}_i \right]$$

$$+ \frac{1}{4} \sum_{i=1}^{N} \left[\left(\underline{E}_i^T P B \underline{\zeta}_{il}^T(z_i, \dot{z}_i) + \frac{1}{\gamma} \dot{\underline{\theta}}_{il}^T \right) \tilde{\underline{\theta}}_{il} \right.$$

$$+ \frac{1}{4} \sum_{i=1}^{N} \left[\left(\underline{E}_i^T P B \underline{\zeta}_{ir}^T(z_i, \dot{z}_i) + \frac{1}{\gamma} \dot{\underline{\theta}}_{ir}^T \right) \tilde{\underline{\theta}}_{ir} \right]$$

$$+ \frac{1}{2} \sum_{i=1}^{N} \left[\underline{w}_i^T B^T P \underline{E}_i + \underline{E}_i^T P B \underline{w}_i \right]. \quad (53)$$

Using adaptation law (48) and the Riccati-like equation (49), the above equation becomes

$$\dot{V} = \frac{1}{2} \sum_{i=1}^{N} \left[-\underline{E}_i^T Q \underline{E}_i - \frac{1}{\rho^2} \underline{E}_i^T P B B^T P \underline{E}_i \right]$$

$$+ \frac{1}{2} \sum_{i=1}^{N} \left[\underline{w}_i^T B^T P \underline{E}_i + \underline{E}_i^T P B \underline{w}_i \right]$$

$$\times \frac{1}{2} \sum_{i=1}^{N} \left[-\underline{E}_i^T Q \underline{E}_i - \left(\frac{1}{\rho} B^T P \underline{E}_i - \rho \underline{w}_i \right)^T \left(\frac{1}{\rho} B^T P \underline{E}_i - \rho \underline{w}_i \right) \right]$$

$$+ \frac{1}{2} \sum_{i=1}^{N} \left[\rho^2 \underline{w}_i^T \underline{w}_i \right] \leq \frac{1}{2} \sum_{i=1}^{N} \left[-\underline{E}_i^T Q \underline{E}_i + \rho^2 \underline{w}_i^T \underline{w}_i \right]. \quad (54)$$

Integrating the above inequality from $t = 0$ to T yields to

$$V(T) - V(0) \leq \frac{1}{2} \sum_{i=1}^{N} \left[-\int_0^T \underline{E}_i^T Q \underline{E}_i \, dt + \rho^2 \int_0^T \underline{w}_i^T \underline{w}_i \, dt \right]. \quad (55)$$

Using the fact that $V(T) \geq 0$ and from (49), the inequality

$$\frac{1}{2} \sum_{i=1}^{N} \left[-\int_0^T \underline{E}_i^T Q \underline{E}_i dt \right]$$

$$\leq \frac{1}{2} \sum_{i=1}^{N} \left[\underline{E}_i(0)^T P \underline{E}_i(0) + \frac{1}{2\gamma} \tilde{\underline{\theta}}(0)_{il}^T \tilde{\underline{\theta}}_{il}(0) + \frac{1}{2\gamma} \tilde{\underline{\theta}}(0)_{ir}^T \tilde{\underline{\theta}}_{ir}(0) \right]$$

$$+ \frac{1}{2} \sum_{i=1}^{N} \left[\rho^2 \int_0^T \underline{w}_i^T \underline{w}_i dt \right] \quad (56)$$

is obtained.

Therefore, the H^∞ tracking equation (50) can be achieved and the proof is completed.

6. Simulation Results

This section presents four simulation examples to illustrate the effectiveness of the proposed control scheme. In the first example, a group of six agents with known dynamics as in (8) is considered. The second example presents the hexagonal formation of six partially unknown agents and an adaptive fuzzy logic system is used to approximate the unknown dynamics. This example proves the system stability under the proposed novel controller. In order to prove the

TABLE 1: Parameter specifications of hexagonal formation.

	$|i - j| = 1$	$|i - j| = 2$	$|i - j| = 3$	$|i - j| = 4$	$|i - j| = 5$
d_{ij}	1.0	1.7	2.0	1.7	1.0

TABLE 2: Agents initial positions.

Agent number	1	2	3	4	5	6
x_0	−2.5	+2.0	−1.0	+1.0	+2.0	+2.5
y_0	+1.0	−2.5	+1.0	−1.0	+2.5	−1.0

controller robustness, in the third example a white Gaussian noise is applied to all measured data and one of the agents is forced to be stationary and still the formation maintains its stabilizing performance. In the forth example one of the agents is chosen as the leader with a constant velocity. It is shown that proposed controller is able to form a dynamic 2D moving hexagon which tracks the leader. All the simulation results are implemented in MATLAB with 0.01 secs as the stepsize.

The unique formation problem used in all five simulation examples is a 2D hexagon with unit radius defined by

$$F = \sum_{i=1}^{5} \sum_{j=i+1}^{6} \left(\left| z_i - z_j \right|^2 - d_{ij} \right)^2, \tag{57}$$

where d_{ij} is specified in Table 1.

In addition six random points in the 2D space are chosen to be the initial positions for six agents. These points are assumed to be fixed in all five numerical simulations (Table 2).

6.1. Example I (Six Agents with Known Dynamics).

Consider a group of six mobile agents with known dynamic models. Based on general model represented in (8), the nonlinear dynamic of the ith robot is considered as

$$\begin{bmatrix} 0.6 & 0 \\ 0 & 0.6 \end{bmatrix} \begin{bmatrix} \ddot{x}_i \\ \ddot{y}_i \end{bmatrix} + \begin{bmatrix} 0.15 & 0 \\ 0 & 0.15 \end{bmatrix} \begin{bmatrix} \dot{x}_i \\ \dot{y}_i \end{bmatrix} + \begin{bmatrix} 0.2 & 0 \\ 0 & 0.2 \end{bmatrix} \begin{bmatrix} \mathrm{sgn}\,(\dot{x}_i) \\ \mathrm{sgn}\,(\dot{y}_i) \end{bmatrix}$$

$$= u_i, \tag{58}$$

and after some manipulations we get

$$\begin{bmatrix} \ddot{x}_i \\ \ddot{y}_i \end{bmatrix} = -\begin{bmatrix} 0.25 & 0 \\ 0 & 0.25 \end{bmatrix} \begin{bmatrix} \dot{x}_i \\ \dot{y}_i \end{bmatrix} - \begin{bmatrix} 0.33 & 0 \\ 0 & 0.33 \end{bmatrix} \begin{bmatrix} \mathrm{sgn}\,(\dot{x}_i) \\ \mathrm{sgn}\,(\dot{y}_i) \end{bmatrix}$$

$$+ \begin{bmatrix} 1.66 & 0 \\ 0 & 1.66 \end{bmatrix} u_i. \tag{59}$$

To give a solution for the formation problem, formation error is defined as (26) and the control law is designed based on (29), where $k_1 = 15$ and $k_2 = 4$. Figure 3(a) shows the formation trajectory of six robots starting from initial

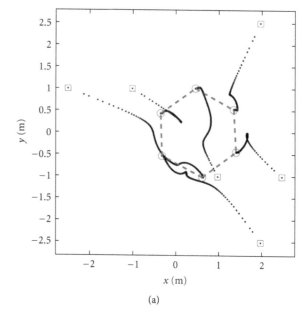

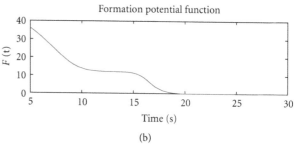

FIGURE 3: Hexagonal formation of six agents with known dynamics. (a) Formation trajectory. (b) Formation potential.

conditions (Table 2) to the final unit hexagon (57) in 30 secs and Figure 3(b) shows the potential value.

The first subfigure (Figure 3(a)) shows how smooth the controller guides all the agents to form the desired hexagon. This geometric formation does not have any fixed position or direction, and it will only be determined by the agents initial position.

The second sub-figure (Figure 3(b)) illustrates the potential decrement through the time. It is shown that the potential is forced to get stabilized in less than 20 secs and it will be shown that the settling time for next simulation examples will more than 20 secs.

6.2. Example II (Six Agents with Partially Unknown Dynamics).

To verify the effectiveness of proposed method the same novel formation error and (26) are chosen, respectively. Consider a group of six agents with the same dynamic models as (59). However, to design the control law, the dynamic model of agents is assumed to be partially unknown (i.e., $C(\cdot)$ and $g(\cdot)$ in (8) are unknown).

Therefore, six fuzzy logic approximators are designed to approximate the unknown dynamic, where each agent approximator just needs the current position and velocity of

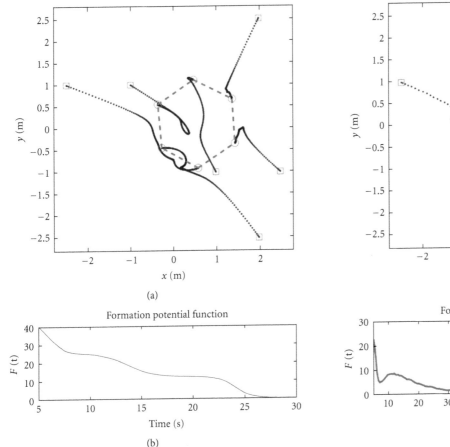

(a)

(b)

FIGURE 4: Hexagonal formation of six agents with partially unknown dynamics. (a) Formation trajectory. (b) Formation potential.

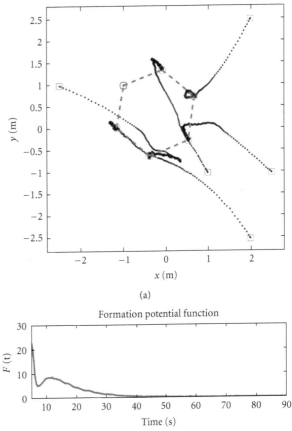

(a)

(b)

FIGURE 5: Hexagonal formation in presence of 20 db noise and one agent failure. (a) Formation trajectory. (b) Formation potential.

itself. Three Gaussian membership functions with unit variance are defined and all $\underline{\theta}$s are initialized from zero vectors. The learning rate in (48) is set to $\gamma = 15$ and the output of the fuzzy system is achieved by choosing singleton fuzzification, center average defuzzification, Mamdani implication in the rule base, and product inference engine [38].

Simulation results of the proposed adaptive fuzzy H^{∞} technique with agents initial positions as shown in Table 2 are shown as following. The motion trajectory in the first 30 secs is illustrated in Figure 4(a) and the formation potential (57) is shown to be stabilized in Figure 4(b).

6.3. Example III (Formation Problem in Presence of Measurement Noise and Agent Failure).
In this example the robustness of proposed controller in presence of measurement noise and agent failure will be proved. The proposed potential function (3) and gradient-based method proposed in Section 2 are able to obtain the exact formation even in the case of one agent failure. Therefore, in this example it will be shown that when Agent #3 ($x_3(0) = -1$, $y_3(0) = +1$) is forced to be stationary with zero velocity, other agents move toward this agent to achieve the hexagon formation. In addition a white Gaussian noise with SNR = 20 db is applied to all the measured data. All of the model characteristics and controller

designs are the same as previous example in Section 6.2. Motion trajectory and formation potential (57) of the first 90 secs of simulation are shown in Figures 5(a) and 5(b), respectively.

6.4. Example IV (Formation Problem While Tracking the Leader).
Previous example illustrated the good performance of formation stabilization, while agent failure (i.e., one agent remains stationary). However, the structure of potential function explained in (3) suggests to exempt one agent from the control law designed in (33), and let it move freely as the leader [8]. Therefore, to run a more general simulation than previous example where one agent was stationary, here one of the agents is chosen as the leader and moves with a constant speed to a predefined direction. Then it is anticipated that, after some transient formation, the agents position achieves the hexagon form in (57). All the problem parameters and controller design are the same as previous examples (i.e., (57), (59) and (42)). Agent #4 ($x_4(0) = +1$, $y_4(0) = -1$) is chosen as the leader, with constant velocity as

$$\dot{x}_4 = +0.030,$$
$$\dot{y}_4 = -0.005. \tag{60}$$

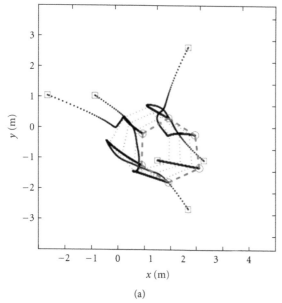

(a)

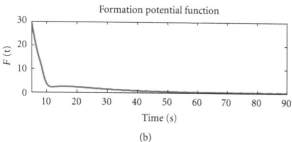

(b)

FIGURE 6: Moving hexagonal formation while tracking the leader. (a) Formation trajectory. (b) Formation potential.

The motion trajectory and formation potential (57) are shown in Figures 6(a) and 6(b), respectively.

Simulation results prove that by using the same control law as (33) even the moving formation can be achieved. It can be seen that the formation is achieved in about 70 secs; however, this numerical simulation contains negligible steady state error (Figure 6(b)).

7. Conclusion

In this paper, the formation control problem of a class of multiagent systems with partially unknown dynamics was investigated. On the basis of the Lyapunov stability theory, a novel decentralized adaptive fuzzy controller with corresponding parameter update law was developed and the stability of the system was proved even in the case of external disturbances and input nonlinearities. All the theoretical results were verified by simulation examples and good performance of the proposed controller was shown even in the case of agent failure, presence of measurement noise, and even moving formations.

References

[1] A. Badawy and C. R. McInnes, "Small spacecraft formation using potential functions," *Acta Astronautica*, vol. 65, no. 11-12, pp. 1783–1788, 2009.

[2] L. E. Barnes, M. A. Fields, and K. P. Valavanis, "Swarm formation control utilizing elliptical surfaces and limiting functions," *IEEE Transactions on Systems, Man, and Cybernetics, Part B*, vol. 39, no. 6, pp. 1434–1445, 2009.

[3] S. H. Kim, C. Park, and F. Harashima, "A self-organized fuzzy controller for wheeled mobile robot using an evolutionary algorithm," *IEEE Transactions on Industrial Electronics*, vol. 48, no. 2, pp. 467–474, 2001.

[4] Y. Chung, C. Park, and F. Harashima, "A position control differential drive wheeled mobile robot," *IEEE Transactions on Industrial Electronics*, vol. 48, no. 4, pp. 853–863, 2001.

[5] J. M. Lee, K. Son, M. C. Lee, J. W. Choi, S. H. Han, and M. H. Lee, "Localization of a mobile robot using the image of a moving object," *IEEE Transactions on Industrial Electronics*, vol. 50, no. 3, pp. 612–619, 2003.

[6] M. J. Er and C. Deng, "Obstacle avoidance of a mobile robot using hybrid learning approach," *IEEE Transactions on Industrial Electronics*, vol. 52, no. 3, pp. 898–905, 2005.

[7] D. Lee and W. Chung, "Discrete-status-based localization for indoor service robots," *IEEE Transactions on Industrial Electronics*, vol. 53, no. 5, pp. 1737–1746, 2006.

[8] J. H. Reif and H. Wang, "Social potential fields: a distributed behavioral control for autonomous robots," *Robotics and Autonomous Systems*, vol. 27, no. 3, pp. 171–194, 1999.

[9] S. Kato, S. Tsugawa, K. Tokuda, T. Matsui, and H. Fujii, "Vehicle control algorithms for cooperative driving with automated vehicles and intervehicle communications," *IEEE Transactions on Intelligent Transportation Systems*, vol. 3, no. 3, pp. 155–160, 2002.

[10] B. A. White, A. Tsourdos, I. Ashokaraj, S. Subchan, and R. Zbikowski, "Contaminant cloud boundary monitoring using network of UAV sensors," *IEEE Sensors Journal*, vol. 8, no. 10, pp. 1681–1692, 2008.

[11] R. Sepulchre, D. A. Paley, and N. E. Leonard, "Stabilization of planar collective motion: all-to-all communication," *Institute of Electrical and Electronics Engineers. Transactions on Automatic Control*, vol. 52, no. 5, pp. 811–824, 2007.

[12] D. V. Dimarogonas and K. J. Kyriakopoulos, "Connectedness preserving distributed swarm aggregation for multiple kinematic robots," *IEEE Transactions on Robotics*, vol. 24, no. 5, pp. 1213–1223, 2008.

[13] M. Proetzsch, T. Luksch, and K. Berns, "Development of complex robotic systems using the behavior-based control architecture iB2C," *Robotics and Autonomous Systems*, vol. 58, no. 1, pp. 46–67, 2010.

[14] K. Peng and Y. Yang, "Leader-following consensus problem with a varying-velocity leader and time-varying delays," *Physica A*, vol. 388, no. 2-3, pp. 193–208, 2009.

[15] H. Takahashi, H. Nishi, and K. Ohnishi, "Autonomous decentralized control for formation of multiple mobile robots considering ability of robot," *IEEE Transactions on Industrial Electronics*, vol. 51, no. 6, pp. 1272–1279, 2004.

[16] M. Defoort, T. Floquet, A. Kökösy, and W. Perruquetti, "Sliding-mode formation control for cooperative autonomous mobile robots," *IEEE Transactions on Industrial Electronics*, vol. 55, no. 11, pp. 3944–3953, 2008.

[17] C. C. Cheah, S. P. Hou, and J. J. E. Slotine, "Region-based shape control for a swarm of robots," *Automatica*, vol. 45, no. 10, pp. 2406–2411, 2009.

[18] V. Gazi, "Swarm aggregations using artificial potentials and sliding-mode control," *IEEE Transactions on Robotics*, vol. 21, no. 6, pp. 1208–1214, 2005.

[19] J. C. Doyle, K. Glover, P. P. Khargonekar, and B. A. Francis, "State-space solutions to standard H_2 and H_∞ control problems," *Institute of Electrical and Electronics Engineers. Transactions on Automatic Control*, vol. 34, no. 8, pp. 831–847, 1989.

[20] B. S. Chen, T. S. Lee, and J. H. Feng, "A nonlinear H_∞ control design in robotic systems under parameter perturbation and external disturbance," *International Journal of Control*, vol. 59, no. 2, pp. 439–461, 1994.

[21] G. Willmann, D. F. Coutinho, L. F. A. Pereira, and F. B. Libano, "Multiple-loop H-Infinity control design for uninterruptible power supplies," *IEEE Transactions on Industrial Electronics*, vol. 54, no. 3, pp. 1591–1602, 2007.

[22] K. H. Kwan, Y. C. Chu, and P. L. So, "Model-based H_∞ control of a unified power quality conditioner," *IEEE Transactions on Industrial Electronics*, vol. 56, no. 7, pp. 2493–2504, 2009.

[23] R. Wang, G. P. Liu, W. Wang, D. Rees, and Y. B. Zhao, "H∞ control for networked predictive control systems based on the switched Lyapunov function method," *IEEE Transactions on Industrial Electronics*, vol. 57, no. 10, pp. 3565–3571, 2010.

[24] A. G. Loukianov, J. Rivera, Y. V. Orlov, and E. Y. Morales Teraoka, "Robust trajectory tracking for an electrohydraulic actuator," *IEEE Transactions on Industrial Electronics*, vol. 56, no. 9, pp. 3523–3531, 2009.

[25] B. S. Chen, C. H. Lee, and Y. C. Chang, "H∞ tracking design of uncertain nonlinear SISO systems: adaptive fuzzy approach," *IEEE Transactions on Fuzzy Systems*, vol. 4, no. 1, pp. 32–43, 1996.

[26] L. A. Zadeh, "Fuzzy sets," *Information and Computation*, vol. 8, pp. 338–353, 1965.

[27] X. D. Sun, K. H. Koh, B. G. Yu, and M. Matsui, "Fuzzy-logic-based V/f control of an induction motor for a DC grid power-leveling system using flywheel energy storage equipment," *IEEE Transactions on Industrial Electronics*, vol. 56, no. 8, pp. 3161–3168, 2009.

[28] N. Yagiz, Y. Hacioglu, and Y. Taskin, "Fuzzy sliding-mode control of active suspensions," *IEEE Transactions on Industrial Electronics*, vol. 55, no. 11, pp. 3883–3890, 2008.

[29] C. Cecati, F. Ciancetta, and P. Siano, "A multilevel inverter for photovoltaic systems with fuzzy logic control," *IEEE Transactions on Industrial Electronics*, vol. 57, no. 12, pp. 4115–4125, 2010.

[30] F.-J. Lin and P.-H. Chou, "Adaptive control of two-axis motion control system using interval type-2 fuzzy neural network," *IEEE Transactions on Industrial Electronics*, vol. 56, no. 1, pp. 178–193, 2009.

[31] P. Shahmaleki, M. Mahzoon, and B. Ranjbar, "Real time experimental study of truck backer upper problem with fuzzy controller," in *Proceedings of the World Automation Congress (WAC'08)*, Hawaii, USA, October 2008.

[32] T. Das and I. N. Kar, "Design and implementation of an adaptive fuzzy logic-based controller for wheeled mobile robots," *IEEE Transactions on Control Systems Technology*, vol. 14, no. 3, pp. 501–510, 2006.

[33] Z. Lin, B. Francis, and M. Maggiore, "Necessary and sufficient graphical conditions for formation control of unicycles," *IEEE Transactions on Automatic Control*, vol. 50, no. 1, pp. 121–127, 2005.

[34] Y. Hu, W. Zhao, and L. Wang, "Vision-based target tracking and collision avoidance for two autonomous robotic fish," *IEEE Transactions on Industrial Electronics*, vol. 56, no. 5, pp. 1401–1410, 2009.

[35] J. Ferruz, V. M. Vega, A. Ollero, and V. Blanco, "Reconfigurable control architecture for distributed systems in the HERO autonomous helicopter," *IEEE Transactions on Industrial Electronics*, vol. 58, no. 12, Article ID 5437249, pp. 5311–5318, 2011.

[36] G. Cai, B. M. Chen, K. Peng, M. Dong, and T. H. Lee, "Modeling and control of the yaw channel of a UAV helicopter," *IEEE Transactions on Industrial Electronics*, vol. 55, no. 9, pp. 3426–3434, 2008.

[37] E. Slotine and W. Li, *Applied Nonlinear Control*, Prentice-Hall, Englewood Cliffs, NJ, USA, 1991.

[38] L. X. Wang, *A Course in Fuzzy Systems and Control*, Prentice-Hall, Englewood Cliffs, NJ, USA, 1997.

[39] H. G. Tanner, A. Jadbabaie, and G. J. Pappas, "Flocking in fixed and switching networks," *Institute of Electrical and Electronics Engineers. Transactions on Automatic Control*, vol. 52, no. 5, pp. 863–868, 2007.

5

Estimate a Flexible Link's Shape by the Use of Strain Gauge Sensors

M. H. Korayem, A. M. Shafei, and F. Absalan

Mechanical Engineering Department, Iran University of Science and Technology, Narmak, Tehran 13114-16846, Iran

Correspondence should be addressed to A. M. Shafei; shafei@iust.ac.ir

Academic Editors: D. K. Pratihar and A. Sabanovic

This paper presents a method for estimating the flexible link's shape by finite number of sensors. The position and orientation of flexible link are expressed as a function of curvature of the link. An interpolation technique gives this continuous curvature function from a finite set of the Wheatstone bridge made with strain gauges. For interpolation we can use different functions to find better way for estimation of link's shape. Comparison between different types of function can show us best corresponding with nature of the link. Our case study is a single flexible link robot. A high-precision data logger is used as data acquisition instrument.

1. Introduction

Research into flexible manipulator fields has become more important for more than a decade on account of new robotic applications in different areas such as industrial tasks in which the trend is to use lightweight materials (e.g., carbon fiber and composites) in the structures of manipulators in order to improve the performance of the industrial robots which are large and heavy. In aerospace applications the lightness of the materials is also an important requirement; the control of large structures, such as boom cranes and fire rescue turntable ladders, which are treated as flexible link robots is discussed by [1, 2]; minimally invasive surgery is performed with thin flexible instruments in which precise automatic manipulators are necessary [3]. These flexible manipulators exhibit important advantages in comparison to rigid ones, such as reduce energy consumption, smaller actuators, safety for humans, and more agility. Moreover, the effects of the collision with obstacles or humans are decreased because of the flexibility of the links. In spite of these advantages, the control problem of the flexible link manipulators becomes more complicated because the structural flexibility has to be controlled in such a way that the vibrations are cancelled if a good tip position and/or force control is to be gained.

Most of the work in the field of elastic robotic manipulator is confined to theoretical investigations. For validation the theoretical results by experimental testbed, it can be pointed out to the works of Cannon and Schmitz [4] as a pioneer in experimental study of single-link elastic robotic manipulator. Naganathan and Soni [5] also prepared an experimental setup composed of a single-link mounted on a stepper motor to verify their FEM results. Bellezza et al. [6] conducted experiments to study quasi-clamped and quasi-pinned end conditioned in slewing links. Luo [7] used a strain gauge sensor to measure the flexible robot arm deflections. Yang [8] presented a modal data-based method to estimate the dynamic response of an elastic robotic manipulator. Martins et al. [9] conducted experiments for a single-link elastic robotic manipulator to validate their suggested FEM based analytical model. More experimental testbed for vibration control of elastic robotic arm can be found in the investigation of Ladkany [10] and Peza Solis et al. [11].

So study and research on deflections and vibration of flexible link robots is an important problem. Increase of accuracy of measurements with finite number of sensors can help us. Flexible link's shapes can be approximated with different functions each one has specific nature. The usage of the best function that correspond nature of flexible link helps us to reduce sensor numbers and increases accuracy.

Research on dynamics and control of flexible robots are dependent on monitoring of link situations. For this purpose many types of sensors can be used such as strain gauges, piezoceramics, accelerometer, and so forth.

2. Kinematics of the Single-Link Elastic Robotic Manipulator

The single-link flexible manipulator system considered in this work is shown in Figure 1, where XYZ and xyz represent the stationary and moving coordinate's frames, respectively.

The position vector of arbitrary differential element Q with respect to the local reference system xyz is shown by $\vec{r}_{Q/o}$. The approach of modal analysis is used to incorporate the deflection of the link. So,

$$\vec{r}_{Q/o} = \vec{\eta} + \{u \quad v \quad w\}^T, \tag{1}$$

where $\vec{\eta} = \{\eta \quad 0 \quad 0\}^T$ is the position vector of differential element Q with respect to o, when the elastic link is unreformed and u, v, and w are small displacements in ox, oy, and oz directions, respectively. To express these small displacements, the approach of assumed mode method is used as

$$\{u \quad v \quad w\}^T = \sum_{i=1}^{m} \delta_i(t) \vec{r}_i(\eta). \tag{2}$$

Here $\vec{r}_i = \{x_i \quad y_i \quad z_i\}^T$ is the Eigen function vector whose components x_i, y_i, and z_i are ith longitudinal and transverse mode shapes of the link; δ_i is the i-th time-dependent modal generalized coordinate of the link, and m is the number of modes used to define the deflection of the link.

The total transverse displacement of the centerline of differential element Q is due to bending and shear. So the total slopes of the deflected centerline about oy and oz directions due to bending and shear deformation can be represented as

$$-\frac{\partial w}{\partial \eta} = \varphi_y + \theta_y,$$

$$\frac{\partial v}{\partial \eta} = \varphi_z + \theta_z, \tag{3}$$

where φ_y and φ_z are the slope of the deflected centerline due to shear and θ_y, θ_z are the slope of the deflected centerline due to bending. Shear has no influence on rotating the differential element Q, and this differential element undertakes rotations only due to bending and torsion. So the rotation of this element in ox, oy, and oz directions can be considered as θ_x, θ_y, and θ_z, respectively. These small angles can be represented by truncated modal expansion as

$$\vec{\theta} = \{\theta_x \quad \theta_y \quad \theta_z\}^T = \sum_{i=1}^{m} \delta_i(t) \vec{\theta}_i(\eta), \tag{4}$$

where $\vec{\theta}_i = \{\theta_{xi} \quad \theta_{yi} \quad \theta_{zi}\}^T$ is the Eigen function vector whose components θ_{xi}, θ_{yi}, and θ_{zi} are i-th rotational mode shapes of the link in ox, oy, and oz directions, respectively.

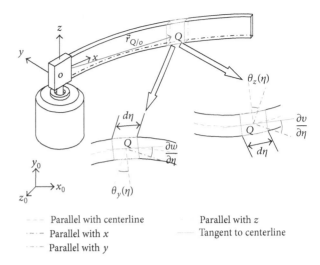

Parallel with centerline
Parallel with x
Parallel with y
Parallel with z
Tangent to centerline

FIGURE 1: Single-link elastic robotic manipulator.

3. The System Gibbs Function and Its Derivatives

In this section the system's acceleration energy and its derivatives with respect to quasi-accelerations are developed for construction the G-A formulation. With the assumption of TBT, the acceleration energy of a differential element Q can be represented as

$$ds = \frac{1}{2} \mu(\eta) \left(\ddot{\vec{r}}_Q^T \cdot \ddot{\vec{r}}_Q \right) d\eta + \frac{1}{2} \ddot{\vec{\theta}}^T \cdot J(\eta) \ddot{\vec{\theta}} d\eta. \tag{5}$$

But with the assumption of EBBT, only the first term of (5) should be preserved. Also $\mu(\eta)$ and $J(\eta)$ are mass per unit length and mass moment of inertia per unit length, respectively. Note that $\ddot{\vec{r}}_Q$ and $\ddot{\vec{\theta}}$ are linear and angular acceleration of differential element Q. These two terms can be stated as

$$\ddot{\vec{r}}_Q = \ddot{\vec{r}}_{Q/o} + 2\vec{\omega} \times \dot{\vec{r}}_{Q/o} + \dot{\vec{\omega}} \times \vec{r}_{Q/o} + \vec{\omega} \times \left(\vec{\omega} \times \vec{r}_{Q/o} \right),$$

$$\ddot{\vec{\theta}} = \sum_{j=1}^{m} \ddot{\delta}_j(t) \vec{\theta}_j(\eta). \tag{6}$$

In the above expressions, $\vec{\omega}$ and $\dot{\vec{\omega}}$ are angular velocity and angular acceleration of the link, respectively. Also $\dot{\vec{r}}_{Q/o}$ and $\ddot{\vec{r}}_{Q/o}$ are velocity and acceleration of differential element Q with respect to the origin of the local reference system, respectively. Inserting (6) into (5) and integrating over the link from 0 to l, the total acceleration energy of the link will be obtained as

$$S = \frac{1}{2} B_1 - 2\vec{\omega}^T \cdot \vec{B}_2 + \dot{\vec{\omega}}^T \cdot \vec{B}_3 - \vec{\omega}^T \cdot B_4 \vec{\omega} + 2\dot{\vec{\omega}}^T \cdot B_5 \vec{\omega}$$

$$+ \frac{1}{2} \dot{\vec{\omega}}^T \cdot B_6 \dot{\vec{\omega}} + \vec{\omega}^T \cdot \tilde{\omega} B_6 \vec{\omega} + \frac{1}{2} B_7 + \text{irrelevant terms}, \tag{7}$$

where $\tilde{\omega}$ is the skew-symmetric tensor associated with $\vec{\omega}$ vector. Also there is a term named as "irrelevant terms."

Motion equation with G-A formulation will be constructed by taking the partial derivatives of Gibbs' function with respect to quasi-accelerations. So, the term in Gibbs' function that does not contain $\ddot{q}$ and $\ddot{\delta}_j$ can be ignored. The variables that appeared in (7) can be calculated as,

$$B_1 = \sum_{j=1}^{m} \sum_{k=1}^{m} \ddot{\delta}_j \ddot{\delta}_k C_{1jk},$$

$$\vec{B}_2 = \sum_{j=1}^{m} \sum_{k=1}^{m} \ddot{\delta}_j \dot{\delta}_k \vec{C}_{2jk},$$

$$\vec{B}_3 = \sum_{j=1}^{m} \ddot{\delta}_j \vec{\alpha}_j,$$

$$B_4 = \sum_{j=1}^{m} \ddot{\delta}_j \beta_j,$$

$$B_5 = \sum_{j=1}^{m} \dot{\delta}_j \beta_j,$$

$$B_6 = C_3 + \sum_{j=1}^{m} \delta_j \left(C_{4j}^T + \beta_j \right),$$

$$B_7 = \sum_{j=1}^{m} \sum_{k=1}^{m} \ddot{\delta}_j \ddot{\delta}_k C_{5jk}.$$

(8)

where

$$C_{1jk} = \int_0^l \mu \vec{r}_j^T \cdot \vec{r}_k d\eta,$$

$$\vec{C}_{2jk} = \int_0^l \mu \tilde{r}_j \vec{r}_k d\eta,$$

$$C_3 = \int_0^l \mu \tilde{\eta}^T \tilde{\eta} d\eta,$$

$$C_{4j} = \int_0^l \mu \, \tilde{\eta}^T \tilde{r}_j d\eta,$$

$$C_{5jk} = \int_0^l \vec{\theta}_j^T \cdot J \vec{\theta}_k d\eta,$$

$$\vec{C}_{6j} = \int_0^l \mu \tilde{\eta} \, \vec{r}_j d\eta,$$

$$C_{7jk} = \int_0^l \mu \vec{r}_j^T \, \tilde{r}_k d\eta,$$

$$\vec{\alpha}_j = \vec{C}_{6j} + \sum_{k=1}^{m} \delta_k \vec{C}_{2kj},$$

$$\beta_j = C_{4j} + \sum_{k=1}^{m} \delta_k C_{7kj}.$$

(9)

In the above equations, $\tilde{\eta}$ and $\tilde{r}_j$ are skew-symmetric tensors associated with $\vec{\eta}$ and $\vec{r}_j$ vectors. As mentioned above, one part of dynamic equations of the system using (G-A) formulation will be obtained by differentiating of Gibbs' function with respect to quasi-accelerations. These two terms can be represented as

$$\frac{\partial S}{\partial \ddot{q}} = \frac{\partial \dot{\vec{\omega}}^T}{\partial \ddot{q}} \cdot \left(\vec{B}_3 + 2B_5 \vec{\omega} + B_6 \dot{\vec{\omega}} + \tilde{\omega} B_6 \vec{\omega} \right),$$

$$\frac{\partial S}{\partial \ddot{\delta}_j} = \sum_{k=1}^{m} \ddot{\delta}_k \left(C_{1jk} + C_{5jk} \right) - 2\vec{\omega}^T \cdot \sum_{k=1}^{m} \dot{\delta}_k \vec{C}_{2jk} - \vec{\omega}^T \cdot \beta_j \vec{\omega}$$

$$+ \dot{\vec{\omega}}^T \cdot \vec{\alpha}_j.$$

(10)

4. The System's Potential Energy and Its Derivatives

The potential energy of the system arises from two sources, first potential energy due to gravity and second potential energy due to the elastic deformations. The corresponding energy due to the gravity can be considered simply by inserting $\ddot{\vec{r}}_O = \vec{g}$, where $\vec{g}$ is the acceleration of gravity.

To express the strain potential energy stored in elastic link, let us assume two theories hold that: TBT and EBBT. For the first assumption the strain potential energy will be expressed in terms of deflections and rotations as

$$V_e = \frac{1}{2} \int_0^l \left[kAG \left(\varphi_y{}^2 + \varphi_z{}^2 \right) + EI_y \left(\frac{\partial \theta_y}{\partial \eta} \right)^2 + EI_z \left(\frac{\partial \theta_z}{\partial \eta} \right)^2 \right.$$

$$\left. + EA \left(\frac{\partial u}{\partial \eta} \right)^2 + GI_x \left(\frac{\partial \theta_x}{\partial \eta} \right)^2 \right] d\eta.$$

(11)

But for the second assumption, the first term in the above integral will be omitted. In (11), E and G are modulus of elasticity and shear modulus, respectively; I_x is the polar area moment of inertia about ox axis; I_y and I_z are area moment of inertia about oy and oz axes, respectively; A is the cross section area of the link and k is shear correction factor.

As noted in the previous section the small angles θ_x, θ_y, θ_z and small displacements u, v, w can be expressed with a truncated modal approximation. By inserting these expressions in (11), the strain potential energy for the link will be obtained as

$$V_e = \frac{1}{2} \sum_{j=1}^{m} \sum_{k=1}^{m} \delta_j(t) \delta_k(t) K_{jk},$$

(12)

where

$$K_{jk} = \int_0^l \left[kAG \left(\varphi_{yj}\varphi_{yk} + \varphi_{zj}\varphi_{zk} \right) + EI_y \frac{\partial \theta_{yj}}{\partial \eta} \frac{\partial \theta_{yk}}{\partial \eta} \right.$$

$$+ EI_z \frac{\partial \theta_{zj}}{\partial \eta} \frac{\partial \theta_{zk}}{\partial \eta} + EA \frac{\partial x_j}{\partial \eta} \frac{\partial x_k}{\partial \eta} \tag{13}$$

$$\left. + GI_x \frac{\partial \theta_{xj}}{\partial \eta} \frac{\partial \theta_{xk}}{\partial \eta} \right] d\eta.$$

For deriving the equations of motion of viscoelastic robotic manipulators, the partial derivatives of strain potential energy with respect to generalized coordinates are needed. These two terms can be represented as

$$\frac{\partial V_e}{\partial q} = 0,$$

$$\frac{\partial V_e}{\partial \delta_j} = \sum_{k=1}^m \delta_k(t) K_{kj}. \tag{14}$$

5. Rayleigh's Dissipation Function and Its Derivatives

An important class of nonconservative forces is the class of forces that dissipate energy. A common way of considering energy-dissipating forces is the assumption of viscous damping. In this model, the viscous damping force is modeled as a force opposing the velocity and proportional to it. The special case of linear proportionality is commonly used, because it is a linear approximation and easier to deal with, mathematically. This approximation is used especially when modeling light amounts of damping. In analytical mechanics, a convenient way of treating viscous damping forces is the use of Rayleigh's dissipation function. Rayleigh's dissipation function associated with these internal and external damping for the flexible link can be represented as

$$D = \frac{1}{2} \int_0^l \gamma \left[\left(\frac{\partial v}{\partial t} \right)^2 + \left(\frac{\partial w}{\partial t} \right)^2 \right] d\eta$$

$$+ \frac{1}{2} \int_0^{l_i} K_v \left[I_z \left(\frac{\partial^3 v}{\partial \eta^2 \partial t} \right)^2 + I_y \left(\frac{\partial^3 w}{\partial \eta^2 \partial t} \right)^2 \right] d\eta, \tag{15}$$

where K_v is the Kelvin-Voigt damping coefficient of the elastic link, and γ is the air damping coefficient. Inserting (2) into (15), Rayleigh's dissipation function for the system will be obtained as

$$D = \frac{1}{2} \sum_{j=1}^m \sum_{k=1}^m \dot{\delta}_j(t) \dot{\delta}_k(t) D_{jk}, \tag{16}$$

where

$$D_{jk} = \int_0^l \gamma \left(y_j y_k + z_j z_k \right) d\eta$$

$$+ \int_0^l K_v \left(I_z \frac{\partial^2 y_j}{\partial \eta^2} \frac{\partial^2 y_k}{\partial \eta^2} + I_y \frac{\partial^2 z_j}{\partial \eta^2} \frac{\partial^2 z_k}{\partial \eta^2} \right) d\eta. \tag{17}$$

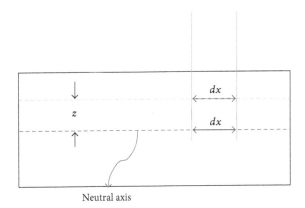

FIGURE 2: Differential element before bending.

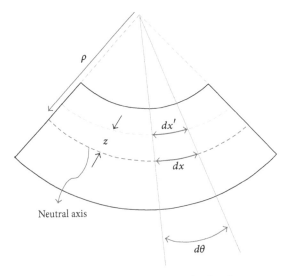

FIGURE 3: Differential element after bending.

Generalized forces due to internal and external damping are obtained by taking partial derivatives of Rayleigh's dissipation function with respect to generalized velocities. These two terms may be presented as

$$\frac{\partial D}{\partial \dot{q}} = 0,$$

$$\frac{\partial D}{\partial \dot{\delta}_j} = \sum_{k=1}^m \dot{\delta}_k(t) D_{kj}. \tag{18}$$

6. Dynamic Equations of Flexible Link Manipulator

Motion equation of viscoelastic robotic manipulators will be completed by considering the generalized forces which are caused by the remaining external force terms. Let us assume that there is no external load on the links of the considered robotic manipulator. So, the generalized forces in the deflection equations will be zero. The generalized force in the joint equations is the torque τ that applies to the joint.

FIGURE 4: The IUST flexible manipulator.

With this assumption, the dynamic equations of motion by (G-A) formulation will be completed as follows

(i) The joint equations of motion:

$$\frac{\partial S}{\partial \ddot{q}} + \frac{\partial D}{\partial \dot{q}} + \frac{\partial V_e}{\partial q} = \tau. \tag{19}$$

(ii) The deflection equations of motion:

$$\frac{\partial S}{\partial \ddot{\delta}_j} + \frac{\partial D}{\partial \dot{\delta}_j} + \frac{\partial V_e}{\partial \delta_j} = 0 \quad j = 1, 2, \dots, m. \tag{20}$$

6.1. Strain and Curvature. If the strain in different sections of an elastic beam is known, the shape of the beam can be estimated by interpolation. The differential element in yellow color in Figures 2 and 3 shows the beam's neutral axis before and after bending, respectively.

The strain of this differential element can be presented as:

$$\varepsilon(x) = \frac{(\rho - z) \cdot d\theta - \rho \cdot d\theta}{\rho \cdot d\theta} = -\frac{z}{\rho}. \tag{21}$$

Based on (21), the strain on the surface of the beam will be obtained as

$$\varepsilon(x) = -\frac{t}{2\rho(x)}, \tag{22}$$

where t is the thickness of the beam. On the other hand from elementary calculus the curvature of a plane curve can be expressed as:

$$\frac{1}{\rho} = \frac{y''(x)}{\left(1 + y'(x)^2\right)^{3/2}}. \tag{23}$$

Thus, the strain of the beam in terms of the function $y(x)$ can be represented as:

$$\varepsilon(x) = -\frac{t \cdot y''(x)}{2\left(1 + y'(x)^2\right)^{3/2}}. \tag{24}$$

But, in the case of the elastic curve of a beam, the slope y' is very small, and its square is negligible compared to unity. So,

$$\varepsilon(x) = -\frac{t \cdot y''(x)^2}{2}. \tag{25}$$

Therefor, the strain is a function of curvature and thickness. The magnitude of strain in x position will be obtained with a strain gauge on that point. As we cannot use infinite number of sensors, the strain is definite only in finite points. We can guess $y(x)$ as a suitable function that can approximate link's shape. The nature of the function must be the same with the nature of the flexible link. If one uses suitable function for link's shape, fewer constants and fewer sensors will be needed. In this paper, the following functions will be used:

$$A \cdot x^4 + B \cdot x^3 + C \cdot x^2 + E \cdot x + F,$$

$$A \cdot x^6 + B \cdot x^5 + C \cdot x^4 + D \cdot x^3 + E \cdot x^2 + F \cdot x + G,$$

$$A \cdot \sin(x) + B \sin(2 \cdot x) + C \cdot \cos(x) + D \cdot \cos(2 \cdot x) + E,$$

$$A \cdot \sin(x) + B \cdot \sin(2 \cdot x) + C \cdot \sin(3 \cdot x) + D \cdot \cos(x)$$
$$+ E \cdot \cos(2 \cdot x) + F \cdot \cos(3 \cdot x) + G,$$

$$A \cdot \sinh(x) + B \cdot \sinh(2 \cdot x) + C \cdot \cosh(x)$$
$$+ D \cdot \cosh(2 \cdot x) + E,$$

$$A \cdot \sinh(x) + B \cdot \sinh(2 \cdot x) + C \cdot \sinh(3 \cdot x)$$
$$+ D \cdot \cosh(x) + E \cdot \cosh(2 \cdot x)$$
$$+ F \cdot \cosh(3 \cdot x) + G. \tag{26}$$

In experimental setup, three full bridge strain gauges attached in three different positions. By the use of (25) and considering the three strain gauge bridges, we can organize three equations. In addition, from boundary condition, slope and deflection at the beginning of the link are zero. So, y and y' in this point will be zero. With these three strains and two boundary conditions, five equations with five unknowns can be solved. But if we consider the boundary conditions at the end point of the link, two more equations will be added. In fact at the end point of the link shear and moment are zero. So, y'' and y''' will be zero in this point. In this condition, we have seven equations with seven unknowns and we can guess a function with more constants and more accuracy.

7. Experimental Setup

The experimental testbed is the flexible manipulator that is prepared at the Department of Mechanical Engineering of the Iran University of Science and Technology Figure 4. The experimental setup consists of a single-link flexible manipulator driven by a servo-tech AC servo motor. This 400 W AC servomotor can be driven in position, speed, and toque mode. In order to remove additional effect of bearing friction, the flexible manipulator is directly attached to

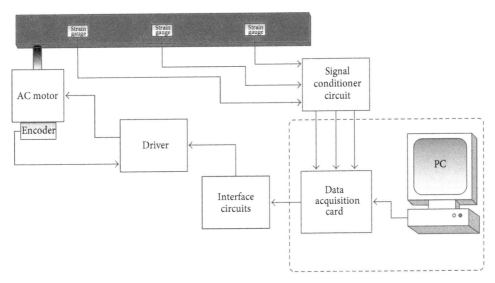

FIGURE 5: Schematic view of the experimental setup.

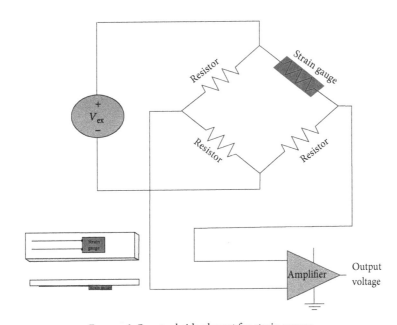

FIGURE 6: Quarter bridge layout for strain gauges.

the motor shaft. In Table 1 the physical properties of the flexible manipulator are summarized. Also, the Schematic diagram of the experimental setup is shown in Figure 5.

The flexible manipulator has a planar motion thus the effect of gravity can be ignored. An incremental encoder with the resolution of 2500 pulse per revolution is used to calculate the rotation angle of the motor. Motor angular velocity is determined by time derivation of the motor angular position data. The tip deflection and vibration of the link are measured by three strain gauge bridges mounted on the link. The analogue signals of the strain gauges amplify through a signal conditioner circuit and sent to a data acquisition card.

A 64-bit personal computer was used for control motor output via an Advantech PCI-1710HG data acquisition card. PCI-1710HG is a multifunction card with 12 bits resolution and 100 kS/s sampling rate.

Strain gauges can be attached in many ways for different purposes. For recording vibrations without temperature compensation, we have three-type layouts. Quarter bridge, half bridge and full bridge layout can be used for this purpose. Quarter bridge (Figure 6) has less sensitivity than two other types. So, it can be economic. But the weakness of signals makes the necessity of expensive signal conditioners.

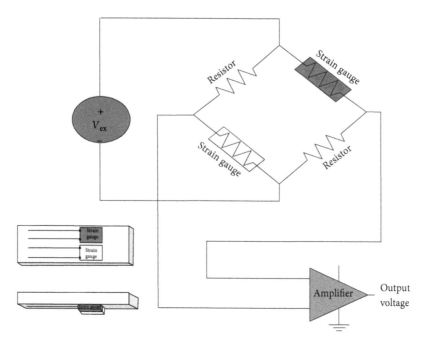

FIGURE 7: Half bridge layout for strain gauges.

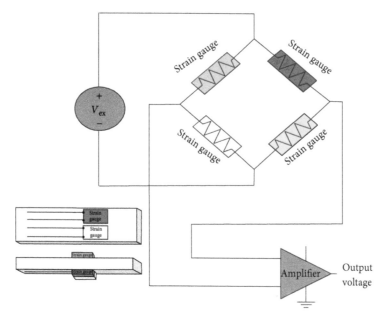

FIGURE 8: Full bridge layout for strain gauges.

Half bridge (Figure 7) and full bridge layouts have more sensitivity but need more number of sensors, respectively. Half bridge layout uses two strain gauges, and if it is required, two other strain gauges in normal directions can be added in order to compensate the temperature effects.

Full bridge layout (Figure 8) uses four strain gauges and has best sensitivity and simplest equation. But as the bridge is full, it is not possible to use temperature compensator in this type.

The following equations can be used for calculation the exact magnitude of strain:

$$\frac{V_o}{V_{\mathrm{Ex}}} = -\frac{GF \cdot \varepsilon}{4}\left(\frac{1}{1 + GF \cdot (\varepsilon/2)}\right),$$

$$\frac{V_o}{V_{\mathrm{Ex}}} = -\frac{GF \cdot \varepsilon}{2}, \qquad (27)$$

$$\frac{V_o}{V_{\mathrm{Ex}}} = -GF \cdot \varepsilon.$$

These three equations show relations between V_o and strain in quarter bridge, half bridge, and full bridge, respectively. It is clear that quarter bridge equation has nonlinear

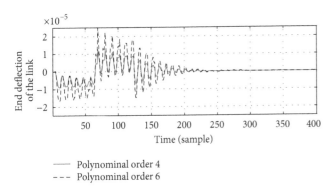

— Polynominal order 4
- - - Polynominal order 6

FIGURE 9: Estimation of end point deflection with 6th-order and 4th-order polynomials.

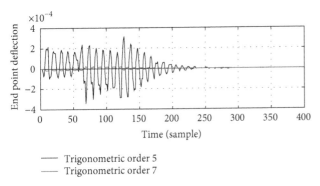

— Trigonometric order 5
— Trigonometric order 7

FIGURE 10: Estimation of end point deflection with 5th and 7th order trigonometric functions.

TABLE 1: Parameters of the flexible link.

Number	Description	Value
1	Length (m)	0.5
2	Height (m)	0.517
3	Thickness (m)	0.0015
4	Bending stiffness (N·m^2)	1.01784
5	Hub inertia (Kg·m^2)	0.0015
6	Shear modulus (N/m^2)	$27e9$

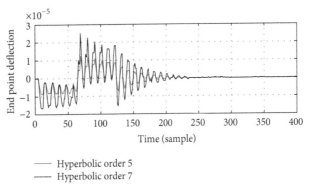

— Hyperbolic order 5
— Hyperbolic order 7

FIGURE 11: Comparison between 5th-and 7th, order hyperbolic functions.

form, but the other two types have linear and simple relations. In the above equations V_{Ex} is excitation voltage exerted on the Wheatstone bridge. V_o in these equations exhibit output voltage. Excitation voltage affects V_o. On the other hand, increasing in excitation voltage causes increasing in output voltage and provides more resolution. But increasing in exoitation voltage causes increasing in ampere. It can generates heat in strain gauges. Generated heat in strain gauges must be compensated with temperature compensator strain gauges. Otherwise, error increases in output voltage.

8. Results and Discussion

In this section, simulation and experimental results of the response of a flexible manipulator and the effect of functions are presented. The torque input implemented to the manipulator is a bang-bang torque with amplitude of $\pm 0.13\,\text{N} \cdot \text{m}$ and duty cycle of 0.3 s. This torque has a positive (acceleration) and a negative (deceleration) period allowing the manipulator to initially accelerates and then decelerates and eventually stops at a target location. There are 400 data from each strain gauge bridges that can help to have a comparison between experimental results and theoretical results. Sampling frequency is 200 Hz.

At first, we compare a sixth-order polynomial with a fourth-order polynomial.

It's clear in Figure 9, 6th-order polynomial exhibits better results from sensors data. If we have free conditions at the end of the link, it's better to use this function.

Figure 10 shows that the interpolation with 5th-order trigonometric function leading to very bad results. The function has no enough agility for tracking vibrations. So the behavior of trigonometric functions is far from link vibrations.

At the next stage, the behavior of hyperbolic functions will be studied. As shown in Figure 11, comparison between hyperbolic functions with different constants shows similar results. Nevertheless, the use of hyperbolic function with seven constants yields better results.

In the next step comparison between trigonometric, hyperbolic, and polynomial functions with seven constants will be shown. As seen in Figure 12 vibration behavior of these functions is the same. Although the nature of these three functions is not similar, very good fitting will be observed.

Continuously experimental results will be compared with the Gibbs-Apple theoretical results. For experimental estimation, hyperbolic function with seven contents is used.

In Figure 13 experimental results follow theoretical results closely. So hyperbolic and polynomials are suitable for estimating flexible links vibrations.

9. Conclusions

In this paper the equation of motion of a single-like flexible manipulator is derived by the Gibbs-Appell formulation. Also an experimental test bed was prepared to verify the simulation results. The obtained results from strain gauges

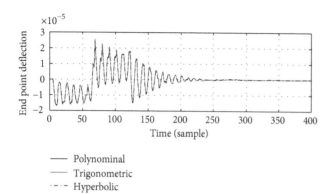

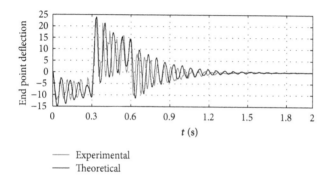

FIGURE 12: Comparison between polynomial, trigonometric, and hyperbolic functions with seven constants.

FIGURE 13: Experiment and theoretical result comparison.

converted to end point deflection by different functions. These functions can be used for monitoring flexible link vibrations. Among these functions, the obtained result from hyperbolic function follows theoretical results much better than the other functions.

References

[1] I. Payo, V. Feliu, and O. D. Cortázar, "Force control of a very lightweight single-link flexible arm based on coupling torque feedback," *Mechatronics*, vol. 19, no. 3, pp. 334–347, 2009.

[2] O. Sawodny, H. Aschemann, and A. Bulach, "Mechatronical designed control of fire-rescue turntable-ladders as flexible link robots," in *Proceedings of the 15th Triennial World Congress International Federation of Automatic Control (IFAC '02)*, Barcelona, Spain, 2002.

[3] R. A. Beasley and R. D. Howe, "Model-based error correction for flexible robotic surgical instruments," in *Proceedings of Robotics: Science and System Conference*, vol. 1, 2005.

[4] R. H. Cannon and E. Schmitz, "Initial experiments on end-point control of a flexible one-link robot," *International Journal of Robotics Research*, vol. 3, no. 3, pp. 62–75, 1984.

[5] G. Naganathan and A. H. Soni, "An analytical and experimental investigation of flexible manipulator performance," in *Proceeding of the IEEE International Conference on Robotic and Automation*, vol. 4, pp. 767–773, 1987.

[6] F. Bellezza, L. Lanari, and G. Ulivi, "Exact modeling of the flexible slewing link," in *Proceedings of the IEEE International Conference on Robotics and Automation*, pp. 734–739, May 1990.

[7] Z. H. Luo, "Direct strain feedback control of flexible robot arms: new theoretical and experimental results," *IEEE Transactions on Automatic Control*, vol. 38, no. 11, pp. 1610–1622, 1993.

[8] Z. Yang, "Prediction of the dynamic response of flexible manipulators from a modal database," *Mechanism and Machine Theory*, vol. 32, no. 6, pp. 679–689, 1997.

[9] J. M. Martins, Z. Mohamed, M. O. Tokhi, J. Sá da Costa, and M. A. Botto, "Approaches for dynamic modelling of flexible manipulator systems," *IEE Proceedings on Control Theory and Applications*, vol. 150, no. 4, pp. 401–411, 2003.

[10] S. G. Ladkany, "The dynamic response of a flexible three-link robot using strain gages and lagrange polynomials," in *Proceedings of the 4th World Conference on Robotics Research*, 1991.

[11] J. F. Peza Solis, G. Silva Navarro, and R. Castro Linares, "Modeling tip position control of a flexible link robot," *Computation y Sistemas*, vol. 12, no. 4, pp. 421–435, 2008.

6

Nontumbling Gait for Multilegged Robots and Its Directional Normalized Energy Stability Margin

Evgeny Lazarenko, Satoshi Kitano, Shigeo Hirose, and Gen Endo

Fukushima Laboratory Department of Mechanical and Aerospace Engineering, Tokyo Institute of Technology, Ishikawadai 1st Building, 2-12-1 I1-52 Ookayama, Meguro-ku, Tokyo 152-8552, Japan

Correspondence should be addressed to Evgeny Lazarenko; lazarenko.e.aa@m.titech.ac.jp

Academic Editors: L. Asplund, R. Bostelman, R. Safaric, and Y. Zhou

This paper discusses the importance of a nontumbling gait, a gait that allows preventing complete tumbling of the robot. Nontumbling gait is made possible by the effect of the swing leg which may contact the ground even when the robot is affected by an external disturbance. Such an effect is present in both static walking and dynamic walking. Stability criterion required to maintain the nontumbling gait is then considered and proposed through generalized directional normalized energy stability margin. The validity of the introduced criterion is evaluated by a tumbling experiment with a simplified walking robot model. The concept is also applied to the gait control of the newly developed walking robot TITAN-XIII.

1. Introduction

Over the past few years the development of various multilegged robots has gained significant traction. However, most of the advances have been made in the direction of mechanical design and high-level control systems. There has been little discussion about such important subject as stability of multi-legged locomotion, and most of the scholars continue to rely on normalized energy stability margin, or NESM [1]. In one of our previous works we proposed a directional normalized energy stability Margin [2], or S_θ, which allowed us to estimate robot's stability at any given direction. In this paper, we will further investigate the properties and possible applications of DNESM S_θ. We will do so through the discussion about the effect that swinging leg may have on the stability of a multi-legged robot during its motion.

2. Nontumbling Gait

When a multi-legged robot cannot maintain a planned stable walking or running due to some disturbance, for example, wind, its movement can be described by one of the two tumbling states: complete tumbling, and partial tumbling (it should be noted that under tumbling we understand

a disruption of a planned walking sequence under the influence of external disturbance). Complete tumbling is a state when robot tumbles until its body hits the ground, whereas partial tumbling is a state when robot inclines, but does not overturn due to the effect of the swing legs which hit the ground and help to maintain standing posture. Figures 1 and 2 illustrate partial tumbling in detail.

Let us assume that the robot is performing a statically stable crawling gait and maintaining stability by forming a supporting triangle with legs P_1, P_3, and P_4. Disturbance energy E_i is applied to the body of the robot as shown in Figure 1(a). When disturbance energy E_i is large, robot may start tumbling around the line connecting P_1 and P_4, and the swing leg P_2 may hit the ground. If disturbance energy is very large, the robot may overturn completely. However, if it is not, robot will maintain a standing posture with a newly formed supporting polygon $P_1P_2P_4$. This latter state is what we call a partial tumbling in a static walking.

Let us assume that the robot is preforming a dynamically stable trot gait and maintaining a planned dynamic motion while keeping the ZMP of the body on the line connecting P_1 and P_4. Disturbance energy E_i is applied as shown in Figure 2(a). If disturbance energy E_i is very large, the robot may tumble completely. However, if it is not, the robot will

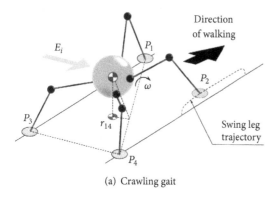

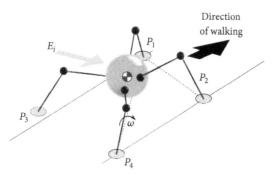

(a) Crawling gait

(b) Crawling gait after the application of disturbing input energy E_i

FIGURE 1: Crawling gait and subsequent rotation after the application of external disturbing energy.

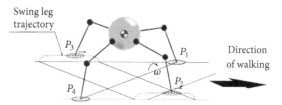

(a) Trotting gait before the application of disturbing energy

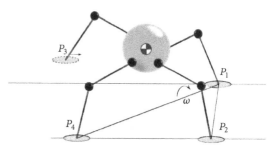

(b) Trotting gait after the application of disturbing energy, case of forward tilting

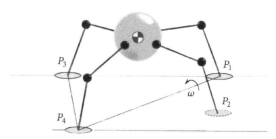

(c) Trotting gait after the application of disturbing energy, case of backward tilting

FIGURE 2: Trotting gait and possible subsequent rotations in case of application of external disturbing energy.

maintain a standing posture with a newly formed supporting polygon $P_1P_2P_4$ in case of Figure 2(b) or $P_1P_3P_4$ in case of Figure 2(c). This latter state is what we call a partial tumbling in a dynamic walking.

Both complete and partial tumbling are, of course, not desirable, and they should be avoided. From practical viewpoint, however, partial tumbling is acceptable, unlike complete tumbling, because it would not damage the body, and resuming normal walking sequence or running in case of partial tumbling is not difficult from the control system standpoint.

Until now, there were many discussions about the stability criteria for statically stable walking, such as: static stability margin [3], energy stability margin [4], normalized energy stability margin [1], energy stability margin accounting for dynamic effects [5, 6], and, finally, directional normalized energy stability margin. But all of these criteria only consider the conditions required to maintain a statically stable posture and never consider the phenomena that happen when tumbling occurs.

As for the stability of dynamic walking, as far as we know, the discussion about it has not been done before, and dynamic walking was considered unstable from the beginning. In this context, an idea about "stability" being an intrinsic property of dynamic walking may sound contradictory.

From practical viewpoint, even if normal planned walking motion is disrupted, it is important to prevent complete tumbling and turn it into partial tumbling, because this may

help to prevent robot's damage and to return to normal static or dynamic walking.

We would like to specifically define the gait that prevents complete tumbling and turns it into partial tumbling as a "nontumbling gait," or "NT gait." We would also like to discuss about the conditions that should be met in order to perform an NT Gait.

3. Generalized Concept of the Directional Normalized Energy Stability Margin, or S_θ

3.1. Definition of Directional Normalized Energy Stability Margin. In order to generate an NT gait resistant to large disturbing forces applied to robot's body from any direction, our first step was to introduce Directional Normalized Stability Margin, a new stability criterion that takes into account the dynamic effects of a tumbling motion, including the effect of the swinging leg when it forms a new ground foothold, as well as a directional disturbing force.

We proposed S_θ before and defined it as the minimum amount of input energy E_i applied in the form of horizontal force with a yaw angular direction θ required to tumble

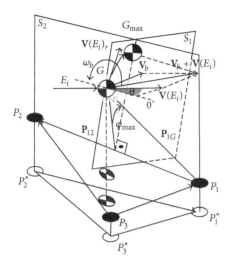

FIGURE 3: Rotation of CG around the edge of the supporting polygon under the influence of external disturbance E_i for robot standing in an arbitrary posture. P_i are footholds, and P_i^* are their projections on a horizontal plane. $\mathbf{V}(E_i)$ is input velocity, created by external disturbance energy E_i, and $\mathbf{V}_b$ is robot's body velocity. S_1 is the plane of CG rotation around P_1P_2, and S_2 is a vertical plane of an unstable equilibrium above P_1P_2. Other variables are defined in Section 3.

an object, divided by weight mg of the robot itself. DNESM S_θ was expressed as follows:

$$S_\theta = \left.\frac{E_i}{mg}\right|_\theta. \tag{1}$$

In this criterion, we assume the phenomenon of instantaneous time, when robot's movement is measured in discrete time snapshots; therefore, even though $\mathbf{V}(E_i)$ is created by a certain input force which is, in turn, caused by an input energy E_i, we may neglect such parameters as acceleration under the influence of that force, feet slipping, and so forth. Input energy E_i is applied to the center of gravity of the object in the form of force $\mathbf{F}(E_i)$ that acts in the horizontal plane on the yaw angle θ and generates velocity $\mathbf{V}(E_i)$.

3.2. Calculation of S_θ. Let us summarize the calculation of S_θ for a walking robot with an n-legged supporting posture.

We assume that a walking robot is affected by an input energy E_i that generates horizontal input velocity $\mathbf{V}(E_i)$ of the CG (Figure 3). Yaw direction θ of $\mathbf{V}(E_i)$ is variable, and its magnitude is defined by the amount of energy required to overturn the robot. Additionally, robot body has a horizontal velocity $\mathbf{V}_b$. Therefore, we are considering that rotational velocity $\mathbf{V}(\mathbf{V}(E_i), \mathbf{V}_b)_r$ is generated by both $\mathbf{V}(E_i)$ and $\mathbf{V}_b$.

P_i and P_j are neighboring ground contact points. Edges of the supporting polygon and CG of the robot may be denoted as $\mathbf{P}_{i,j}$ and $G(x_G, y_G, z_G)$ correspondingly.

Main condition for overturning the robot is moving its CG from initial position G to a position $G_{(i,j)\max}$—an unstable equilibrium in rotation around $\mathbf{P}_{i,j}$ axis.

Thus, S_θ for the edge of the supporting polygon connecting ith and jth foothold may be easily computed through (2):

$$S_\theta = \frac{1}{2g}\left(\frac{\sqrt{2gH_{i,j}}}{Z_{i,j}} - V_b\frac{B_{i,j\,\text{body}}}{B_{i,j}}\right)^2. \tag{2}$$

Variables, necessary for computation of S_θ via (2), can be calculated through the following equations.

(1) $H_{i,j}$, height difference between original CG position G and its highest possible position $G_{(i,j)\max}$ above $\mathbf{P}_{i,j}$:

$$H_{i,j} = G_{(i,j)\max z} - G_z, \tag{3}$$

where

$$\begin{aligned}
\mathbf{G}_{(i,j)\max} &= \frac{C_{i,j}}{\|\mathbf{P}_{i,j}\|}\widehat{\mathbf{P}}_{i,j} \\
&+ \cos\varphi_{\max}\left(\mathbf{P}_{iG} - \frac{C_{i,j}}{\|\mathbf{P}_{i,j}\|}\widehat{\mathbf{P}}_{i,j}\right) \\
&+ \sin\varphi_{\max}\frac{\mathbf{A}_{i,j}}{\|\mathbf{P}_{i,j}\|} + \mathbf{P_i},
\end{aligned} \tag{4}$$

for which

$$\mathbf{A}_{i,j} = \begin{bmatrix} (y_j - y_i)(z_G - z_i) - (y_G - y_i)(z_j - z_i) \\ -(x_j - x_i)(z_G - z_i) + (x_G - x_i)(z_j - z_i) \\ (x_j - x_i)(y_G - y_i) - (x_G - x_i)(y_j - y_i) \end{bmatrix}, \tag{5}$$

$$\begin{aligned}
C_{i,j} &= (x_G - x_i)(x_j - x_i) + (y_G - y_i)(y_j - y_i) \\
&+ (z_G - z_i)(z_j - z_i).
\end{aligned}$$

Also, a maximum angular displacement of robot's CG $\varphi_{\max_{i,j}}$ can be found as

$$\varphi_{\max_{i,j}} = \arctan(D_{ij}), \tag{6}$$

where

$$D_{i,j} = \frac{(x_j - x_i)(y_G - y_i) - (x_G - x_i)(y_j - y_i)}{\|\mathbf{P}_{i,j}\|(z_G - z_i) - (C_{i,j}/\|\mathbf{P}_{i,j}\|)(z_j - z_i)}. \tag{7}$$

(2) Coefficient $Z_{i,j}$ for a $\mathbf{P}_{i,j}$ axis:

$$Z_{i,j}^2 = \left(\frac{B_{i,j}}{\|\mathbf{P}_{i,j}\times\mathbf{P}_{iG}\|^2}\right)^2\mathbf{A}_{i,j}^T\mathbf{A}_{i,j}, \tag{8}$$

for which coefficient

$$\begin{aligned}
B_{i,j} &= \left[\left((y_j - y_i)(z_G - z_i) - (y_G - y_i)(z_j - z_i)\right)\cos\theta\right. \\
&+ \left.\left(-(x_j - x_i)(z_G - z_i) + (x_G - x_i)(y_j - y_i)\right)\sin\theta\right].
\end{aligned} \tag{9}$$

(3) Similarly, coefficient $B_{i,j\,body}$:

$$
\begin{aligned}
B_{i,j\,body} = &\left[\left(\left(y_j - y_i\right)\left(z_G - z_i\right) - \left(y_G - y_i\right)\left(z_j - z_i\right)\right)\cos\gamma\right.\\
&+ \left(-\left(x_j - x_i\right)\left(z_G - z_i\right)\right.\\
&\left.\left.+ \left(x_G - x_i\right)\left(y_j - y_i\right)\right)\sin\gamma\right],
\end{aligned}
$$

$$(10)$$

where γ is the direction angle of robot's body velocity $\mathbf{V}_b$.

3.3. Expansion of S_θ for the Generalized Case of Partial Tumbling.
As it was explained above, in presence of the swinging leg, when disturbing force is high enough to cause robot's rotation around a given edge of the supporting polygon, the leg may block robot's motion. In order to explain this tumbling sequence in detail, let us refer to Figure 1. There are two possible stages of rotation, and we will refer to them as "first rotation" and "second rotation."

We will be using the case of a crawling gait pictured in Figure 1 as an illustration to our explanation and subsequent calculations.

In case of Figure 1, first rotation is a rotation of robot's CG around P_1P_4 edge of the supporting polygon $P_1P_3P_4$ (top view diagram shown in Figure 4(a)). If input energy E_i is sufficient, and so is input velocity $\mathbf{V}(E_i)$, it may force the robot to overturn around P_1P_4. If that is the case, leg P_3 loses its contact with the ground, while leg P_2, on contrary, gains it. This motion results in a change of the supporting polygon from $P_1P_3P_4$ to $P_1P_4P_2$ (Figures 1(b) and 4(b)).

If initial disturbing energy E_i is high enough, robot's movement can continue in a second rotation phase either around P_2P_4 (in S_2 plane, Figure 4(b)) or around P_1P_2 (in S_3 plane, Figure 5), depending on the position of the swinging leg P_2 and direction of motion of the CG.

For the purpose of illustration, let us suppose that second rotation occurs around P_2P_4, as in Figure 4(b). Let us discuss the process of calculation of S_θ in such case in detail.

3.3.1. Calculation of S_θ for the First Rotation.
For the first rotation, we will not be calculating a typical S_θ as the one we discussed before. This is because previously we were suggesting that disturbance input energy E_i should be sufficient to rotate CG around P_1P_4 edge on angle φ_{max}. But in case of partial tumbling, the motion of robot's CG is constrained by existing swing leg (e.g., P_2). Thus, it needs to be moved on angle δ, or the angular distance which swing leg P_2 should travel before hitting the ground (Figure 6).

In such case, we can substitute angle θ_{max} with angle δ. Therefore, we must first calculate angle δ based on the coordinates of swing leg P_2 before its collision with the ground. It can be expressed as

$$\delta = \arctan\left(\frac{z_2}{d_2}\right), \qquad (11)$$

where z_2 is the height of the swing leg P_2 and d_2 is the distance between projection of P_2 on a horizontal plane and P_1P_4 edge of the supporting polygon.

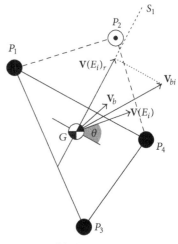

(a) First rotation

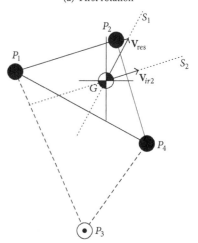

(b) Second rotation, variant with tumbling around P_2P_4 line

FIGURE 4: Sequence of destabilized motion (partial tumbling) after the application of disturbing input energy E_i.

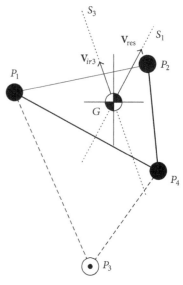

FIGURE 5: Second rotation, variant with tumbling around P_1P_2 line.

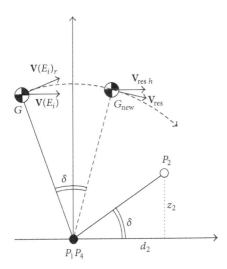

FIGURE 6: Side view of the first rotation.

In turn, distance d_2 can be easily calculated as

$$d_2 = \frac{(y_1 - y_4)\, x_2 + (x_4 - x_1)\, y_2 + (x_1 y_4 - x_4 y_1)}{\sqrt{(y_1 - y_4)^2 + (x_4 - x_1)^2}}. \tag{12}$$

New position of robot's CG in rotation around $P_1 P_4$ edge can be calculated from (4) by substituting $\varphi_{\max}$ with δ which can be found through (11) and (12):

$$
\begin{aligned}
\mathbf{G}_{\text{first}} &= \frac{C_{1,4}}{\|\mathbf{P}_{1,4}\|} \widehat{\mathbf{P}}_{1,4} \\
&\quad + \cos\delta \left(\mathbf{P}_{1G} - \frac{C_{1,4}}{\|\mathbf{P}_{1,4}\|} \widehat{\mathbf{P}}_{1,4} \right) \\
&\quad + \sin\delta \, \frac{\mathbf{A}_{1,4}}{\|\mathbf{P}_{1,2}\|} + \mathbf{P_1}.
\end{aligned}
\tag{13}
$$

Knowing G_{first}, the new position of CG, we can calculate the height difference $H_{1,4}$ between it and initial position G:

$$H_{1,4} = G_{\text{first}\, z} - G_z. \tag{14}$$

Also, from (9), we can define coefficient $B_{1,4}$, and, from (8), we can calculate $Z_{1,4}$. Subsequently, from (2), it is easy to find $S_{\theta_{\text{first}}}$ for $P_1 P_4$ edge of the supporting polygon:

$$S_{\theta_{\text{first}}} = \frac{1}{2g} \left(\frac{\sqrt{2g H_{1,4}}}{Z_{1,4}} - V_b \frac{B_{1,4\,\text{body}}}{B_{1,4}} \right)^2. \tag{15}$$

3.3.2. Calculation of S_θ for the Second Rotation. It is important to highlight that after the first rotation, the robot's body acquires a residual velocity $\mathbf{V}_{\text{res}}$ (Figures 4(b) and 6). Projection of this residual velocity on a horizontal plane represents a body velocity $\mathbf{V}_{b\,\text{second}}$, which is an initial condition for the second rotation.

Another important point is that we cannot vary angle θ_{second} (direction of the input velocity $\mathbf{V}_{\text{second}}(E_i)$) during

the second rotation. This is because robot's motion in this stage is not independent but is only a continuation of the motion initiated at the stage of first rotation under the influence of previously applied disturbance energy E_i. Thus, the directions of $\mathbf{V}_{\text{res}\,h}$, horizontal projection of residual velocity, and input velocity for the second rotation $\mathbf{V}_{\text{second}}(E_i)$ coincide. Therefore, the physical meaning of S_θ for the second rotation is how much energy is required to overturn the robot around the edge of the supporting polygon *in addition* to the existing residual energy from the first rotation (represented in the form of residual velocity $\mathbf{V}_{\text{res}}$).

In such case, $S_{\theta_{\text{second}}}$ can be calculated through (2), with a consideration that $\theta_{\text{second}} = \gamma_{\text{second}}$, and $\mathbf{V}_b = \mathbf{V}_{\text{res}\,h}$. Thus, $B_{2,4} = B_{2,4\,\text{body}}$, and equation for its calculation will look like

$$
\begin{aligned}
B_{2,4} = \big[& ((y_4 - y_2)(z_G - z_2) \\
& - (y_G - y_2)(z_4 - z_2)) \cos\theta_{\text{second}} \\
& + (-(x_4 - x_2)(z_G - z_2) \\
& + (x_G - x_2)(y_4 - y_2)) \sin\theta_{\text{second}} \big].
\end{aligned}
\tag{16}
$$

Height difference $H_{2,4}$ must be calculated in regard to G_{first}, position of CG after the first rotation:

$$H_{2,4} = G_{2,4\,z} - G_{\text{first}\, z}. \tag{17}$$

Finally, (2) for calculation of $S_{\theta_{\text{second}}}$ can be written as

$$S_{\theta_{\text{second}}} = \frac{1}{2g} \left(\frac{\sqrt{2g H_{2,4}}}{Z_{2,4}} - V_{\text{res}\,h} \right)^2. \tag{18}$$

After all those calculations, computed S_θ for both rotations, expressed in (15) and (18), can be combined, thus giving an understanding of total dynamic normalized energy stability margin for a given posture in presence of the swinging leg:

$$S_{\theta_{\text{total}}} = S_{\theta_{\text{first}}} + S_{\theta_{\text{second}}}, \tag{19}$$

where $S_{\theta_{\text{first}}}$ represents an energy required to perform first rotation and $S_{\theta_{\text{second}}}$ represents an additional energy required for robot to continue tumbling motion.

4. Basic Tumbling Experiment with Consideration about the Swinging Leg

As in our previous study on Directional Normalized Energy Stability Margin [2], we validated the calculation of S_θ by performing a numerical simulation and then conducting a tumbling experiment with a simple model of a robot, measuring S_θ manually and comparing our results with a simulation for the same model.

In order to perform a validation of S_θ with swinging leg consideration, we conducted an experiment with a similar, but slightly modified setup.

Tumbling experiment setup is shown in Figure 7(a). It consisted of the following elements: a pendulum with a hammer 1 (mass: 470 g) attached to a connecting rod 2 and

(1) Hammer   (5) Supporting pillars
(2) Connecting rod   (6) Rotary table
(3) Shaft   (7) Scale
(4) Robot model

(a) Impact table

(b) Robot body model 4 (swing   (c) Robot body model after first
leg height is 5 mm), before first   rotation
rotation

FIGURE 7: Experimental setup.

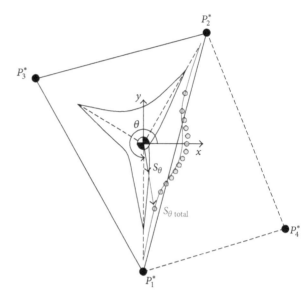

FIGURE 8: Experimental results (shown as dots) and derived S_θ accounting for existence of the swinging leg (shown as a red line). DNESM S_θ for $P_1P_2P_3$ supporting polygon without swinging leg consideration is presented for comparison (shown in black).

FIGURE 9: TITAN-XIII walking robot.

rotating on a shaft 3; a robot model 4 (mass: 490 g) with lightweight legs (mass of each leg is 2.3 g), Figure 7(b); as mass of the legs is small compared to mass of the body, they can be neglected; supporting pillars 5; rotary table 6 for positioning the body against hammer 1, and a vertical scale 7 for measuring the value of S_θ.

For the purpose S_θ validation, body 4 also had an additional "swinging" leg—a shorter leg elevated 5 mm above the surface. After the application of impact force and subsequent first rotation around an edge of the existing supporting polygon, swinging leg prevented overturning and helped to create a secondary supporting polygon (second rotation stage).

Experimental process was done to measure the lowest height of the pendulum that defined a corresponding potential energy required to overturn the body around the edge of a secondary supporting polygon. After several iterations for each angular position, we were able to make a measurement of S_θ with a certain precision.

Results of the experiment were then compared to the results of numerical simulation for the tumbling model and are shown in Figure 8.

5. Discussion about Actual Application of S_θ

Currently, we are developing a new walking robot, TITAN-XIII (Figure 9). This is a lightweight machine built specifically for research on gait control and stability of multi-legged locomotion. Although work on the robot is not yet completed, we decided to apply the theory of S_θ and examine stability of TITAN-XIII beforehand.

To do that, we developed a numerical simulation based on the geometry of TITAN-XIII performing a trotting gait, and calculated S_θ in all stages of motion for all edges of all possible supporting polygons. Main purpose of such simulation was to measure the minimum of S_θ throughout the motion sequence and suggest ways to improve locomotion stability, thus creating a Non-Tumbling gait for a particular robot.

Subsections below discuss the specifics of the simulation and its results.

5.1. Simulation Assumptions. Similar to previous simulations, walking simulation was done with the following assumptions.

(i) External energy E_i is supplied to the system in a horizontal plane, and, thus, $\mathbf{V}(E_i)$ lays in the horizontal plane as well.

(ii) Friction in the footholds is infinite, and slipping does not occur.

(iii) Legs are massless, and robot's mass is concentrated in the body.

(iv) Angular velocity of the body $\omega_b = 0$.

(v) Simulation is conducted with an assumption that the surface is flat.

(vi) In simulated trotting gait, change of the supporting pair of legs happens instantaneously.

5.2. Parameters of Robot's Motion. The equations used to control CG position and its velocity are as follows.

Position of CG is calculated as

$$G_x(t) = Ae^{st} + Be^{-st}, \qquad (20)$$

where $A = (V_0/s + x_0)/2$, $B = (-V_0/s + x_0)/2$, $s = \sqrt{g/G_z(t)}$.

CG velocity is calculated as

$$V_b(t) = s\left(Ae^{st} - Be^{st}\right), \qquad (21)$$

and minimum initial velocity is $V_0 = -G_{x_0}\sqrt{g/G_{z_0}}$.

As it is clear from (21) and Figure 11, robot's body velocity is the highest in the beginning of each step. As the motions progress, it decreases, and, at the point when robot's CG is located above the supporting line, robot's body velocity reaches its minimum. After this, it enters a phase of acceleration and reaches minimum initial velocity V_0 towards the end of the current step and the beginning of the next step.

Such sophisticated velocity control, despite introducing rapid acceleration and deceleration, allows achieving greater speed and greater stability of the posture. Specifics of this approach are discussed in [7].

In the context of validation of S_θ, consideration of robot's body velocity $\mathbf{V}_b$ brings the simulation closer to real life and allows making better judgements about the applicability of S_θ.

We have conducted several types of simulation where robot was performing a step of a trot gait. Simulation types are as follows.

(i) Varying swing leg height.

(ii) Varying CG height.

(iii) Varying velocity simulations.

5.3. Locomotion Stability Map. Simulation that we performed, was based on a trot gait with a fixed stride (150 mm). We were calculating the minimum S_θ throughout the motion sequence. By varying the wideness of the posture, we obtained different minimum measurements of S_θ. Each simulation was conducted in 30 different configuration positions across the service area for that particular stride (service area for 150 mm stride is shown in dark grey in Figure 10, and M is the middle point of the stride).

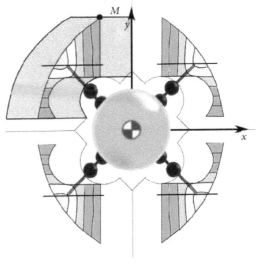

$h_{\text{swing}} = 10\,\text{mm}$ $S_\theta > 30\,\text{mm}$
$CG_h = 232\,\text{mm}$ $S_\theta = 30\cdots20\,\text{mm}$
               $S_\theta = 20\cdots10\,\text{mm}$
               $S_\theta = 10\cdots1\,\text{mm}$

FIGURE 10: Areas of minimum S_θ for TITAN-XIII walking robot performing a trotting gait with a fixed stride. The best $S_\theta = 0.055$ m.

Position of a stride's middle point M defined the posture.

Simulation allowed us to generate a stability map, a simple representation of safe and unsafe postures and footholds (Figure 10). Light green areas represent zones with most stable postures, while pinkish areas show most unstable postures.

5.4. Direction of Minimum S_θ during Motion. Firstly, we studied basic behavior of S_θ, such as the changes in direction of minimum S_θ during a step of our model of TITAN-XIII. Although walking cycle consists of two steps performed by interchanging pairs of legs, due to symmetrical nature of the examined walk, it is enough to consider only one step.

Changes of S_θ throughout one step of a simulated TITAN-XIII walking robot performing trot gait are presented in Figure 11, and actual contour of S_θ for each measurement can be seen in Figure 12.

It is interesting to notice that, during the motion, direction of minimum S_θ changes (Figure 12). From Figure 11, it is clear that this happens because of the changes of robot's velocity (Figure 11). Additionally, the way S_θ changes throughout the step is not trivial. In points 0 to 2, stability is low as the velocity is high and directed forward. As the decrease of body velocity $\mathbf{V}_b$ becomes significant, stability increases (points 3 to 5), achieving its maximum in point 5, where velocity is minimum, and posture is effectively a square. S_θ starts decreasing in point 6 and achieves a local minimum in point 8, but because a pair of swinging legs is moved forward and velocity is not yet high enough, the minimum stability is directed backwards.

A sudden increase of stability in point 9 is of particular interest. It occurs because of the increase of velocity (directed

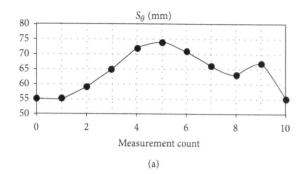

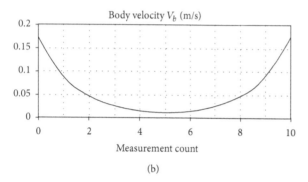

FIGURE 11: Behavior of S_θ throughout the step of TITAN-XIII walking robot.

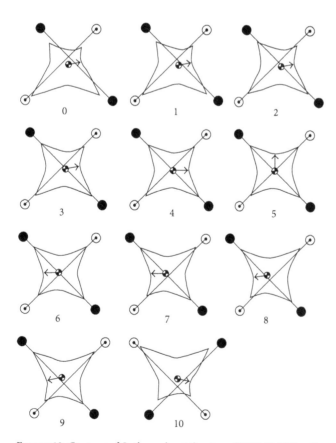

FIGURE 12: Contour of S_θ throughout the step of TITAN-XIII walking robot.

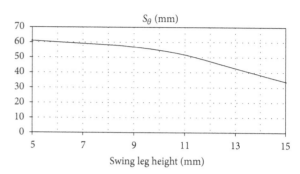

FIGURE 13: Behavior of S_θ in case of increasing swing leg height.

forward) that counteracts the negative effect of the swinging pair of legs which affect S_θ and decrease it in the backward direction.

Finally, at point 10, when the step is finished and another pair of legs becomes supporting, S_θ equals to measurement in point 0, and contours in 0 and 10 are symmetrical.

It is important to highlight that this simple analysis shows that Directional Normalized Energy Stability Margin (or S_θ) can be used to estimate stability of multi-legged robot in *every* moment throughout the motion. Not only it provides the insights about which phase of the step is most stable and unstable, but it also shows interesting effects that posture and velocity control may have on stability during walking.

5.5. Varying Height of the Swing Leg. In order to gain more insights about how different parameters of robot's posture influence S_θ, we performed a simulation with varying swing leg height: 5, 10, and 15 mm above the ground for each series of the simulation. Position of robot's CG remained at 232 mm above the ground.

Dependency between S_θ and height of the swing leg is shown in Figure 13. It is clear that the increase of swing leg height results in decrease of multi-legged locomotion stability, as indicated by S_θ.

5.6. Varying Height of Robot's CG. Previous simulations were conducted with a consideration that robot's center of gravity has a constant height of 232 mm above the surface (default height of the CG of TITAN-XIII). In order to understand how the decrease of CG height influences locomotion stability, we performed a set of experiments where CG height was gradually decreased to 200 mm.

As one can see from results of the simulation presented in Figure 14, decrease of robot's CG height allows achieving a significant increase in locomotion safety. By lowering CG we were able to increase minimum S_θ to 73 mm. Thus, 16% decrease in CG, height resulted in 33% increase in S_θ.

5.7. Varying Constant Velocity. Finally, in order to understand the effect which body velocity has on safety margin, we performed a series of simulations where robot's velocity was

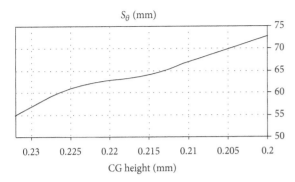

FIGURE 14: Behavior of S_θ in case of decreasing CG height.

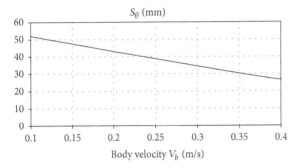

FIGURE 15: Linear decline of S_θ caused by the increase of robot's body velocity.

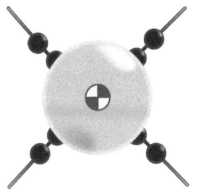

(a) Insect type posture (wide; CG height is low)

(b) Mammal type posture (narrow/elongated; CG is elevated)

FIGURE 16: Insect and mammal postures.

constant throughout the motion sequence but was incrementally increased in each modeling session. Four velocities considered were 0.1 m/s, 0.2 m/s, 0.3 m/s, and 0.4 m/s (maximum possible velocity for TITAN-XIII walking robot is 0.7 m/s).

It is obvious that an increase in the velocity would result in a decline of safety. Results of the simulation are shown in Figure 15. As one can see from the plot, the decrease of stability caused by increase in velocity is essentially linear.

5.8. S_θ as a Source of Insights about Design of Multilegged Robots. TITAN-XIII walking robot, shown in Figure 9, was specifically designed for experiments in gait control and locomotion stability of multi-legged vehicles. Before building the robot, we agreed that from design standpoint, it would be better to pursue an insect-type construction, instead of a more widespread mammal type. By insect type (Figure 16(a)), we mean a robot design which allows wide postures with an ability to position center of gravity at a low height. Mammal-type design, on the contrary, presupposes a narrow posture (Figure 16(b)) and high position of the CG.

Insect-type design of TITAN-XIII was justified by the fact that insects, due to their wide postures, have greater stability than mammals. However, such proposition lacked scientific backing. So far, there has been no significant research that aimed at studying quantitative estimation of the advantage which insect-type design has over mammal type in terms of stability.

Now, Directional Normalized Energy Stability Margin gives us an insight into how significantly different those two

types of design/postures are in terms of stability. We have compared stability of insect and mammal postures presented in Figure 16. Apart from one being wider than the other, insect-type posture featured a CG height of 200 mm, while mammal-type posture had 232 mm height (not the highest TITAN-XIII is capable of, but, nevertheless, suitable for illustration).

As a result, minimum stability margin for insect posture was 73 mm, and minimum stability margin for mammal posture was only 11 mm, which constitutes only 15,1% of the stability of an insect-type posture.

Stability map provided in Figure 10 may serve as an additional illustration of the fact that not only more narrow postures have reduced stability as we suspected before, but that in case of narrow mammal-type postures, stability is reduced radically.

6. Conclusion and Future Work

In this paper, we discussed the effect that swing leg has on stability of multi-legged robots. We introduced the idea of Non-Tumbling Gait, which relies on the phenomenon occurring during tumbling of the robots when the swing leg contacts the ground and prevents overturning of the robot.

We have also explored the relationship between Non-Tumbling Gait and Directional Normalized Energy Stability Margin, or S_θ. S_θ was suggested as a stability criterion suitable for maintaining Non-Tumbling Gait. The validity of this choice was evaluated by a tumbling experiment with a simplified model of a walking robot. Additionally, the concepts of Non-Tumbling Gait and S_θ were applied to searching an optimal posture for the new quadruped walking robot, TITAN-XIII.

In our future work we will further study the application of Non-Tumbling Gait and S_θ in different settings, both in numerical simulations, with additional dynamic effects (e.g., compliance in the joints, ground friction, etc.), and also on various types of walking robots available at Fukushima Robotics Lab.

Nomenclature

E_i:	Input energy, external disturbance
$\mathbf{V}(E_i)$:	Input velocity generated by input energy
$\mathbf{V}_b$:	Body velocity
P_i, P_j, P_k:	Ground contact points, heights of the supporting polygon
$\mathbf{P}_{i,j}$:	Edge of the supporting polygon formed by P_i and P_j contact points
G:	Position of the center of gravity (CG)
$\mathbf{P}_{iG}$:	Vector from ground contact point P_i to robot's center of gravity G
x_i, y_i, z_i:	Coordinates in Cartesian coordinate system
θ:	Direction angle of disturbing input energy
$\varphi_{\max}$:	Angular distance from current position of robot's CG to the position above the edge of the supporting polygon (unstable equilibrium)
H:	Height difference between original CG position G and its highest possible position $G_{\max}$
A, B, C, D, Z:	Numerical coefficients introduced to simplify calculations.

References

[1] S. Hirose, H. Tsukagoshi, and K. Yoneda, "Normalized energy stability margin: generalized stability criterion for walking vehicles," in *Proceedings of the International Conference on Climbing and Walking Robot*, pp. 71–76, Brussels, Belgium, 1998.

[2] S. Hirose, E. Lazarenko, and G. Endo, "Directional normalized energy stability margin," in *Proceedings of the 2nd IFToMM Asian Conference on Mechanism and Machine Science*, 2012.

[3] R. B. McGhee and A. A. Frank, "On the stability properties of quadruped creeping gaits," *Mathematical Biosciences*, vol. 3, no. 1-2, pp. 331–351, 1968.

[4] D. A. Messuri and C. A. Klein, "Automatic body regulation for maintaining stability of a legged vehicle during rough-terrain locomotion," *IEEE Journal of Robotics and Automation*, vol. 1, no. 3, pp. 132–141, 1985.

[5] E. Garcia and P. G. de Santos, "An improved energy stability margin for walking machines subject to dynamic effects," *Robotica*, vol. 23, no. 1, pp. 13–20, 2005.

[6] P. Gonzalez de Santos, E. Garcia, and J. Estemera, *Quadrupedal Locomotion. An Introduction to the Coltrol of Four-Legged Robots*, Springer, 2006.

[7] S. Kitano, G. Endo, and S. Hirose, "Development of light weight quadruped robot TITAN XIII," in *Proceedings of the Robotics and Mechatronics Conference*, 2013.

7

Flocking for Multiple Ellipsoidal Agents with Limited Communication Ranges

K. D. Do

Department of Mechanical Engineering, Curtin University of Technology, Perth, WA 6845, Australia

Correspondence should be addressed to K. D. Do; duc@curtin.edu.au

Academic Editors: G.-C. Luh, K. A. Mcisaac, and F. Torres

This paper contributes a design of distributed controllers for flocking of mobile agents with an ellipsoidal shape and a limited communication range. A separation condition for ellipsoidal agents is first derived. Smooth step functions are then introduced. These functions and the separation condition between the ellipsoidal agents are embedded in novel pairwise potential functions to design flocking control algorithms. The proposed flocking design results in (1) smooth controllers despite of the agents' limited communication ranges, (2) no collisions between any agents, (3) asymptotic convergence of each agent's generalized velocity to a desired velocity, and (4) boundedness of the flock size, defined as the sum of all distances between the agents, by a constant.

1. Introduction

Flocking, referred to as a collective motion of a large number of self-propelled entities, has attracted a lot of attention of researchers in biology, physics, and computer science [1–4]. Engineering applications of flocking include search, rescue, coverage, surveillance, sensor networks, and cooperative transportation [5–14].

In 1987, Reynolds [2] introduced three rules of flocking: (1) separation: avoid collision with nearby flock-mates; (2) alignment: attempt to match velocity with nearby flock-mates; (3) cohesion: attempt to stay close to nearby flock-mates. Since then, there has been a number of modifications and extensions of the above three rules and additional rules to result in many algorithms to realize these rules. The graph theory and the Lyapunov direct method were used to solve consensus problems in [15–17]. Local artificial potentials between neighboring agents were used to deal with separation (collision avoidance) and cohesion problems in [12, 13, 18–23]. The leader-follower approach to a target tracking problem was used in [24, 25]. Other related work includes geometric formation optimization [26, 27], pattern formation [28], and task allocation [29]. In all the above cited references, the agents are considered as a single point, a circular disk, or a sphere.

In practice, many agents have a nonspherical, especially long and narrow, shape. If these agents are fitted to spheres, there is a problem of the large conservative volume. To illustrate this problem, we look at an example of fitting a cylindrical agent with a radius of r_c and a length of $2l_c$ to an ellipsoid with semiaxes of a, b, and c, and a sphere with a radius of r_s as shown Figure 1. By shrinking the space along the direction of the major axis of the ellipsoid, we can find $a = \sqrt{2}l_c$, $b = c = \sqrt{2}r_c$, and $r_s = \sqrt{r_c^2 + l_c^2}$. Therefore, the conservative volume, V_{con}, defined as the difference between the volumes enclosed by the sphere and the ellipsoid, is given by $V_{\text{con}} = (4\pi r_c^3/3)[(l_c^2/r_c^2 + 1)\sqrt{l_c^2/r_c^2 + 1} - 2\sqrt{2}(l_c/r_c)]$. This means that the conservative volume is always nonnegative and is proportional to cubic of the half-length l_c over the radius r_c of an agent.

A spherical approximation of the shape of long and narrow agents can adversely affect performance of a flocking algorithm. An example is the case where it is a must to flock a group of long and narrow agents through a long and narrow passageway. In some cases, a spherical approximation of the agents's shape can result in failure of a flocking algorithm. As an illustration, we consider two cylindrical agents with a length of $2l_1$ and $2l_2$, and a radius of r_1 and r_2. Assuming that r_1 and r_2 are much less than l_1 and l_2, respectively, that is, the

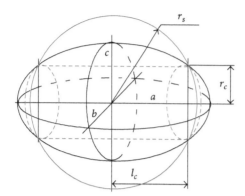

FIGURE 1: Fitting an cylindrical agent to a sphere and an ellipsoid.

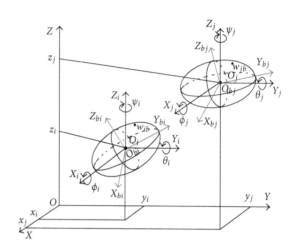

FIGURE 2: Two ellipsoids and their coordinates.

two agents have a long and narrow shape. We now require these two agents to flock in a way that they do not collide with each other and the distance d_{12} between them is such that $(r_1 + r_2) + \epsilon_{12} < d_{12} < (l_1 + l_2) - \epsilon_{12}$ with ϵ_{12} being a feasible positive constant. Clearly, a spherical approximation of the agents' shape is not applicable in this case for a flocking algorithm. On the other hand, an ellipsoidal approximation can be applicable. In addition, an ellipsoidal approximation of the agents' shape for collision avoidance between the agents in a flocking algorithm covers a spherical approximation of the agents' shape by setting the semiaxes of the ellipsoid equal, but not vice versa. The above discussion indicates that it is much more efficient to use an ellipsoidal approximation of the agents with a long and narrow shape for collision avoidance in designing flocking algorithms.

Despite of the above advantages of an ellipsoidal approximation of the agents' shape, flocking for ellipsoidal agents has not been addressed in the literature except for a recent paper [30] on coordination control of multiple ellipsoidal agents. This is partially due to difficulties in determining a separation condition between two ellipsoids. There have been two main methods to determine a separation condition between ellipsoids. The first method in [31, 32] consists of determining the intersection of the ellipsoids with the plane containing the line joining their centers and rotating the plane. The distance of closest approach [33] of the two ellipses formed by the intersection is a periodic function of the plane orientation, of which the maximum value corresponds to the closest distance between the two ellipsoids. The second method [34] is based on the discriminant of their characteristic polynomial. Both methods are too complicated for an application in flock control. If these methods are applied for collision avoidance, the condition, for which the minimum distance between two disks or the discriminant of their characteristic polynomial is positive, is extremely complicated to be embedded in a proper potential function for designing a flocking algorithm. In [35], a design of distributed controllers for flocking of mobile agents with an elliptical shape and with limited communication ranges was addressed. As it will be seen later, the design of a flocking algorithm in two dimensional space (i.e., elliptical agents are considered) is much harder than that in three-dimensional space (i.e., ellipsoidal agents are considered).

The aforementioned observations motivate contributions of this paper on a design of flocking algorithms for mobile agents with an ellipsoidal shape and limited communication ranges. The paper's contributions include (1) a new condition for separation between two ellipsoids, see Section 2.1; (2) smooth step functions; (3) a new pairwise potential function for two ellipsoidal agents, see Section 4.1.1; (4) a derivation of flocking algorithms based on the pairwise potential functions, see Section 4.4.

2. Preliminaries

2.1. Separation Condition Between Two Ellipsoids. This section presents a condition for separation of two ellipsoids applicable for collision avoidance in the flock control design later. As such, we consider two ellipsoids i and j shown in Figure 2. In this figure, $OXYZ$ is the earth-fixed frame, $O_i X_i Y_i Z_i$ is the body-fixed frame attached to ellipsoid i, $\mathbf{q}_i = [x_i \ y_i \ z_i]^T$ denotes the position of the center O_i, and $\boldsymbol{\eta}_i = [\phi_i \ \theta_i \ \psi_i]^T$ denotes the orientation (roll, pitch and yaw angles) of the ellipsoid i. Moreover, (a_i, b_i, c_i) denote the semiaxes of the ellipsoids i. These notations are similar to the ellipsoid j.

Lemma 1. *Consider two ellipsoids i and j, which have semiaxes of (a_i, b_i, c_i) and (a_j, b_j, c_j), and orientation vectors $\boldsymbol{\eta}_j = [\phi_i \ \theta_i \ \psi_i]^T$ and $\boldsymbol{\eta}_j = [\phi_j \ \theta_j \ \psi_j]^T$, and are centered at $\mathbf{q}_i = [x_i \ y_i \ z_i]^T$ and $\mathbf{q}_j = [x_j \ y_j \ z_j]^T$, respectively, see Figure 2. Define the transformed distance Δ_{ij} between the ellipsoids i and j as*

$$\Delta_{ij} = \sqrt{\frac{\left\| \mathbf{Q}_{ij}\overline{\mathbf{q}}_{ij} \right\|^2 + \left\| \mathbf{Q}_{ji}\overline{\mathbf{q}}_{ji} \right\|^2}{2}} - 1, \tag{1}$$

where

$$\mathbf{Q}_{ij} = \mathbf{I}_{3\times3} - \left(\mathbf{I}_{3\times3} + \kappa_{ij}\mathbf{T}_j \right)^{-1},$$
$$\overline{\mathbf{q}}_{ij} = \mathbf{P}_i\mathbf{q}_{ij}, \tag{2}$$

with $\mathbf{I}_{3\times3}$ being a 3×3 identity matrix, and

$$\mathbf{q}_{ij} = \mathbf{q}_i - \mathbf{q}_j,$$

$$\mathbf{P}_i = -\mathbf{A}_i^{-1}\mathbf{R}^{-1}(\boldsymbol{\eta}_i), \qquad (3)$$

$$\mathbf{A}_i = \mathrm{diag}(a_i, b_i, c_i).$$

The matrix $\mathbf{R}(\bullet)$ represents the three-dimensional rotational matrix with respect to the vector $\bullet$. The matrix $\mathbf{T}_j$ is given by

$$\mathbf{T}_j = \begin{bmatrix} T_{j11} & T_{j12} & T_{j13} \\ T_{j12} & T_{j22} & T_{j23} \\ T_{j13} & T_{j23} & T_{j33} \end{bmatrix}, \qquad (4)$$

where

$$T_{j11} = a_{11}^2 + a_{21}^2 + a_{31}^2, \qquad T_{j12} = a_{11}a_{12} + a_{21}a_{22} + a_{31}a_{32},$$

$$T_{j22} = a_{12}^2 + a_{22}^2 + a_{32}^2, \qquad T_{j13} = a_{11}a_{13} + a_{21}a_{23} + a_{31}a_{33},$$

$$T_{j33} = a_{13}^2 + a_{23}^2 + a_{33}^2, \qquad T_{j23} = a_{12}a_{13} + a_{22}a_{23} + a_{32}a_{33},$$

$$(5)$$

with a_{mn} for $m = 1,2,3$ and $n = 1,2,3$ being the element (m,n) of the matrix $(\mathbf{A}_i^{-1}\mathbf{R}(\boldsymbol{\eta}_{ij})\mathbf{A}_j)^{-1}$ with

$$\boldsymbol{\eta}_{ij} = \boldsymbol{\eta}_i - \boldsymbol{\eta}_j,$$
$$\mathbf{A}_j = \mathrm{diag}(a_j, b_j, c_j). \qquad (6)$$

The variable κ_{ij} is the largest root (the right most root) of the following equation:

$$F_{ij}(\kappa_{ij}) := \overline{\mathbf{q}}_{ij}^T(\mathbf{I}_{3\times3} + \kappa_{ij}\mathbf{T}_j)^{-T}\mathbf{T}_j(\mathbf{I}_{3\times3} + \kappa_{ij}\mathbf{T}_j)^{-1}\overline{\mathbf{q}}_{ij} - 1 = 0,$$
$$(7)$$

where $(\mathbf{I}_{3\times3} + \kappa_{ij}\mathbf{T}_j)^{-T}$ denotes the transpose of $(\mathbf{I}_{3\times3} + \kappa_{ij}\mathbf{T}_j)^{-1}$.

The vector $\mathbf{q}_{ji}$ and the matrix $\mathbf{Q}_{ji}$ are defined accordingly. The two ellipsoids are externally separated, that is, the ellipsoids are outside of each other and do not contact with each other like Figure 2, if

$$\Delta_{ij} > 0. \qquad (8)$$

Remark 2. The transformed distance Δ_{ij} is symmetric, that is, $\Delta_{ij} = \Delta_{ji}$. Moreover, Δ_{ij} is a smooth function of $\mathbf{q}_{ij}$, $\boldsymbol{\eta}_i$, $\boldsymbol{\eta}_j$, and $\boldsymbol{\eta}_{ij}$. Alternatively, Δ_{ij} is a smooth function of $\overline{\mathbf{q}}_{ij}$, $\overline{\mathbf{q}}_{ji}$, and $\boldsymbol{\eta}_{ij}$.

Proof. see Appendix A. □

2.2. Smooth Step Function.
This section gives a definition of the smooth step function followed by a construction of this function. The smooth step function is to be embedded in a pairwise potential function to avoid discontinuities in the control law due to the agents' communication limitation ranges in solving the collision avoidance problem.

Definition 3. A scalar function $h(x,a,b,c)$ is said to be a smooth step function if it possesses the following properties:

(1) $h(x,a,b,c) = 0, \quad \forall x \in (-\infty, a]$,

(2) $h(x,a,b,c) = 1, \quad \forall x \in [b, \infty)$,

(3) $0 < h(x,a,b,c) < 1, \quad \forall x \in (a,b)$,

(4) $h(x,a,b,c)$ is smooth,

(5) $h'(x,a,b,c) > 0, \quad \forall x \in (a,b)$,

(6) $h''(x,a,b,c) = 0$ at $x = x^* \in (a,b)$,

$$(9)$$

where $h'(x,a,b,c) = \partial h(x,a,b,c)/\partial x$, $h''(x,a,b,c) = \partial^2 h(x,a,b,c)/\partial x^2$, a and b are constants such that $a < b$, and c is a positive constant.

Lemma 4. Let the scalar function $h(x,a,b,c)$ be defined as

$$h(x,a,b,c) = \frac{f(\tau)}{f(\tau) + cf(1-\tau)} \quad \text{with } \tau = \frac{x-a}{b-a}, \quad (10)$$

where

$$f(\tau) = 0 \quad \text{if } \tau \leq 0, \quad f(\tau) = e^{-1/\tau} \quad \text{if } \tau > 0, \qquad (11)$$

with a and b being constants such that $a < b$, and c being a positive constant. Then the function $h(x,a,b,c)$ is a smooth step function.

Proof (see [30]). An alternative "symmetric" (i.e., $c = 1$) smooth step function is available in [14] but it requires a numerical integration. The introduction of the positive constant c in the smooth step function in Lemma 4 is to shift the location at which $h'(x,a,b,c)$ attains its extremum value. An illustration of a smooth step function ($a = 0, b = 3, c = 2$) is given in Figure 3. □

2.3. Barbalat-Like Lemma.
The following Barbalat-like lemma is to be used in stability analysis of the closed-loop system.

Lemma 5. Assume that a nonnegative scalar differentiable function $f(t)$ satisfies the following conditions:

(1) $\left| \dfrac{d}{dt} f(t) \right| \leq k_1 f(t), \quad \forall t \geq 0$,

(2) $\displaystyle\int_0^\infty f(t)\, dt \leq k_2$,

$$(12)$$

where k_1 and k_2 are positive constants, then $\lim_{t \to \infty} f(t) = 0$.

Proof (see [7]). Lemma 5 differs from Barbalat's lemma found in [36]. While Barbalat's lemma assumes that $f(t)$ is uniformly continuous, Lemma 5 assumes that $|(d/dt)f(t)|$ is bounded by $k_1 f(t)$. Lemma 5 is useful in proving convergence of $f(t)$ when it is difficult to prove uniform continuity of $f(t)$. □

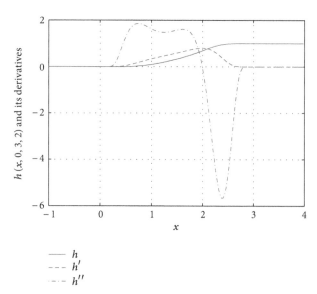

FIGURE 3: A smooth step function and its first and second derivatives.

3. Problem Statement

3.1. Agent Dynamics. As mentioned before, this paper mainly focuses on difficulties caused by the ellipsoidal shape of the agents in designing flocking algorithms, we therefore assume that each ellipsoidal agent i has the following dynamics:

$$\dot{\mathbf{q}}_i = \mathbf{u}_i,$$
$$\dot{\boldsymbol{\eta}}_i = \boldsymbol{\omega}_i, \quad i \in \mathbb{N}, \tag{13}$$

where $\mathbb{N}$ is the set of all agents in the group, $\mathbf{u}_i = \begin{bmatrix} u_{xi} & u_{yi} & u_{zi} \end{bmatrix}^T$ and $\boldsymbol{\omega}_i = \begin{bmatrix} \omega_{\phi i} & \omega_{\theta i} & \omega_{\psi i} \end{bmatrix}^T$ are the control input vectors of the agent i. It is recalled that $\mathbf{q}_i = \begin{bmatrix} x_i & y_i & z_i \end{bmatrix}^T$ with (x_i, y_i, z_i) being the position coordinates of the center of the agent i and $\boldsymbol{\eta}_i = \begin{bmatrix} \phi_i & \theta_i & \psi_i \end{bmatrix}^T$ with $(\phi_i, \theta_i, \psi_i)$ being the orientation angles of the agent i, see Figure 2. For agents with higher order dynamics, the backstepping technique [37] can be used because we will design the control input vectors $\mathbf{u}_i$ and $\boldsymbol{\omega}_i$ such that they are smooth.

3.2. Flock Control Objective. In order to design a flocking algorithm for a group of ellipsoidal agents, there is a need to specify a common goal for the group, some communication between the agents, and initial position and orientation of the agents. We therefore impose the following assumption on the flocking rendezvous trajectory, communication, and initial conditions between the agents.

Assumption 1. (1) The agents i and j have spherical communication spaces, which are centered at the points O_i and O_j, and have radii of R_i and R_j. The radii R_i and R_j are sufficiently large in the sense that

$$\Delta_{ijR}^m > 0, \tag{14}$$

where Δ_{ijR}^m is the greatest lower bound of Δ_{ij} when the agents i and j are within their communication ranges, that is,

$$\Delta_{ijR}^m = \inf\left(\Delta_{ij}\right) \quad \text{s.t.} \quad \begin{cases} \boldsymbol{\eta}_{ij} \in \mathbb{R}^3, \\ \|\mathbf{q}_{ij}\| = \min\left(R_i, R_j\right), \end{cases} \tag{15}$$

for all $(i, j) \in \mathbb{N}$ and $j \neq i$.

(2) The agents i and j can exchange their trajectories, $(\mathbf{q}_i, \boldsymbol{\eta}_i)$ and $(\mathbf{q}_j, \boldsymbol{\eta}_j)$ if these agents are in their communication spaces.

(3) At the initial time $t_0 \geq 0$, all the agents in the group are sufficiently far away from each other in the sense that the following condition holds

$$\Delta_{ij}\left(t_0\right) > 0, \tag{16}$$

where $\Delta_{ij}(t_0)$ is given in (1) evaluated at $(\mathbf{q}_i = \mathbf{q}_i(t_0), \boldsymbol{\eta}_i = \boldsymbol{\eta}_i(t_0))$ and $(\mathbf{q}_j = \mathbf{q}_j(t_0), \boldsymbol{\eta}_j = \boldsymbol{\eta}_j(t_0))$, and we have abused the notation of $\Delta_{ij}(\mathbf{q}_{ij}(t_0), \boldsymbol{\eta}_i(t_0), \boldsymbol{\eta}_j(t_0))$ as $\Delta_{ij}(t_0)$ for simplicity of presentation.

(4) The flocking rendezvous position and orientation trajectory, $\mathbf{q}_{od} = \begin{bmatrix} x_{od}, y_{od}, z_{od} \end{bmatrix}^T$ and $\boldsymbol{\eta}_{od} = \begin{bmatrix} \phi_{od}, \theta_{od}, \psi_{od} \end{bmatrix}^T$, for the flock to follow has bounded derivatives $\dot{\mathbf{q}}_{od}$ and $\dot{\boldsymbol{\eta}}_{od}$, and is available for all the agents.

Remark 6. (1) In item (1), the condition (14) holds if there exists a positive constant ϱ_i such that $R_i \geq \varrho_i + \sup(a_i + a_j, a_i + b_j, a_i + c_j, b_i + a_j, b_i + b_j, b_i + c_j, c_i + a_j, c_i + b_j, c_i + c_j)$, for all $(i, j) \in \mathbb{N}$ and $j \neq i$.

(2) Items (1) and (2) in Assumption 1 specify the way each agent communicates with other agents in the group within its communication range. In other words, the agents in the group are connected if they are inside their communication ranges.

(3) Item (3) in Assumption 1 implies from Lemma 1 that at the initial time t_0 there is no collision between any agents in the group.

(4) Items (1), (2), and (3) in Assumption 1 do not guarantee overall connectivity among all the agents in the group in general. Under item (4) in Assumption 1, we do not require overall connectivity among all the agents to design a flocking algorithm.

(5) Item (4) in Assumption 1 means that all the agents are aware of the flocking rendezvous trajectory. This item together with items (1) and (2) in Assumption 1 were also required in [13] to design a nonfragmentation flocking algorithm for *point* agents based on an attractive/repulsive potential field. In [13] Olfati-Saber also showed that under items (1) and (2) if all the agents are not aware of the flocking rendezvous trajectory, the flocking algorithm works only for a very restricted set of initial states and a small number of agents. In [21], a further analysis of the flocking algorithm proposed in [13] was carried out for the case where only several agents in a group are aware of the flocking rendezvous trajectory. It was shown in [21] that the agents, which are not aware of the flocking rendezvous trajectory and stay disconnected from the other agents in the group sufficiently long, would stay disconnected from the agents, which are aware of the flocking rendezvous trajectory, that is, the flocking algorithm leads to fragmentation. This represents a

real situation. For example, the chance for a bird that has gone away from its flock a sufficiently long time coming back to the flock is very low. Hence, this paper imposes item (4) in Assumption 1 to design a flocking algorithm for elliptical agents. It is possible to use the analysis technique in [21] to analyze the flocking algorithm to be proposed later in this paper for ellipsoidal agents when only several agents are aware of the flocking rendezvous trajectory. This is because the flocking algorithm to be designed in this paper is also based on an attractive/repulsive potential field. However, since this paper focuses on solving difficulties due to an ellipsoidal shape of the agents for collision avoidance in a flocking algorithm, all the agents are assumed to be aware of the flocking rendezvous trajectory.

Flock Control Objective. Under Assumption 1, for each agent i design the smooth control input vectors $\mathbf{u}_i$ and $\boldsymbol{\omega}_i$ to achieve a desired flocking including: (1) no collisions between any agents; (2) asymptotic convergence of each agent's generalized velocity to a desired velocity; (3) boundedness of the flock size $F_L(t) = \sum_{j=i+1}^{N} \sum_{j=1}^{i-1} \Delta_{ij}(t)$ by a constant when the time t tends to infinity.

4. Flock Control Design

4.1. Potential Function

4.1.1. Pairwise Potential Function.
This section defines and constructs pairwise potential functions that will be used in a Lyapunov function for the flock control design.

Definition 7. Let φ_{ij} be a scalar function of the transformed distance Δ_{ij} given in (1) between the ellipsoidal agents i and j. The function φ_{ij} is said to be a pairwise potential function if it has the following properties:

(1) $\varphi_{ij} = k_{ij}, \quad \varphi_{ij}' = 0, \quad \varphi_{ij}'' = 0, \quad \forall \Delta_{ij} \in [\Delta_{ijR}^M, \infty)$,

(2) $\varphi_{ij} > 0, \quad \forall \Delta_{ij} \in (0, \Delta_{ijR}^M)$,

(3) $\lim_{\Delta_{ij} \to 0} \varphi_{ij} = \infty, \quad \lim_{\Delta_{ij} \to 0} \varphi_{ij}' = -\infty$,

(4) φ_{ij} is smooth, $\quad \forall \Delta_{ij} \in (0, \infty)$,

(5) φ_{ij} has a unique minimum value at $\Delta_{ij} = \Delta_{ijd}$,

$$\forall \Delta_{ij} \in (0, \Delta_{ijR}^M), \tag{17}$$

where $\varphi_{ij}' = \partial \varphi_{ij}/\partial \Delta_{ij}$, $\varphi_{ij}'' = \partial^2 \varphi_{ij}/\partial \Delta_{ij}^2$, and k_{ij} is a positive constant. The positive constant Δ_{ijd} is referred to as the desired transformed distance between the agents i and j, and satisfies the condition

$$0 < \Delta_{ijd} < \Delta_{ijR}^m, \tag{18}$$

with Δ_{ijR}^m defined in (15). The constant Δ_{ijR}^M is the least upper bound of the transformed distance Δ_{ij} when the agents i and j are within their communication ranges, that is,

$$\Delta_{ijR}^M = \sup(\Delta_{ij}) \quad \text{s.t.} \quad \begin{cases} \boldsymbol{\eta}_{ij} \in \mathbb{R}^3, \\ \|\mathbf{q}_{ij}\| = \min(R_i, R_j). \end{cases} \tag{19}$$

Remark 8. Property (1) implies that the function φ_{ij} is constant when the agents i and j are outside of their communication ranges. Property (2) implies that the function φ_{ij} is positive definite when the agents i and j are inside of their communication ranges. By Lemma 1, Property (3) means that the function φ_{ij} is equal to infinity when a collision between the agents i and j occurs. Property (4) allows us to use control design and stability analysis methods found in [36] for continuous systems instead of techniques for switched and discontinuous systems found in [38] to handle the collision avoidance problem under the agents' limited communication ranges. Property (5) makes it effective to use a gradient-based method for the flock control design.

Lemma 9. Let the scalar function φ_{ij} be defined as

$$\varphi_{ij} = (\Delta_{ij} - \Delta_{ijd})^2 \frac{1 - h(\Delta_{ij}, a_{ij}, b_{ij}, c_{ij})}{\Delta_{ij}^2} \tag{20}$$

$$+ k_{ij} h(\Delta_{ij}, a_{ij}, b_{ij}, c_{ij}),$$

where the positive constants a_{ij} and b_{ij} satisfy the condition

$$a_{ij} = \Delta_{ijd}, \quad a_{ij} < b_{ij} < \Delta_{ijR}^M, \tag{21}$$

and c_{ij} is a positive constant. The positive constant k_{ij} is chosen such that

$$\varphi_{ij}' > 0, \quad \forall \Delta_{ij} \in (\Delta_{ijd}, \Delta_{ijR}^M), \tag{22}$$

where

$$\varphi_{ij}' = 2(\Delta_{ij} - \Delta_{ijd}) \frac{1 - h(\bullet)}{\Delta_{ij}^2}$$

$$- (\Delta_{ij} - \Delta_{ijd})^2 \frac{h'(\bullet) + 2(1 - h(\bullet))}{\Delta_{ij}^3} + k_{ij} h'(\bullet). \tag{23}$$

The function $h(\bullet)$ with $\bullet$ stood for $(\Delta_{ij}, a_{ij}, b_{ij}, c_{ij})$ is a smooth step function defined in Definition 3.
Then the function φ_{ij} is a pairwise potential function.

Proof (see Appendix B). A pairwise potential function φ_{ij} with $\Delta_{ijd} = 5$, $\Delta_{ijR}^M = 10$, $a_{ij} = \Delta_{ijd}$, $b_{ij} = 0.9\Delta_{ijR}^M$, and $c_{ij} = 1$ is plotted in Figure 4. □

4.1.2. Potential Function.
Having constructed the pairwise potential function φ_{ij} for the agents i and j, the potential

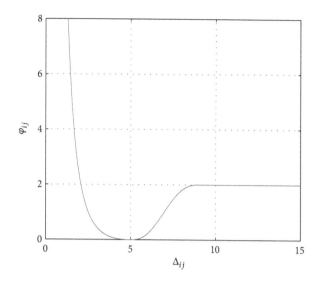

FIGURE 4: A pairwise potential function.

function φ for all the agents in the group is the sum of all the pairwise potential functions, that is,

$$\varphi = \sum_{i=1}^{N-1} \sum_{j=i+1}^{N} \varphi_{ij}, \qquad (24)$$

where φ_{ij} is given in (20).

4.2. Derivative of Potential Function. To prepare for the flock control design later, we calculating the derivative of φ by differentiating both sides of (24) to obtain

$$\dot{\varphi} = \sum_{i=1}^{N-1} \sum_{j=i+1}^{N} \varphi'_{ij} \dot{\Delta}_{ij}. \qquad (25)$$

It is noted that Δ_{ij} is a smooth function of $\mathbf{q}_{ij}, \boldsymbol{\eta}_i, \boldsymbol{\eta}_j$, and $\boldsymbol{\eta}_{ij}$, see Remark 2. However, there is a difficulty in determining an explicit dependence of Δ_{ij} on $\mathbf{q}_{ij}, \boldsymbol{\eta}_i, \boldsymbol{\eta}_j$, and $\boldsymbol{\eta}_{ij}$ via the matrix $\mathbf{Q}_{ij}$, see (1) and (2), because κ_{ij} cannot be solved explicitly. To avoid this difficulty, we treat Δ_{ij} as a smooth function of κ_{ij}, $\overline{\mathbf{q}}_{ij}, \overline{\mathbf{q}}_{ji}$, and $\boldsymbol{\eta}_{ij}$.

We first calculate the first time derivative of κ_{ij}. From (7), we have

$$\dot{\kappa}_{ij} = -\left(\frac{\partial F_{ij}}{\partial \kappa_{ij}}\right)^{-1} \left(\left(\frac{\partial F_{ij}}{\partial \overline{\mathbf{q}}_{ij}}\right)^T \dot{\overline{\mathbf{q}}}_{ij} + \left(\frac{\partial F_{ij}}{\partial \boldsymbol{\eta}_{ij}}\right)^T \dot{\boldsymbol{\eta}}_{ij}\right). \qquad (26)$$

It is noted that $\partial F_{ij}/\partial \kappa_{ij}$ is always nonzero, see A.10. Hence, the first time derivative of Δ_{ij} is

$$\dot{\Delta}_{ij} = \mathbf{G}_{ij} \dot{\overline{\mathbf{q}}}_{ij} + \mathbf{G}_{ji} \dot{\overline{\mathbf{q}}}_{ji} + \mathbf{H}_{ij} \dot{\boldsymbol{\eta}}_{ij} + \mathbf{H}_{ji} \dot{\boldsymbol{\eta}}_{ji}, \qquad (27)$$

where

$$\mathbf{G}_{ij} = \left[\frac{\partial \Delta_{ij}}{\partial \overline{\mathbf{q}}_{ij}} - \frac{\partial \Delta_{ij}}{\partial \kappa_{ij}} \left(\frac{\partial F_{ij}}{\partial \kappa_{ij}}\right)^{-1} \frac{\partial F_{ij}}{\partial \overline{\mathbf{q}}_{ij}}\right]^T,$$

$$\mathbf{G}_{ji} = \left[\frac{\partial \Delta_{ij}}{\partial \overline{\mathbf{q}}_{ji}} - \frac{\partial \Delta_{ij}}{\partial \kappa_{ji}} \left(\frac{\partial F_{ji}}{\partial \kappa_{ji}}\right)^{-1} \frac{\partial F_{ji}}{\partial \overline{\mathbf{q}}_{ji}}\right]^T,$$

$$\hspace{10cm} (28)$$

$$\mathbf{H}_{ij} = \left[\frac{\partial \Delta_{ij}}{\partial \boldsymbol{\eta}_{ij}} - \frac{\partial \Delta_{ij}}{\partial \kappa_{ij}} \left(\frac{\partial F_{ij}}{\partial \kappa_{ij}}\right)^{-1} \frac{\partial F_{ij}}{\partial \boldsymbol{\eta}_{ij}}\right]^T,$$

$$\mathbf{H}_{ji} = \left[\frac{\partial \Delta_{ij}}{\partial \boldsymbol{\eta}_{ji}} - \frac{\partial \Delta_{ij}}{\partial \kappa_{ji}} \left(\frac{\partial F_{ji}}{\partial \kappa_{ji}}\right)^{-1} \frac{\partial F_{ji}}{\partial \boldsymbol{\eta}_{ji}}\right]^T.$$

From definition of $\overline{\mathbf{q}}_{ij}$ in (2), we have

$$\dot{\overline{\mathbf{q}}}_{ij} = \mathbf{P}_i \dot{\mathbf{q}}_{ij} + \dot{\mathbf{P}}_i \mathbf{q}_{ij},$$
$$= \mathbf{P}_i \left(\dot{\mathbf{q}}_{ij} + \mathbf{S}_i \mathbf{q}_{ij} + \mathbf{S}_j \left(\mathbf{q}_j - \mathbf{q}_{od}\right) - \mathbf{S}_j \left(\mathbf{q}_j - \mathbf{q}_{od}\right)\right), \qquad (29)$$

where $\mathbf{S}_i = \mathbf{P}_i^{-1} \dot{\mathbf{P}}_i$ and $\mathbf{S}_j = \mathbf{P}_j^{-1} \dot{\mathbf{P}}_j$, and we have added and subtracted $\mathbf{S}_j (\mathbf{q}_j - \mathbf{q}_{od})$ to the first line of (29) to result in the second line. Now substituting $\mathbf{q}_{ij} = [\mathbf{q}_i - \mathbf{q}_{od}] - [\mathbf{q}_j - \mathbf{q}_{od}]$ into (29) gives

$$\dot{\overline{\mathbf{q}}}_{ij} = \mathbf{P}_i \left(\left[\dot{\mathbf{q}}_i - \dot{\mathbf{q}}_{od} + \overline{\mathbf{S}}_i \boldsymbol{\eta}_i\right] - \left[\dot{\mathbf{q}}_j - \dot{\mathbf{q}}_{od} + \overline{\mathbf{S}}_j \boldsymbol{\eta}_j\right]\right)$$
$$- \mathbf{P}_i \left(\overline{\mathbf{S}}_{ij} \dot{\boldsymbol{\eta}}_i - \overline{\mathbf{S}}_j \dot{\boldsymbol{\eta}}_j\right), \qquad (30)$$

where the matrices $\overline{\mathbf{S}}_i, \overline{\mathbf{S}}_j$, and $\overline{\mathbf{S}}_{ij}$ are defined by

$$\mathbf{S}_i \left(\mathbf{q}_i - \mathbf{q}_{od}\right) = \overline{\mathbf{S}}_i \dot{\boldsymbol{\eta}}_i,$$
$$\mathbf{S}_j \left(\mathbf{q}_j - \mathbf{q}_{od}\right) = \overline{\mathbf{S}}_j \dot{\boldsymbol{\eta}}_j, \qquad (31)$$
$$\mathbf{S}_i \left(\mathbf{q}_j - \mathbf{q}_{od}\right) = \overline{\mathbf{S}}_{ij} \dot{\boldsymbol{\eta}}_i.$$

Similarly, we have

$$\dot{\overline{\mathbf{q}}}_{ji} = \mathbf{P}_j \left(\left[\dot{\mathbf{q}}_j - \dot{\mathbf{q}}_{od} + \overline{\mathbf{S}}_j \boldsymbol{\eta}_j\right] - \left[\dot{\mathbf{q}}_i - \dot{\mathbf{q}}_{od} + \overline{\mathbf{S}}_i \boldsymbol{\eta}_i\right]\right)$$
$$- \mathbf{P}_j \left(\overline{\mathbf{S}}_{ji} \dot{\boldsymbol{\eta}}_j - \overline{\mathbf{S}}_i \dot{\boldsymbol{\eta}}_i\right). \qquad (32)$$

Substituting (30) and (32) into (27) results in the following:

$$\dot{\Delta}_{ij} = \boldsymbol{\Gamma}_{ij} \left(\dot{\mathbf{q}}_i - \dot{\mathbf{q}}_{od} + \overline{\mathbf{S}}_i \boldsymbol{\eta}_i\right) + \boldsymbol{\Lambda}_{ij} \dot{\boldsymbol{\eta}}_i$$
$$+ \boldsymbol{\Gamma}_{ji} \left(\dot{\mathbf{q}}_j - \dot{\mathbf{q}}_{od} + \overline{\mathbf{S}}_j \boldsymbol{\eta}_j\right) + \boldsymbol{\Lambda}_{ji} \dot{\boldsymbol{\eta}}_j, \qquad (33)$$

where

$$\boldsymbol{\Gamma}_{ij} = \mathbf{G}_{ij} \mathbf{P}_i - \mathbf{G}_{ji} \mathbf{P}_j, \qquad \boldsymbol{\Gamma}_{ji} = \mathbf{G}_{ji} \mathbf{P}_j - \mathbf{G}_{ij} \mathbf{P}_i,$$

$$\boldsymbol{\Lambda}_{ij} = -\mathbf{G}_{ij} \mathbf{P}_i \overline{\mathbf{S}}_{ij} + \mathbf{G}_{ji} \mathbf{P}_j \overline{\mathbf{S}}_i + \mathbf{H}_{ij} - \mathbf{H}_{ji}, \qquad (34)$$

$$\boldsymbol{\Lambda}_{ji} = -\mathbf{G}_{ji} \mathbf{P}_j \overline{\mathbf{S}}_j + \mathbf{G}_{ij} \mathbf{P}_i \overline{\mathbf{S}}_j + \mathbf{H}_{ji} - \mathbf{H}_{ij}.$$

Substituting (33) into (25) gives

$$\dot{\varphi} = \sum_{i=1}^{N} \left[\left(\sum_{j \neq i} \varphi'_{ij} \Gamma_{ij} \right) (\dot{\mathbf{q}}_i - \dot{\mathbf{q}}_{od} + \overline{\mathbf{S}}_i \dot{\boldsymbol{\eta}}_i) + \left(\sum_{j \neq i} \varphi'_{ij} \Lambda_{ij} \right) \dot{\boldsymbol{\eta}}_i \right].$$

(35)

Remark 10. The transformed distance Δ_{ij} depends not only on the relative distance vector $\mathbf{q}_{ij}$ and the relative orientation vector $\boldsymbol{\eta}_{ij}$ but also on the individual orientation vectors $\boldsymbol{\eta}_i$ and $\boldsymbol{\eta}_j$ of the ellipsoidal agents i and j. This dependence creates a difficulty in designing flocking control algorithms using a gradient-based approach since it is hard to write the derivative of the potential function φ as a summation of the product of each individual agent's potential gradient and its state derivative. To overcome this difficulty, we have carefully calculated the derivative of the transformed distance by adding and subtracting the term $\mathbf{S}_j(\mathbf{q}_j - \mathbf{q}_{od})$ to the first line of (29). As a result, the expression of $\dot{\varphi}$ has been obtained in a feasible form, see (35), for the flocking control design later.

The expression of $\dot{\varphi}$ in (35) deserves some discussion. If we define $\varphi = \sum_{i=1}^{N} \varphi_i$, where φ_i is the potential function for each agent i. We then have $\dot{\varphi}_i = (\sum_{j \neq i} \varphi'_{ij} \Gamma_{ij})(\dot{\mathbf{q}}_i - \dot{\mathbf{q}}_{od} + \overline{\mathbf{S}}_i \dot{\boldsymbol{\eta}}_i) + (\sum_{j \neq i} \varphi'_{ij} \Lambda_{ij}) \dot{\boldsymbol{\eta}}_i$, where the term $(\sum_{j \neq i} \varphi'_{ij} \Gamma_{ij})$ can be regarded as the gradient of φ_i with respect to the relative distance, which is rotated by the orientation vector $\boldsymbol{\eta}_i$, from the agent i to the rendezvous trajectory $\mathbf{q}_{od}$. The term $(\sum_{j \neq i} \varphi'_{ij} \Lambda_{ij})$ can be considered as the gradient of φ_i with respect to $\boldsymbol{\eta}_i$.

4.3. Lyapunov Function. Since the derivative of the potential function φ is the summation of the term $(\sum_{j \neq i} \varphi'_{ij} \Gamma_{ij})(\dot{\mathbf{q}}_i - \dot{\mathbf{q}}_{od} + \overline{\mathbf{S}}_i \dot{\boldsymbol{\eta}}_i)$ instead of $(\sum_{j \neq i} \varphi'_{ij} \Gamma_{ij})(\dot{\mathbf{q}}_i - \dot{\mathbf{q}}_{od})$, and the term $(\sum_{j \neq i} \varphi'_{ij} \Lambda_{ij}) \dot{\boldsymbol{\eta}}_i$ instead of $(\sum_{j \neq i} \varphi'_{ij} \Lambda_{ij})(\dot{\boldsymbol{\eta}}_i - \dot{\boldsymbol{\eta}}_{od})$, it is not possible to use a Lyapunov function candidate as a summation of the potential function φ and the square of all errors $\mathbf{q}_i - \mathbf{q}_{od}$ and $\boldsymbol{\eta}_i - \boldsymbol{\eta}_{od}$ for the flock control design.

To overcome the aforementioned impossibilities, we will construct a Lyapunov function candidate as a sum of the potential function φ in (24) and the square of errors $\mathbf{P}_i(\mathbf{q}_i - \mathbf{q}_{od})$ and $\boldsymbol{\eta}_i - \boldsymbol{\eta}_{id}$. The vector $\boldsymbol{\eta}_{id}$ is considered as the virtual rendezvous orientation vector to be designed such that $\lim_{t \to \infty} \boldsymbol{\eta}_{id}(t) = \boldsymbol{\eta}_{od}(t)$. As such, the Lyapunov function candidate for the flock control design in the next section is constructed as follows:

$$V = \varphi + \frac{1}{2} \sum_{i=1}^{N} \left[c_1 \| \mathbf{P}_i (\mathbf{q}_i - \mathbf{q}_{od}) \|^2 + c_2 \| \boldsymbol{\eta}_i - \boldsymbol{\eta}_{id} \|^2 \right],$$

(36)

where c_1 and c_2 are positive constants. Differentiating both sides of (36) along the solutions of (35) and recalling from (13) that $\dot{\mathbf{q}}_i = \mathbf{u}_i$ and $\dot{\boldsymbol{\eta}}_i = \boldsymbol{\omega}_i$ results in the folowing:

$$\dot{V} = \sum_{i=1}^{N} \left(\left[\boldsymbol{\Omega}_i^T (\mathbf{u}_i - \dot{\mathbf{q}}_{od} + \overline{\mathbf{S}}_i \boldsymbol{\omega}_i) + \boldsymbol{\Xi}_i^T (\boldsymbol{\omega}_i - \dot{\boldsymbol{\eta}}_{id}) \right] \right.$$

$$\left. + \left(\sum_{j \neq i} \varphi'_{ij} \Lambda_{ij} \right) \dot{\boldsymbol{\eta}}_{id} \right),$$

(37)

where we added and subtracted $\sum_{i=1}^{N} (\sum_{j \neq i} \varphi'_{ij} \Lambda_{ij}) \dot{\boldsymbol{\eta}}_{id}$ to the right hand side of the equation (35) before substituting this equation into the derivative of V. In (37), we have defined

$$\boldsymbol{\Omega}_i = \left[\sum_{j \neq i} \varphi'_{ij} \Gamma_{ij} + c_1 (\mathbf{P}_i (\mathbf{q}_i - \mathbf{q}_{od}))^T \mathbf{P}_i \right]^T,$$

$$\boldsymbol{\Xi}_i = \left[\sum_{j \neq i} \varphi'_{ij} \Lambda_{ij} + c_2 (\boldsymbol{\eta}_i - \boldsymbol{\eta}_{id})^T \right]^T.$$

(38)

4.4. Control Law. We first deal with the terms inside the square bracket in the right hand side of (37). As such, to avoid a large control effort when an agent in the group is close to the agent i due to Property (3) of the function φ_{ij}, see (17), for collision avoidance, we design a control law for $\mathbf{u}_i$ and $\boldsymbol{\omega}_i$ as follows:

$$\mathbf{u}_i = -k_1 \mathbf{W}(\boldsymbol{\Omega}_i) + \dot{\mathbf{q}}_{od} - \overline{\mathbf{S}}_i (-k_2 \mathbf{W}(\boldsymbol{\Xi}_i) + \dot{\boldsymbol{\eta}}_{id}),$$

$$\boldsymbol{\omega}_i = -k_2 \mathbf{W}(\boldsymbol{\Xi}_i) + \dot{\boldsymbol{\eta}}_{id},$$

(39)

where k_1 and k_2 are positive constants. The vector $\mathbf{W}(\chi)$ denotes a vector of bounded and differentiable functions of elements of χ in the sense that $\mathbf{W}(\chi) = [w(\chi_1) \ldots, w(\chi_l), \ldots, w(\chi_n)]^T$ with χ_l the lth element of χ, that is, $\chi = [\chi_1 \ldots, \chi_l, \ldots, \chi_n]^T$. The function $w(\chi)$ is a scalar, differentiable and bounded function, and satisfies

(1) $|w(\chi)| \leq M_1$,

(2) $w(\chi) = 0$ if $\chi = 0$, $\quad \chi w(\chi) > 0 \quad$ if $\chi \neq 0$,

(3) $w(-\chi) = -w(\chi)$, $\quad (\chi - \omega)[w(\chi) - w(\omega)] \geq 0$,

(4) $\left| \dfrac{w(\chi)}{\chi} \right| \leq M_2$, $\quad \left| \dfrac{\partial w(\chi)}{\partial \chi} \right| \leq M_3$,

$\left. \dfrac{\partial w(\chi)}{\partial \chi} \right|_{\chi=0} = 1$,

(40)

for all $\chi \in \mathbb{R}$, $\omega \in \mathbb{R}$, where M_1, M_2, M_3 are positive constants. Some functions that satisfy the above properties are $\arctan(\chi)$ and $\tanh(\chi)$.

We now deal with the term $(\sum_{j \neq i} \varphi'_{ij} \Lambda_{ij}) \dot{\boldsymbol{\eta}}_{id}$ in the right hand side of (37). This term seems to be troublesome because

$\dot{\eta}_{id}$ is nonzero in general since we are considering a time-varying rendezvous trajectory. To get around this problem, we will design an update law $\dot{\eta}_{id}$ such that

$$\left(\sum_{j \neq i} \varphi'_{ij} \Lambda_{ij}\right) \dot{\eta}_{id} = 0, \qquad (41)$$

holds for all time. Moreover, it is desired to have the virtual rendezvous orientation vector η_{id} asymptotically approached the desired rendezvous orientation vector η_{od}. As such, we utilize the smooth step function to design an update law $\dot{\eta}_{id}$ as follows:

$$\dot{\eta}_{id} = \left(\prod_{j \neq i} h\left(\Delta_{ij}, a_{ijd}, b_{ijd}, c_{ijd}\right)\right)\left(-k_d\left(\eta_{id} - \eta_{od}\right) + \dot{\eta}_{od}\right), \qquad (42)$$

where k_d is a positive constant, and $\eta_{id}(t_0) = \eta_{od}(t_0)$. The function $h(\Delta_{ij}, a_{ijd}, b_{ijd}, c_{ijd})$ is a smooth step function with the constants a_{ijd}, b_{ijd}, and c_{ijd} chosen as

$$a_{ijd} = b_{ij}, \quad a_{ijd} < b_{ijd} \leq \Delta^M_{ijR}, \quad c_{ijd} > 0, \qquad (43)$$

where b_{ij} is chosen as in (21), and Δ^M_{ijR} is given in (19). Using properties of the smooth step function, the choice of the constants a_{ij}, b_{ij}, a_{ijd}, and b_{ijd} in (21) and (43) results in $h'\left(\Delta_{ij}, a_{ij}, b_{ij}, c_{ij}\right) h(\Delta_{ij}, a_{ijd}, b_{ijd}, c_{ijd}) = 0$ and $(1 - h(\Delta_{ij}, a_{ij}, b_{ij}, c_{ij})) h(\Delta_{ij}, a_{ijd}, b_{ijd}, c_{ijd}) = 0$. These equalities imply that (41) holds as long as $\Delta_{ij} > 0$, which is to be guaranteed by our control design. Moreover, the choice of the constants a_{ijd} and b_{ijd} in (43) ensures that the function $h(\Delta_{ij}, a_{ijd}, b_{ijd}, c_{ijd})$ approaches 1 whenever Δ_{ij} approaches a value larger than b_{ijd}. The inequality $\Delta_{ij} > 0$ and the limit $\lim_{t \to \infty}(\sum_{j \neq i} \varphi'_{ij}(t) \Lambda_{ij}(t)) = 0$ will be guaranteed by our designed control input vectors $\mathbf{u}_i$ and ω_i in (39). This will be shown in the proof of the main result.

Remark 11. (1) The control vectors $\mathbf{u}_i$ and ω_i in (39) of the agent i are smooth and depend on only its own state and the rendezvous trajectory, and the states of other agents j in the communication range of the agent i due to Property (1) of the pairwise potential function φ_{ij} in (17).

(2) The update law $\dot{\eta}_{id}$ in (42) ensures that when the collision avoidance is active, the virtual rendezvous orientation vector η_{id} is not updated. This implies that the control vectors $\mathbf{u}_i$ and ω_i give priority to the collision avoidance mission or the rendezvous orientation tracking mission whenever which mission is more important.

Substituting the control vectors $\mathbf{u}_i$ and ω_i in (39) and the update law $\dot{\eta}_{id}$ in (42) into (37) results in

$$\dot{V} = -\sum_{i=1}^{N} \vartheta_i, \qquad (44)$$

where

$$\vartheta_i = k_1 \Omega_i^T \mathbf{W}(\Omega_i) + k_2 \Xi_i^T \mathbf{W}(\Xi_i). \qquad (45)$$

On the other hand, substituting the control vectors $\mathbf{u}_i$ and ω_i in (39) and the update law $\dot{\eta}_{id}$ in (42) into (13) results in the closed-loop system:

$$\dot{\mathbf{q}}_i = -k_1 \mathbf{W}(\Omega_i) + \dot{\mathbf{q}}_{od} - \bar{\mathbf{S}}_i\left(-k_2 \mathbf{W}(\Xi_i) + \dot{\eta}_{id}\right),$$
$$\dot{\eta}_i = -k_2 \mathbf{W}(\Xi_i) + \dot{\eta}_{id}, \qquad (46)$$

for all $i \in \mathbb{N}$. We now present the main result of our paper in the following theorem.

Theorem 12. *Under Assumption 1, the smooth control vectors $\mathbf{u}_i$ and ω_i in (39) and the update law $\dot{\eta}_{id}$ in (42) for the agent i solve the flocking control objective. In particular, the following results hold*

(1) There are no collisions between any agents and the closed-loop system (46) is forward complete;

(2) The relative distance between each agent i and the flocking rendezvous trajectory $\mathbf{q}_{od}$ is bounded, that is, $\|\mathbf{q}_i(t) - \mathbf{q}_{od}(t)\| \leq A_0$ for all $t \geq t_0 \geq 0$ with A_0 a constant depending on the initial conditions;

(3) The generalized velocity of each agent i asymptotically tends to the generalized flocking rendezvous velocity, that is,

$$\lim_{t \to \infty}\left(\dot{\mathbf{q}}_i - \dot{\mathbf{q}}_{od} + \bar{\mathbf{S}}_i \dot{\eta}_{id}\right) = 0, \qquad (47)$$

where $\dot{\eta}_{id}$ is given in (42).

(4) The flock size $F_L(t) = \sum_{j=i+1}^{N} \sum_{j=1}^{i-1} \Delta_{ij}(t)$ is bounded by a positive constant as time tends to infinity, that is,

$$\lim_{t \to \infty} F_L(t) = F_{Lc}, \qquad (48)$$

with $F_{Lc} \leq c_0$ where c_0 is a positive constant.

Proof. See Appendix C. □

5. Simulation Results

In this section, we provide a numerical simulation to illustrate the effectiveness of the proposed flocking control design stated in Theorem 12. We use $N = 6$ ellipsoidal agents with the geometric parameters as $a_i = 3$ and $b_i = c_i = 1$ for all $i = 1, \ldots, N$. The initial position and orientation of these agents are chosen as follows: $\mathbf{q}_i(0) = 15[\cos(2\pi(i - 1)/N) \quad \sin(2\pi(i - 1)/N) \quad 0]^T$ and $\eta_i(0) = [0 \quad 0 \quad 0]^T$. All the agents have the same communication range of $R_i = 25$. The control design parameters are chosen as follows: $k_{ij} = 10$, $\Delta_{ijd} = 5, a_{ij} = \Delta_{ijd}, b_{ij} = 1.5a_{ij}, c_1 = 1, c_2 = 1, k_1 = 20, k_2 = 20$, $a_{ijd} = b_{ij}, b_{ijd} = 1.2a_{ijd}, k_d = 1$. The function $w(\cdot)$ is chosen as $\arctan(\cdot)$. The flocking rendezvous trajectory is chosen as $\dot{\mathbf{q}}_{od} = [1 \quad 1 \quad 1]^T$ with $\mathbf{q}_{od}(0) = [0, 0, 0]^T$. This choice implies that the flocking rendezvous trajectory is a angled straight line. A calculation shows that the above initial conditions and the above choice of control design parameters satisfy all the conditions (14), (16), (18), (21), (22).

Simulation results are plotted in Figures 5 and 6. In Figure 5, several snapshots of the position and orientation of all agents are plotted. The representative $\Delta^*_{ij} = \left(\Pi_{j \in \mathbb{N} j \neq i} \Delta_{ij}\right)^{1/5}$

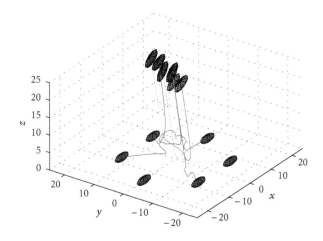

FIGURE 5: Snapshots of the agents' position and orientation.

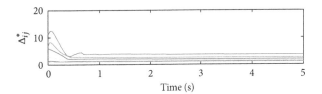

(a)

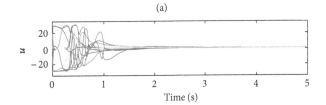

(b)

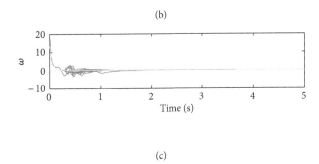

(c)

FIGURE 6: Representative Δ_{ij}^* and control inputs.

is plotted in the first subfigure of Figure 6. The control inputs $\mathbf{u} = [\mathbf{u}_1, \ldots, \mathbf{u}_i, \ldots, \mathbf{u}_N]^T$ and $\boldsymbol{\omega} = [\boldsymbol{\omega}_1, \ldots, \boldsymbol{\omega}_i, \ldots, \boldsymbol{\omega}_N]^T$ are plotted in the second and third subfigures of Figure 6. It is clearly seen from Figures 5 and 6 that there is no collision between any agents as indicated by $\Delta_{ij}^* > 0$ for all $i \in \mathbb{N}$. Moreover, all the agents manage to track the generalized flocking rendezvous trajectory $\mathbf{q}_{od}$. The mismatched velocity can be seen from the second and third subfigures of Figure 6.

6. Conclusions

Flocking of N mobile agents with an ellipsoidal shape and limited communication ranges was studied. The flock control design is based on a separation condition for ellipsoidal agents, smooth step functions, and novel pairwise potential functions. The proposed flock algorithms achieved desired flocking behaviors including smooth controllers despite of agents' limited communication ranges, no collisions between any agents, asymptotic convergence of each agent's velocity to a desired velocity, and boundedness of the flock size by a constant. The keys to success of our proposed flocking algorithm include the symmetric transformed distance Δ_{ij} between two ellipsoids, smooth cut-off pairwise potential function φ_{ij}, and a careful derivation of the derivative of the potential function φ. An extension of the proposed flock control design and those controllers designed for single underactuated underwater vehicles in [39] to provide a flock control system for multiple underactuated underwater vehicles is under consideration.

Appendix

A. Proof of Lemma 1

From Figure 2, the boundaries of the ellipsoids i and j (equations of the points w_{ib} and w_{jb}) coordinated in

the $O_{bi}X_{bi}Y_{bi}Z_{bi}$ frame attached to the ellipsoid i can be described by

$$
\begin{aligned}
E_i &: \mathbf{q}_{ib}^T \mathbf{A}_i^{-2} \mathbf{q}_{ib} = 1, \\
E_j &: \mathbf{q}_{jb} = -\mathbf{R}^{-1}(\boldsymbol{\eta}_i)\,\mathbf{q}_{ij} + \mathbf{R}^{-1}(\boldsymbol{\eta}_{ij})\,\mathbf{A}_j \boldsymbol{\varrho}_j,
\end{aligned}
\tag{A.1}
$$

where $\mathbf{A}_i$, $\mathbf{A}_j$, $\mathbf{q}_{ij}$, and $\boldsymbol{\eta}_{ij}$ are defined in (3) and (6) and $\boldsymbol{\varrho}_j = [\cos(\alpha_j)\cos(\beta_j)\ \ \cos(\alpha_j)\sin(\beta_j)\ \ \sin(\alpha_j)]^T$ with $\alpha_j \in [-\pi/2, \pi/2]$ and $\beta_j \in [-\pi, \pi]$ are auxiliary angles and $\mathbf{q}_{ib}$ and $\mathbf{q}_{jb}$ are vectors denoting position of the points w_{ib} and w_{jb}, respectively. The ideas to prove Lemma 1 consists of two steps: (1) transforming the ellipsoids i and j to a unit sphere and an ellipsoid; (2) calculating the distance between the transformed sphere and the transformed ellipsoid.

1. Transformation. We transform the ellipsoids i and j to a unit sphere and an ellipsoid by the following coordinate transformation:

$$
\begin{aligned}
\bar{\mathbf{q}}_{ib} &= \mathbf{A}_i^{-1}\left(\mathbf{q}_{ib} + \mathbf{R}^{-1}(\boldsymbol{\eta}_i)\,\mathbf{q}_{ij}\right), \\
\bar{\mathbf{q}}_{jb} &= \mathbf{A}_i^{-1}\left(\mathbf{q}_{jb} + \mathbf{R}^{-1}(\boldsymbol{\eta}_i)\,\mathbf{q}_{ij}\right).
\end{aligned}
\tag{A.2}
$$

With the above coordinate transformation, the ellipsoids (A.1) are transformed to a unit sphere and an ellipsoid as follows:

$$\overline{E}_i : \left(\overline{\mathbf{q}}_{ib} + \overline{\mathbf{q}}_{ij}\right)^T \left(\overline{\mathbf{q}}_{ib} + \overline{\mathbf{q}}_{ij}\right) = 1,$$
$$\overline{E}_j : \overline{\mathbf{q}}_{jb} = \mathbf{A}_i^{-1}\mathbf{R}\left(\boldsymbol{\eta}_{ij}\right)\mathbf{A}_j\boldsymbol{\varrho}_j. \tag{A.3}$$

Now, the ellipsoid E_i has become the unit sphere $\overline{E}_i$ centered at the point O_{usi} whose coordinates are described by the first equation in (A.3). The ellipsoid E_j has become another ellipsoid $\overline{E}_j$ centered at the origin of the $O_{bi}X_{bi}Y_{bi}Z_{bi}$ frame, that is, the point O_{bi}.

For convenience of calculating the distance between the unit sphere $\overline{E}_i$ and the ellipsoid $\overline{E}_j$, we will rewrite the ellipsoid $\overline{E}_j$ in an implicit form instead of parametric form given in the second equation of (A.3). By squaring both sides of each row of $\overline{\mathbf{q}}_{jb} = \mathbf{A}_i^{-1}\mathbf{R}(\boldsymbol{\eta}_{ij})\mathbf{A}_j\boldsymbol{\varrho}_j$ then adding the results together, we have $\overline{\mathbf{q}}_{jb}^T\mathbf{T}_j\overline{\mathbf{q}}_{jb} = 1$, where $\mathbf{T}_j$ is defined in (4). Hence, the unit sphere and the ellipsoid defined in (A.3) can be rewritten as

$$\overline{E}_i : \left(\overline{\mathbf{q}}_{ib} + \overline{\mathbf{q}}_{ij}\right)^T \left(\overline{\mathbf{q}}_{ib} + \overline{\mathbf{q}}_{ij}\right) = 1,$$
$$\overline{E}_j : \overline{\mathbf{q}}_{jb}^T\mathbf{T}_j\overline{\mathbf{q}}_{jb} = 1. \tag{A.4}$$

2. Distance Δ_{ij}. We now calculate the distance from the center of the unit sphere $\overline{E}_i$ described by the first equation in (A.4), that is, from the point O_{usi} to the ellipsoid $\overline{E}_j$ described by the second equation in (A.4). A necessary condition for a point $\overline{\mathbf{q}}_{jb}$ to be the closest point to the point O_{usi} is that $\overline{\mathbf{q}}_{ij} - \overline{\mathbf{q}}_{jb}$ is perpendicular to the tangent plane to the ellipsoid $\overline{E}_j$ at $\overline{\mathbf{q}}_{jb}$. Since the surface gradient $\partial f(\overline{\mathbf{q}}_{jb})/\partial \overline{\mathbf{q}}_{jb}$ with $f(\overline{\mathbf{q}}_{jb}) := (1/2)(\overline{\mathbf{q}}_{jb}^T\mathbf{T}_j\overline{\mathbf{q}}_{jb} - 1)$ is normal to the ellipsoid's surface, the algebraic condition for the closest point $\overline{\mathbf{q}}_{ib}$ is

$$\overline{\mathbf{q}}_{ij} - \overline{\mathbf{q}}_{jb} = \kappa_{ij}\frac{\partial f\left(\overline{\mathbf{q}}_{jb}\right)}{\partial \overline{\mathbf{q}}_{jb}}. \tag{A.5}$$

For the point O_{usi} outside the ellipsoid $\overline{E}_j$, there is only one point on the ellipsoid whose normal points toward the point O_{usi}. However, there can be as many as five other points whose surface normals point directly away from O_{usi}. The point on the ellipsoid whose normal points toward the point O_{usi} corresponds to the largest root κ_{ij} of (A.5). Moreover, $\overline{\mathbf{q}}_{jb}$ must satisfy the ellipsoid equation, that is, the second equation of (A.4).

From (A.5), we have

$$\overline{\mathbf{q}}_{jb} = \left(\mathbf{I}_{3\times3} + \kappa_{ij}\mathbf{T}_j\right)^{-1}\overline{\mathbf{q}}_{ij}, \tag{A.6}$$

which is substituted into the second equation in (A.4) results in (7).

Now the distance from the point O_{usi} to the closest point $\overline{\mathbf{q}}_{jb}$ on the ellipsoid $\overline{E}_j$ described by the second equation in (A.4) is given by

$$d_{ij} = \left\|\overline{\mathbf{q}}_{ij} - \overline{\mathbf{q}}_{jb}\right\| - 1, \tag{A.7}$$

where $\overline{\mathbf{q}}_{jb}$ is the solution of (A.5) and the second equation of (A.4) with κ_{ij} being the largest root. Substituting $\overline{\mathbf{q}}_{jb}$ in (A.6) and $\overline{\mathbf{q}}_{ij}$ in (2) into (A.7) results in the following:

$$d_{ij} = \left\|\mathbf{Q}_{ij}\mathbf{q}_{ij}\right\| - 1, \tag{A.8}$$

where $\mathbf{Q}_{ij}$ is given in (2).

It is noted that after $\overline{\mathbf{q}}_{jb}$ is found, we can determine the intersection point with coordinates $\overline{\mathbf{q}}_{ib}$ on the unit sphere $\overline{E}_i$ between the line from the point O_{usi} to the point with coordinates $\overline{\mathbf{q}}_{jb}$ and the unit sphere $\overline{E}_i$. Once we obtain the coordinates $\overline{\mathbf{q}}_{ib}$ and $\overline{\mathbf{q}}_{jb}$ with respect to the closest distance between the unit sphere $\overline{E}_i$ and the transformed ellipsoid $\overline{E}_j$, the corresponding coordinates $\mathbf{q}_{ib}$ and $\mathbf{q}_{jb}$ with respect to the shortest distance between the original ellipsoids E_i and E_j on the original ellipsoids E_i and E_j can be directly determined from (A.2). The actual distance between the original ellipsoids E_i and E_j is $\|\mathbf{q}_{ib} - \mathbf{q}_{jb}\|$. For a flocking control application, the transformed distance d_{ij} is sufficient because from the transformation (A.2) we can see that $d_{ij} > 0$ implies that $\|\mathbf{q}_{ib} - \mathbf{q}_{jb}\| > 0$ and vice versa.

Similarly, we transform the two ellipsoids j and i to a unit sphere $\overline{E}_j$ and an ellipsoid $\overline{E}_i$. The distance from the center of the unit sphere $\overline{E}_j$, whose coordinates are $\overline{\mathbf{q}}_{ji}$, to the closest point $\overline{\mathbf{q}}_{ib}$ on the ellipsoid $\overline{E}_i$ (which is transformed from the ellipsoid i) is

$$d_{ji} = \left\|\mathbf{Q}_{ji}\mathbf{q}_{ji}\right\| - 1. \tag{A.9}$$

Therefore, two ellipsoids i and j are separated if either $d_{ij} > 0$ or $d_{ji} > 0$. Moreover, $d_{ij} > 0$ implies $d_{ji} > 0$ and vice versa. Hence it is sufficient that the two ellipsoids are separated if the condition (8) holds. The reason why we use the distance Δ_{ij} in (1) instead of $\Delta_{ij} = d_{ij}$ or $\Delta_{ij} = d_{ji}$ is to create a symmetrical Δ_{ij}, see Remark 2. This is crucial for the success of our flocking design.

3. Solution of (7). We first show that (7) has a unique root on the domain of interest. Let us define κ_{ij}^L be the largest root of the equation $\det(\mathbf{I}_{3\times3} + \kappa_{ij}\mathbf{T}_j) = 0$. This is a cubic equation and can be solved for its roots explicitly. We now observe that for any $\overline{\mathbf{q}}_{ij}$ such that $\|\overline{\mathbf{q}}_{ij}\| > 0$, the following inequalities and limits hold

$$\frac{\partial F\left(\kappa_{ij}\right)}{\partial \kappa_{ij}} < 0, \quad \frac{\partial^2 F\left(\kappa_{ij}\right)}{\partial \kappa_{ij}^2} > 0, \quad \forall \kappa_{ij} \in \left(\kappa_{ij}^L, \infty\right),$$
$$\lim_{\kappa_{ij}\to\kappa_{ij}^L} F_{ij}\left(\kappa_{ij}\right) = \infty, \quad \lim_{\kappa_{ij}\to\infty} F_{ij}\left(\kappa_{ij}\right) = -1, \tag{A.10}$$

because the matrix $\mathbf{T}_j$ is symmetric and positive definite with its elements given in (5). Properties of $F_{ij}(\kappa_{ij})$ in (A.10) imply that the function $F_{ij}(\kappa_{ij})$ is strictly decreasing from ∞ to -1 on the domain $\kappa_{ij} \in (\kappa_{ij}^L, \infty)$. Therefore, (7) has a unique root on the domain of interest. Moreover, this root is also the largest root of (7).

Given an initial value $\kappa_{ij}(0) = \kappa_{ij}^L + \epsilon$, where ϵ is a positive constant such that $F_{ij}(\kappa_{ij}^L + \epsilon) > 0$, a numerical procedure using the Newton method to calculate the largest root κ_{ij} is given as follows [40]:

$$\kappa_{ij}(n+1) = \kappa_{ij}(n) - \frac{F_{ij}(\kappa_{ij}(n))}{F'_{ij}(\kappa_{ij}(n))}, \qquad (A.11)$$

where $F'_{ij}(\kappa_{ij}(n)) = \partial F_{ij}(\kappa_{ij})/\partial \kappa_{ij}|_{\kappa_{ij}=\kappa_{ij}(n)}$ and $F_{ij}(\kappa_{ij}(n)) = F_{ij}(\kappa_{ij})|_{\kappa_{ij}=\kappa_{ij}(n)}$ with $F_{ij}(\kappa_{ij})$ given in (7). The algorithm (A.11) provides a quadratic convergence of $\kappa_{ij}(n)$ to the largest root κ_{ij} of (7), since $\partial F(\kappa_{ij})/\partial \kappa_{ij}$ is nonzero and $\partial^2 F(\kappa_{ij})/\partial \kappa_{ij}^2$ is bounded in the domain of interest, see Theorem 1.1 in [40] for a proof. Indeed, after the largest root κ_{ij} is found, $\bar{\mathbf{q}}_{jb}$ is obtained from (A.6). Proof of Lemma 1 is completed.

B. Proof of Lemma 9

We first show that there exists a positive constant k_{ij} such that the condition (22) holds. To do so, we partition the interval $(\Delta_{ijd}, \Delta_{ijR}^M)$ into two intervals $(\Delta_{ijd}, \Delta_{ij}^*]$ and $(\Delta_{ij}^*, \Delta_{ijR}^M)$ with Δ_{ij}^* being such that

$$\left((\Delta_{ij} - \Delta_{ijd}) - \frac{(\Delta_{ij} - \Delta_{ijd})^2}{\Delta_{ij}} \right) \Bigg|_{\forall \Delta_{ij} \in (\Delta_{ijd}, \Delta_{ij}^*]} > 0. \qquad (B.1)$$

It is trivial to show that there exists $\Delta_{ij}^* \in (\Delta_{ijd}, \Delta_{ijR}^M)$ such that (B.1) holds.

For all $\Delta_{ij} \in (\Delta_{ijd}, \Delta_{ij}^*]$, we rewrite (23) as

$$\varphi'_{ij} = 2\frac{1-h(\bullet)}{\Delta_{ij}^2}\left(\Delta_{ij} - \Delta_{ijd} - \frac{(\Delta_{ij} - \Delta_{ijd})^2}{\Delta_{ij}} \right)$$
$$+ h'(\bullet)\left(k_{ij} - \frac{(\Delta_{ij} - \Delta_{ijd})^2}{\Delta_{ij}^2} \right). \qquad (B.2)$$

Since $(1-h(\bullet))/\Delta_{ij}^2 > 0$ and $h'(\bullet) > 0$ for all $\Delta_{ij} \in (\Delta_{ijd}, \Delta_{ij}^*]$, we choose the constant k_{ij} such that

$$k_{ij} \geq \sup\left(\frac{(\Delta_{ij} - \Delta_{ijd})^2}{\Delta_{ij}^2} \right), \quad \forall \Delta_{ij} \in (\Delta_{ijd}, \Delta_{ij}^*]. \qquad (B.3)$$

The above choice of k_{ij} makes the condition (22) hold for all $\Delta_{ij} \in (\Delta_{ijd}, \Delta_{ij}^*]$.

For all $\Delta_{ij} \in (\Delta_{ij}^*, \Delta_{ijR}^M)$, we rewrite (23) as

$$\varphi'_{ij} = 2(\Delta_{ij} - \Delta_{ijd})\frac{1-h(\bullet)}{\Delta_{ij}^2}$$
$$+ h'(\bullet)\left(k_{ij} - \frac{(\Delta_{ij} - \Delta_{ijd})^2}{\Delta_{ij}^2}\left(1 + \frac{2(1-h(\bullet))}{h'(\bullet)} \right) \right). \qquad (B.4)$$

Since $(\Delta_{ij} - \Delta_{ijd})((1-h(\bullet))/\Delta_{ij}^2) > 0$ and $h'(\bullet) > 0$ for all $\Delta_{ij} \in (\Delta_{ij}^*, \Delta_{ijR}^M)$, we can choose the constant k_{ij} such that

$$k_{ij} \geq \sup\left(\frac{(\Delta_{ij} - \Delta_{ijd})^2}{\Delta_{ij}^2}\left(1 + \frac{2(1-h(\bullet))}{h'(\bullet)} \right) \right), \qquad (B.5)$$
$$\forall \Delta_{ij} \in \Delta_{ij} \in (\Delta_{ij}^*, \Delta_{ijR}^M).$$

The above choice of k_{ij} makes condition (22) hold for all $\Delta_{ij} \in (\Delta_{ij}^*, \Delta_{ijR}^M)$. Since a_{ij} and b_{ij} satisfy condition (21), and $\Delta_{ij}^* \in (\Delta_{ijd}, \Delta_{ijR}^M)$, we have $(1-h(\bullet))/(h'(\bullet))$ is bounded by some constant for all $\Delta_{ij} \in (\Delta_{ij}^*, \Delta_{ijR}^M)$. This implies that the value of k_{ij} satisfying (B.5) is finite.

Therefore, the positive constant k_{ij} that satisfies both conditions (B.3) and (B.5) makes condition (22) holds for all $\Delta_{ij} \in (\Delta_{ijd}, \Delta_{ijR}^M)$.

To prove Lemma 9, we show that the pairwise function φ_{ij} defined in (20) satisfies all properties listed in (17). Proof of Properties (1)–(4) is trivial using properties of the smooth function $h_{ij}(\Delta_{ij}, a_{ij}, b_{ij})$ listed in (9). We focus on proving Property (5).

Since the function φ_{ij} is smooth, Property (5) holds if

$$\varphi'_{ij} < 0, \quad \forall \Delta_{ij} \in (0, \Delta_{ijd}), \quad \varphi'_{ij} = 0, \quad \text{if } \Delta_{ij} = \Delta_{ijd},$$
$$\varphi'_{ij} > 0, \quad \forall \Delta_{ij} \in (\Delta_{ijd}, \Delta_{ijR}^M), \quad \varphi'_{ij} = 0, \quad \forall \Delta_{ij} \in [\Delta_{ijR}^M, \infty). \qquad (B.6)$$

The above conditions mean that the smooth function φ_{ij} is decreasing for all $\Delta_{ij} \in (0, \Delta_{ijd})$, is increasing for all $\Delta_{ij} \in (\Delta_{ijd}, \Delta_{ijR}^M)$, and is constant for all $\Delta_{ij} \in [\Delta_{ijR}^M, \infty)$.

For all $\Delta_{ij} \in (0, \Delta_{ijd})$, we have from (23) that

$$\varphi'_{ij} = \frac{2\Delta_{ijd}}{\Delta_{ij}^3}(\Delta_{ij} - \Delta_{ijd}), \qquad (B.7)$$

where we have used $h(\bullet) = 0$ and $h'(\bullet) = 0$ for all $\Delta_{ij} \in (0, \Delta_{ijd})$ because a_{ij} and b_{ij} satisfy condition (21). Therefore $\varphi'_{ij} < 0$, for all $\Delta_{ij} \in (0, \Delta_{ijd})$. For $\Delta_{ij} = \Delta_{ijd}$, clearly $\varphi'_{ij} = 0$ since $a_{ij} = \Delta_{ijd}$, see (21). For all $\Delta_{ij} \in (\Delta_{ijd}, \Delta_{ijR}^M)$, we have already proved that $\varphi'_{ij} > 0$. For all $\Delta_{ij} \in [\Delta_{ijR}^M, \infty)$, we have $h(\Delta_{ij}, a_{ij}, b_{ij}) = 1$ because a_{ij} and b_{ij} satisfy condition (21). Hence, from (20) we have $\varphi_{ij} = k_{ij}$, which implies that $\varphi'_{ij} = 0$ for all $\Delta_{ij} \in [\Delta_{ijR}^M, \infty)$. Proof of Lemma 9 is completed.

C. Proof of Theorem 12

1. Proof of No Collisions and Complete Forwardness of the Closed Loop System. It is seen from (44) that $\dot{V} \leq 0$. Integrating $\dot{V} \leq 0$ from t_0 to t and using the definition of V in (36) with φ in (24) and φ_{ij} in (20) result in $V(t) \leq V(t_0)$, where $V(t) = \sum_{i=1}^{N-1}\sum_{j=i+1}^{N}\varphi_{ij}(t) + (1/2)\sum_{i=1}^{N}(c_1\|\mathbf{P}_i(\mathbf{q}_i - \mathbf{q}_{od})\|^2 + c_2\|\boldsymbol{\eta}_i - \boldsymbol{\eta}_{id}\|^2)$, and $V(t_0)$ is $V(t)$ with t replaced by t_0, for all $t \geq t_0 \geq 0$. From the condition specified in item

(4) of Assumption 1, and Property (3) of φ_{ij}, we have $V(t_0)$ is bounded by a positive constant depending on the initial conditions. Boundedness of $V(t_0)$ implies that $V(t)$ must be also bounded. As a result, $\varphi_{ij}(\Delta_{ij}(t))$ must be smaller than some positive constant depending on the initial conditions for all $t \geq t_0 \geq 0$. From properties of φ_{ij}, see (17), $\Delta_{ij}(t)$, for all $(i, j) \in \mathbb{N}$ and $i \neq j$, must be larger than 0 for all $t \geq t_0 \geq 0$. This in turn implies from Lemma 1 that there are no collisions between any agents for all $t \geq t_0 \geq 0$. Boundedness of $V(t)$ also implies that of $\mathbf{P}_i(t)(\mathbf{q}_i(t) - \mathbf{q}_{od}(t))$ and $\boldsymbol{\eta}_i(t) - \boldsymbol{\eta}_{id}(t)$ for all $t \geq t_0 \geq 0$. Since we have already proved that $\Delta_{ij}(t) > 0$, the update law $\dot{\boldsymbol{\eta}}_{id}$ in (42) implies that $\boldsymbol{\eta}_{id}(t) - \boldsymbol{\eta}_{od}(t)$ is also bounded. Therefore, the closed-loop system (46) is forward complete. Moreover, from $V(t) \leq V(t_0)$ we have $\|\mathbf{q}_i(t) - \mathbf{q}_{od}(t)\| \leq (2\lambda_{\max}(\mathbf{A}_i)/\min(c_1, c_2))V(t_0) := A_0$ where $\lambda_{\max}(\mathbf{A}_i)$ denotes the maximum eigenvalue of $\mathbf{A}_i$. Hence we have proved the first two results listed in Theorem 12.

2. Mismatched Velocity Analysis. We first use Lemma 5 to find the equilibrium set, which the trajectories of the closed loop system (46) converge to. Integrating both sides of (44) yields $\int_0^\infty \sum_{i=1}^N \vartheta_i(t)dt = \varphi(t_0) - \varphi(\infty) \leq \varphi(t_0)$, where ϑ_i is given in (45). Indeed, the function $\sum_{i=1}^N \vartheta_i(t)$ is scalar, nonnegative, and differentiable. Now differentiating $\sum_{i=1}^N \vartheta_i(t)$ along the solutions of the closed loop system (46) and using the properties of the function φ_{ij} given in (17) and the function $w(\cdot)$ in (40) readily show that $|d\sum_{i=1}^N \vartheta_i(t)/dt| \leq M\sum_{i=1}^N \vartheta_i(t)$ with M being a positive constant. Therefore, Lemma 5 results in $\lim_{t \to \infty} \sum_{i=1}^N \vartheta_i(t) = 0$, which implies that $\lim_{t \to \infty} \vartheta_i(t) = 0$. Hence, from the expression of $\vartheta_i(t)$ in (45) we have $\lim_{t \to \infty}(\boldsymbol{\Omega}_i(t), \boldsymbol{\Xi}_i(t)) = 0$. Hence the position and orientation trajectory $(\mathbf{q}_i, \boldsymbol{\eta}_i)$ of the agent i 'almost globally' converges to an (moving with $(\mathbf{q}_{od}, \boldsymbol{\eta}_{od})$ equilibrium set, $\mathbf{Y_c}$, asymptotically. In the equilibrium set $\mathbf{Y_c}$, we have $\boldsymbol{\Omega}_i(t) = 0$ and $\boldsymbol{\Xi}_i(t) = 0$ for all $i \in \mathbb{N}$. The term "almost globally" refers to the fact that the agents start from a set, in which the condition (16) holds. Now substituting the limit $\lim_{t \to \infty}(\boldsymbol{\Omega}_i(t), \boldsymbol{\Xi}_i(t)) = 0$ into the time limit both sides of the closed-loop system (46) to ∞ gives (47). Moreover, it is seen from the update law (42) that when the transformed distance Δ_{ij} is larger than b_{ijd} (noting that $\Delta_{ijd} < b_{ijd}$, see (43) and (21)), we have $\lim_{t \to \infty}(\boldsymbol{\eta}_{id}(t) - \boldsymbol{\eta}_{od}(t)) = 0$ and $\lim_{t \to \infty}(\dot{\boldsymbol{\eta}}_{id}(t) - \dot{\boldsymbol{\eta}}_{od}(t)) = 0$.

3. Flock Size. Let $(\mathbf{q}_{ic}, \boldsymbol{\eta}_{ic})$, for all $i \in \mathbb{N}$, be the equilibrium state of the agent i, that is, $(\mathbf{q}_{ic}, \boldsymbol{\eta}_{ic}) \in \mathbf{Y_c}$ where $\mathbf{Y_c}$ is the equilibrium set as defined above. In the set $\mathbf{Y_c}$, we have $\boldsymbol{\Omega}_i(t) = 0$ and $\boldsymbol{\Xi}_i(t) = 0$ for all $i \in \mathbb{N}$. Hence, from the expression of $\boldsymbol{\Omega}_i$ and $\boldsymbol{\Xi}_i$ in (38), we have

$$\sum_{j \neq i} \varphi_{ijc}' \boldsymbol{\Gamma}_{ijc} + c_1 \left(\mathbf{P}_{ic}\left(\mathbf{q}_{ic} - \mathbf{q}_{od}\right)\right)^T \mathbf{P}_{ic} = 0,$$

$$\sum_{j \neq i} \varphi_{ijc}' \boldsymbol{\Lambda}_{ijc} + c_2 \left(\boldsymbol{\eta}_{ic} - \boldsymbol{\eta}_{id}\right)^T = 0,$$

(C.1)

where $\boldsymbol{\Gamma}_{ijc}$, $\boldsymbol{\Lambda}_{ijc}$, and $\mathbf{P}_{ic}$ are $\boldsymbol{\Gamma}_{ij}$, $\boldsymbol{\Lambda}_{ij}$, and $\mathbf{P}_i$ with $(\mathbf{q}_i, \boldsymbol{\eta}_i)$ replaced by $(\mathbf{q}_{ic}, \boldsymbol{\eta}_{ic})$ for all $i \in \mathbb{N}$. From (C.1), we have

$$\mathbf{q}_{ijc} = \frac{\left(\mathbf{P}_{ic}^T \mathbf{P}_{ic}\right)^{-1}}{c_1} \sum_{l \neq i} \varphi_{ilc}' \boldsymbol{\Gamma}_{ilc}^T - \frac{\left(\mathbf{P}_{jc}^T \mathbf{P}_{jc}\right)^{-1}}{c_1} \sum_{k \neq j} \varphi_{jkc}' \boldsymbol{\Gamma}_{jkc}^T,$$

$$\boldsymbol{\eta}_{ijc} = \boldsymbol{\eta}_{ijd} + \frac{1}{c_2} \sum_{l \neq i} \varphi_{ilc}' \boldsymbol{\Lambda}_{ilc} - \frac{1}{c_2} \sum_{k \neq i} \varphi_{jkc}' \boldsymbol{\Lambda}_{jkc},$$

(C.2)

where $\mathbf{q}_{ijc} = \mathbf{q}_{ic} - \mathbf{q}_{jc}$ for all $(i, j) \in \mathbb{N}$, $j \neq i$.

We make the following observations. All the terms $\boldsymbol{\Gamma}_{ijc}$ and $\boldsymbol{\Lambda}_{ijc}$ are vector functions of $\mathbf{q}_{ijc}$, and bounded functions (sin and cos) of elements of $\boldsymbol{\eta}_{ic}$, $\boldsymbol{\eta}_{ic}$, and $\boldsymbol{\eta}_{jc}$ only for all $(i, j) \in \mathbb{N}$, $j \neq j$, see (28) and (34) for the expression of $\boldsymbol{\Gamma}_{ij}$ and $\boldsymbol{\Lambda}_{ij}$ with a note that $(\mathbf{q}_i, \boldsymbol{\eta}_i$ are replaced by $(\mathbf{q}_{ic}, \boldsymbol{\eta}_{ic}$ for all $i \in \mathbb{N}$. Moreover, from (42), we can see that $\lim_{t \to \infty} \boldsymbol{\eta}_{ijd}(t)$ tends to a value depending on $\boldsymbol{\Gamma}_{ijc}$ and $\boldsymbol{\Lambda}_{ijc}$ only.

The above observations imply from (C.2) that $\mathbf{q}_{ijc}$ and $\boldsymbol{\eta}_{ijc}$ must be bounded and depend on bounded functions (sin and cos) of elements of $\boldsymbol{\eta}_{ic}$ only with $i = 1, \ldots, N$. On the other hand, the flock size $F_L = \sum_{j=i+1}^N \sum_{j=1}^{i-1} \Delta_{ij}$ is a function which depends on $\mathbf{q}_{ij}$, and bounded functions (sin and cos) of elements of $\boldsymbol{\eta}_{ijc}$, $\boldsymbol{\eta}_{ic}$, and $\boldsymbol{\eta}_{jc}$ only for all $(i, j) \in \mathbb{N}$, $j \neq j$. Therefore in the equilibrium set $\mathbf{Y_c}$, the flock size, F_{Lc} being F_L with $(\mathbf{q}_i, \boldsymbol{\eta}_i)$ replaced by $(\mathbf{q}_{ic}, \boldsymbol{\eta}_{ic})$, is a function that depends bounded functions (sin and cos) of elements of $\boldsymbol{\eta}_{ic}$ only with $i = 1, \ldots, N$. Moreover, the flock size is bounded whenever its arguments $\mathbf{q}_{ij}$ and bounded functions (sin and cos) of elements of $\boldsymbol{\eta}_{ijc}$, $\boldsymbol{\eta}_{ic}$, and $\boldsymbol{\eta}_{jc}$ are bounded.

Hence, in the equilibrium set $\mathbf{Y_c}$, the flock size is bounded by a function of bounded functions (sin and cos) of elements of $\boldsymbol{\eta}_{ijc}$, $\boldsymbol{\eta}_{ic}$, and $\boldsymbol{\eta}_{jc}$. Since functions sin and cos are bounded by -1 and 1, there exist a positive constant c_0 such that $F_c \leq c_0$. This completes proof of Theorem 12.

References

[1] A. Okubo, "Dynamical aspects of animal grouping: swarms, schools, flocks, and herds," *Advances in Biophysics*, vol. 22, no. C, pp. 1–94, 1986.

[2] C. W. Reynolds, "Flocks, herds, and schools: a distributed behavioral model," *Computer Graphics (ACM)*, vol. 21, no. 4, pp. 25–34, 1987.

[3] J. Toner and Y. Tu, "Flocks, herds, and schools: a quantitative theory of flocking," *Physical Review E*, vol. 58, no. 4, pp. 4828–4858, 1998.

[4] H. Sridhar, G. Beauchamp, and K. Shanker, "Why do birds participate in mixed-species foraging flocks? A large-scale synthesis," *Animal Behaviour*, vol. 78, no. 2, pp. 337–347, 2009.

[5] I. F. Akyildiz, W. Su, Y. Sankarasubramaniam, and E. Cayirci, "A survey on sensor networks," *IEEE Communications Magazine*, vol. 40, no. 8, pp. 102–105, 2002.

[6] D. M. Stipanović, G. Inalhan, R. Teo, and C. J. Tomlin, "Decentralized overlapping control of a formation of unmanned aerial vehicles," *Automatica*, vol. 40, no. 8, pp. 1285–1296, 2004.

[7] K. D. Do, "Bounded controllers for formation stabilization of mobile agents with limited sensing ranges," *IEEE Transactions on Automatic Control*, vol. 52, no. 3, pp. 569–576, 2007.

[8] D. V. Dimarogonas, S. G. Loizou, K. J. Kyriakopoulos, and M. M. Zavlanos, "A feedback stabilization and collision avoidance scheme for multiple independent non-point agents," *Automatica*, vol. 42, no. 2, pp. 229–243, 2006.

[9] K. D. Do, "Formation tracking control of unicycle-type mobile robots with limited sensing ranges," *IEEE Transactions on Control Systems Technology*, vol. 16, no. 3, pp. 527–538, 2008.

[10] P. Ögren, E. Fiorelli, and N. E. Leonard, "Cooperative control of mobile sensor networks: adaptive gradient climbing in a distributed environment," *IEEE Transactions on Automatic Control*, vol. 49, no. 8, pp. 1292–1302, 2004.

[11] H. G. Tanner and A. Kumar, "Towards decentralization of multi-robot navigation functions," in *Proceedings of the IEEE International Conference on Robotics and Automation*, pp. 4132–4137, Barcelona, Spain, April 2005.

[12] S. S. Ge and Y. J. Cui, "New potential functions for mobile robot path planning," *IEEE Transactions on Robotics and Automation*, vol. 16, no. 5, pp. 615–620, 2000.

[13] R. Olfati-Saber, "Flocking for multi-agent dynamic systems: algorithms and theory," *IEEE Transactions on Automatic Control*, vol. 51, no. 3, pp. 401–420, 2006.

[14] K. D. Do, "Output-feedback formation tracking control of unicycle-type mobile robots with limited sensing ranges," *Robotics and Autonomous Systems*, vol. 57, no. 1, pp. 34–47, 2009.

[15] W. Ren and R. W. Beard, "Consensus seeking in multiagent systems under dynamically changing interaction topologies," *IEEE Transactions on Automatic Control*, vol. 50, no. 5, pp. 655–661, 2005.

[16] R. Olfati-Saber and R. M. Murray, "Consensus problems in networks of agents with switching topology and time-delays," *IEEE Transactions on Automatic Control*, vol. 49, no. 9, pp. 1520–1533, 2004.

[17] Y. Hong, L. Gao, D. Cheng, and J. Hu, "Lyapunov-based approach to multiagent systems with switching jointly connected interconnection," *IEEE Transactions on Automatic Control*, vol. 52, no. 5, pp. 943–948, 2007.

[18] V. Gazi and K. M. Passino, "A class of attractions/repulsion functions for stable swarm aggregations," *International Journal of Control*, vol. 77, no. 18, pp. 1567–1579, 2004.

[19] D. E. Koditschek and E. Rimon, "Robot navigation functions on manifolds with boundary," *Advances in Applied Mathematics*, vol. 11, no. 4, pp. 412–442, 1990.

[20] V. Gazi and K. M. Passino, "Stability analysis of social foraging swarms," *IEEE Transactions on Systems, Man, and Cybernetics B*, vol. 34, no. 1, pp. 539–557, 2004.

[21] H. Su, X. Wang, and Z. Lin, "Flocking of multi-agents with a virtual leader," *IEEE Transactions on Automatic Control*, vol. 54, no. 2, pp. 293–307, 2009.

[22] F. Cucker and S. Smale, "Emergent behavior in flocks," *IEEE Transactions on Automatic Control*, vol. 52, no. 5, pp. 852–862, 2007.

[23] F. Cucker and J. G. Dong, "Avoiding collisions in flocks," *IEEE Transactions on Automatic Control*, vol. 55, no. 5, pp. 1238–1243, 2010.

[24] A. K. Das, R. Fierro, V. Kumar, J. P. Ostrowski, J. Spletzer, and C. J. Taylor, "A vision-based formation control framework," *IEEE Transactions on Robotics and Automation*, vol. 18, no. 5, pp. 813–825, 2002.

[25] D. Gu and Z. Wang, "Leader-follower flocking: algorithms and experiments," *IEEE Transactions on Control Systems Technology*, vol. 17, no. 5, pp. 1211–1219, 2009.

[26] J. Cortés, S. Martínez, T. Karataş, and F. Bullo, "Coverage control for mobile sensing networks," *IEEE Transactions on Robotics and Automation*, vol. 20, no. 2, pp. 243–255, 2004.

[27] I. Suzuki and M. Yamashita, "Distributed anonymous mobile robots: formation of geometric patterns," *SIAM Journal on Computing*, vol. 28, no. 4, pp. 1347–1363, 1999.

[28] A. Jadbabaie, J. Lin, and A. S. Morse, "Coordination of groups of mobile autonomous agents using nearest neighbor rules," *IEEE Transactions on Automatic Control*, vol. 48, no. 6, pp. 988–1001, 2003.

[29] J. Cortés, S. Martínez, and F. Bullo, "Spatially-distributed coverage optimization and control with limited-range interactions," *ESAIM Control, Optimisation and Calculus of Variations*, no. 11, pp. 691–719, 2005.

[30] K. D. Do, "Coordination control of multiple ellipsoidal agents with collision avoidance and limited sensing ranges," *Systems and Control Letters*, vol. 61, no. 1, pp. 247–257, 2012.

[31] X. Zheng, W. Iglesias, and P. Palffy-Muhoray, "Distance of closest approach of two arbitrary hard ellipsoids," *Physical Review E*, vol. 79, no. 5, Article ID 057702, 2009.

[32] W. Wang, Y. K. Choi, B. Chan, M. S. Kim, and J. Wang, "Efficient collision detection for moving ellipsoids using separating planes," *Computing*, vol. 72, no. 1-2, pp. 235–246, 2004.

[33] X. Zheng and P. Palffy-Muhoray, "Distance of closest approach of two arbitrary hard ellipses in two dimensions," *Physical Review E*, vol. 75, no. 6, Article ID 061709, 2007.

[34] Y. K. Choi, J. W. Chang, W. Wang, M. S. Kim, and G. Elber, "Continuous collision detection for ellipsoids," *IEEE Transactions on Visualization and Computer Graphics*, vol. 15, no. 2, pp. 311–324, 2009.

[35] K. D. Do, "Flocking for multiple elliptical agents with limited communication ranges," *IEEE Transactions on Robotics*, vol. 27, no. 5, pp. 931–942, 2011.

[36] H. Khalil, *Nonlinear Systems*, Prentice Hall, 2002.

[37] M. Krstic, I. Kanellakopoulos, and P. Kokotovic, *Nonlinear and Adaptive Control Design*, John Wiley & Sons, New York, NY, USA, 1995.

[38] D. Liberzon, *Switching in Systems and Control*, Birkauser, 2003.

[39] K. D. Do and J. Pan, *Control of Ships and Underwater Vehicles: Design for Underactuated and Nonlinear Marine Systems*, Springer, 2009.

[40] C. T. Kelley, *Solving Nonlinear Equations with Newton's Method*, SIAM, 2003.

8

Application of Online Iterative Learning Tracking Control for Quadrotor UAVs

Pong-in Pipatpaibul and P. R. Ouyang

Department of Aerospace Engineering, Ryerson University, Toronto, ON, Canada

Correspondence should be addressed to P. R. Ouyang; pouyang@ryerson.ca

Academic Editors: Z. Bi, J.-S. Liu, R. Safaric, and Y. Zhou

Quadrotor unmanned aerial vehicles (UAVs) have attracted considerable interest for various applications including search and rescue, environmental monitoring, and surveillance because of their agilities and small sizes. This paper proposes trajectory tracking control of UAVs utilizing online iterative learning control (ILC) methods that are known to be powerful for tasks performed repeatedly. PD online ILC and switching gain PD online ILC are used to perform a variety of manoeuvring such as take-off, smooth translation, and various circular trajectory motions in two and three dimensions. Simulation results prove the ability and effectiveness of the online ILCs to perform successfully certain missions in the presence of disturbances and uncertainties. It also demonstrates that the switching gain PD ILC is much effective than the PD online ILC in terms of fast convergence rates and smaller tracking errors.

1. Introduction

Unmanned aerial vehicles (UAVs) have become very popular among researchers and developers in the last decade, owing to their capabilities of various applications such as meteorological surveillance, disaster monitoring, and military purposes. Depending on their applications, UAVs vary in sizes, shapes, and operating ranges. UAVs are complicated for control considering the nonlinearity of the system, no supervision of pilots, and external disturbances that need sophisticated control system to deal with.

A quadrotor UAV is a special UAV that has four rotors with a symmetric shape to generate thrust. A quadrotor UAV can vertically take-off, hover, swiftly manoeuvre in any direction and carry a large payload comparing to its own weight . In addition, a quadrotor UAV is normally small compared with other types of UAVs, which makes it simple and cheap, and accessible indoors or in urban constrained areas.

In order to achieve autonomous control, many studies and experiments have been performed for UAVs. However, due to their nonlinearity, multi-input and coupling characteristics, traditional control methods such as PID control may perform poorly under uncertainty and wind disturbances for UAVs, as shown in [1–3]. As an optimization technique with feedback control, Linear Quadratic Regulator (LQR) and its variation of State Dependent Riccati Equation (SDRE) control were proved to perform well for UAVs without disturbances [4, 5]. Comparisons and implementation of Sliding Mode Control (SMC) and Backstepping control were presented in [6–8]. The SMC methods were found to be robust against uncertainties, but they are still relatively complicated and it might cause chattering problems. An H-infinity control [9] was proposed to deal with the problem of stabilization of a rotorcraft with small external disturbances. An adaptive-fuzzy control was developed in [10] with robustness but limited to stabilization applications only. Neural Network control methods were implemented in [11, 12] that proved to perform well, but intensive computations are required for training NN that may limit their real applications. A testbed for the development and demonstration of control systems and trajectory planning optimization of UAVs was set up and discussed in MIT [13, 14].

On the other hand, iterative learning control (ILC) [16] is based on simple PD/PID control and adopts the idea of human learning process, and it is mainly used in robotic manipulators where their tasks are performed repeatedly. ILC

FIGURE 1: An example of a quadrotor UAV [15].

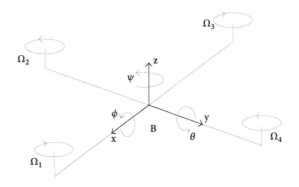

FIGURE 2: Coordinate system of UAV.

can improve tracking performances when a specific task is done again and again, and it is robust against uncertainties and disturbances. ILC was originally proposed by Arimoto [16], where only derivative part (D-type) and information from previous iteration(s) were used to determine the control input for current iteration (offline ILC). Some variations of ILC such as P-type [17], PD-type [18, 19], PI-type [20, 21], and PID-type [22, 23] were studied, but most of them cannot assure monotonic convergence for nonlinear systems. Faster convergence rates can be achieved by using current iteration errors (online ILC) in [24–27] or a combination of both online and offline ILCs in [28–31]. An even faster monotonic convergence rate and less tracking error can be achieved by using switching gain learning control developed in [32, 33]. Performance comparison of various types of ILCs was conducted in [34].

Many control methods have been developed to deal with the control problems of UAVs. The majority of those controllers focused heavily on the stabilization problem which is the first step toward successfully autonomous flights. Some of them also handled position maintaining or velocity holding in order to fulfill certain manoeuvrings and thus full autonomous control. Some researches focused on the trajectory tracking control of UAVs through developing different control methods [35–37]. Based on gain-scheduling control theory, the nonlinear problem of UAV dynamics was represented as piece-wise error dynamics over a predefined set of operating regions in [35], and the design and performance evaluation of a trajectory tracking controller were discussed. LQR control was applied as a trajectory follower to minimize errors between the real trajectory and the reference trajectory in [36]. A switching control method was introduced for trajectory tracking of fixed-wing UAVs in [37].

To the best of our knowledge, there is rare application of ILC on the control of UAVs. The contribution of this work to the UAV field consists in the exploration of different online ILCs on trajectory tracking control of quadrotor UAVs for the first time, focusing on performance improvements under conditions of uncertainty and disturbances. The capability of online ILCs to reject random disturbances and noise is examined and demonstrated. The research can be viewed as a new application of online ILCs. In this research, two

competitive types of ILCs, namely, PD online ILC and switching gain PD (SPD online ILC), are employed in order to control a quadrotor UAV to follow various desired trajectories in the presence of disturbances and uncertainties. Nonlinear dynamic model of the quadrotor UAV is established where major aerodynamic and gyroscopic effects are included. Simulations are conducted to verify the capability of performing various missions repeatedly with some constraints.

2. Quadrotor UAV: Dynamic Model and Parameters

As named, a quadrotor UAV consists of four rotors producing thrust upward against its own weight and payloads. Usually, payloads are placed at the center of the UAV, and rotors propelled by DC motors with or without gearbox. Figure 1 shows an example of a quadrotor UAV and Figure 2 illustrates the coordinate system and positions of rotors used in this paper. The rotors are divided into two pairs; one pair rotates in the opposite direction of the other pair. Increasing the thrust on one side and decreasing the thrust on the other side of the same pair will result in rotation in the pitch or roll direction and the quadrotor will tend to translate toward the direction that it inclines to. Simply increasing thrust equally in one pair and decreasing thrust in the other pair will result in the rotation of the yaw angle while maintaining the position and altitude.

According to the coordinate system shown in Figure 2, a nonlinear translational and rotational dynamic model for the quadrotor UAV can be expressed as [12]

$$\tau = J\dot{\omega} + \omega \left(J\omega + J_r \Omega_r e_3 \right) + d_\tau,$$
$$m\dot{v} = RT - mge_3 - d_T, \tag{1}$$

where τ is a torque vector of the three axes; J is the inertia tensor of a quadrotor; ω is an angular velocity vector; J_r is the moment of inertia of rotor; $\Omega_r = \Omega_1 - \Omega_2 + \Omega_3 - \Omega_4$ is the total rotor speed; $e_3 = \begin{bmatrix} 0 & 0 & 1 \end{bmatrix}^T$ is a unit vector in the inertial frame; R is the rotation matrix; T is a force vector; d_τ and d_T are the disturbance vectors for rotations and translations, respectively.

Table 1: Parameters of a quadrotor UAV.

Parameters	Description	Value
l	Quadrotor arm length	0.232 m
b	Rotor thrust coefficient	3.13×10^{-5} N $\cdot$ s^2
d	Rotor drag coefficient	7.5×10^{-7} m $\cdot$ s^2
m	Total quadrotor mass	0.52 kg
I_x	Moment of inertia about X axis	6.228×10^{-3} kg $\cdot$ m^2
I_y	Moment of inertia about Y axis	6.225×10^{-3} kg $\cdot$ m^2
I_z	Moment of inertia about Z axis	1.121×10^{-2} kg $\cdot$ m^2
J_r	Moment of inertia of the rotors	6×10^{-5} kg $\cdot$ m^2
Ω_{max}	Maximum rotor speed	279 rad/s

The equations of motion, along with control inputs, can be described in each axis based on (1) as [12]

$$\ddot{X} = -\sin\theta\cos\phi\left(\frac{b}{m}\right)u_1 - \frac{d_x}{m}, \tag{2}$$

$$\ddot{Y} = \sin\phi\left(\frac{b}{m}\right)u_1 - \frac{d_y}{m}, \tag{3}$$

$$\ddot{Z} = -g + \cos\theta\cos\phi\left(\frac{b}{m}\right)u_1 - \frac{d_z}{m}, \tag{4}$$

$$\ddot{\phi} = \dot{\theta}\dot{\psi}\frac{I_y - I_z}{I_x} - \dot{\theta}\Omega_r\frac{J_r}{I_x} + \frac{lb}{I_x}u_2 - \frac{d_\phi}{I_x}, \tag{5}$$

$$\ddot{\theta} = \dot{\phi}\dot{\psi}\frac{I_z - I_x}{I_y} + \dot{\phi}\Omega_r\frac{J_r}{I_y} + \frac{lb}{I_y}u_3 - \frac{d_\theta}{I_y}, \tag{6}$$

$$\ddot{\psi} = \dot{\theta}\dot{\phi}\frac{I_x - I_y}{I_z} + \frac{d}{I_z}u_4 - \frac{d_\psi}{I_z}, \tag{7}$$

where l is the span of the quadrotor; b is the thrust coefficient; d is the drag coefficient, which relates to torque in the yaw angle.

The control inputs related to each rotor speed are defined as follows:

$$\mathbf{u} = \begin{Bmatrix} u_1 \\ u_2 \\ u_3 \\ u_4 \end{Bmatrix} = \begin{bmatrix} 1 & 1 & 1 & 1 \\ 0 & -1 & 0 & 1 \\ 1 & 0 & -1 & 0 \\ 1 & -1 & 1 & -1 \end{bmatrix} \begin{Bmatrix} \Omega_1^2 \\ \Omega_2^2 \\ \Omega_3^2 \\ \Omega_4^2 \end{Bmatrix}. \tag{8}$$

Note that (2)–(4) are derived using the rotation matrix of R_{ZXY} instead of R_{ZYX} as used by most robotic applications. Design parameters and some limitations of a quadrotor UAV are referred from a real application in [15] and listed in Table 1.

To design a control system for the quadrotor UAV, it is more convenient to establish a state-space model. First, we define a state variable vector as follows:

$$\mathbf{x} = \begin{bmatrix} X & Y & Z & \phi & \theta & \psi & \dot{X} & \dot{Y} & \dot{Z} & \dot{\phi} & \dot{\theta} \end{bmatrix}^T. \tag{9}$$

Then the state space system for the UAV dynamic model described in (2)–(7) can be expressed as

$$\dot{\mathbf{x}} = \begin{pmatrix} x_7 \\ x_8 \\ x_9 \\ x_{10} \\ x_{11} \\ x_{12} \\ -\sin x_5 \cos x_4 \left(\dfrac{b}{m}\right)u_1 - \dfrac{d_x}{m} \\ \sin x_4 \left(\dfrac{b}{m}\right)u_1 - \dfrac{d_y}{m} \\ -g + \cos x_5 \cos x_4 \left(\dfrac{b}{m}\right)u_1 - \dfrac{d_z}{m} \\ a_1 x_{11}x_{12} - a_2\Omega_r x_{11} - a_{11}u_2 - \dfrac{d_\phi}{I_x} \\ a_3 x_{10}x_{12} + a_4\Omega_r x_{10} - a_{22}u_3 - \dfrac{d_\theta}{I_y} \\ a_5 x_{10}x_{11} + a_{33}u_4 - \dfrac{d_\psi}{I_z} \end{pmatrix}, \tag{10}$$

$$\mathbf{y} = I_{12\times12}\mathbf{x},$$

where

$$a_1 = \frac{I_y - I_z}{I_x}, \quad a_2 = \frac{J_r}{I_x}, \quad a_3 = \frac{I_z - I_x}{I_y}, \quad a_4 = \frac{J_r}{I_y},$$

$$a_5 = \frac{I_x - I_y}{I_z}, \quad a_{11} = \frac{l}{I_x}, \quad a_{22} = \frac{l}{I_y}, \quad a_{33} = \frac{d}{I_z}. \tag{11}$$

In this paper, the disturbances given in (10) have wind disturbance components along the X and Y directions that are modeled by a correlated Gauss-Markov process [9]. In all other directions, some random noises are added to simulate the disturbances and the uncertainties of the dynamics.

3. Different ILCS: Basics and Convergence Conditions

ILC can improve tracking performance of a nonlinear system through iterative operations when a specific task is performed repeatedly. Consider a nonlinear time varying system with the following form:

$$\dot{x}_k(t) = f(x_k(t), t) + B(t)U_k(t) + d_k,$$

$$y_k(t) = C(t)x_k(t), \tag{12}$$

where subscription k denotes the iteration number.

A general form of the control update law for ILCs involving online and offline learning technique can be written

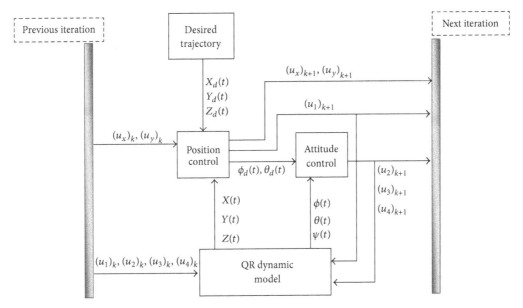

FIGURE 3: Control scheme for PD online ILC and SPD ILC.

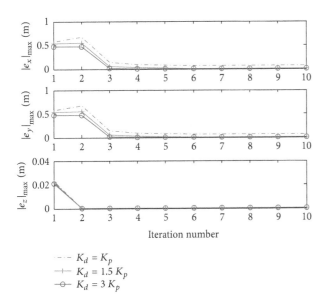

FIGURE 4: Effect of K_d on tracking errors for PD online ILCs.

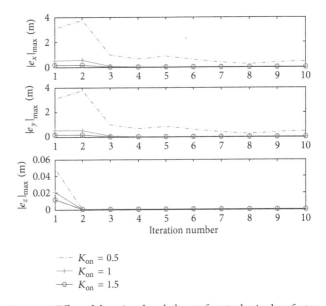

FIGURE 5: Effect of changing the whole set of control gains by a factor of 0.5 and 1.5.

as

$$U_{k+1} = U_k + K_{p\,\text{on}} e_{k+1}(t) + K_{i\,\text{on}} \int_0^t e_{k+1}(t)\,dt$$

$$+ K_{d\,\text{on}} \dot{e}_{k+1}(t) + K_{p\,\text{off}} e_k(t)$$

$$+ K_{i\,\text{off}} \int_0^t e_k(t)\,dt + K_{d\,\text{off}} \dot{e}_k(t), \tag{13}$$

where $e(t) = y_d(t) - y(t)$ and $\dot{e}(t) = \dot{y}_d(t) - \dot{y}(t)$. K_p, K_i, and K_d are PID control gains, and subscriptions on and off represent online (feedback, using errors from the current iteration) and offline (feed-forward, using errors from the previous iteration), respectively. Based on the selection of the control gains, ILCs can be mainly classified as three types, namely, offline, online, and online-offline. In the following sections, the convergence conditions and the convergence rate are discussed.

3.1. Offline ILCs. Traditional ILCs belong to offline learning control, where only the errors from previous iterations have been included in the control law:

$$U_{k+1} = U_k + K_{p\,\text{off}} e_k(t) + K_{i\,\text{off}} \int_0^t e_k(t)\,dt$$

$$+ K_{d\,\text{off}} \dot{e}_k(t). \tag{14}$$

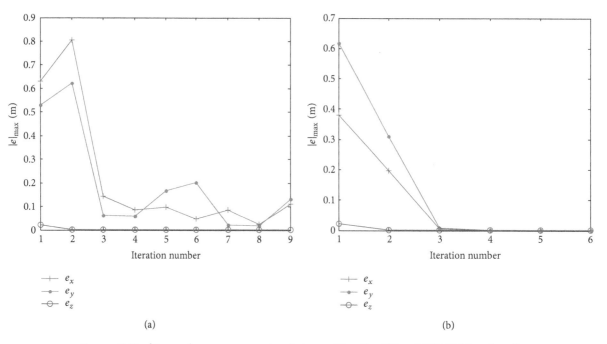

FIGURE 6: Tracking performance comparison between PD online ILC and SPD ILC for take-off.

In the case that only a proportional part is utilized (P-ILCs), the control law can be expressed as

$$U_{k+1} = U_k + K_{p\,\text{off}}e_k(t). \tag{15}$$

For a P-type ILC, the convergence condition for the controlled system (12) is [17]

$$\rho_{p\,\text{off}} = \left\| I - K_{p\,\text{off}}CB \right\| < 1. \tag{16}$$

Whenever a derivative part is involved in an ILC, including D-ILC, PD-ILC, and PID-ILC, the convergence condition is [16, 18, 19]

$$\rho_{d\,\text{off}} = \left\| I - K_{d\,\text{off}}CB \right\| < 1. \tag{17}$$

The two aforementioned convergence conditions imply that offline learning gains are upper bounded, which means that only a certain range of control gains can be chosen. Therefore, offline ILCs have a relatively slow convergence rate.

3.2. Online ILCs. On the other hand, online ILCs only rely on current iteration errors:

$$U_{k+1} = U_k + K_{p\,\text{on}}e_{k+1}(t) + K_{i\,\text{on}}\int_0^t e_{k+1}(t)\,dt \\ + K_{d\,\text{on}}\dot{e}_{k+1}(t) \tag{18}$$

and their convergence conditions are [27–29]

$$\rho_{p\,\text{on}} = \left\| \left(I + K_{p\,\text{on}}CB\right)^{-1} \right\| < 1 \quad (\text{P-type only}),$$
$$\rho_{d\,\text{on}} = \left\| \left(I + K_{d\,\text{on}}CB\right)^{-1} \right\| < 1 \quad (\text{D-type involved}). \tag{19}$$

It is noticed that the learning gains are unbounded for online ILCs from (19), which makes it very flexible to choose control gains. Furthermore, it is demonstrated that the larger the online control gains, the faster the system convergence rate.

In addition to ordinary online ILCs, one might utilize switching gain learning control to increase the convergence rate by increasing online learning gains for each iteration. The convergence conditions then become [32]

$$\rho_{p\,\text{on}} = \left\| \left(I + K_{p\,\text{on}}(0)\,CB\right)^{-1} \right\| < 1 \quad (\text{P-type only}),$$
$$\rho_{d\,\text{on}} = \left\| \left(I + K_{d\,\text{on}}(0)\,CB\right)^{-1} \right\| < 1 \quad (\text{D-type involved}). \tag{20}$$

3.3. Online-Offline ILCs. When online and offline ILCs are combined and used simultaneously, it simply turns into online-offline ILCs. Convergence conditions are then a combination of both types and can be expressed as [31]

$$\begin{aligned} \rho_{p\,\text{off}} &< 1 \\ \rho_{p\,\text{on}} &< 1 \end{aligned} \quad (\text{P-type only}) \quad \text{or}$$
$$\begin{aligned} \rho_{d\,\text{off}} &< 1 \\ \rho_{d\,\text{on}} &< 1 \end{aligned} \quad (\text{D-type involved}). \tag{21}$$

4. Controller Design for Quadrotor UAV

In this paper, the integral part of PID control in (13) will be neglected as ILC itself has the feature of integration, by adding control actions from previous iterations to the current one. Furthermore, offline and online-offline ILCs are not

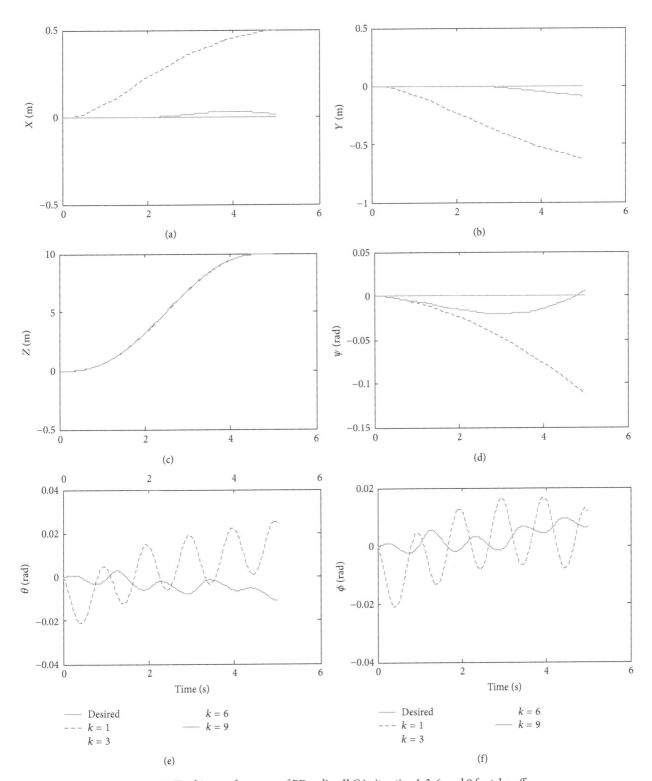

FIGURE 7: Tracking performance of PD online ILC in iteration 1, 3, 6, and 9 for take-off.

considered as many researchers have demonstrated a superior performance of online ILCs over offline ILCs. Figure 3 shows a scheme of a control diagram for online ILCs. Only ordinary PD online ILCs and SPD online ILCs will be tested and compared in this research.

According to (8), there are four control inputs for the UAV system. Based on the state variables defined in (9), the control variables are defined as x_3 to x_6, corresponding to Z axis and three rotation angles; their corresponding derivatives are x_9 to x_{12}. The control inputs of the UAV are calculated using the

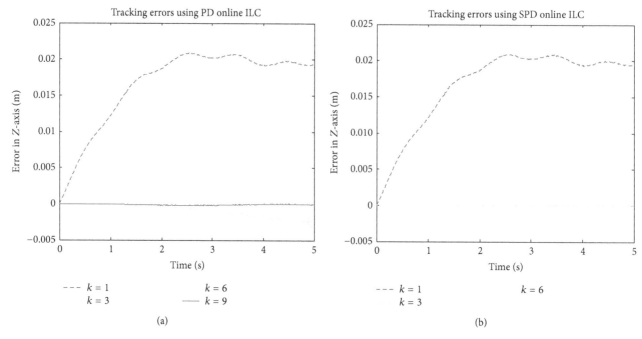

FIGURE 8: Tracking performance improvement comparison for take-off.

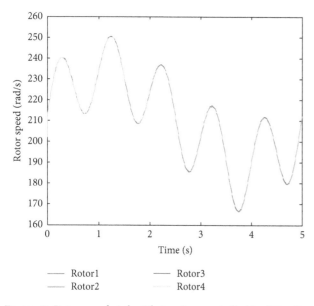

FIGURE 9: Rotor speed at the 9th iteration controlled by PD online ILC for take-off.

following ILC update law:

$$u_{i,k+1} = u_{i,k} + \left(K_{p\,on}\right)_{i+2}\left(x_{i+2,d} - x_{i+2}\right)_{k+1}$$
$$+ \left(K_{d\,on}\right)_{i+2}\left(x_{i+8,d} - x_{i+8}\right)_{k+1}$$
$$\text{for } i = 1, 2, 3, 4,$$

$$(22)$$

where $\left(K_{p\,on}\right)_j$ and $\left(K_{d\,on}\right)_j$ are the corresponding online learning proportional and derivative gains.

If the Z direction needs to be controlled, from (22), we can see that $x_{3,d}$ and $x_{9,d}$ are the only desired states determined by the desired trajectories. In order to find properly desired states as a function of time for the rest of state variables, two dummy control inputs for the X and Y direction motions are defined as

$$u_{x,k+1} = u_{x,k} + \left(K_{p\,on}\right)_1\left(x_{1,d} - x_1\right)_{k+1}$$
$$+ \left(K_{d\,on}\right)_1\left(x_{7,d} - x_7\right)_{k+1},$$
$$u_{y,k+1} = u_{y,k} + \left(K_{p\,on}\right)_2\left(x_{2,d} - x_2\right)_{k+1}$$
$$+ \left(K_{d\,on}\right)_2\left(x_{8,d} - x_8\right)_{k+1},$$

$$(23)$$

where $x_{1,d}$, $x_{2,d}$, $x_{7,d}$, and $x_{8,d}$ are the desired trajectories in the X and Y directions and their derivatives, respectively; $\left(K_{p\,on}\right)_j$ and $\left(K_{d\,on}\right)_j$ are the online learning gains. Based on the defined rotation matrix $\mathbf{R}$, the desired angles can be calculated from

$$\phi_d = x_{4,d} = a\sin\left(u_y\right),$$

$$\dot{\phi}_d = x_{10,d} = \frac{1}{\sqrt{1 - u_y^2}}\dot{u}_y,$$

$$\theta_d = x_{5,d} = -a\sin\left(\frac{u_x}{\cos\left(x_4\right)}\right),$$

$$\dot{\theta}_d = x_{11,d} = -\frac{\dot{u}_x + \tan\left(x_4\right)x_{10}u_x}{\cos\left(x_4\right)\sqrt{1 - \left(u_x/\cos\left(x_4\right)\right)^2}}.$$

$$(24)$$

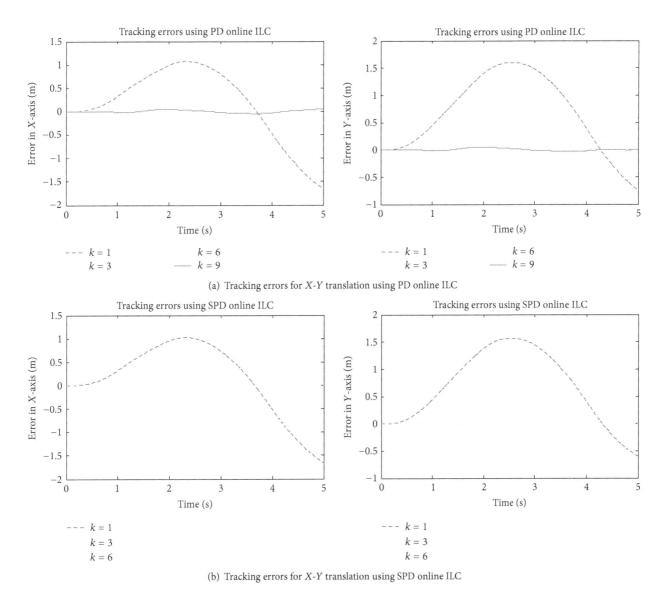

FIGURE 10: Tracking errors from iteration to iteration for X-Y translation ($S = 10$ m, $T = 5$ sec.).

Since a quadrotor UAV is very agile and is able to maneuver in any direction, the yaw angle in this paper is defined as

$$\psi_d = x_{6,d} = \dot{\psi}_d = x_{12,d} = 0. \qquad (25)$$

According to (19), the convergence conditions for online ILCs are only related to matrices $\mathbf{B}$ (input matrix) and $\mathbf{C}$ (output matrix) and are not related to function $f(x,t)$ in (12). This feature provides the robustness of the control law to deal with the mismatch in modeling the system. Also, the choices of control gains in (22)-(23) are flexible because they are unbounded as long as (19) is satisfied. It should be noticed that, in the developed control law (22)-(23), the angular positions and angular speeds should be measured by sensors. A fibre optic gyroscope sensor can be used for this purpose because of its high accuracy, fast response, and low weight.

Note that in the SPD ILC, the online learning gains are defined as functions of iteration number and are chosen as

$$K_{p\,\mathrm{on}}(k) = s(k) * K_{p\,\mathrm{on}}(0)$$

$$K_{d\,\mathrm{on}}(k) = s(k) * K_{d\,\mathrm{on}}(0) \qquad (26)$$

$$s(k) = k, \quad \text{for } k \geq 1.$$

The switching action here occurs in iteration domain rather than in time domain. For traditional switching control, the switching action may cause problems in transient process of the switched system, while this phenomenon does not occur in iteration domain.

5. Simulation Results

In order to obtain a smooth trajectory, that is, continuous in position, velocity, and acceleration, a 5th order polynomial

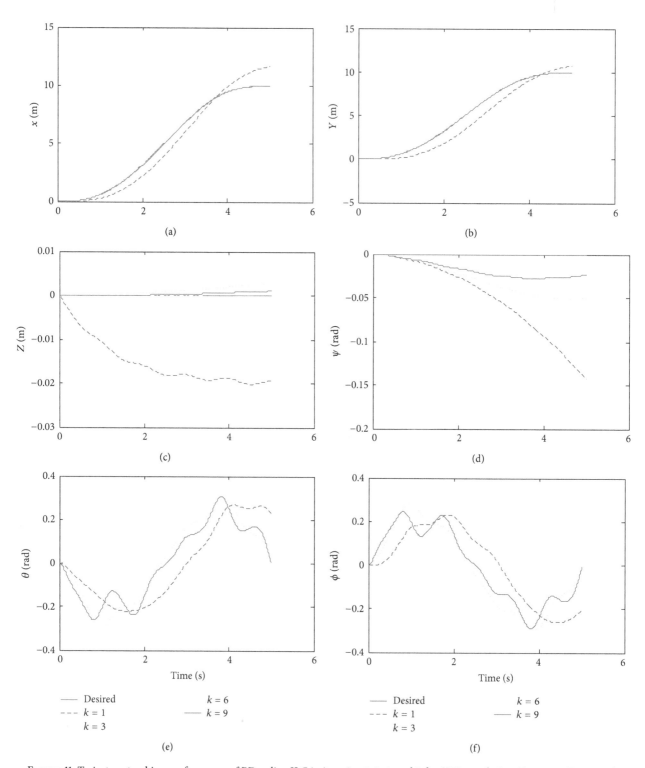

FIGURE 11: Trajectory tracking performance of PD online ILC in iteration 1, 3, 6, and 9 for X-Y translation ($S = 10$ m, $T = 5$ sec.).

function of time is used for each desired trajectory in our simulation studies. With the boundary conditions of $f(0) = 0$, $f(T) = 1$, $f'(0) = f'(T) = f''(0) = f''(T) = 0$, the following polynomial function [38] is used to generate the desired trajectory:

$$f(t) = 10\left(\frac{t}{T}\right)^3 - 15\left(\frac{t}{T}\right)^4 + 6\left(\frac{t}{T}\right)^5, \quad t \in [0,1]. \quad (27)$$

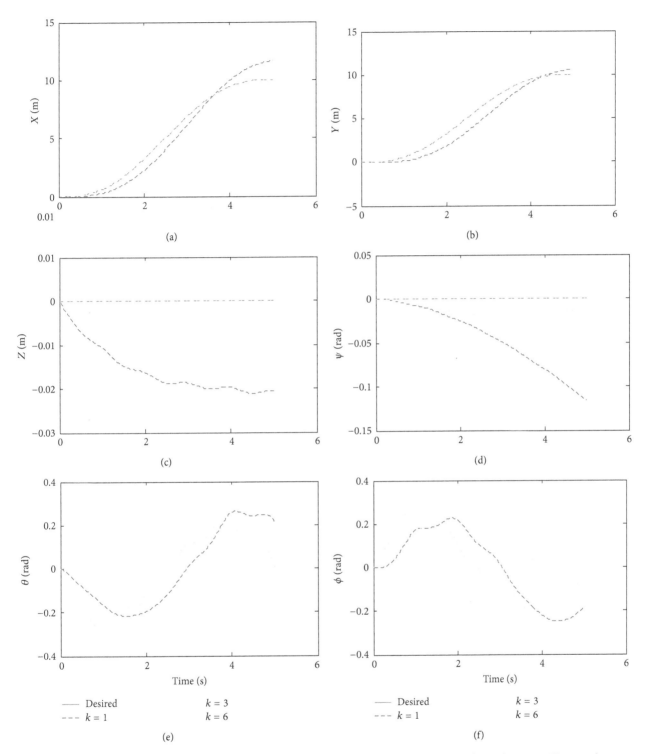

FIGURE 12: Trajectory tracking performance of SPD ILC in iteration 1, 3, and 6 for X-Y translation ($S = 10$ m, $T = 5$ sec.).

In the simulation studies, two different types of disturbances are introduced to deal with different environmental effects on different direction motions of the quadrotor UAV.

For the X and Y direction motions, external disturbances caused by wind gusts are described by stochastic functions where a Gauss-Markov process is chosen to simulate the wind

effect to the UAV system

$$d_x\left(t_j\right) = d_x\left(t_{j-1}\right) + A * \text{rand}\left(\right),$$
$$d_y\left(t_j\right) = d_y\left(t_{j-1}\right) + A * \text{rand}\left(\right).$$

(28)

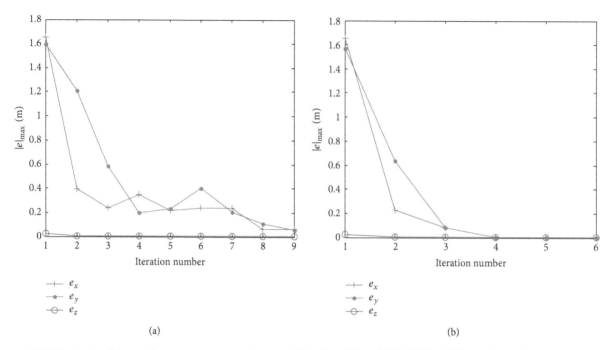

(a)

(b)

FIGURE 13: Trajectory tracking performance comparison between PD online ILC and SPD ILC for X-Y translation ($S = 10$ m, $T = 5$ sec.).

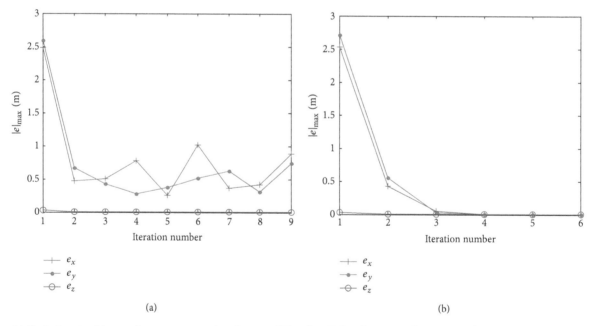

(a)

(b)

FIGURE 14: Trajectory tracking performance comparison between PD online ILC and SPD ILC for X-Y translation ($S = 100$ m, $T = 15$ sec.).

Throughout all the simulations, disturbances in the Z direction and all three angles are presented in (29). Note that the disturbances with random noise are very large compared to the components of the dynamic model

$$D = 10 + 20 \sin(2\pi t) + \text{rand}(),$$

$$d_z = 0.1D,$$

$$d_\phi = D,$$

$$d_\theta = D,$$

$$d_\psi = 0.001D.$$

(29)

To demonstrate tracking performance and robustness of online ILCs, the following simulation will cover main missions of a quadrotor UAV, that is, take-off, hovering, and moving in various trajectories.

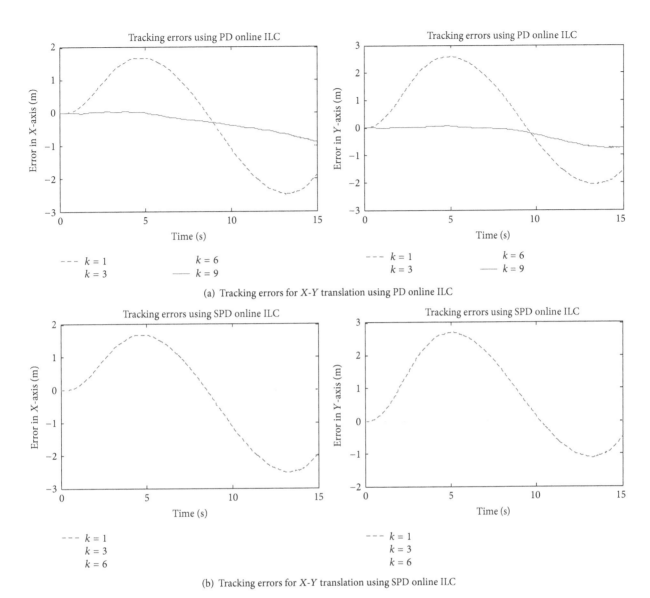

(a) Tracking errors for X-Y translation using PD online ILC

(b) Tracking errors for X-Y translation using SPD online ILC

FIGURE 15: Tracking errors from iteration to iteration for X-Y translation ($S = 100$ m, $T = 15$ sec.).

5.1. Take-Off Control.

In a take-off mission, the quadrotor UAV is commanded to smoothly take-off and ultimately hover at a desired height $h_d = 10$ m within a time duration of $T = 5$ sec. The desired trajectory is defined as

$$Z_d(t) = h_d \left[10\left(\frac{t}{T}\right)^3 - 15\left(\frac{t}{T}\right)^4 + 6\left(\frac{t}{T}\right)^5 \right],$$

$$X_d = Y_d = 0, \quad t \in [0, T] \tag{30}$$

and a set of online learning gains is chosen as

$$K_{p\,\mathrm{on}} = K_{\mathrm{on}} \begin{bmatrix} 0.1 & 0.1 & 50 & 5 & 5 & 500 \end{bmatrix},$$

$$K_{d\,\mathrm{on}} = 1.5 K_{p\,\mathrm{on}}, \tag{31}$$

where $K_{\mathrm{on}} = 0.5, 1, 1.5$ for different control gains. For most simulations conducted in this research, we set $K_{\mathrm{on}} = 1$

unless otherwise stated. The choice of control gains above was based on trial and error, with regard to stability and trajectory tracking performance.

The constant K_{on} is used to demonstrate the effect of increasing-decreasing the whole gain set by a factor. A variation of learning gains and its trajectory tracking performance for take-off are listed in Table 2. It should be mentioned that, in order to get fair comparison results, the disturbances and uncertainties for each simulation in the same iteration are assumed to be the same.

As shown in Table 2, reducing $(K_{p\,\mathrm{on}})_1$ and $(K_{p\,\mathrm{on}})_2$ by a factor of 10 significantly reduces the convergence rate and yields much larger errors in the first three iterations. Likewise, decreasing $(K_{p\,\mathrm{on}})_4$ and $(K_{p\,\mathrm{on}})_5$ by a factor of 10 yields similar results. This is due to a slower reaction in attitude control, making the quadrotor UAV away from the desired position

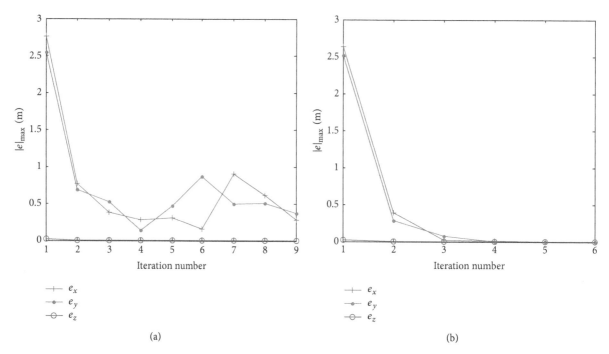

FIGURE 16: Trajectory tracking performance comparison between PD online ILC and SPD ILC for X-Y-Z translation.

TABLE 2: Effect of each control gain on tracking errors.

Control gain	k	$\|e_x\|$ (m)	$\|e_y\|$ (m)	$\|e_z\|$ (m)	$\|\phi\|$ (deg)	$\|\theta\|$ (deg)	$\|\psi\|$ (deg)
[0.1 0.1 50 5 5 500] $K_{\text{on}} = 1$	1	$5.423e-1$	$5.423e-1$	$2.228e-2$	$1.244e0$	$1.244e0$	$6.8584e0$
	3	$5.857e-2$	$5.856e-2$	$1.157e-5$	$4.632e-1$	$4.636e-1$	$4.7586e0$
	5	$1.532e-2$	$1.529e-2$	$1.151e-5$	$3.287e-1$	$3.286e-1$	$3.0638e0$
	9	$5.261e-3$	$5.258e-3$	$1.141e-5$	$2.415e-1$	$2.415e-1$	$1.3656e0$
[0.01 0.01 50 5 5 500] $K_{\text{on}} = 1$	1	$7.472e0$	$7.471e0$	$2.229e-2$	$2.331e0$	$2.330e0$	$6.8584e0$
	3	$2.627e0$	$2.627e0$	$2.099e-5$	$2.101e0$	$2.104e0$	$4.7586e0$
	5	$1.204e0$	$1.204e0$	$1.693e-5$	$1.298e0$	$1.298e0$	$3.0638e0$
	9	$5.748e-1$	$5.750e-1$	$1.244e-5$	$1.727e0$	$1.727e0$	$1.3656e0$
[0.1 0.15 5 5 500] $K_{\text{on}} = 1$	1	$5.429e-1$	$5.429e-1$	$2.214e-1$	$1.243e0$	$1.243e0$	$6.8584e0$
	3	$5.951e-2$	$5.950e-2$	$2.414e-4$	$4.638e-1$	$4.642e-1$	$4.7586e0$
	5	$1.569e-2$	$1.566e-2$	$3.032e-5$	$3.307e-1$	$3.307e-1$	$3.0638e0$
	9	$5.281e-3$	$5.278e-3$	$1.784e-5$	$2.442e-1$	$2.442e-1$	$1.3656e0$
[0.1 0.1 50 0.5 0.5 500] $K_{\text{on}} = 1$	1	$5.132e0$	$5.152e0$	$2.231e-2$	$1.296e1$	$1.288e1$	$6.8584e0$
	3	$5.954e-1$	$5.955e-1$	$1.224e-4$	$5.599e0$	$5.687e0$	$4.7586e0$
	5	$1.487e-1$	$1.453e-1$	$2.560e-5$	$3.962e0$	$3.879e0$	$3.0638e0$
	9	$5.173e-2$	$5.130e-2$	$1.298e-5$	$2.955e0$	$2.891e0$	$1.3656e0$
[0.1 0.1 50 5 5 50] $K_{\text{on}} = 1$	1	$5.421e-1$	$5.422e-1$	$2.213e-2$	$1.247e0$	$1.247e0$	$7.9413e0$
	3	$5.940e-2$	$5.938e-2$	$1.085e-5$	$4.627e-1$	$4.632e-1$	$7.6792e0$
	5	$1.577e-2$	$1.568e-2$	$1.062e-5$	$3.272e-1$	$3.273e-1$	$7.4223e0$
	9	$5.360e-3$	$5.315e-3$	$1.062e-5$	$2.421e-1$	$2.424e-1$	$6.9237e0$

in the presence of disturbances. Lastly, reducing $(K_{p\,\text{on}})_6$ by a factor of 10 shows a considerable decrease in yaw angle stability and a slower convergence rate. The effect of changes in $K_{d\,\text{on}}$ on the performance is illustrated in Figure 4. For the X and Y axes tracking, when $K_{d\,\text{on}} = K_{p\,\text{on}}$ the system yields larger errors and tends to produce steady errors. For $K_{d\,\text{on}} = 1.5K_{p\,\text{on}}$ and $K_{d\,\text{on}} = 3K_{p\,\text{on}}$, the results are much better in terms of maximum errors and final steady errors. These results strongly show the importance of the derivative gains. For the Z direction, the results are merely identical.

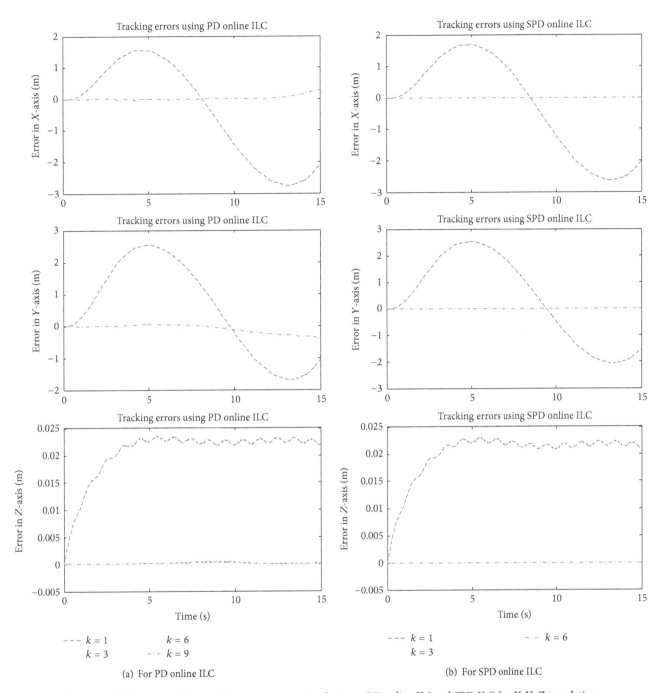

(a) For PD online ILC   (b) For SPD online ILC

FIGURE 17: Trajectory tracking performance comparison between PD online ILS and SPD ILC for X-Y-Z translation.

TABLE 3: Maximum tracking errors in the Z direction for take-off under LQR control.

Low Q ($10^6 \mathbf{I}$)	Middle Q ($10^7 \mathbf{I}$)	Large Q ($10^8 \mathbf{I}$)
0.0802	0.0327	0.0105

Figure 5 shows how changing the whole set of gains by a factor affects trajectory tracking performances. With $K_{\mathrm{on}} = 0.5$, for the X and Y directions, it is obvious that the control gains are not high enough to ensure monotonic convergence and yield large errors. On the other hand, when $K_{\mathrm{on}} = 1$ and $K_{\mathrm{on}} = 1.5$, the system is monotonically convergent and even faster for the latter case. Again, the effect is hardly detected in the Z direction. This is because control in the Z direction depends solely on u_1, while the X and Y motions also depend on the attitude of the quadrotor UAV.

To compare the performances of ILCs with traditional control such as LQR control, take-off simulations were fulfilled. Table 3 lists the maximum tracking errors under different LQR performance indices where an approach for the design of LQR controller discussed in [4] is used. Comparing the maximum errors in Z direction shown in Table 3 with those listed in Table 2, it is clearly shown that the ILC

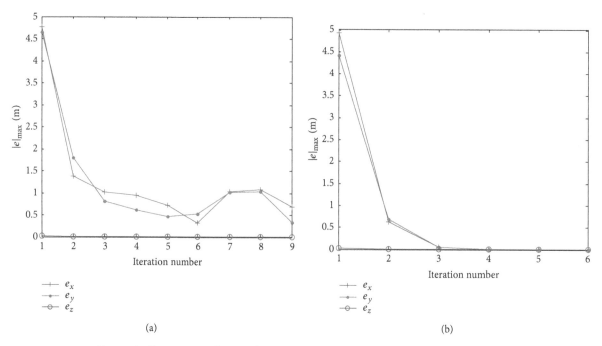

FIGURE 18: Trajectory tracking performance comparisons for X-Y plane circular motion.

performed much better than the LQR. Such a result would be expected as the ILCs is a kind of nonlinear learning control while the LQR is a linearized control for a nonlinear system.

After finishing the initial comparison study on the performance improvements by changing online control gains, some take-off simulation studies with wind disturbances and uncertainties are conducted. Figure 6 shows the maximum tracking errors from iteration to iteration controlled by both PD online ILCs and SPD ILCs. In the presence of disturbances, there are small errors for the X and Y direction motions controlled by the PD online ILC because of the existence of wind disturbance. But SPD ILCs outperform PD online ILCs with their incredibly fast convergence rates, and achieve very good performances in all three translation motions after 3 iterations. It demonstrates the capability of dealing with disturbances in SPD ILC.

Trajectory tracking performance in translations and orientations controlled by PD online ILCs is shown in Figure 7 for different iterations. It can be seen that the quadrotor UAV can smoothly take-off, with some errors in the X and Y directions that were caused by the wind disturbances. It is also noticed that the PD online ILCs and SPD ILCs can reject disturbances in orientations. Figure 8 shows the tracking performance improvements in Z direction from iteration to iteration for both online ILCs. It clearly shows the significant differences between the PD online ILC and the SPD ILC after the first iteration. Rotor speed in the 9th iteration is depicted in Figure 9 for the PD online ILC, which shows that all four rotors operate in the specified ranges.

5.2. Smooth Translation Tracking. To demonstrate a good trajectory tracking performance for an X-Y plane translation

motion, desired trajectories are chosen as follows:

$$X_d(t) = Y_d(t) = S\left[10\left(\frac{t}{T}\right)^3 - 15\left(\frac{t}{T}\right)^4 + 6\left(\frac{t}{T}\right)^5\right],$$

$$Z_d(t) = 0, \quad t \in [0, T]. \tag{32}$$

Two sets of simulations are performed here. The first simulation is set for a short range linear translation motion with $S = 10$ m and $T = 5$ sec., and the second one is for a long range translation motion at a higher speed with $S = 100$ m and $T = 15$ sec.

For the first set motion, it shows that the PD online ILCs tend to take more iterations, as many as 9, to converge to approximate zero errors in X and Y directions while SPD ILCs take 6 iterations. Trajectory tracking errors from iteration to iteration are shown in Figure 10. It clearly shows that the SPD ILC can ensure less tracking errors and faster convergence rates.

Figures 11 and 12 show the tracking performance improvements from iteration to iteration for both PD online ILC and SPD ILC. The effectiveness of the online ILCs in terms of tracking error reductions and resistance to disturbances is clearly shown.

Note that shown in Figure 13, there are relatively large errors in the X and Y directions for the first iteration and then they converge to stable error boundaries for the PD ILC, but the SPD ILCs obtained very good tracking performance with very small ($<10^{-2}$ m) tracking errors in all three directions even under the wind gust disturbance conditions.

For the second set test with large motion ranges and fast speeds, the maximum tracking errors from iteration to iteration are depicted in Figure 14 for both PD online ILC

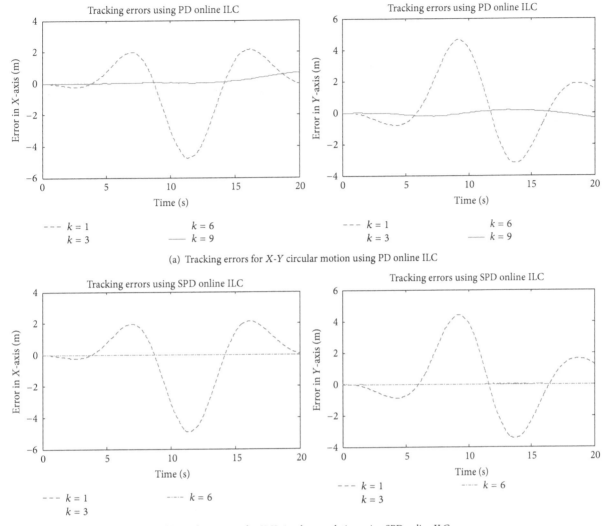

(a) Tracking errors for X-Y circular motion using PD online ILC

(b) Tracking errors for X-Y circular translation using SPD online ILC

FIGURE 19: Tracking performance comparison for X-Y circular motion.

and SPD ILC. It is shown that the PD online ILCs obtain acceptable tracking performance (the tracking errors are around 1 m for both X and Y directions), while the SPD ILCs still perform much better than the PD online ILCs.

Figure 15 shows the tracking errors in the X and Y directions from iteration to iteration for both PD online ILC and SPD online ILC. Considering the long range motions and relatively higher speed than the previous short range motion case, it is clearly shown that, after a few iterations, the quadrotor can obtain smooth and good motions that follow the desired trajectories, especially for the SPD ILC.

Furthermore, to examine the tracking performance for a three dimensional translation motion based on the ILCs, a simulation of linear motion from point A (0, 0, 0) to point B (100, 100, 10) in 15 seconds is conducted. Figure 16 shows the maximum tracking errors from iteration to iteration controlled by these two different online ILCs. It is clearly shown that the SPD ILCs performed much better than the PD online ILCs in terms of fast convergent rate, small tracking errors, and good capability to compensate the disturbances

and uncertainties. It also shows that the tracking performance in the Z direction was controlled very well for both online ILCs. Figure 17 shows the tracking errors from iteration to iteration for both PD online ILC and SPD online ILC for 3D translation motions. It demonstrates the effectiveness of the online ILCs and the better tacking performance obtained by the SPD online ILC.

5.3. Circular Trajectories Tracking. To prove that the quadrotor UAV can freely maneuver a complex trajectory, a circular trajectory tracking test is performed by using the online ILCs. In this mission, the quadrotor revolves the X-Y plane with a radius $R = 20$ m for a time duration $T = 20$ sec., smoothly starting from and ending at the velocity of 0. The desired trajectories are

$$X_d(t) = R\cos\left(2\pi\left[10\left(\frac{t}{T}\right)^3 - 15\left(\frac{t}{T}\right)^4 + 6\left(\frac{t}{T}\right)^5\right] + \pi\right)$$
$$+ R,$$

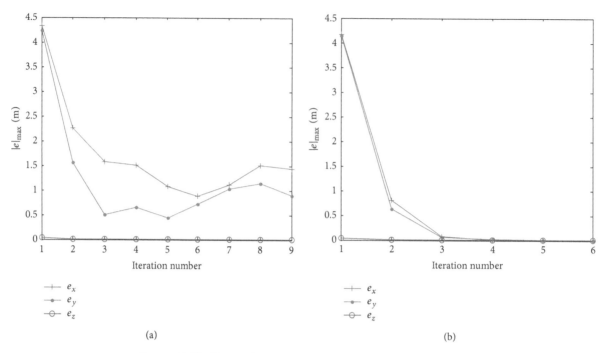

FIGURE 20: Tracking performance comparisons for 3D circular motion.

$$Y_d(t) = R \sin\left(2\pi\left[10\left(\frac{t}{T}\right)^3 - 15\left(\frac{t}{T}\right)^4 + 6\left(\frac{t}{T}\right)^5\right] + \pi\right),$$

$$Z_d(t) = 25, \qquad X_d \in [0, 2R], \qquad Y_d \in [-R, R]$$

$$t \in [0, T].$$

$$(33)$$

Figure 18 shows the performance improvements from iteration to iteration for both PD online ILCs and SPD ILCs. Once again, it demonstrated the effectiveness of the SPD ILCs. Figure 19 shows the tracking errors controlled by PD online ILCs and SPD ILCs for the X-Y plane circular trajectory, respectively. It can be observed that PD online ILCs can obtain acceptable tracking performances through iterative learning processes, and SPD ILCs converge to approximate zero errors at the 3rd iteration while PD online ILCs still have small bounded tracking errors. Therefore, it can be seen that SPD ILCs perform much better in yaw angle than the PD online ILCs.

By adding the Z direction motion (20 m) accordingly with the X-Y plane circular motion discussed above, a 3D circular tracking case was formed and used to examine the effectiveness of the online ILCs. Figure 20 shows the maximum tracking errors in three axes for the PD online ILCs and the SPD ILCs, while Figure 21 shows the tracking performance improvements from iteration to iteration for both online ILCs. It demonstrates again that the SPD ILCs can obtain much better tracking performances than the PD online ILCs under the existence of disturbances and uncertainties.

6. Conclusion and Discussion

Iterative learning control is simple to build, easy to implement, and robust to uncertainties and disturbances. In order to perform some fundamental missions for a quadrotor UAV, some trajectory tracking control for a UAV was conducted based on online ILCs in this paper. Different trajectory tracking tasks using PD online ILCs and SPD ILCs were simulated and compared. It was proven that tracking performances can be improved by choosing large control gains for the online ILCs. In addition, the choice of control gains is very flexible. Despite nonlinearity of the system and the presence of disturbances, both types of online ILCs demonstrated good tracking capabilities of smooth take-off, straight-line, and circular motions in two and three dimensions and provided good performances after a few iterations. Simulation results demonstrated that SPD ILCs performed much better than PD online ILCs in terms of convergence rate and disturbance rejection.

The online ILCs have been successfully applied to trajectory tracking control of a quadrotor UAV through simulations for different missions. To deal with the real application of online ILCs, it should be mentioned that a PD feedback control is applied to control the quadrotor UAV in the first iteration, as there is no previous experimental learning process. The PD feedback control was proved to provide the stability of the UAV system, even with some big tracking errors. The control input information obtained from the first iteration will be stored and used as a feedforward control for the next iterations. In case the state of the system cannot be measured directly, the online ILCs update law could include

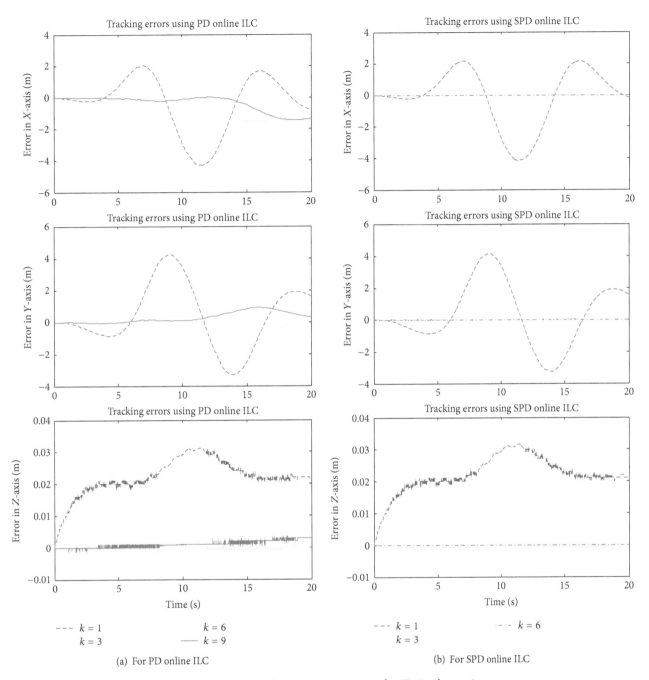

(a) For PD online ILC

(b) For SPD online ILC

Figure 21: Tracking performance improvement for 3D circular motion.

a Kalman filter to estimate the states. With all the aspects shown above, implementation to a real application seems to be practical, and it is a future work.

Acknowledgment

This research is supported by the Natural Sciences and Engineering Research Council of Canada (NSERC) through a Discovery Grant to the second author.

References

[1] Y. Wu, *Development and implementation of a control system for a quadrotor UAV [Ph.D. thesis]*, University of Applied Science Ravensburg-Weingarten, 2009.

[2] G. M. Hoffmann, S. L. Waslander, and C. J. Tomlin, "Quadrotor helicopter trajectory tracking control," in *AIAA Guidance, Navigation and Control Conference and Exhibit*, Honolulu, Hawaii, USA, August 2008.

[3] K. Miller, "Path tracking control for quadrotor helicopters," 2008.

[4] I. D. Cowling, O. A. Yakimenko, J. F. Whidborne, and A. K. Cooke, "A prototype of an autonomous controller for a quadrotor UAV," in *European Control Conference*, 2007.

[5] H. Voos, "Nonlinear state-dependent riccati equation control of a quadrotor UAV," in *Proceedings of IEEE Conference on Control Applications (CCA '06)*, pp. 2547–2552, Munich, Germany, October 2006.

[6] P. Adigbli, C. Grand, J.-B. Mouret, and S. Doncieux, "Nonlinear attitude and position control of a micro quadrotor using sliding mode and backstepping techniques," in *European Micro Air Vehicle Conference and Flight Competition*, Toulouse, France, 2007.

[7] S. Bouabdallah and R. Siegwart, "Backstepping and sliding-mode techniques applied to an indoor micro Quadrotor," in *Proceedings of IEEE International Conference on Robotics and Automation*, pp. 2247–2252, April 2005.

[8] G. Hoffmann, D. G. Rajnarayan, S. L. Waslander, D. Dostal, J. S. Jang, and C. J. Tomlin, "The Stanford testbed of autonomous rotorcraft for multi agent control (STARMAC)," in *Proceedings of the 23rd Digital Avionics Systems Conference*, vol. 2, pp. 121–130, October 2004.

[9] J. Gadewadikar, F. L. Lewis, K. Subbarao, K. Peng, and B. M. Chen, "H-infinity static output-feedback control for rotorcraft," *Journal of Intelligent and Robotic Systems: Theory & Applications*, vol. 54, no. 4, pp. 629–646, 2009.

[10] C. Coza and C. J. B. Macnab, "A new robust adaptive-fuzzy control method applied to quadrotor helicopter stabilization," in *Proceedings of the Annual Meeting of the North American Fuzzy Information Processing Society (NAFIPS '06)*, pp. 475–479, June 2006.

[11] T. Dierks and S. Jagannathan, "Output feedback control of a quadrotor UAV using neural networks," *IEEE Transactions on Neural Networks*, vol. 21, no. 1, pp. 50–66, 2010.

[12] C. Nicol, C. J. B. Macnab, and A. Ramirez-Serrano, "Robust neural network control of a quadrotor helicopter," in *Proceedings of IEEE Canadian Conference on Electrical and Computer Engineering (CCECE '08)*, pp. 1233–1237, May 2008.

[13] J. How, E. King, and Y. Kuwata, "Flight demonstrations of cooperative control for UAV teams," in *Collection of Technical Papers—AIAA 3rd "Unmanned-Unlimited" Technical Conference, Workshop, and Exhibit*, pp. 505–513, September 2004.

[14] J. P. How, B. Bethke, A. Frank, D. Dale, and J. Vian, "Real-time indoor autonomous vehicle test environment," *IEEE Control Systems Magazine*, vol. 28, no. 2, pp. 51–64, 2008.

[15] S. Bouabdallah and R. Siegwart, "Towards intelligent miniature flying robots," *Springer Tracts in Advanced Robotics*, vol. 25, pp. 429–440, 2006.

[16] S. Arimoto, S. Kawamura, and F. Miyazaki, "Bettering operation of robots by learning," *Journal of Robotic Systems*, vol. 1, pp. 123–140, 1984.

[17] K. L. Moore, "An observation about monotonic convergence in discrete-time, P-type iterative learning control," in *Proceedings of IEEE International Symposium on Intelligent Control (ISIC '01)*, pp. 45–49, Mexico City, Mexico, September 2001.

[18] C. Chen and J. Hwang, "PD-type iterative learning control for the trajectory tracking of a pneumatic X-Y table with disturbances," *JSME International Journal, Series C*, vol. 49, no. 2, pp. 520–526, 2006.

[19] K. Park, "An average operator-based PD-type iterative learning control for variable initial state error," *IEEE Transactions on Automatic Control*, vol. 50, no. 6, pp. 865–869, 2005.

[20] Y. Chen and K. L. Moore, "An optimal design of PD-type iterative learning control with monotonic convergence," in *Proceedings of IEEE International Symposium on Intelligent Control*, pp. 55–60, Vancouver, Canada, October 2002.

[21] Y. Chen and K. L. Moore, "PI-type iterative learning control revisited," in *Proceedings of the American Control Conference*, pp. 2138–2143, Anchorage, Alaska, USA, May 2002.

[22] K. Park, Z. Bien, and D. Hwang, "A study on the robustness of a PID-type iterative learning controller againts initial state error," *International Journal of Systems Science*, vol. 30, no. 1, pp. 49–59, 1999.

[23] A. Madady, "PID type iterative learning control with optimal gains," *International Journal of Control, Automation and Systems*, vol. 6, no. 2, pp. 194–203, 2008.

[24] C. Chien and J. Liu, "P-type iterative learning controller for robust output tracking of nonlinear time-varying systems," in *Proceedings of the American Control Conference*, pp. 2595–2599, July 1994.

[25] X. G. Yan, I. M. Chen, and J. Lam, "D-type learning control for nonlinear time-varying systems with unknown initial states and inputs," *Transactions of the Institute of Measurement and Control*, vol. 23, no. 2, pp. 69–82, 2001.

[26] S. Yu, S. Xiong, and J. Bai, "Design of iterative learning controller combined with feedback control for electrohydraulic servo system," in *Proceedings of the 4th International Conference on Natural Computation (ICNC '08)*, vol. 2, pp. 622–626, October 2008.

[27] P. R. Ouyang, W. J. Zhang, and M. M. Gupta, "PD-type on-line learning control for systems with state uncertainties and measurement disturbances," *Control and Intelligent Systems*, vol. 35, no. 4, pp. 351–358, 2007.

[28] "Iterative learning control for uncertain nonlinear discrete-time systems using current iteration tracking error," in *Iterative LearnIng Control*, vol. 248, chapter 4, Springer, Berlin, Germany, 1999.

[29] J. Shou, D. Pi, and W. Wang, "Sufficient conditions for the convergence of open-closed-loop PID-type iterative learning control for nonlinear time-varying systems," in *Proceedings of IEEE International Conference on Systems, Man and Cybernetics*, vol. 3, pp. 2557–2562, October 2003.

[30] S. Yu, J.-H. Wu, and X.-W. Yan, "A PD-type open-closed-loop iterative learning control and its convergence for discrete systems," in *Proceedings of the 1st International Conference on Machine Learning and Cybernetics*, pp. 659–662, Beijing, China, November 2002.

[31] P. R. Ouyang, "PD-PD type learning control for uncertain nonlinear systems," in *Proceedings of the ASME International Design Engineering Technical Conferences and Computers and Information in Engineering Conference (DETC '09)*, pp. 699–707, San Diego, Calif, USA, September 2009.

[32] P. R. Ouyang, B. A. Petz, and F. F. Xi, "Iterative learning control with switching gain feedback for nonlinear systems," *Journal of Computational and Nonlinear Dynamics*, vol. 6, no. 1, Article ID 011020, 7 pages, 2011.

[33] P. R. Ouyang, W. J. Zhang, and M. M. Gupta, "An adaptive switching learning control method for trajectory tracking of robot manipulators," *Mechatronics*, vol. 16, no. 1, pp. 51–61, 2006.

[34] P. R. Ouyang and P. Pong-in, "Iterative learning control: a comparison study," in *Proceedings of ASME International Mechanical Engineering Congress & Exposition*, Vancouver, Canada, 2010.

[35] B. Guerreiro, C. Silvestre, R. Cunha, and D. Antunes, "Trajectory tracking H2 controller for autonomous helicopters: an application to industrial chimney inspection," in *Proceedings of the 17th IFAC Symposium on Automatic Control in Aerospace (ACA '07)*, pp. 431–436, June 2007.

[36] R. Beard, D. Kingston, M. Quigley et al., "Autonomous vehicle technologies for small fixed-wing UAVs," *Journal of Aerospace Computing, Information and Communication*, vol. 2, no. 1, pp. 92–108, 2005.

[37] I. D. Cowling, O. A. Yakimenko, J. F. Whidborne, and A. K. Cooke, "A prototype of an autonomous controller for a quadrotor UAV," in *European Control Conference*, Kos, Greece, July 2007.

[38] E. Dombre and W. Khalil, "Trajectory generation," in *Modeling, Performance Analysis and Control of Robot Manipulators*, p. 191, ISTE Ltd., 2007.

9

Flight Control Laws Verification Using Continuous Genetic Algorithms

A. Al-Asasfeh,[1] **N. Hamdan,**[2] **and Z. Abo-Hammour**[3]

[1] *Department of Mechanical Engineering, The University of Jordan, P.O. Box 962069, Sport City, Amman 11196, Jordan*
[2] *Mechanical Engineering Department, King Faisal University, Al Hofuf, Saudi Arabia*
[3] *Department of Mechatronics Engineering, The University of Jordan, Amman, Jordan*

Correspondence should be addressed to N. Hamdan; naderhamdan@hotmail.com

Academic Editors: A. Hamzaoui and K. Watanabe

This work is concerned with the application of a continuous genetic algorithm (CGA) to solve the nonlinear optimization problem that results from the clearance process of nonlinear flight control laws. The CGA is used to generate a pilot command signal that governs the aircraft performance around certain points in the flight envelope about which the aircraft dynamics were trimmed. The performance of the aircraft model due to pitch and roll pilot commands is analyzed to find the worst combination that leads to a nonallowable load factor. The motivations for using the CGA to solve this type of optimization problem are due to the fact that the pilot command signals are smooth and correlated, which are difficult to generate using the conventional genetic algorithm (GA). Also the CGA has the advantage over the conventional GA method in being able to generate smooth solutions without the loss of significant information in the presence of a rate limiter in the controller design and the time delay in response to the actuators. Simulation results are presented which show superior convergence performance using the CGA compared with conventional genetic algorithms.

1. Introduction

A validation and verification (clearance) process of flight control laws is required to prove and guarantee that the aircraft response is safe and stable for any possible failure case such as engine or actuator failures. In addition, the clearance process must take into account possible variations of flight parameters (e.g., large variations in mass, inertia, center of gravity positions, highly nonlinear aerodynamics, aerodynamic tolerances, and air data system tolerances). Also it is required to prove that pilot commands will not drive the aircraft response to critical operating points. It is noted that the aircraft flight quality and performance requirement are specified in the form of sets of stability performance and handling requirement criteria [3]. Consideration of all of these requirements makes the clearance process computationally complex, time consuming, and extremely expensive [2]. Therefore, the approach commonly used by investigator is to clear each performance/handling criterion individually. For a given performance/handling criterion, the clearance

process requires finding for all possible configurations and for all combinations of parameter variations, and uncertainties, the worst-case scenario that violates the specified criterion in a specified flight envelope [3].

To date, very little research has been reported in the literature on the flight control law (FCL) clearance for time-varying pilot command inputs. Skoogh et al. [4] used a parameterization of pilot command inputs where the pilot signals are represented as low-order piecewise polynomials. Menon et al. [5] employed a sequence of discretized pilot command inputs and a sequence of pilot command inputs called Clonk. The resulting nonlinear optimization problems by using the above-mentioned signals were solved using the genetic algorithm and the differential evolution algorithm. These two approaches apply many restrictions on the shape of the pilot command inputs. Due to the presence of a rate limiter in the controller design and the time delay in response of the actuators, it is suitable to use smooth and correlated commands. Other investigators treated the pilot command inputs as predetermined step inputs and

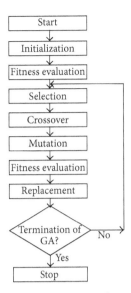

FIGURE 1: Block diagram for a typical genetic algorithm.

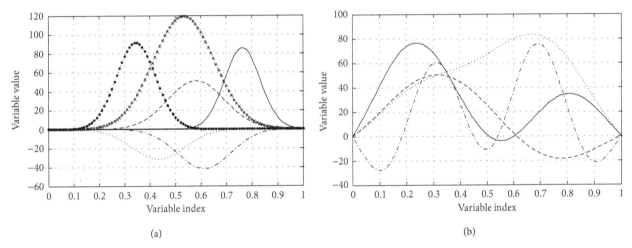

FIGURE 2: The initialization functions used in the continuous genetic algorithm: (a) modified Gauss function and (b) modified Sinc function.

evaluated the clearance criteria based on evaluation of system parameter uncertainties.

The continuous genetic algorithm (CGA), explained in the next section, is one of the stochastic population methods for global optimization which operates on a population of solution vectors [6]. It is an efficient method for the solution of optimization problems in which the parameters to be optimized are correlated with each other or the smoothness of the solution curve should be achieved. The advantage of this approach is the ability to find the global optimal solution for nonlinear optimal problem having multiple solutions such as the clearance process found in flight control validation. The advantages of using this method, in comparison with other available techniques, to solve optimal control problems have been demonstrated in several linearized model of control problems such as chemical reactors, tracking systems, and multidegree-of-freedom manipulator [7]. Based on the previous work in applying this technique to solve the above-mentioned optimal control problems [8], the present work will explore applying this technique to the analysis of

the nonlinear flight control laws clearance process. To the authors knowledge, the application of this technique to flight control laws clearance process has not been addressed in the open literature.

Military aircrafts are usually, due to performance reasons, naturally unstable, and therefore a flight control system which provides a required artificial stability is essential for their operation. Because the performance of the aircraft is dependent on the controller, and this performance affects the safety of the pilot and reliability of the aircraft structure and components, it must be proven to the aviation authorities that a controller performance will be correctly acceptable throughout a specified flight envelope in all possible failure conditions and in the presence of all possible system parameter variations [1, 2].

2. Continuous Genetic Algorithm

2.1. General Description. Genetic algorithms (GAs) are adaptive heuristic search algorithms premised on the evolutionary

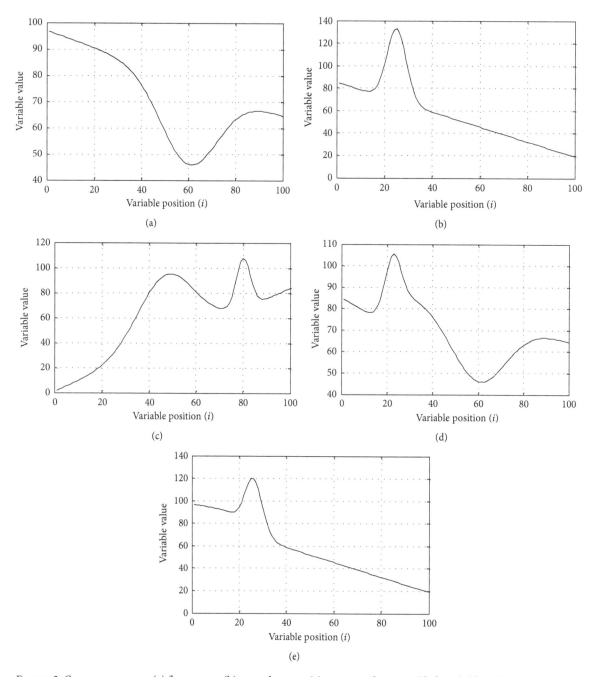

FIGURE 3: Crossover process: (a) first parent, (b) second parent, (c) crossover function, (d) first child, and (e) second child.

ideas of natural selection and genetics [9]. The basic concept of GAs is designed to simulate processes in natural system necessary for evolution, specifically those that follow the principles first laid down by Charles Darwin of the survival of the fittest. As such, these algorithms represent an intelligent exploitation of a random search within a defined search space to solve a problem.

First pioneered by John Holland in the 1960s [9], genetic algorithms have been widely studied, experimented, and applied in many fields in the engineering world. Not only do GAs provide an alternative method to solving problem, but also outperform other traditional methods in most of the problems considered. Many of the real-world problems

have proven difficult for traditional methods but ideal for GAs.

The GA procedural steps are illustrated in Figure 1. An initial population is created containing a predefined number of individuals (or solutions), incorporating the variable information. Each individual has an associated fitness measure, typically representing an objective value. The concept that the fittest (or best) individuals in a population will produce fitter offspring is then implemented in order to reproduce the next population. Selected individuals are chosen for crossover at each generation, with an appropriate mutation factor to randomly modify the genes of an individual in order to develop the new population. The result is another

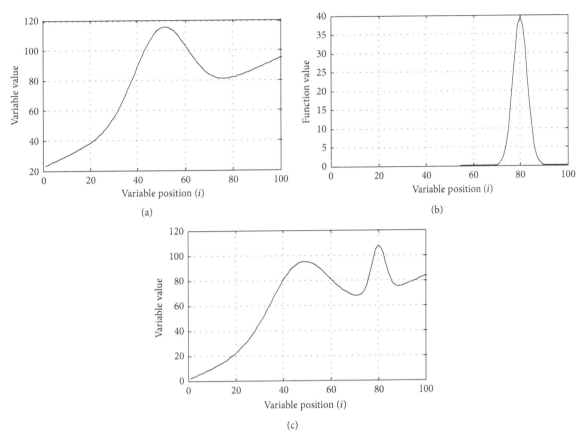

FIGURE 4: Mutation process: (a) offspring, (b) mutation function, and (c) offspring after mutation.

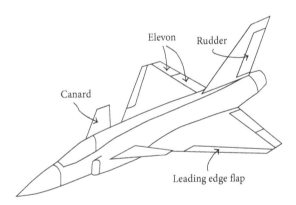

FIGURE 5: Principal layout of the control surface configuration.

set of individuals based on the original population leading to subsequent populations with better (min. or max.) individual fitness. Therefore, the algorithm identifies the individuals with the high fitness values, and those with lower fitness will naturally get discarded from the population [9, 10].

The CGA was shown to be an efficient method for the solution of optimization problems in which the parameters to be optimized are correlated with each other or the smoothness of the solution curve should be achieved. As indicated above, this procedure has been successfully applied in the motion planning of robot manipulators in the field of robotics [6], in the numerical solution of boundary value problems in

TABLE 1: The selected operating points in flight envelope.

Point no.	Speed (Mach)	Altitude (m)
1	0.3	1000
2	0.6	6000
3	0.8	3000
4	1	5000
5	1.2	3000
6	1.2	6000

TABLE 2: Maximum load factor ($n_{z\max}$) results obtained using a modified Gauss function and the population size of 64 individuals.

Mach	Alt.	Run 1		Run 2		Run 3		Run 4		Max value
		Iter. no.	n_z	Iter. no.	n_z	Iter. no.	n_z	Iter. no.	n_z	
0.3	1000	158	10.5582	189	10.4209	319	10.5693	138	10.4263	10.5693
0.6	6000	368	10.4260	133	10.4495	169	10.6645	256	10.3020	10.6645
0.8	3000	213	10.6005	301	10.5697	257	10.4085	179	10.5354	10.6005
1	5000	202	10.5085	154	10.2681	320	10.4363	176	10.4696	10.5085
1.2	3000	189	10.4260	401	10.4495	188	10.6645	147	10.3020	10.6645
1.2	6000	198	10.4260	180	10.4495	152	10.6645	137	10.3020	10.6645

TABLE 3: Same as Table 2, but using modified Sinc function.

Mach	Alt.	Run 1		Run 2		Run 3		Run 4		Max value
		Iter. no.	n_z	Iter. no.	n_z	Iter. no.	n_z	Iter. no.	n_z	
0.3	1000	160	10.4049	295	10.4432	313	10.4736	171	10.4206	10.4736
0.6	6000	142	10.4843	275	10.5461	250	10.4613	177	10.4852	10.5461
0.8	3000	269	10.4258	401	10.5404	195	10.6252	137	10.6064	10.6252
1	5000	155	10.4702	225	10.4961	143	10.3488	246	10.6615	10.6615
1.2	3000	215	10.5534	262	10.4596	245	10.8290	214	10.4406	10.8290
1.2	6000	194	10.6149	184	10.4595	209	10.3111	310	10.5633	10.6149

TABLE 4: Same as Table 2, but for a population size of 128 individuals.

Mach	Alt.	Run 1		Run 2		Run 3		Run 4		Max value
		Iter. no.	n_z	Iter. no.	n_z	Iter. no.	n_z	Iter. no.	n_z	
0.3	1000	143	10.6429	183	10.3990	200	10.7130	208	10.6184	10.7130
0.6	6000	139	10.6506	381	10.8285	207	10.6122	195	10.5630	10.8285
0.8	3000	285	10.7417	293	10.6393	228	10.6686	256	10.9005	**10.9005**
1	5000	180	10.8291	202	10.6537	196	10.8093	239	10.8391	10.8391
1.2	3000	189	10.6367	401	10.5831	188	10.8135	147	10.7866	10.8135
1.2	6000	152	10.4815	168	10.6388	247	10.8049	190	10.5147	10.8049

the field of applied mathematics [7], and as optimal control problem solver for both linear and nonlinear systems [8].

Before going to the detailed description of the CGA, the conditions concerning the continuous functions that can be used in such algorithms should be clearly stated. In relation to the initialization function, any smooth function that is close enough to the expected solution curve can be used. It is to be noted that the closer the initialization function to the final solution, the faster the convergence speed since the coarse tuning stage of CGA in this case will be bypassed and the algorithm will jump to the fine tuning stage. In the case that there is no prior information about the expected solution curves, then any smooth function can be used. Furthermore, a mixture of functions can be used which is beneficial in this case as it allows one to obtain a diverse initial population. The effect of the initial population usually dies after few tens of generations and the convergence speed after that is governed by the selection mechanism, crossover and mutation operators [8]. The crossover function, as shown later on, is within the range [0, 1] such that the offspring solution curve will start with the solution curve of the first parent and gradually change its values until they reach the solution curve of the second parent at the other end. The mutation function may be any continuous function. However, both the crossover and mutation functions should satisfy any problem-specific constraints if such constraints exist.

2.2. CGA Steps. The continuous genetic algorithm consists of the following main steps.

(1) Initialization. In this phase, an initial population comprising of N_p smooth individuals is randomly generated. In this work, two smooth functions are used for initializing the population: the modified Gaussian function and the modified Sinc function (Figures 2(a) and 2(b)). The modified Gaussian function $P_j(h, i)$ is defined as follows:

$$P_j(h, i) = u_{\text{left}}(h) + \frac{u_{\text{right}}(h) - u_{\text{left}}(h)}{N_t - 1}(i - 1)$$

$$+ A * \exp\left[\frac{-(i - \mu)^2}{2\sigma^2}\right], \tag{1}$$

TABLE 5: Maximum load factor ($n_{z\mathrm{max}}$) results obtained using a modified Sinc function and the population size of 128 individuals.

Mach	Alt.	Run 1		Run 2		Run 3		Run 4		Max value
		Iter. no.	n_z	Iter. no.	n_z	Iter. no.	n_z	Iter. no.	n_z	
0.3	1000	275	10.6571	299	10.5299	204	10.5714	401	10.7866	10.5092
0.6	6000	255	10.4802	237	10.7215	216	10.8129	210	10.5034	10.5174
0.8	3000	189	10.3804	401	10.5431	188	10.7358	147	10.3020	10.6630
1	5000	401	10.6885	223	10.6571	211	10.4816	294	10.5633	10.5110
1.2	3000	122	10.5953	148	10.7304	278	10.8423	136	10.5147	10.5034
1.2	6000	235	10.6007	204	10.7166	280	10.6554	381	10.7092	10.7092

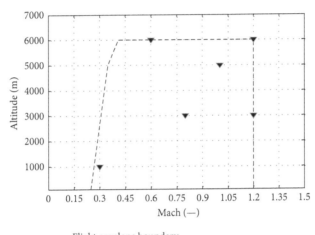

--- Flight envelope boundary
▼ Selected FE points

FIGURE 6: The selected operating points in flight envelope.

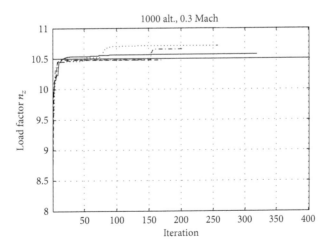

—— Number of population: 64, init. function: G
--- Number of population: 64, init. function: S
······ Number of population: 128, init. function: G
·-·- Number of population: 128, init. function: S

FIGURE 7: Maximum load factor ($n_{z\,\mathrm{max}}$) versus the iteration (generation). Result using CGA with population sizes of 64 and 128 and both initialization functions: modified Gauss function (G) and modified Sinc function (S). Aircraft model trimmed at 1000 m altitude and 0.3 Mach speed.

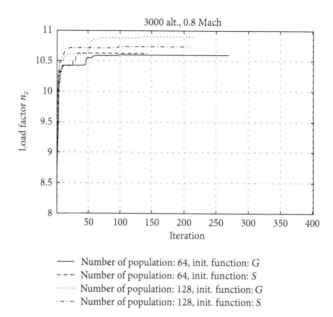

FIGURE 8: Same as Figure 7, but the aircraft model trimmed at 3000 m altitude and 0.8 Mach speed.

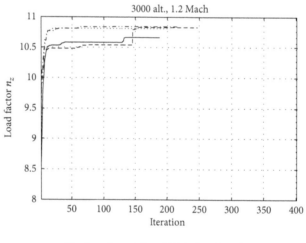

FIGURE 9: Same as Figure 7, but the aircraft model trimmed at 3000 m altitude and 1.2 Mach speed.

and the modified Sinc function $P_j(h, i)$ is given by the following equation:

$$P_j(h, i) = u_{\text{left}}(h) + \frac{u_{\text{right}}(h) - u_{\text{left}}(h)}{N_t - 1}(i - 1) \\ + \text{sinc}(x_s - i) * i, \tag{2}$$

where $1 \leq h \leq N_c$, $1 \leq i \leq N_t$, $P_j(h, i)$ is the ith node value of the hth curve for the jth parent, $u_{\text{left}}(h)$ is the value of the leftmost variable of the hth curve, $u_{\text{right}}(h)$ is the value of the rightmost variable of the hth curve, $u_{\text{left}}(h)$ and $u_{\text{right}}(h)$ are randomly generated subject to the problem constraints, N_t is the total number of nodes along each solution curve, A represents a random number within the range $[-3R(h), 3R(h)]$, with $R(h) = |u_{\text{right}}(h) - u_{\text{left}}(h)|$, μ is a random number within the range $[1, N_t]$, and σ is a random number within the range $[1, N_t/6]$, $x_s = f(x_v, N_t)$, index series at which to interpolate, and x_v is random number between 1 and 5.

(2) *Evaluation*. The fitness (F) is calculated for each individual in the population. In the present clearance process, F is given by

$$F = \max(\xi), \tag{3}$$

where ξ is the angle of attack or the load factor.

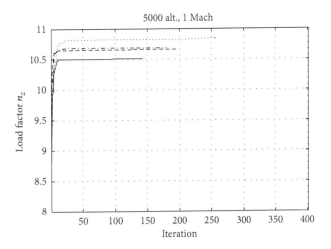

FIGURE 10: Same as Figure 7, but the aircraft model trimmed at 5000 m altitude and 1.0 Mach speed.

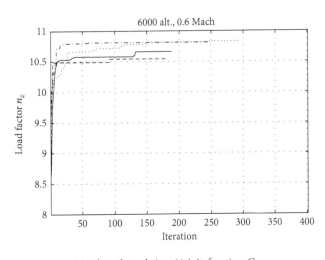

FIGURE 11: Same as Figure 7, but the aircraft model trimmed at 6000 m altitude and 0.6 Mach speed.

(3) *Selection.* In this step, individuals from the current population are selected to mate according to their relative fitness so that best individuals receive more copies in subsequent generations.

(4) *Crossover.* Crossover is the way through which information is shared among the population. The crossover process combines the features of two parent individuals, say j and k, to form two children individuals, say L and $L + 1$, as given by the following equations:

$$C_L(h, i) = W(h, i) P_j(h, i) + [1 - W(h, i)] P_k(h, i)$$

$$C_{L+1}(h, i) = [1 - W(h, i)] P_j(h, i) + W(h, i) P_k(h, i)$$

$$W(h, i) = 0.5 \left[1 + \tanh\left(\frac{i - \mu}{\sigma}\right) \right]$$

(4)

for all $1 \leq h \leq N_c$, $1 \leq i \leq N_t$, where P_j and P_k represent the two parents chosen from the mating pool, C_L and C_{L+1} are the two children obtained through crossover process, W represents the crossover weighting function within the range $[0, 1]$, μ is a random number within the range $[1, N_t]$, and σ is a random number within the range $[1, N_t/6]$.

The crossover operator in CGA is applied in the same way as in conventional GA except that smooth continuous representation of the individuals is used in the CGA while in

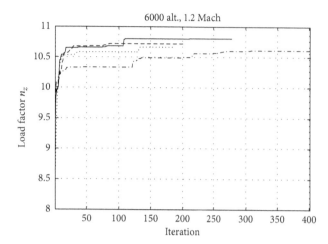

··•·· Number of population: 64, init. function: G
·-•- Number of population: 64, init. function: S
—•— Number of population: 128, init. function: G
--- Number of population: 128, init. function: S

FIGURE 12: Same as Figure 7, but the aircraft model trimmed at 6000 m altitude and 1.2 Mach speed.

the GA binary code representation for individuals is used. In the CGA, pairs of individuals are crossed with probability P_{ci}. Within the pair of parents that should undergo crossover process, individual curves are crossed with probability P_{cc}. That is, the hth smooth curve of the first parent is crossed with the hth smooth curve of the second parent with P_{cc} probability. If P_{ci} value is set to 0.5 and P_{cc} value is set to 0.5, then one pair of parents between two pairs is likely to be crossed, and within that pair, $N_c/2$ of the curves are likely to be crossed. Figure 3 shows the crossover process between two random solution curves. It is clear that new information is incorporated in the children while maintaining the smoothness of the resulting solution curves.

(5) *Mutation.* The function of mutation is used to introduce occasional perturbations to the variables to maintain the diversity within the population. The mutation process in CGA is governed by the following formulas:

$$C_j^m (h, i) = C_j (h, i) + d \times M (h, i),$$

$$M (h, i) = \exp \left[\frac{-(i - \mu)^2}{2\sigma^2} \right], \tag{5}$$

where C_j represents the jth child produced through the crossover process, C_j^m is the mutated jth child, M is the Gaussian mutation function, d represents a random number within the range $[-\text{range}(h), \text{range}(h)]$, with range($h$)representing the difference between the minimum and maximum values of the hth smooth curve of child C_j, and μ and σ are as given in the crossover process.

In the mutation process, each individual child undergoes mutation with probability P_{mi}. However, for each child that should undergo a mutation process, individual curves are

mutated with probability P_{mc}. If P_{mi} value is set to 0.5 and P_{mc} value is set to 0.5, then one child out of two children is likely to be mutated, and within that child, $N_c/2$ of the solution curves are likely to be mutated. Figure 4 shows the mutation process in a solution curve of a certain child. As in the crossover process, some new information is incorporated in the children while maintaining the smoothness of the resulting solution curves.

(6) *Replacement.* In this step, the parent population is totally or partially replaced by the offspring population depending on the replacement scheme used. This completes the "life cycle" of population.

(7) *Termination.* CGA is terminated when some convergence criterion is met. Possible convergence criteria are the fitness of the best individual so far found exceeds a threshold value, the maximum number of generations is reached, or the progress limit (the improvement in the fitness value of the best member of the population over a specified number of generations being less than some predefined threshold) is reached. After terminating the algorithm, the optimal solution of the problem is the best individual so far found.

To summarize the evolution process in CGA, an individual is a candidate solution of the required solution curves; that is, each individual consists of N_c solution curves, each consisting of N_t variables. This results in a two-dimensional array of the size $N_c \times N_t$. The population undergoes the selection process, which results in a mating pool among which pairs of individuals are crossed with probability P_{ci}. Within that pair of parents, individual solution curves are crossed over with probability P_{cc}. This process results in an offspring generation where every individual child undergoes mutation with probability P_{mi}. Within that child, individual solution curves are mutated with probability P_{mc}. After that, the next generation is produced according to the replacement strategy applied.

This process is repeated till the convergence criterion is met where the N_c solution curves of the best individual are the required solution curves. The final goal of discovering the required solution curves is translated into finding the fittest individual in genetic terms. It is to be noted that the two functions used in the initialization phase of the CGA will smoothly oscillate between the two ends with a maximum number of single oscillations. If the final solution curves have more smooth oscillations than one oscillation, then this will be done during the crossover and mutation mechanisms throughout the evolution process. This is actually done by those two operators during the run of the CGA while solving a problem. However, the evaluation step in the CGA will automatically decide whether they have rejected or accepted modification because of their fitness function value.

In addition to the previous operator, the elitism operator is introduced to enhance the performance of the algorithm. The preservation of the best solution or solutions and moving it or them to the next generation is vital to the effectiveness of GA [11, 12]. Elitism is utilized to ensure that the fitness of the best candidate solution in the current population is larger than or equal to that in the previous population.

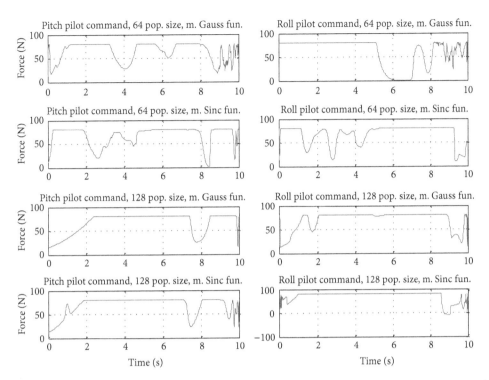

FIGURE 13: Pitch and roll pilot command obtained from CGA represents the pilot command that generates the maximum load factor ($n_{z\,max}$) value. The aircraft model trimmed at 1000 m altitude and 0.3 Mach speed.

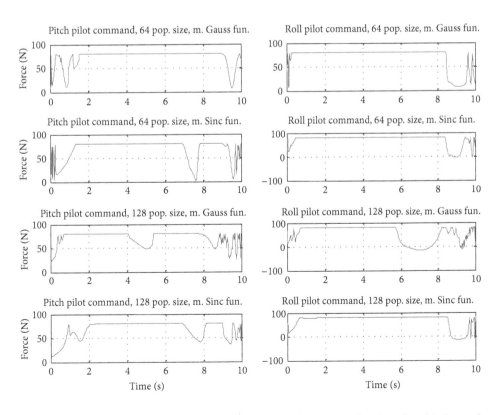

FIGURE 14: Same as Figure 13, but the aircraft model trimmed at 6000 m altitude and 0.6 Mach speed.

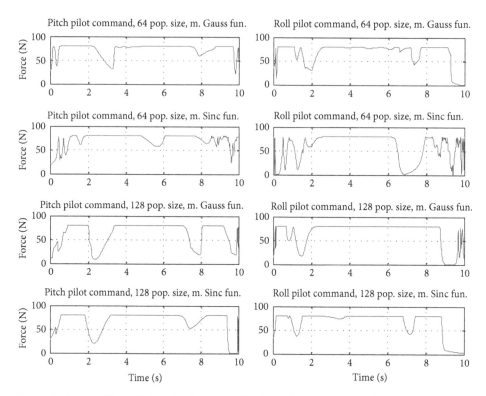

FIGURE 15: Same as Figure 13, but the aircraft model trimmed at 3000 m altitude and 0.8 Mach speed.

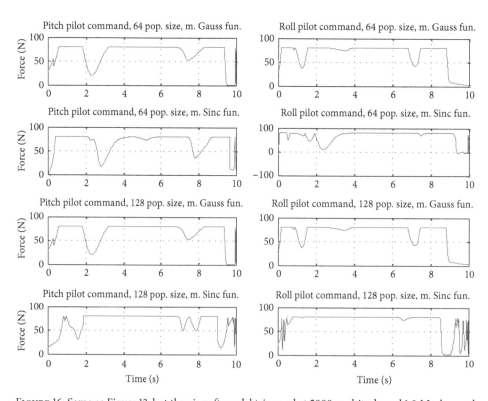

FIGURE 16: Same as Figure 13, but the aircraft model trimmed at 5000 m altitude and 1.0 Mach speed.

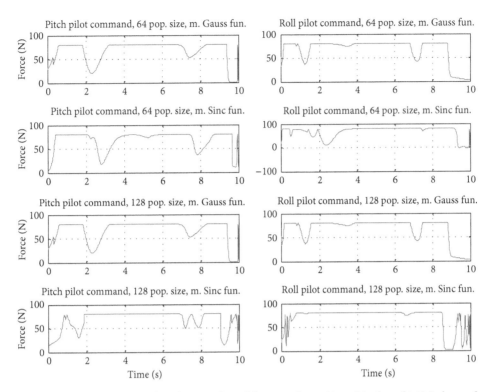

FIGURE 17: Same as Figure 13, but the aircraft model trimmed at 3000 m altitude and 1.2 Mach speed.

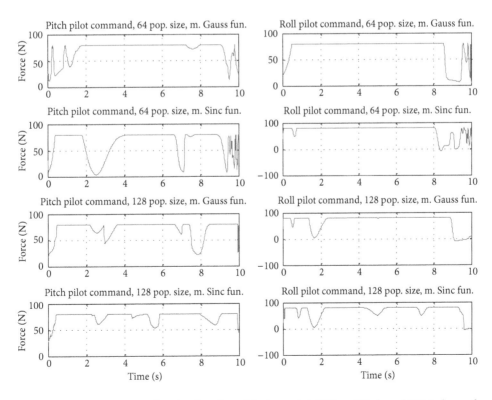

FIGURE 18: Same as Figure 13, but the aircraft model trimmed at 6000 m altitude and 1.2 Mach speed.

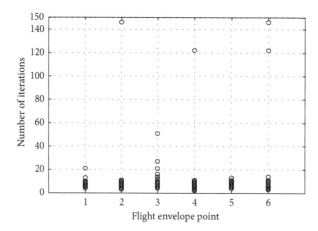

FIGURE 19: The convergence performance of CGA, flight envelope points corresponding to number of iterations with load factor achieve 97.5% of maximum value of it.

TABLE 6: The results using a modified Gauss function and the population size of 64 individuals.

Mach	Alt.	Run 1		Run 2		Run 3		Run 4		Max value
		Iter. no.	AOA	Iter. no.	AOA	Iter. no.	AOA	Iter. no.	AOA	
0.3	1000	208	20.39536	214	19.86801	171	19.35071	209	20.75794	20.75794
0.6	6000	140	19.39938	187	19.80721	148	18.83285	147	19.34686	19.80721
0.8	3000	221	20.04925	282	20.60796	308	21.66616	172	18.59303	21.66616
1	5000	179	20.00234	201	19.7998	150	19.12577	182	20.94341	20.94341
1.2	3000	276	17.59301	185	19.37977	162	20.19032	271	20.91565	20.91565
1.2	6000	212	21.90015	229	15.17864	208	20.39536	208	20.39536	**21.90015**

TABLE 7: Same as Table 6, but using a modified Sinc function.

Mach	Alt.	Run 1		Run 2		Run 3		Run 4		Max value
		Iter. no.	AOA	Iter. no.	AOA	Iter. no.	AOA	Iter. no.	AOA	
0.3	1000	182	19.30103	170	19.04308	251	20.60302	166	19.00672	20.60302
0.6	6000	210	20.24026	207	20.67776	262	20.89506	208	19.15628	20.89506
0.8	3000	175	13.64315	239	21.17564	210	20.24026	207	20.67776	**21.17564**
1	5000	210	20.24026	207	20.67776	262	20.89506	209	18.92149	20.89506
1.2	3000	200	21.0805	364	14.64127	192	19.00408	255	12.94459	21.0805
1.2	6000	450	20.90201	257	12.77573	178	19.91921	181	15.52381	20.90201

In other words, it guarantees that the best fitness in the population is a monotonically nondecreasing function. The above procedure will be closely followed in this work to solve the clearance problem using the ADMIRE aircraft model which is described next.

3. ADMIRE Aircraft Model

The aircraft model used in this work is the ADMIRE (aerodata Model in a Research Environment). It is a non-linear, six-degree-of-freedom simulation model developed by the Swedish Aeronautical Research Institute using aerodata obtained from a generic single-seat, single-engine fighter aircraft with a delta canard configuration. This model is augmented with a flight control system and includes engine dynamics and actuator models and number of uncertain parameters [13]. In state space, this model is represented by a set of twelve first-order coupled nonlinear differential equations [13]:

$$\dot{x}(t) = f(x(t), u(t), \Delta), \tag{6}$$

$$y(t) = h(x(t), u(t)), \tag{7}$$

where $x(t)$ is the state vector with twelve components (velocity, angle of attack, sideslip angle angular rate vector, attitude angles, position, etc.), Δ represent uncertain parameters, $y(t)$ is the output vector, $u(t)$ is the control input vector, whose components are left and right canard deflection angles, left and right inboard/outboard elevator deflection angles, leading edge flap deflection angle, rudder deflection angle, and vertical and horizontal thrust vectoring (see Figure 5 for illustration). The control input is given by

$$u(t) = g(x(t), y_{\text{ref}}(t)), \tag{8}$$

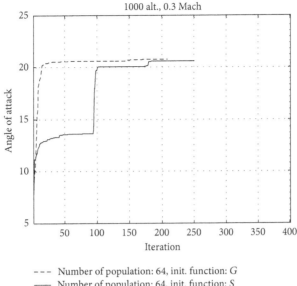

FIGURE 20: Maximum angle of attack versus the iteration (generation). Result using CGA with population size of 64 and both initialization functions: modified Gauss function (G) and modified Sinc function (S). Aircraft model trimmed at 1000 m altitude and 0.3 Mach speed.

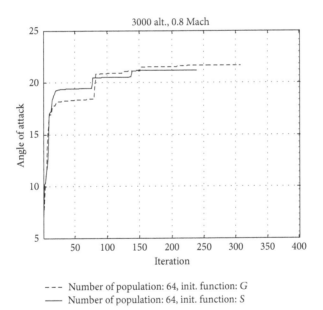

FIGURE 21: Same as Figure 20, but the aircraft model trimmed at 3000 m altitude and 0.8 Mach speed.

where $g(\cdot, \cdot)$ is a standard flight control law, which is set by the ADMIRE model, and $y_{\text{ref}}(t)$ is the reference demand that consists of the pilot inputs such as pitch and roll stick demands. Equations (6), (7), and (8) represent the closed loop dynamics of the aircraft with the flight control law in the loop.

The ADMIRE is augmented with a flight control system, FCS, in order to provide stability and sufficient handling qualities within the operational envelope. The FCS contains a longitudinal and a lateral part. The function of the longitudinal controller is pitch rate control q_{com} below Mach number 0.58 and load factor control n_{zcom} above Mach number 0.62. A blending function is used in the region in between in order

to switch between the two different modes. The longitudinal controller also contains a speed control V_{Tcom}. The lateral controller enables the pilot to perform roll control around the velocity vector of the aircraft $P_{\omega com}$ and to control the sideslip angle β_{com} [13].

The augmented ADMIRE operational flight envelope is defined up to 1.2 Mach and 6000 meter altitude [13]. The longitudinal control law is the gain scheduled over the whole flight envelope with respect to Mach and altitude variations and is designed to ensure robust stability and handling qualities over the entire flight envelope. The model also contains rate limiting and saturation blocks as well as

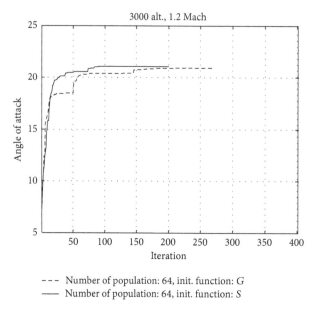

FIGURE 22: Same as Figure 20, but the aircraft model trimmed at 3000 m altitude and 1.2 Mach speed.

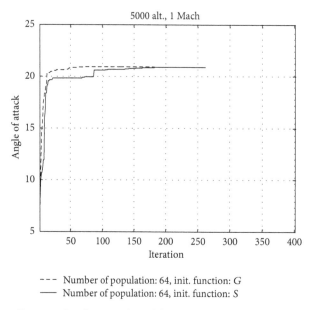

FIGURE 23: Same as Figure 20, but the aircraft model trimmed at 5000 m altitude and 1.0 Mach speed.

nonlinear stick shaping elements in its forward path; more details are found in [13].

4. Results

The CGA as described in Section 2 was used in this work to generate the pilot input signals for both pitch and roll pilot commands. These two command inputs were used during the simulation of ADMIRE model to find the aircraft response. The load factor was extracted from the aircraft response and is used as fitness function in the GCA. The CGA algorithm coupled with ADMIRE aircraft model described in Section 3 was implemented and programmed using the MATLAB platform.

The initial setting of the CGA-related parameters are as follows: the population size was set to 64 and 128 individuals, the crossover probability was set to 0.5, and the mutation probability was set also to 0.5. During the iteration, the initialization of new population was taking place and shared the offspring population by 12.5% of population size. The passed offspring population to the next generation from crossover process was 25% of population size. The rank-based selection strategy was used where the rank-based ratio was set to 10%.

Immigration operator was applied when the improvement in the fitness value of the best individual of the population over 20 generation is less than $1e-6$. The CGA was stopped when one of the following conditions is met. First,

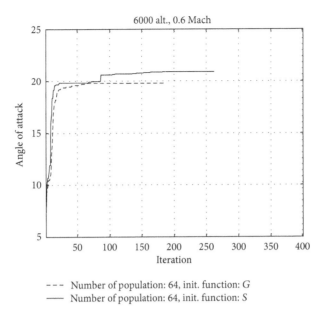

FIGURE 24: Same as Figure 20, but the aircraft model trimmed at 6000 m altitude and 0.6 Mach speed.

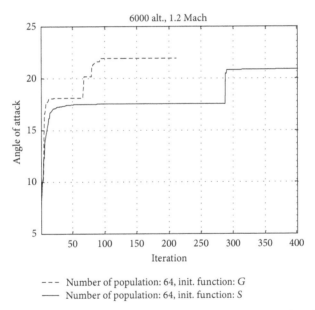

FIGURE 25: Same as Figure 20, but the aircraft model trimmed at 6000 m altitude and 1.2 Mach speed.

the number of immigration processes taking place is more than 100 times and second, when the generation number exceeds 400. Due to the stochastic nature of CGA, a total of four runs were performed for every point in the flight envelope.

Table 1 shows the selected points in the flight envelope used in the present investigation. Four of these points are located on the flight envelope boundary and two are inside it. The selection of these points is similar to that used by other investigators [3–5]. The aircraft model was trimmed to the selected altitude and speed value after that the pilot command inputs generated from the CGA algorithm was applied to aircraft model for 10 seconds.

The simulation was performed using two initialization functions which are the modified Gauss function and the modified Sinc function. For both of these functions the population size is 64 and 128 individuals. Tables 2, 3, 4, and 5 show the results obtained from this simulation. The number of iterations (generation) required to obtain the maximum load factor value are presented in Tables 2–5 for each selected point in the flight envelope, Figure 6. Figures 7, 8, 9, 10, 11, and 12 show the convergence performance of CGA for the selected points in the flight envelope. Each of these figures shows the convergence performance for the cases that results in using the two initialization modified Gauss and modified Sinc functions and two deferent values for the population

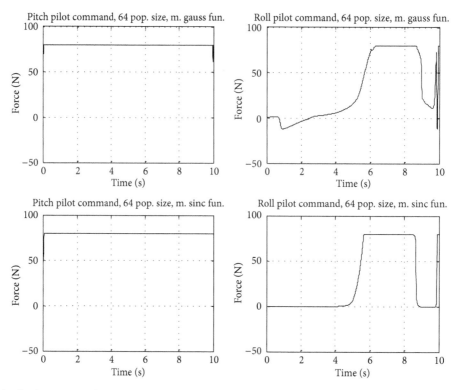

FIGURE 26: Pitch and roll pilot command obtained from CGA represent the pilot command that generate the maximum angle of attack value. The aircraft model trimmed at 1000 m altitude and 0.3 Mach speed.

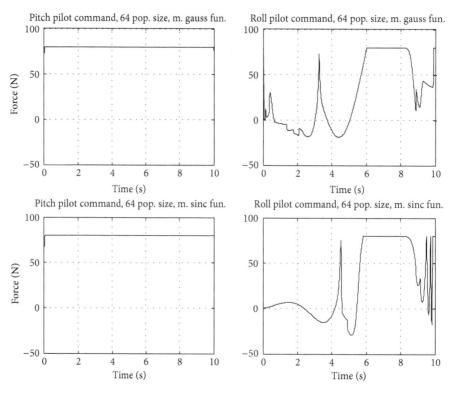

FIGURE 27: Same as Figure 26, but the aircraft model trimmed at 6000 m altitude and 0.6 Mach speed.

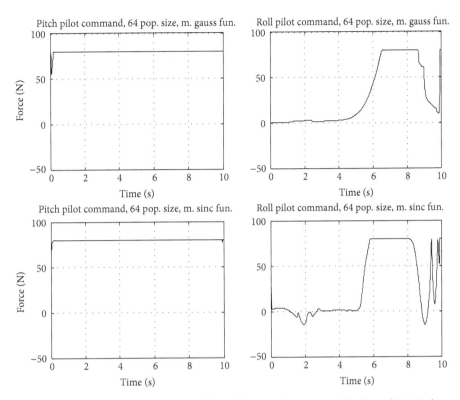

FIGURE 28: Same as Figure 26, but the aircraft model trimmed at 3000 m altitude and 0.8 Mach speed.

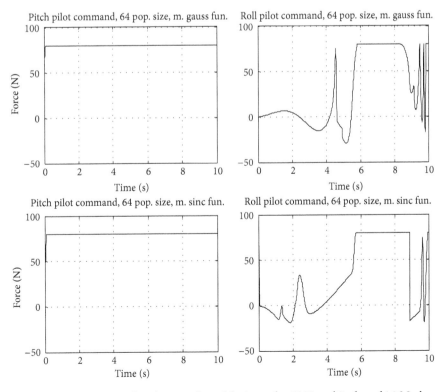

FIGURE 29: Same as Figure 26, but the aircraft model trimmed at 5000 m altitude and 1.0 Mach speed.

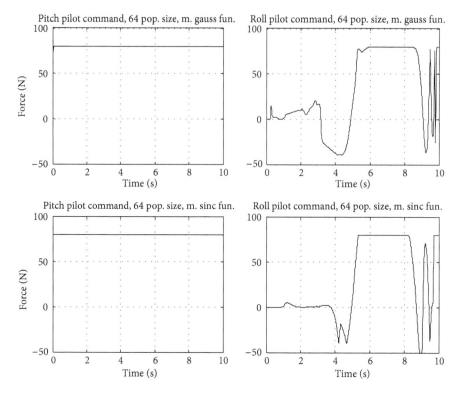

FIGURE 30: Same as Figure 26, but the aircraft model trimmed at 3000 m altitude and 1.2 Mach speed.

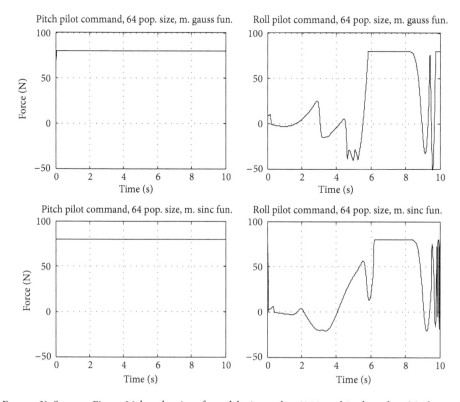

FIGURE 31: Same as Figure 26, but the aircraft model trimmed at 6000 m altitude and 1.2 Mach speed.

sizes: 64 and 128 individuals. Pitch and roll pilot commands obtained from CGA which represent the pilot command that generate the maximum load factor ($n_{z\,max}$) value are shown in Figures 13, 14, 15, 16, 17, and 18. These results show that the maximum value for the load factor is about 10.9 g obtained at 3000 m attitude and 0.8 Mach speed. This means that the load factor criterion exceeds the limit ($-3\,g$–$9\,g$) specified by the clearance process [3]. This result agrees with that obtained by other investigators using other optimization methods [1–5].

The previously mentioned results show that the CGA has a significant convergence speed to the maximum value of the clearance criteria. For example, Figure 19 shows the number of iterations (generations) in the above simulation results in Figures 7–12 for the clearance criteria to reach 97.5% of the maximum value. As can be seen from this figure, the majority of the simulation iterations reached 97.5% of the maximum value in about 20 iterations or less.

Tables 6 and 7 and Figures 20, 21, 22, 23, 24, 25, 26, 27, 28, 29, 30, and 31 show the simulation results when considering the angle of attack as fitness function in CGA. These results show that the maximum value for the angle of attack is 21.9 obtained at 6000 m altitude and 1.2 Mach speed. This means that the angle of attack criteria is within the limit ($-10°$–$26°$) specified by the clearance process [3]. This result also agrees with that obtained by other investigators using other optimization methods [1–5].

5. Discussion and Conclusions

In this work, the CGA was used as a global optimization problem solver to study the clearance process of flight control laws. The CGA was used to find the worst-case pilot inputs found based on the load factor and angle of attack exceedance criteria, for a given speed and altitude, that might stall the aircraft or exceed its structural stress limit. The results presented in this work agreed well with those obtained by other investigators using other optimization methods. In addition, the results in this investigation show that the CGA has a significant convergence speed to the maximum value of the considered clearance criteria for angle of attack and load factor.

Several researches used conventional genetic algorithms and other optimization methods to find the worst-case combination but with some restriction on the pilot command signal such as parameterizing the pilot signals and then solving the resulting optimization problem. But here in CGA, there is no any restriction on the shape of the pilot command signal.

The parallel implementation of the CGA is currently under consideration by the authors to reduce the computational burden of genetic algorithms.

References

[1] M. Selier, C. Fielding, U. Korte, and R. Luckner, "New analysis techniques for clearance of flight control laws," in *AIAA Guidance, Navigation and Control Conference*, pp. 11–14, Austin, Tex, USA, August 2003.

[2] P. P. Menon, J. Kim, D. G. Bates, and I. Postlethwaite, "Improved clearance of flight control laws using hybrid optimisation," in *Proceedings of the IEEE Conference on Cybernetics and Intelligent Systems*, pp. 676–681, Singapore, December 2004.

[3] C. Fielding, A. Varga, S. Bennani, and M. Selier, Eds., *Advanced Techniques for Clearance of Flight Control Laws*, Springer, 2002.

[4] D. Skoogh, P. Eliasson, F. Berefelt, R. Amiree, D. Tourde, and L. Forssell, "Clearance of flight control laws for time varying pilot input signals," in *Proceedings of the 6th IFAC Symposium on Robust Control Design*, pp. 16–18, Haifa, Israel, June 2009.

[5] P. P. Menon, J. Kim, D. G. Bates, and I. Postlethwaite, "Computation of worst-case pilots for clearance of flight control laws," in *Proceedings of the 16th Triennial World Congress*, Prague, Czech Republic, 2005.

[6] Z. S. Abo-Hammour, N. M. Mirza, S. M. Mirza, and M. Arif, "Cartesian path generation of robot manipulators using continuous genetic algorithms," *Robotics and Autonomous Systems*, vol. 41, no. 4, pp. 179–223, 2002.

[7] Z. S. Abo-Hammour, M. Yusuf, N. M. Mirza, S. M. Mirza, M. Arif, and J. Khurshid, "Numerical solution of second-order, two-point boundary value problems using continuous genetic algorithms," *International Journal for Numerical Methods in Engineering*, vol. 61, no. 8, pp. 1219–1242, 2004.

[8] Z. S. Abo-Hammour, A. G. Asasfeh, A. M. Al-Smadi, and O. M. K. Alsmadi, "A novel continuous genetic algorithm for the solution of optimal control problems," *Optimal Control Applications and Methods*, vol. 32, no. 4, pp. 414–432, 2011.

[9] D. E. Goldberg, *Genetic Algorithms in Search, Optimization, and Machine Learning*, Addison-Wesley, 1989.

[10] D. Sarkar and J. M. Modak, "Genetic algorithms with filters for optimal control problems in fed-batch bioreactors," *Bioprocess and Biosystems Engineering*, vol. 26, no. 5, pp. 295–306, 2004.

[11] Z. Michalewicz, C. Z. Janikow, and J. B. Krawczyk, "A modified genetic algorithm for optimal control problems," *Computers and Mathematics with Applications*, vol. 23, no. 12, pp. 83–94, 1992.

[12] Z. Michalewicz, J. B. Krawczyk, M. Kazemi, and C. Z. Janikow, "Genetic algorithms and optimal control problems," in *Proceedings of the 29th IEEE Conference on Decision and Control*, pp. 1664–1666, December 1990.

[13] L. S. Forssell, G. Hovmark, A. Hyden, and F. Johansson, "The aero-data model in a research environment (ADMIRE) for flight control robustness evaluation," GARTUER/TP-119-7, 2001.

10

An Introduction to Swarm Robotics

Iñaki Navarro and Fernando Matía

ETSI Industriales, Universidad Politécnica de Madrid, c/José Gutiérrez Abascal, 2, 28006 Madrid, Spain

Correspondence should be addressed to Iñaki Navarro; inaki.navarro@upm.es

Academic Editors: C. A. G. Soerensen and A. Zavala-Rio

Swarm robotics is a field of multi-robotics in which large number of robots are coordinated in a distributed and decentralised way. It is based on the use of local rules, and simple robots compared to the complexity of the task to achieve, and inspired by social insects. Large number of simple robots can perform complex tasks in a more efficient way than a single robot, giving robustness and flexibility to the group. In this article, an overview of swarm robotics is given, describing its main properties and characteristics and comparing it to general multi-robotic systems. A review of different research works and experimental results, together with a discussion of the future swarm robotics in real world applications completes this work.

1. Introduction

Swarm robotics is the study of how to coordinate large groups of relatively simple robots through the use of local rules. It takes its inspiration from societies of insects that can perform tasks that are beyond the capabilities of the individuals. Beni [1] describes this kind of robots' coordination as follows:

> *The group of robots is not just a group. It has some special characteristics, which are found in swarms of insects, that is, decentralised control, lack of synchronisation, simple and (quasi) identical members.*

This paper summarises the research performed during the last years in this field of multi-robotic systems. The aim is to give a glimpse of swarm robotics and its applications. In Section 2, the motivation and inspiration of swarm robotics taken from social insects is explained. Section 3 continues addressing the main characteristics of swarm robotics. The relationship of swarm robotics with multi-robotic systems in general is stated in Section 4. Different robotic platforms and simulators suitable for swarm-robotic experimentation are described in Section 5. Section 6 surveys the different results in solving tasks and performing basic behaviours using a swarm-robotic approach. Present and future real applications are depicted in Section 7. Lastly, in Section 8 the main ideas of this survey are summarised.

2. Social Insect Motivation and Inspiration

The collective behaviours of social insects, such as the honeybee's dance, the wasp's nest-building, the construction of the termite mound, or the trail following of ants, were considered for a long time strange and mysterious aspects of biology. Researchers have demonstrated in recent decades that individuals do not need any representation or sophisticated knowledge to produce such complex behaviours [2]. In social insects, the individuals are not informed about the global status of the colony. There exists no leader that guides all the other individuals in order to accomplish their goals. The knowledge of the swarm is distributed throughout all the agents, where an individual is not able to accomplish its task without the rest of the swarm.

Social insects are able to exchange information, and for instance, communicate the location of a food source, a favourable foraging zone or the presence of danger to their mates. This interaction between the individuals is based on the concept of locality, where there is no knowledge about the overall situation. The implicit communication through changes made in the environment is called stigmergy [3, 4]. Insects modify their behaviours because of the previous

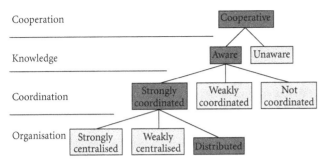

FIGURE 1: Taxonomy from Iocchi et al. [6]. For each level the corresponding type of system is marked in dark grey for a swarm-robotic system.

changes made by their mates in the environment. This can be seen in the nest construction of termites, where the changes in the behaviours of the workers are determined by the structure of the nest [5].

Organisation emerges from the interactions between the individuals and between individuals and the environment. These interactions are propagated throughout the colony and therefore the colony can solve tasks that could not be solved by a sole individual. These collective behaviours are defined as self-organising behaviours. Self-organisation theories, borrowed from physics and chemistry domains, can be used to explain how social insects exhibit complex collective behaviour that emerges from interactions of individuals behaving simply [5]. Self-organisation relies on the combination of the following four basic rules: *positive feedback, negative feedback, randomness,* and *multiple interactions* [5].

Şahin [7] lists some properties seen in social insects as desirable in multi-robotic systems: robustness, the robot swarm must be able to work even if some of the individuals fail, or there are disturbances in the environment; flexibility, the swarm must be able to create different solutions for different tasks, and be able to change each robot role depending on the needs of the moment; scalability, the robot swarm should be able to work in different group sizes, from few individuals to thousands of them.

3. Main Characteristics

In order to understand what swarm robotics is, a definition taken from Sahin [7] is given:

> Swarm robotics is the study of how large number of relatively simple physically embodied agents can be designed such that a desired collective behaviour emerges from the local interactions among agents and between the agents and the environment.

This definition is complemented with a set of criteria in order to have a better understanding and be able to differentiate it from other multi-robot types of systems [7].

(i) The robots of the swarm must be autonomous robots, able to sense and actuate in a real environment.

(ii) The number of robots in the swarm must be large or at least the control rules allow it.

(iii) Robots must be homogeneous. There can exist different types of robots in the swarm, but these groups must not be too many.

(iv) The robots must be incapable or inefficient respect to the main task they have to solve, this is, they need to collaborate in order to succeed or to improve the performance.

(v) Robots have only local communication and sensing capabilities. It ensures the coordination is distributed, so scalability becomes one of the properties of the system.

4. Swarm Robotics and Multi-Robotic Systems

In this section, we classify and characterise swarm robotics using the most known taxonomies and classifications in the multi-robotic systems' literature. Dudek et al. define a taxonomy [8] in which different axes are used to characterise multi-robotic architectures using their properties. The taxonomy axes are summarised in Table 1, directly extracted from the author. Using this classification, properties are assigned to each one of the axes, for a generic swarm-robotic architecture, although these properties would depend on the concrete architecture. *Collective Size* is SIZE-INF, that is, number of robots $N \gg 1$, in opposition to SIZE-LIM, where the number of robots N is small compared to the size of the task or environment. This expresses the scalability aimed in swarm-robotic systems. *Communication Range* is COM-NEAR, robots can only communicate with robots which are close enough. *Communication Topology* for a swarm system would be generally TOP-GRAPH, robots are linked in a general graph. *Communication Bandwidth* is BAND-MOTION, communication costs are of the same magnitude as the cost of moving the robot between locations. *Collective Reconfigurability* is generally ARR-COMM, this is, coordinated rearrangement with members that communicate; but it could also be ARR-DYN, dynamic arrangement, positions can change arbitrarily. *Process Ability* is PROC-TME, where computational model is a turing machine equivalent. Lastly, *Collective Composition* is CMP-HOM, meaning that robots are homogeneous.

Iocchi et al. present a taxonomy [6] structured in different levels. The first level is *Cooperation*, which includes a situation in which several robots perform a common task. Second level is *Knowledge*, which distinguishes whether robots know of the existence of other robots (*Aware*) or not (*Unaware*). Third level is *Coordination*, to differentiate the degree in which robots take into account the actions executed by other robots. According to the authors of the taxonomy this can be: *Strongly Coordinated, Weakly Coordinated,* or *Not Coordinated.* The last level is *Organisation*, which distinguishes between *Centralised* systems, where there exists a robot that is in charge of organising other robots' work, and *Distributed* systems, where robots are autonomous in their decisions, that is, there are no leaders. According to this taxonomy, swarm-robotic systems are: *Cooperative, Aware, Strongly Coordinated*

TABLE 1: Taxonomy axes and explanation from Dudek et al. [8].

Axis	Description
Collective size	Number of robots in the collective.
Communication range	Maximum communication range.
Communication topology	Of the robots in the communication range, those which can be communicated with.
Communication Bandwidth	How much information the robots can send to each other.
Collective reconfigurability	The rate at which the organisation of the collective can be modified.
Process ability	The computational model used by the robots.
Collective composition	Are the robots homogeneous or heterogeneous.

(they could also be *Weakly Coordinated*), and *Distributed*. A schematic of the taxonomy is shown in Figure 1, where for each level the corresponding type of system is marked in dark grey for a swarm-robotic system.

Cao et al. define a not so complete taxonomy [9]. It differentiates among *centralised* and *decentralised* architectures. *Decentralised* can be *distributed*, if all robots are equal with respect to control; or *hierarchical* if there exists a local centralisation. It also identifies between *homogeneous* and *heterogeneous* individuals. Using this taxonomy swarm systems are: *decentralised*, *distributed*, and *homogeneous*.

Some of the characteristics of multi-robotic systems can be extrapolated to swarm-robotic systems. We borrow here from Ronald Arkin [10] a list of advantages and disadvantages of multi-robotic systems compared to single-robot systems. Advantages of multi-robotic approaches are the following.

(i) Improved performance: if tasks can be decomposable then by using parallelism, groups can make tasks to be performed more efficiently.

(ii) Task enablement: groups of robots can do certain tasks that are impossible for a single robot.

(iii) Distributed sensing: the range of sensing of a group of robots is wider than the range of a single robot.

(iv) Distributed action: a group a robots can actuate in different places at the same time.

(v) Fault tolerance: under certain conditions, the failure of a single robot within a group does not imply that the given task cannot be accomplished, thanks to the redundancy of the system.

Drawbacks are the following.

(i) Interference: robots in a group can interfere between them, due to collisions, occlusions, and so forth.

(ii) Uncertainty concerning other robots' intentions: coordination requires to know what other robots are doing. If this is not clear robots can compete instead of cooperate.

(iii) Overall system cost: the fact of using more than one robot can make the economical cost bigger. This is ideally not the case of swarm-robotic systems, which intend to use many cheap and simple robots which total cost is under the cost of a more complex single robot carrying out the same task.

5. Experimental Platforms in Swarm Robotics

In this section, the different experimental platforms used in the most relevant swarm-robotic experiments found in literature are described, including robotic platforms and simulators.

5.1. Robotic Platforms. Several robotic platforms used in swarm-robotic experiments in different laboratories are summarised in Table 2. These platforms are the following.

(i) Khepera robot [11], for research and educational purposes, developed by École Polytechnique Fédérale de Lausanne (EPFL, Switzerland), widely used in the past, nowadays has fallen in disuse;

(ii) Khepera III robot (http://www.k-team.com/) [12], designed by K-Team together with EPFL;

(iii) e-puck robot (http://www.e-puck.org/) [13], designed at EPFL for educational purposes;

(iv) The miniature Alice robot [14] also developed at EPFL;

(v) Jasmine robot (http://www.swarmrobot.org/) [15], developed under the I-swarm project;

(vi) I-Swarm robot (http://www.i-swarm.org/) [16], very small, also developed by the I-swarm project;

(vii) S-Bot (http://www.swarm-bots.org/) [17], very versatile, with many actuators, developed in the Swarm-bots project;

(viii) Kobot (http://www.kovan.ceng.metu.edu.tr/) [18], designed by Middle East Technical University (Turkey);

(ix) SwarmBot (http://www.irobot.com/) [19], designed by i-Robot company for research.

In Table 2, the column *Relative Positioning System* indicates if the robots possess the ability to determine the relative positions of their nearby robots. This sensor is quite useful and necessary in many swarm-robotic tasks. Some of them are based on the emission of an infrared signal by a robot and the estimate of the distance by its neighbours depending on the strength of the received signal [12, 20]. Others work by emitting an ultrasound pulse at the same time than a radio signal, and estimating the distance taking into account the time difference in the reception of both signals [21, 22]. There are also robots that use a camera to detect and estimate the

TABLE 2: Summary of the main robotic platforms used in swarm experiments.

Name	Size (mm) (diam.) or ($l \times w$)	Actuators	Computing capabilities	Sensors	Communications	Relative positioning system	Development
Khepera	55	Wheeled (differential drive)	Motorola MC68331	8 IR	RS232 Wired link	—	Research Commercial
Khepera III	120	Wheeled (differential drive)	PXA-255 (400 MHz) Linux and dsPICs	11 IR 5 ultra sound	WIFI and bluetooth	Expansion (IR based)	Research Commercial
e-puck	75	Wheeled (differential drive)	dsPIC	11 infrared (IR) Contact ring Colour camera	Bluetooth	Expansion (IR based)	Open source Commercial Research and Edu.
Alice	20×20	Wheeled (differential drive)	Microchip PIC	IR proximity and light Linear camera	Radio (115 kbit/s)	—	Research Non commercial
Jasmine	23×23	Wheeled (differential drive)	2 ATMega microcontrollers	8 IR	IR	Integrated (IR based)	Open source Research
I-Swarm robot	3×3	Micro legged	[a]	[a]	[a]	—	Research Non commercial
S-Bot	120	Wheeled (differential drive) 2 Grippers	XSclae (400 Mhz) Linux PICs	15 Proximity OmniCamera Microphone, Temp.	WIFI	Camera based	Research Non commercial
Kobot	120	Wheeled (differential drive)	PXA-255 (200 MHz) and PICs	8 IR Colour camera	Zigbee	Integrated (IR based)	Research Non commercial
SwarmBot	127×127	Wheeled (differential drive)	ARM (40 Mhz) and FPGA 200 kgate	IR, light sensors Contact, camera	IR based (Local)	Integrated (IR based)	Research Non commercial

[a]Information not available.

position of nearby robots that are equipped with markers [23–25].

5.2. Simulators.

There exist many mobile robotic simulators available which can be used for multi-robotic experiments, and more concretely for swarm-robotic experiments. They differ not only in their technical aspects but also in the license and cost. We summarise them, along with comments on their use on swarm-robotic applications in the following paragraphs.

Player/Stage/Gazebo (http://playerstage.sourceforge.net/) [26] is an open source simulator with multi-robotic capabilities and a wide set of available robots and sensors ready to use. The use for swarm-robotic experiments is analysed for 2D simulations [27] with very good results. Runtime scales approximately linearly with population sizes up to at least 100,000 simple robots. It works on real time for 1000 robots running a simple program. It is a good solution for swarm robotic experiments.

Webots (http://www.cyberbotics.com/) [28] is a realistic, commercial mobile simulator that allows multi-robot simulation, with already built models of real robots. It is 3D, simulating physics and collisions. According to our experience, its performance when working with more than 100 robots decreases very fast, making the simulations with a large number of robots difficult.

Microsoft Robotics Studio [29] is a simulator developed by Microsoft Corporation. It allows multi-robotic simulation. It requires a Windows platform to run.

SwarmBot3D [17] is a simulator for multi-robotics but designed specifically for the S-Bot robot of the SwarmBot project.

6. Experimental Basic Behaviours and Tasks in Swarm Robotics

A collection of the most representative experimental works in Swarm Robotics is depicted in this section. The different experimental results are organised grouping them depending on the tasks or behaviours carried out by the swarms. Some of the behaviours, such as *aggregation* and *collective movement*, are quite basic and constitute a previous level for more complex tasks. They are presented in increasing order of complexity.

6.1. Aggregation.

In order to perform other tasks, such as collective movement, self-assembly and pattern formation, or to exchange information, robots must initially gather. This aggregation problem has been studied from a swarm-robotic approach by several researchers.

Trianni et al. [30] perform experiments using an evolutionary algorithm on simulated S-Bot robots. The sensory inputs are the proximity sensors and the microphones. The actuators are the motors and the speakers. One of the evolved solutions is scalable. Bahçeci and Şahin [31] also use evolutionary algorithms and simulated S-bot robots, leading to scalable results, although their work is rather focused on evolutionary algorithms than on aggregation.

Soysal and Sahin [32] use an algorithm based on a probabilistic finite state machine for aggregation. They develop a macroscopic model of it and compares it with simulation results. Dimarogonas and Kyriakopoulos [33] propose a distributed aggregation algorithm based on potential functions consisting on: a repulsive force for obstacle avoidance and a attractive force for aggregation. They analyse mathematically its convergence and carry out simulated experiments with nine robots. Lastly, Garnier et al. [34] implement a biological model based on cockroach aggregation on Alice robots.

6.2. Dispersion.

The aim of dispersion is to distribute the robots in space to cover it as much area as possible, usually without losing the connectivity between them. The swarm can work, when dispersed, as a distributed sensor, but also as a means for exploration.

Dispersion has been studied by different researchers both using real robots and in simulation. Howard et al. [35] present a potential field algorithm for the deployment of robots, in which robots are repelled by obstacles and other robots. The approach is distributed and does not require centralised localisation, leading to a scalable solution. The work is conducted only in simulation.

In [36], the authors propose and test in simulation a distributed algorithm for dispersion based on the read wireless intensity signals and a potential field approach. According to them, and although robots do not have information about the bearing to neighbouring robots, the algorithm successfully disperses the robots. Ludwig and Gini [37] and Damer et al. [38] also only use the wireless intensity for dispersion of a swarm of robots. They use a more elaborated algorithm that takes into account a graph of the neighbouring robots and the received signal intensities. They reach successful results in more complicated environments than the proposed in [36]. The fact that just wireless signal intensities are needed in these algorithms makes them quite attractive since they can be used with very simple robots not provided with relative positioning systems.

McLurkin and Smith [39] show the performance of a set of distributed algorithms for the dispersion of a large group of robots, where only inter-robot communications and sensing of other robots' positions is used. The network connection of the swarm is maintained, creating a route to the initial positions where chargers were placed. The dispersion allows robots to explore large indoor environments. Experiments were run with up to 108 real SwamBots, showing the algorithm's scalability.

In [40], a distributed algorithm for dispersing a set of robots in the environment at the same time that robots aggregate in areas of interest is presented and tested. Experiments done with 16 real SwarmBot robots show the success of the algorithm.

The coverage problem is related to dispersion. Robots need to disperse and detect the borders of the environment. Correll et al. [41] present a set of distributed and scalable algorithms for covering the boundaries of elements placed in a regular pattern. They show based on experimental results and using up to 30 Alice robots that coverage performance is improved with increasing number of robots.

6.3. Pattern Formation.

Pattern formation is the problem of creating a global shape by changing the positions of the individual robots. Since we are here interested in a swarm-robotic approach, the explained examples will have just local information.

In [42], a swarm of particles form a lattice with both an internal and external defined shape. All the rules that make the particles/robots to aggregate in the desired formation are local, but a global external shape emerges, without having any global information. The algorithm uses virtual springs between neighbouring particles, taking into account how many neighbours they have.

Martinson and Payton [43] describe an algorithm that using a common reference orientation for the robots and local control laws acting in orthogonal axes creates square lattices.

Chaimowicz et al. [44] show an algorithm for placing robots in different shapes and patterns defined by implicit functions. Robots use a distributed approach based on local information to place themselves in the desired contour. Algorithms are tested both in simulation and with real robots.

In [45], a framework to assemble a swarm of robots given a morphology is shown. Using the robots' capability of attaching they demonstrate how S-bot robots self-assemble forming global morphologies. The algorithm is completely distributed, and just local information is used.

6.4. Collective Movement.

Collective movement is the problem of how to coordinate a group of robots and move them together as a group in a cohesive way [46]. It can also serve as a basic behaviour for more complicate tasks. It can be classified into two types: formations and flocking. In the former, robots must maintain predetermined positions and orientations among them. On the other hand, in flocking, robots' relative positions are not strictly enforced.

There exist many architectures for collective movement but only those allowing scalability with increasing number of robots are of interest here. In [47–49], the *Physicomimetics Framework* (PF), which allows to create a self-organised formation by using control laws inspired by physics, is presented and analysed. The controller is fully decentralised; each robot perceives the relative positions of its neighbours and reacts to attractive or repulsive forces, forming triangular lattices. The algorithm is scalable, working for dozens of robots.

Lee and Nak [50] propose a distributed algorithm for collective movement based on lattices. Its convergence is proved using Lyapunov's theorem. In [51], a decentralised algorithm for the collective movement based on lattice formations is proposed. The stability of the algorithm in a particular case of study is proved. Obstacle avoidance is implemented by partitioning the plane into Voronoi regions.

Turgut et al. [52] propose and study a scalable and distributed algorithm for robot flocking. It is based on the heading alignment of the robots and the inter-robot distance control. The algorithm is tested in simulation with up to 1000 robots and with a small group of real robots.

6.5. Task Allocation.

The problem of labour division is not a task as the previous ones, but a problem that can arise in multi-robotic systems and particularly in swarm robotics.

Jones and Matarić [53] present a distributed and scalable algorithm for labour division in swarms of robots. Each robot maintains a history of the activities performed by other robots based on observation, and independently performs a division of labour using this history. It then can modify its own behaviour to accommodate to this division.

In [54], authors propose two different methods for task allocation in a robotic swarm. Tasks are previously announced by certain robots and a number of them must attend to them simultaneously. The first algorithm is based on a gossip communication scheme, and it has better performance than the other, but due to limited robustness to packet loss it might be less scalable. The second is simple and reactive, based on interaction through light signals.

McLurkin and Yamins [55] describe four different algorithms for task allocation and test them using 25 SwarmBot real robots. The four of them result successful and scalable, although needing of different communication requirements.

In [56], a group of robots must solve a complex foraging task that is divided in a collection of subtasks. The authors propose and test with real robots a distributed algorithm based on a state machine that solves the main problem by self-assigning each robot a desired task.

6.6. Source Search.

Swarm robotics can be very useful in search tasks, especially those in which the spatial pattern of the source can be complex as in the case of sound or odour. The odour localisation problem is studied in [57], where robots look for the odour source using a distributed algorithm. Experiments are conducted both in simulation and with real robots.

In [58], authors describe and test a distributed algorithm for localising stationary, time-invariant sources. They use feedback controls motivated by function minimisation theory. They explore two situations: one with global communications, in which robots are able to find the global maximum source; and a second one restricted to local communication, where local maxima are found. Experiments are run in simulation.

6.7. Collective Transport of Objects.

Swarm robotics is very promising in solving the problem object transportation. The use of many robots can represent an advantage because of cooperation handling one object. In addition, the possible parallelism dealing with different objects by several robots at the same time might improve the performance.

Kube and Bonabeau [59] take as inspiration the ant collective transport of preys, where individuals wait for other mates if the transported object is too heavy. In their experiments, performed with real robots, a group of 6 robots is able to collectively push an object towards a destination in a purely distributed way.

Groß and Dorigo [60] solve the problem of transporting different objects by groups of S-Bot robots that self-assemble to cooperate. The algorithms were synthesised using an evolutionary algorithm. The experimental results in simulation show that the algorithm scales with heavier objects by using larger groups of robots (up to 16). But the performance does not scale with the group size, since the mass transported per robot decreases with the number of robots.

In [61], authors discuss and propose the collective transport of objects by collecting them and storing them for later transport. The robots of the swarm would have two different tasks: collecting the objects and placing them in a cart; and collectively move the cart carrying objects.

6.8. Collective Mapping. The problem of collective mapping has not yet been widely studied by the swarm-robotic community. In [62], a set of algorithms for the exploration and mapping of big indoor areas using large amounts of robots is described. In their experiments, they use up to 80 robots spread in a $600\,\text{m}^2$ area. Nevertheless, the mapping is carried out by two groups of two robots that eventually exchange and merge their maps, so it cannot be considered swarm mapping.

Rothermich et al. [63] propose and test (in simulation and with real robots) a method for distributed mapping using a swarm of robots. Each robot can assume two roles: *moving* or *landmark* that are exchanged for the movement of the swarm. In addition, robots have a certain confidence in their localisation estimated position. Using this information, localisation estimates of other robots and sensor measurements they build a collective map.

7. Towards Real World Applications

In the first sections of this paper many interesting and promising properties of swarm robotics have been enlightened. Nevertheless, currently there exist no real commercial applications. The reasons for it are varied. Sahin and Winfield [64] enumerate three of them as follows.

Algorithm Design. Swarm robotics must design both the physical robots and the behaviours of the individual robots, so the global collective behaviour emerges from their interactions. At the moment, no general method exists to go from the individuals to the group behaviour.

Implementation and Test. The use of many real robots needs of good laboratory infrastructure to be able to perform experiments.

Analysis and Modeling. Swarm-robotic systems are usually stochastic, nonlinear, so building mathematical models for validation and optimisation is hard. These models might be necessary for creating safety real world applications.

Winfield et al. [65] discuss the concept of *swarm engineering*, studying the dependability of swarm-robotic systems through a case of study. According to them, some of the future work needed from a dependability point of view is the following.

(i) Mathematical modelling of swarm-robotic systems.

(ii) Work on *safety* analysis at robot and swarm level.

(iii) Develop an approach to the design of emergence.

(iv) Develop methodologies and practises for the testing of swarm systems.

Higgins et al. [66] address the main security challenges that swarm-robotic systems should face in a future. They state that due to the simplicity of swarm-robotic architectures they have to deal with the following problems.

(i) Physical capture of the robots.

(ii) Identity and authentication, robot must know if it is interacting with a robot from its swarm or from an intruder robot.

(iii) Communication attacks, communications can be intercepted or disturbed by an attacker.

The possible real applications of swarm robotics will take special importance when robots get to be mass produced and the costs of building swarms of robots decrease. This is the objective of I-swarm project [67] which aimed at building a swarm of micro robots. The development of technologies such as MEMS (Micro-Electro-Mechanical Systems) will allow to create small and cheap robots.

Swarm robots can perform tasks in which the main goal is to cover a wide region. The robots can disperse and perform monitoring tasks, for example, in forests, lakes, and so forth. It can be really useful for detecting hazardous events, like a leakage of a chemical substance. The main advantage over a sensor network is that the swarm can move and focus on the problem and even act to prevent the consequences of that problem.

In this way swarms of robots can be really useful for dangerous tasks. For example, for mining detection and cleaning. It can be more useful than a unique specialised robot, mainly because of the robustness of the swarm: if one robot fails and the mine explodes, the rest of the swarm continues working. In the case of a single robot this is not possible.

The number of possible applications is really promising, but still the technology must firstly be developed both in the algorithmic and modelling part, and also in the miniaturisation technologies.

8. Summary

An overview of swarm robotics has been given for a better understanding of this field of multi-robot research. The first sections have made an introduction to the topic, showing its main properties and characteristics and placing the field in relation to more general multi-robotic systems. The main tasks and experimental results in swarm robotics and the platforms used have been then summarised. Lastly, the future promising applications together with the problems to overcome in order to reach them have been explained and analysed.

References

[1] G. Beni, "From swarm intelligence to swarm robotics," in *Swarm Robotics Workshop: State-of-the-Art Survey*, E. Şahin and W. Spears, Eds., no. 3342, pp. 1–9, Springer, Berlin, Germany, 2005.

[2] S. Garnier, J. Gautrais, and G. Theraulaz, "The biological principles of swarm intelligence," *Swarm Intelligence*, vol. 1, no. 1, pp. 3–31, 2007.

[3] O. Holland and C. Melhuish, "Stigmergy, self-organization, and sorting in collective robotics," *Artificial Life*, vol. 5, no. 2, pp. 173–202, 1999.

[4] S. Franklin, "Coordination without communication," 2010, http://www.msci.memphis.edu/~franklin/coord.html.

[5] E. Bonabeau, M. Dorigo, and G. Theraulaz, *Swarm Intelligence: From Natural to Artificial Systems*, Oxford University Press, New York, NY, USA, 1999.

[6] L. Iocchi, D. Nardi, and M. Salerno, "Reactivity and deliberation: a survey on multi-robot systems," in *Balancing Reactivity and Social Deliberation in Multi-Agent Systems. From RoboCup to Real-World Applications*, pp. 9–32, Springer, Berlin, Germany, 2001.

[7] E. Şahin, "Swarm robotics: from sources of inspiration to domains of application," in *Swarm Robotics Workshop: State-of-the-Art Survey*, E Şahin and W. Spears, Eds., Lecture Notes in Computer Science, no. 3342, pp. 10–20, Berlin, Germany, 2005.

[8] G. Dudek, M. R. M. Jenkin, E. Milios, and D. Wilkes, "A taxonomy for multi-agent robotics," *Autonomous Robots*, vol. 3, no. 4, pp. 375–397, 1996.

[9] Y. U. Cao, A. S. Fukunaga, and A. B. Kahng, "Cooperative mobile robotics: antecedents and directions," *Autonomous Robots*, vol. 4, no. 1, pp. 226–234, 1997.

[10] C. Ronald Arkin, *Behavior-Based Robotics*, MIT Press, Cambridge, Mass, USA, 1998.

[11] F. Mondada, E. Franzi, and A. Guignard, "The development of Khepera," in *Proceedings of the 1st International Khepera Workshop*, vol. 64 of *HNI-Verlagsschriftenreihe, Heinz Nixdorf Institut*, pp. 7–14, 1999.

[12] J. Pugh, X. Raemy, C. Favre, R. Falconi, and A. Martinoli, "A fast onboard relative positioning module for multirobot systems," *IEEE/ASME Transactions on Mechatronics*, vol. 14, no. 2, pp. 151–162, 2009.

[13] F. Mondada, M. Bonani, and X. Raemy, "The e-puck, a robot designed for education in engineering," in *Proceedings of the 9th Conference on Autonomous Robot Systems and Competitions*, vol. 1, pp. 59–65, 2009.

[14] G. Caprari and R. Siegwart, "Mobile micro-robots ready to use: alice," in *Proceedings of the IEEE IRS/RSJ International Conference on Intelligent Robots and Systems (IROS '05)*, pp. 3845–3850, Edmonton, Canada, August 2005.

[15] S. Kornienko, O. Kornienko, and P. Levi, "Minimalistic approach towards communication and perception in microrobotic swarms," in *Proceedings of the IEEE IRS/RSJ International Conference on Intelligent Robots and Systems (IROS '05)*, pp. 2228–2234, August 2005.

[16] P. Valdastri, P. Corradi, A. Menciassi et al., "Micromanipulation, communication and swarm intelligence issues in a swarm microrobotic platform," *Robotics and Autonomous Systems*, vol. 54, no. 10, pp. 789–804, 2006.

[17] F. Mondada, L. M. Gambardella, D. Floreano, S. Nolfi, J.-L. Deneubourg, and M. Dorigo, "The cooperation of swarm-bots: physical interactions in collective robotics," *IEEE Robotics and Automation Magazine*, vol. 12, no. 2, pp. 21–28, 2005.

[18] A. E. Turgut, F. Gökçe, H. C. Çelikkanat, L. Bayindir, and E. Şahin, "Kobot: a mobile robot designed speci cally for swarm robotics research," Tech. Rep., KOVAN Research Lab, Department of Computer Engineering, Middle East Technical University, 2007.

[19] J. McLurkin, *Stupid robot tricks: a behavior-based distributed algorithm library for programming swarms of robots [M.S. thesis]*, Massachusetts Institute of Technology, 2004.

[20] Á. Gutiérrez, A. Campo, M. Dorigo, D. Amor, L. Magdalena, and F. Monasterio-Huelin, "An open localization and local communication embodied sensor," *Sensors*, vol. 8, no. 11, pp. 7545–7568, 2008.

[21] W. M. Spears, J. C. Hamann, P. M. Maxim et al., "Where are you?" *Lecture Notes in Computer Science*, vol. 4433, pp. 129–143, 2007.

[22] L. E. Navarro-Serment, C. J. J. Paredis, and P. K. Khosla, "A beacon system for the localization of distributed robotic teams," in *Proceedings of the International Conference on Field and Service Robots*, pp. 232–237, Pittsburgh, Pa, USA, September 1999.

[23] S. Nouyan, A. Campo, and M. Dorigo, "Path formation in a robot swarm: self-organized strategies to find your way home," *Swarm Intelligence*, vol. 2, no. 1, pp. 1–23, 2008.

[24] L. E. Parker, B. Kannan, X. Fu, and Y. Tang, "Heterogeneous mobile sensor net deployment using robot herding and line-of-sight formations," in *Proceedings of the IEEE/RSJ International Conference on Intelligent Robots and Systems*, pp. 2488–2493, October 2003.

[25] A. K. Das, R. Fierro, V. Kumar, J. P. Ostrowski, J. Spletzer, and C. J. Taylor, "A vision-based formation control framework," *IEEE Transactions on Robotics and Automation*, vol. 18, no. 5, pp. 813–825, 2002.

[26] B. P. Gerkey, R. T. Vaughan, and A. Howard, "The player/stage project: Tools for multirobot and distributed sensor systems," in *Proceedings of the International Conference on Advanced Robotics*, pp. 317–323, Coimbra, Portugal, July 2003.

[27] R. Vaughan, "Massively multi-robot simulation in stage," *Swarm Intelligence*, vol. 2, no. 2-4, pp. 189–208, 2008.

[28] O. Michel, "Webots: professional mobile robot simulation," *Journal of Advanced Robotics Systems*, vol. 1, no. 1, pp. 39–42, 2004.

[29] J. Jackson, "Microsoft robotics studio: a technical introduction," *IEEE Robotics and Automation Magazine*, vol. 14, no. 4, pp. 82–87, 2007.

[30] V. Trianni, R. Groß, T. H. Labella, E. Şahin, and M. Dorigo, "Evolving aggregation behaviors in a swarm of robots," in *Proceedings of the 7th European Conference on Artificial Life (ECAL '03)*, W. Banzhaf, T. Christaller, P. Dittrich, J. T. Kim, and J. Ziegler, Eds., vol. 2801 of *Lecture Notes in Artificial Intelligence*, pp. 865–874, Springer, Heidelberg, Germany, 2003.

[31] E. Bahçeci and E. Şahin, "Evolving aggregation behaviors for swarm robotic systems: a systematic case study," in *Proceedings of the IEEE Swarm Intelligence Symposium*, pp. 333–340, June 2005.

[32] O. Soysal and E. Şahin, "A macroscopic model for self-organized aggregation in swarm robotic systems," *Lecture Notes in Computer Science*, vol. 4433, pp. 27–42, 2007.

[33] D. V. Dimarogonas and K. J. Kyriakopoulos, "Connectedness preserving distributed swarm aggregation for multiple kinematic robots," *IEEE Transactions on Robotics*, vol. 24, no. 5, pp. 1213–1223, 2008.

[34] S. Garnier, C. Jost, R. Jeanson et al., "Aggregation behaviour as a source of collective decision in a group of cockroach-like-robots," *Lecture Notes in Computer Science*, vol. 3630, pp. 169–178, 2005.

[35] A. Howard, J. Maja Mataric, and S. Gaurav Sukhatme, "Mobile sensor network deployment using potential elds: a distributed, scalable solution to the area coverage problem," in *Proceedings of the 6th International Symposium on Distributed Autonomous Robotics Systems (DARS02)*, Fukuoka, Japan, June 2002.

[36] E. Ugur, A. E. Turgut, and E. Şahin, "Dispersion of a swarm of robots based on realistic wireless intensity signals," in *Proceedings of the 22nd International Symposium on Computer and Information Sciences*, pp. 1–6, November 2007.

[37] L. Ludwig and M. Gini, "Robotic swarm dispersion using wireless intensity signals," in *Distributed Autonomous Robotic Systems*, vol. 7, pp. 135–144, Springer, Tokyo, Japan, 2007.

[38] S. Damer, L. Ludwig, M. A. Lapoint, M. Gini, N. Papanikolopoulos, and J. Budenske, "Dispersion and exploration algorithms for robots in unknown environments," in *Proceedings of the Unmanned Systems Technology VIII*, vol. 6230, no. 1, April 2006.

[39] J. McLurkin and J. Smith, "Distributed algorithms for dispersion in indoor environments using a swarm of autonomous mobile robots," in *Distributed Autonomous Robotic System*, vol. 6, pp. 399–408, Springer, Tokyo, Japan, 2007.

[40] M. Schwager, J. McLurkin, J. J. E. Slotine, and D. Rus, "From theory to practice: distributed coverage control experiments with groups of robots," in *Proceedings of International Symposium on Experimental Robotics*, Athens, Greece, July 2008.

[41] N. Correll, S. Rutishauser, and A. Martinoli, "Comparing coordination schemes for miniature robotic swarms: a case study in boundary coverage of regular structures," in *Proceedings of the 10th International Symposium on Experimental Robotics (ISER '08)*, Springer, 2006.

[42] K. Fujibayashi, S. Murata, K. Sugawara, and M. Yamamura, "Self-organizing formation algorithm for active elements," in *Proceedings of the 21st IEEE Symposium on Reliable Distributed Systems (SRDS '02)*, pp. 416–421, IEEE Computer Society, Washington, DC, USA, October 2002.

[43] E. Martinson and D. Payton, "Lattice formation in mobile autonomous sensor arrays," in *Proceedings of the Swarm Robotics Workshop: State-of-the-art Survey*, E. Şahin and W. Spears, Eds., no. 3342, pp. 98–111, Berlin, Germany, 2005.

[44] L. Chaimowicz, N. Michael, and V. Kumar, "Controlling swarms of robots using interpolated implicit functions," in *Proceedings of the IEEE International Conference on Robotics and Automation (ICRA '05)*, pp. 2487–2492, April 2005.

[45] A. L. Christensen, R. O'Grady, and M. Dorigo, "Morphology control in a multirobot system," *IEEE Robotics and Automation Magazine*, vol. 14, no. 4, pp. 18–25, 2007.

[46] I. Navarro and F. Matía, "A survey of collective movement of mobile robots," Tech. Rep., Universidad Polit ecnica de Madrid, 2010.

[47] W. M. Spears, D. F. Spears, and R. Heil, "A formal analysis of potential energy in a multi-agent system," in *Proceedings of the 3rd International Workshop on Formal Approaches to Agent-Based Systems (FAABS '04)*, pp. 131–145, April 2004.

[48] W. M. Spears, D. F. Spears, J. C. Hamann, and R. Heil, "Distributed, physics-based control of swarms of vehicles," *Autonomous Robots*, vol. 17, no. 2-3, pp. 137–162, 2004.

[49] W. M. Spears, D. F. Spears, R. Heil, W. Kerr, and S. Hettiarachchi, "An overview of physicomimetics," in *Swarm Robotics Workshop: State-of-the-Art Survey*, E. Şahin and W. Spears, Eds., vol. 3342, no. 3342, pp. 84–97, Springer, Berlin, Germany, 2005.

[50] G. Lee and Y. C. Nak, "Self-configurable mobile robot swarms with hole repair capability," in *Proceedings of the IEEE/RSJ International Conference on Intelligent Robots and Systems (IROS '08)*, pp. 1403–1408, September 2008.

[51] M. Lindhé and K. H. Johansson, "A formation control algorithm using voronoi regions," in *CTS-HYCON Workshop on Nonlinear and Hybrid Control*, 2005.

[52] A. E. Turgut, H. Çelikkanat, F. Gökçe, and E. Şahin, "Self-organized flocking in mobile robot swarms," *Swarm Intelligence*, vol. 2, no. 2–4, pp. 97–120, 2008.

[53] C. Jones and M. J. Matarić, "Adaptive division of labor in large-scale minimalist multi-robot systems," in *Proceedings of the IEEE/RSJ International Conference on Intelligent Robots and Systems*, pp. 1969–1974, Las Vegas, Nev, USA, October 2003.

[54] F. Ducatelle, A. Foerster, G. A. Di Caro, and L. M. Gambardella, "New task allocation methods for robotic swarms," in *Proceedings of the 9th IEEE/RAS Conference on Autonomous Robot Systems and Competitions*, Castelo Branco, Portugal, May 2009.

[55] J. McLurkin and D. Yamins, "Dynamic task assignment in robot swarms," in *Proceedings of Robotics: Science and Systems*, Cambridge, Mass, USA, June 2005.

[56] R. Groß, S. Nouyan, M. Bonani, F. Mondada, and M. Dorigo, "Division of labour in selforganised groups," in *Proceedings of the 10th International Conference on Simulation of Adaptive Behavior (SAB '08)*, vol. 5040 of *Lecture Notes in Computer Science*, pp. 426–436, Berlin, Germany, 2008.

[57] A. T. Hayes, A. Martinoli, and R. M. Goodman, "Swarm robotic odor localization: off-line optimization and validation with real robots," *Robotica*, vol. 21, no. 4, pp. 427–441, 2003.

[58] J. E. Hurtado, R. D. Robinett, C. R. Dohrmann, and S. Y. Goldsmith, "Decentralized control for a swarm of vehicles performing source localization," *Journal of Intelligent and Robotic Systems*, vol. 41, no. 1, pp. 1–18, 2004.

[59] C. R. Kube and E. Bonabeau, "Cooperative transport by ants and robots," *Robotics and Autonomous Systems*, vol. 30, no. 1, pp. 85–101, 2000.

[60] R. Groß and M. Dorigo, "Towards group transport by swarms of robots," *International Journal of Bio-Inspired Computation*, vol. 1, no. 1-2, pp. 1–13, 2009.

[61] A. Decugnière, B. Poulain, A. Campo et al., "Enhancing the cooperative transport of multiple objects," in *Proceedings of the Sixth International Conference on Ant Colony Optimization and Swarm Intelligence (ANTS '08)*, vol. 5217 of *Lecture Notes in Computer Science*, pp. 307–314, Springer, September 2008.

[62] A. Howard, L. E. Parker, and G. S. Sukhatme, "The SDR experience: experiments with a large-scale heterogeneous mobile robot team," in *Proceedings of the th International Symposium on Experimental Robotics*, pp. 121–130, Singapore, June 2004.

[63] J. A. Rothermich, M. I. Ecemiş, and P. Gaudiano, "Distributed localization and mapping with a robotic swarm," E. Şahin and W. Spears, Eds., vol. 3342 of *Lecture Notes in Computer Science*, pp. 58–69, Springer, Berlin, Germany.

[64] E. Şahin and A. Winfield, "Special issue on swarm robotics," *Swarm Intelligence*, vol. 2, no. 2–4, pp. 69–72, 2008.

[65] A. Winfield, C. Harper, and J. Nembrini, "Towards dependable swarms and a new discipline of swarm engineering," in *Swarm Robotics Workshop: State-of-the-Art Survey*, E. Şahin and W. Spears, Eds., vol. 3342, pp. 126–142, Berlin, Germany, 2005.

[66] F. Higgins, A. Tomlinson, and K. M. Martin, "Survey on security challenges for swarm robotics," in *Proceedings of the 5th International Conference on Autonomic and Autonomous Systems (ICAS '09)*, pp. 307–312, IEEE Computer Society, Los Alamitos, CA, USA, April 2009.

[67] J. Seyfried, M. Szymanski, N. Bender, R. Estana, M. Thiel, and H. Worn, "The i-swarm project: intelligent small world autonomous robots for micro-manipulation," in *Swarm Robotics Workshop: State-of-the-Art Survey*, E. Şahin and W. Spears, Eds., vol. 3342, pp. 70–83, Springer, Berlin, Germany, 2005.

11

A Theoretical and Experimental Approach of Fuzzy Adaptive Motion Control for Wheeled Autonomous Nonholonomic Vehicles

Maurizio Melluso

CIRIAS-C.I. di Ricerca dell'Automazione e dei Sistemi, University of Palermo, Palermo 90128, Italy

Correspondence should be addressed to Maurizio Melluso; maurizio.melluso@alice.it

Academic Editors: L. Moreno, L. Qinchuan, A. Sabanovic, and K.-T. Song

A new fuzzy adaptive control is applied to solve a problem of motion control of nonholonomic vehicles with two independent wheels actuated by a differential drive. The major objective of this work is to obtain a motion control system by using a new fuzzy inference mechanism where the Lyapunov stability can be ensured. In particular the parameters of the kinematical control law are obtained using a fuzzy mechanism, where the properties of the fuzzy maps have been established to have the stability above. Due to the nonlinear map of the intelligent fuzzy inference mechanism (i.e., fuzzy rules and value of the rule), the parameters above are not constant, but, time after time, based on empirical fuzzy rules, they are updated in function of the values of the tracking errors. Since the fuzzy maps are adjusted based on the control performances, the parameters updating ensures a robustness and fast convergence of the tracking errors. Also, since the vehicle dynamics and kinematics can be completely unknown, dynamical and kinematical adaptive controllers have been added. The proposed fuzzy controller has been implemented for a real nonholonomic electrical vehicle. Therefore, system robustness and stability performance are verified through simulations and experimental studies.

1. Introduction

In recent years much attention has been focused upon the position and orientation control of nonholonomic mechanical systems. Nonholonomic mechanics describe the motion of systems constrained by nonintegrable constraints, that is, constraints on the system velocities that do not arise from constraints on the configurations alone. A mobile autonomous wheeled vehicle with two wheels actuated by a differential drive mechanism, that is, two independent electric DC motors with common axis, is usually studied as a typical nonholonomic system. Kinematical nonholonomic constraints arise in wheeled vehicles under the no-slip constraints. Due to nonholonomic motion, the vehicle above is also underactuated [1]. In fact there are three generalized coordinates that is, lateral position, longitudinal position, and vehicle orientation to be controlled, while there are two control inputs only, that is, steering and longitudinal inputs. Several approaches have been proposed for the synthesis of kinematical controllers for vehicles with nonholonomic

constraints on the motion [2–4]. The kinematical controller is essential to guarantee the vehicle motion along the direction of the orientation. The main idea behind these algorithms is to define velocity control inputs which stabilize the closed loop system. However, in many works [4–6] the parameters of the kinematical control laws are constant and they must be chosen suitably to guarantee the asymptotical stability of the tracking errors. About the dynamical control, backstepping methodologies were treated [4, 7, 8]. Backstepping method is very important since we aim to convert a speed control (high-level control) into a torque control (low-level control) for the wheels. The classical backstepping control for nonholonomic vehicles implies the knowledge of the kinematical and dynamical parameters. Wavelet network-based controller and techniques of "adaptive backstepping" control have been proposed to solve the problem of unknown parameters and/or unstructured unmodeled dynamics [5, 6, 8]. Relatively few results have been presented about the robustness of the motion control of nonholonomic vehicles [9], that is, the problem of vehicle control where there are perturbations of the nonholonomic constraints. About the fuzzy systems, the modern literature is focusing on developing a theory based on Lyapunov stability. Some researchers [10, 11] provide an interesting theory of stability for fuzzy Mamdani control systems. About the fuzzy control applied to nonholonomic vehicles, there are several approaches [12–16]. However, the Lyapunov stability is not assured. A case of study with Lyapunov stability is proposed in [17]. Also the works above are based only on the steering kinematics and assume that there exists *perfect velocity tracking*, that is, the control signals affect the vehicle velocities instantaneously and this is not true. Some works developed adaptive fuzzy controller with Lyapunov stability analysis for manipulators control [18, 19]. About applications to nonholonomic vehicles of fuzzy control with Lyapunov stability, relatively few results have been obtained [20, 21].

In this paper, in order to continue this research line, a fuzzy controller is used to design a stable adaptive kinematical and dynamical control system for a problem of motion control of wheeled autonomous nonholonomic vehicles actuated by a differential drive. This work is an extension of the control strategy proposed in [21].

The contributions of this work include the following:

(1) The use of a new Fuzzy inference mechanism to determine the values of the parameters of the kinematical control laws generating the angular velocities for right and left wheels. So the parameters above are not constant, but they depend on the tracking errors through an intelligent fuzzy system inference, that is, a set of empirical rules and values of the rules. This assures a good robustness and very good convergence of the motion errors;

(2) Exhibiting the formal asymptotical stability proof of the motion errors by employing the Lyapunov's theorem and Barbalat's Lemma based on the input-output properties of the fuzzy inference system;

(3) Taking the full nonholonomic vehicle dynamics, disturbance and unmodeled dynamics into consideration in the vehicle model and fuzzy control;

(4) The extension with an adaptive kinematical and dynamical control and asymptotical stability proof of the adaptive control scheme. In this way the kinematical and dynamical parameters of the vehicle model can be unknown;

(5) Simulation to verify the robustness and the asymptotical stability of the motion errors;

(6) Implementation of the controller and application to a real nonholonomic vehicle to verify the validity of the method.

This paper is organized as follows. Section 2 describes the kinematic and dynamic model of a vehicle with nonholonomic constraints. Section 3.1 presents the fundamental innovation of this paper, that is, the new adaptive fuzzy speed system for motion control of nonholonomic autonomous vehicles. The inputs of the fuzzy system are the tracking errors of the motion control system, while the crisp outputs are the parameters of the kinematic control law. Due to the road conditions and contact between the wheels and the ground, the impact of the vehicle with the environment can cause slipping of the wheels with consequential perturbations violating the nonholonomic constraints. By using our fuzzy solution, the constant parameters of the classical kinematic control law [4] are obviated. In fact, in our approach, the parameters above are nonlinear functions of the tracking errors and this assures a certain robustness with respect to the perturbations above and faster convergence than the adaptive controller shown in [6]. In particular, by inserting the input-output functions of the fuzzy map without approximation into kinematic control law suitably, the input-output properties of the fuzzy system are determined to guarantee the asymptotical stability of the tracking errors which has been proved in Section 3.2. Section 3.3 adds an adaptive kinematical control with stability proof. So the kinematical parameters of the vehicle model may be unknown. In Section 4 a dynamical extension and an adaptive control are presented with stability proof. Several parameters of the dynamic model (i.e., mass, friction, and other disturbances) are unknown; therefore, an adaptation is explained by employing the adaptive backstepping method suitably. In Section 5 some simulation tests in MATLAB environment illustrate the robustness and the asymptotical stability of the tracking errors for the proposed fuzzy control system and we compare our results with the adaptive control without fuzzy proposed in [6]. Section 6 shows experimental results obtained by an implementation of the proposed control system for a real nonholonomic vehicle. Section 7 presents our conclusion.

2. Dynamic and Kinematic Model of a Constrained Nonholonomic Vehicle

In this section forms of the kinematic and dynamic model of a nonholonomic vehicle are presented to develop the control system of the next sections.

Let us consider a mobile nonholonomic vehicle (see Figure 1) with generalized coordinates $\mathbf{q} \in \mathbb{R}^n$, subject to m constraints. The well-known dynamic model [4] is

$$\mathbf{M}(\mathbf{q})\,\ddot{\mathbf{q}} + \mathbf{C}(\mathbf{q},\dot{\mathbf{q}})\,\dot{\mathbf{q}} + \tau_d = \mathbf{E}(\mathbf{q})\,\tau - \mathbf{A}^{\mathbf{T}}(\mathbf{q})\,\lambda, \qquad (1)$$

where $\mathbf{M}(\mathbf{q}) \in \mathbb{R}^{n \times n}$ is a symmetric, positive definite matrix; $\mathbf{C}(\mathbf{q},\dot{\mathbf{q}}) \in \mathbb{R}^{n \times n}$ is the centripetal Coriolis matrix; $\tau_d \in \mathbb{R}^n$ is a bounded unknown disturbance including unstructured and unmodeled dynamics; $\tau \in \mathbb{R}^r$ is the input vector including torques applied to right and left wheel; $\mathbf{A}(\mathbf{q}) \in \mathbb{R}^{m \times n}$ is the matrix of nonholonomic constraints; $\mathbf{E}(\mathbf{q}) \in \mathbb{R}^{n \times r}$ is the input transformation matrix; $\lambda \in \mathbb{R}^m$ is the Lagrange multiplier vector of constraint forces.

Supposing that the m constraints are time invariant, it yields

$$\mathbf{A}(\mathbf{q})\,\dot{\mathbf{q}} = \mathbf{0}. \qquad (2)$$

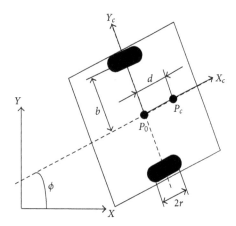

FIGURE 1: Nonholonomic vehicle and coordinate systems.

Let $\mathbf{S}(\mathbf{q})$ be the Jacobian matrix with full rank $n \times (n - m)$ and made up by a set of smooth and linearly independent vectors spanning the null space of $\mathbf{A}(\mathbf{q})$, that is,

$$\mathbf{A}(\mathbf{q})\,\mathbf{S}(\mathbf{q}) = \mathbf{0}. \tag{3}$$

It is possible to find an $(n - m)$ velocity vector $\mathbf{v}$ as it follows

$$\mathbf{v}^{\mathbf{T}} = \begin{bmatrix} u & \omega \end{bmatrix}, \tag{4}$$

where u and ω are the linear and angular body-fixed (Xc, Yc) velocities of the nonholonomic vehicle (see Figure 1). About the kinematical parameters, let r and b be the ray of the wheels and the distance between the driving wheels and the axis of symmetry. The P_0 coordinates, that is, the intersection of the axis of symmetry with the driving wheel axis (see Figure 1), are indicated by (x_0, y_0), while the vehicle orientation is indicated by ϕ. In this way we focus only on three variables x, y, and ϕ, excluding the angular velocities of the right wheel ($\dot{\theta}_r$) and of the left wheel ($\dot{\theta}_l$). The relationship between the vector $[u \ \omega]$ and the vector $[\dot{\theta}_r \ \dot{\theta}_l]$ is the following:

$$\begin{bmatrix} \dot{\theta}_r \\ \dot{\theta}_l \end{bmatrix} = \begin{bmatrix} \dfrac{1}{r} & \dfrac{b}{r} \\ \dfrac{1}{r} & \dfrac{-b}{r} \end{bmatrix} \begin{bmatrix} u \\ \omega \end{bmatrix}. \tag{5}$$

Equations (5) can be rewritten as follows:

$$\boldsymbol{\eta} = \begin{bmatrix} \dfrac{1}{r} & \dfrac{b}{r} \\ \dfrac{1}{r} & \dfrac{-b}{r} \end{bmatrix} \mathbf{v}, \tag{6}$$

where

$$\boldsymbol{\eta}^{\mathbf{T}} = \begin{bmatrix} \dot{\theta}_r & \dot{\theta}_l \end{bmatrix}. \tag{7}$$

Therefore, the model of a nonholonomic vehicle can be described employing five generalized coordinates,

$$\mathbf{q}^{\mathbf{T}} = \begin{bmatrix} x_0 & y_0 & \phi & \theta_r & \theta_l \end{bmatrix}. \tag{8}$$

In the condition of pure rolling and nonslipping, the vehicle can move in perpendicular direction to the driving wheels axis. So we have three constraint equations of the vehicle motion

$$\dot{x}_0 \sin \phi - \dot{y}_0 \cos \phi = 0,$$

$$\dot{x}_0 \cos \phi + \dot{y}_0 \sin \phi + b\dot{\phi} = r\dot{\theta}_r, \tag{9}$$

$$\dot{x}_0 \cos \phi + \dot{y}_0 \sin \phi - b\dot{\phi} = r\dot{\theta}_l.$$

The constraints above can be written in the *Pfaffian* form (2). From (3), the Jacobian matrix $\mathbf{S}(\mathbf{q})$ is

$$\mathbf{S}^{\mathbf{T}}(\mathbf{q}) = \begin{bmatrix} cb \cos \phi & cb \sin \phi & c & 1 & 0 \\ cb \cos \phi & cb \sin \phi & -c & 0 & 1 \end{bmatrix}, \tag{10}$$

where $c = r/2b$.

One of three constraints (9) is holonomic [22]. In fact, by comparing the second and third of (9), it follows

$$\dot{\phi} = c\left(\dot{\theta}_r - \dot{\theta}_l\right). \tag{11}$$

The constraint (11) is integrable. Therefore, by eliminating ϕ or θ_r and θ_l in vector (8), two new vectors of generalized coordinates can be defined as follows

$$\mathbf{q}_1^{\mathbf{T}} = \begin{bmatrix} x_0 & y_0 & \theta_r & \theta_l \end{bmatrix} \tag{12}$$

or

$$\mathbf{q}_2^{\mathbf{T}} = \begin{bmatrix} x_0 & y_0 & \phi \end{bmatrix}. \tag{13}$$

In cases (12) and (13) $\mathbf{A}(\mathbf{q})$ matrix presents nonholonomic constraints only. In particular, in case (12), a new Jacobian matrix is obtained as it follows

$$\mathbf{S}_1^{\mathbf{T}}(\mathbf{q}_1) = \begin{bmatrix} c^2 b \cos\left(\theta_r - \theta_l\right) & c^2 b \sin\left(\theta_r - \theta_l\right) & 1 & 0 \\ c^2 b \cos\left(\theta_r - \theta_l\right) & c^2 b \sin\left(\theta_r - \theta_l\right) & 0 & 1 \end{bmatrix}. \tag{14}$$

In this way the kinematic model is

$$\dot{\mathbf{q}}_1 = \mathbf{S}_1(\mathbf{q}_1)\,\boldsymbol{\eta}. \tag{15}$$

In case (13) the kinematic model is

$$\begin{bmatrix} \dot{x}_0 \\ \dot{y}_0 \\ \dot{\phi} \end{bmatrix} = \begin{bmatrix} cb \cos \phi & cb \cos \phi \\ cb \sin \phi & cb \sin \phi \\ c & -c \end{bmatrix} \begin{bmatrix} \dot{\theta}_r \\ \dot{\theta}_l \end{bmatrix}. \tag{16}$$

From (4) and (13) and by substituting (6) into (16), it yields

$$\dot{\mathbf{q}}_2 = \mathbf{S}_2(\mathbf{q}_2)\,\mathbf{v}, \tag{17}$$

where

$$\mathbf{S}_2(\mathbf{q}_2) = \begin{bmatrix} \cos \phi & 0 \\ \sin \phi & 0 \\ 0 & 1 \end{bmatrix}. \tag{18}$$

About the dynamical parameters, let P_c be the mass center of the vehicle which is on the x-axis, let d be the distance from P_0 to P_c (see Figure 1). For the later description, m_c is the mass of the vehicle without the driving wheels, m_w is the mass of each driving wheels, and I_c, I_w, and I_m are the inertia moments of the body around a vertical axis through P_0, of the wheel with a motor around the wheel axis and of the wheel with a motor around the wheel diameter, respectively. Now the dynamical model in body-fixed coordinates (Xc, Yc) is obtained by differentiating (15), replacing it into (1) and performing additional operations with $\mathbf{S_1}$. It follows

$$\mathbf{S}_1^T \mathbf{M}(\mathbf{q_1}) \mathbf{S_1}\dot{\eta} + \mathbf{S}_1^T \left(\mathbf{M}(\mathbf{q_1}) \dot{\mathbf{S}}_1 + \mathbf{C}(\mathbf{q_1}, \dot{\mathbf{q}}_1) \mathbf{S_1} \right) \eta$$
$$= \mathbf{S}_1^T \mathbf{E}(\mathbf{q_1}) \tau - \mathbf{S}_1^T \tau_{\mathbf{d}} \tag{19}$$

or

$$\overline{\mathbf{M}}\dot{\eta} + \overline{\mathbf{V}}_{\mathbf{m}}(\eta)\eta = \mathbf{B}\tau - \mathbf{S}_1^T \tau_d, \tag{20}$$

where

$$\overline{\mathbf{M}} = \begin{bmatrix} b^2 c^2 m + c^2 I + I_w & b^2 c^2 m - c^2 I \\ b^2 c^2 m - c^2 I & b^2 c^2 m + c^2 I + I_w \end{bmatrix},$$

$$\overline{\mathbf{V}}_{\mathbf{m}}(\eta) = \begin{bmatrix} 0 & 2bc^3 dm_c \left(\dot{\theta}_r - \dot{\theta}_l \right) \\ -2bc^3 dm_c \left(\dot{\theta}_r - \dot{\theta}_l \right) & 0 \end{bmatrix} \tag{21}$$

$$\mathbf{B} = \begin{bmatrix} 1 & 0 \\ 0 & 1 \end{bmatrix}; \qquad \tau = \begin{bmatrix} \tau_r \\ \tau_l \end{bmatrix}$$

and m and I are the dynamical parameters as it follows

$$m = m_c + 2m_w; \qquad I = m_c d^2 + I_c + 2m_w b^2 + 2I_m. \tag{22}$$

Also $\overline{\mathbf{M}} \in \mathbb{R}^{(n-m) \times (n-m)}$ is a symmetric and definite positive matrix, while $\overline{\mathbf{V}}_{\mathbf{m}}(\eta)\eta \in \mathbb{R}^{(n-m) \times 1}$.

3. Adaptive Fuzzy Kinematic Motion Control of Nonholonomic Vehicles and Lyapunov Stability Analysis

In this section the fundamental innovation of this paper is presented, that is, a new fuzzy adaptive motion control system for electric nonholonomic vehicles with two independent wheels.

3.1. Fuzzy Kinematical Motion Control and Preliminary Input-Output Properties of the Fuzzy System for the Lyapunov Stability. Let the references of velocities and positions for a nonholonomic vehicle be

$$\dot{x}_r = u_r \cos \phi_r$$
$$\dot{y}_r = u_r \sin \phi_r \tag{23}$$
$$\dot{\theta}_r = \omega_r,$$

where $u_r > 0$ is the reference linear velocity and ω_r is the reference angular velocity. The tracking errors between the reference position $\mathbf{q_r^T} = [x_r, y_r, \phi_r]$ and the actual position $\mathbf{q^T} = [x, y, \phi]$ can be expressed in the vehicle local frame (Xc, Yc) as [4]

$$\mathbf{e} = \begin{bmatrix} e_x \\ e_y \\ e_\phi \end{bmatrix} = \begin{bmatrix} \cos \phi & \sin \phi & 0 \\ -\sin \phi & \cos \phi & 0 \\ 0 & 0 & 1 \end{bmatrix} \begin{bmatrix} x_r - x \\ y_r - y \\ \phi_r - \phi \end{bmatrix}, \tag{24}$$

where e_x and e_y are the lateral and longitudinal position errors, while e_ϕ is the vehicle orientation error. Note that, time after time, the vector $\mathbf{q_r}(t)$ is the reference motion for the vehicle, while $\mathbf{q}(t)$ is the real motion of the vehicle above. So, differentiating equation system (24) and applying two auxiliary inputs

$$u_1 = -u_c + u_r \cos e_\phi; \qquad u_2 = \omega_r - \omega_c, \tag{25}$$

where u_c and ω_c are the kinematic control laws in terms of steering and longitudinal velocities lead to

$$\begin{bmatrix} \dot{e}_x \\ \dot{e}_y \\ \dot{e}_\phi \end{bmatrix} = \begin{bmatrix} 0 & \omega_c & 0 \\ -\omega_c & 0 & 0 \\ 0 & 0 & 0 \end{bmatrix} \begin{bmatrix} e_x \\ e_y \\ e_\phi \end{bmatrix} + \begin{bmatrix} 0 \\ u_r \sin e_\phi \\ 0 \end{bmatrix} + \begin{bmatrix} 1 & 0 \\ 0 & 0 \\ 0 & 1 \end{bmatrix} \begin{bmatrix} u_1 \\ u_2 \end{bmatrix}. \tag{26}$$

Now a new fuzzy kinematic control law is proposed

$$u_c = u_r \cos e_\phi + k_x(t) e_x,$$
$$\omega_c = \omega_r + u_r \left(k_y(t) e_y + k_\phi(t) \sin e_\phi \right). \tag{27}$$

This control law depends on the error vector (24) and on the following parameters:

$$\mathbf{k^T} = \begin{bmatrix} k_x(t) & k_y(t) & k_\phi(t) \end{bmatrix}. \tag{28}$$

Parameters (28) are provided by a fuzzy controller. The fuzzy controller is used because, in this way, the parameters of the kinematic control law are not constant as in the controllers proposed in [4, 6], but they are nonlinear functions of the tracking errors (24) through an intelligent fuzzy inference system, that is, empirical fuzzy rules and values of the rules. In other words, since the model of the nonholonomic vehicle is highly nonlinear, it is convenient to have nonlinear functions of the tracking errors in the control laws. Since the fuzzy maps are adjusted based on the control performance, the updating of the parameters (28) assures a good robustness and fast convergence. Now the Fuzzy inference system is described. The input and output membership functions are shown in Figures 2 and 3, respectively. The fuzzy rules are shown in Table 1. The input and output memberships are *generalized bell* functions and three linguistic labels are defined as S: small, M: medium, H: High, Opp: opposite.

The inputs of the fuzzification process (see Figure 2) are the absolute values of the tracking errors (cf. (24)), while the outputs of the input memberships are the degree of membership in the qualifying linguistic sets (always the interval between 0 and 1). The input set is a fuzzy singleton. The implemented methods for the logical and for the implication are the "minimum" and the "fuzzy minimum," respectively.

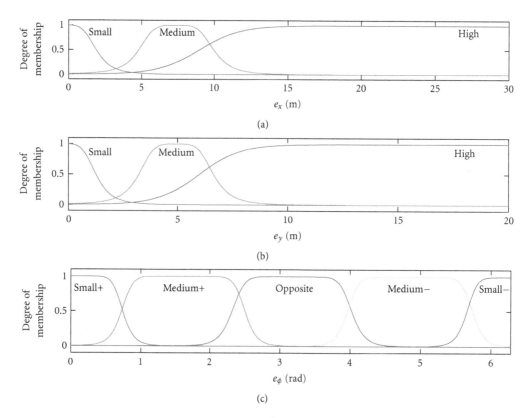

FIGURE 2: Input membership functions.

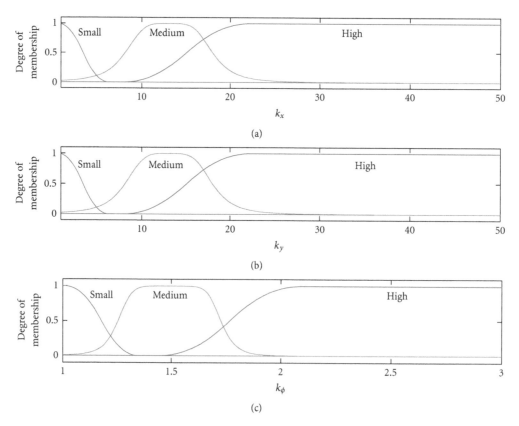

FIGURE 3: Output membership functions.

TABLE 1: Controller rules.

No. Rules	E_x	E_y	E_ϕ	K_x	K_y	K_ϕ
1	S	S	S+	S	S	S
2	S	M	S+	S	M	S
3	S	H	S+	M	H	S
4	M	S	S+	M	S	S
5	M	M	S+	M	M	S
6	M	H	S+	M	H	S
7	H	S	S+	H	M	S
8	H	M	S+	H	M	S
9	H	H	S+	H	H	S
10	S	S	M+	M	M	M
11	S	M	M+	M	M	M
12	S	H	M+	M	H	M
13	M	S	M+	M	M	M
14	M	M	M+	M	M	M
15	M	H	M+	M	H	M
16	H	S	M+	H	M	M
17	H	M	M+	H	M	M
18	H	H	M+	H	H	M
19	S	S	OPP	M	M	H
20	S	M	OPP	M	M	H
21	S	H	OPP	M	H	H
22	M	S	OPP	M	M	H
23	M	M	OPP	M	M	H
24	M	H	OPP	M	H	H
25	H	S	OPP	H	M	H
26	H	M	OPP	H	M	H
27	H	H	OPP	H	H	H
28	S	S	M−	M	M	M
29	S	M	M−	M	M	M
30	S	H	M−	M	H	M
31	M	S	M−	M	M	M
32	M	M	M−	M	M	M
33	M	H	M−	M	H	M
34	H	S	M−	H	M	M
35	H	M	M−	H	M	M
36	H	H	M−	H	H	M
37	S	S	S−	S	S	S
38	S	M	S−	S	M	S
39	S	H	S−	M	H	S
40	M	S	S−	M	S	S
41	M	M	S−	M	M	S
42	M	H	S−	M	H	S
43	H	S	S−	H	M	S
44	H	H	S−	H	H	S
45	H	H	S−	H	H	S

The "fuzzy minimum," method truncates the output fuzzy set opportunely. Since decisions are based on testing of all the

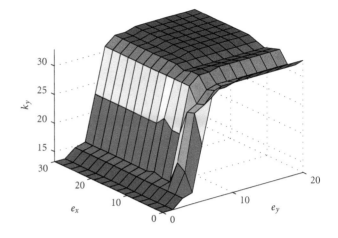

FIGURE 4: k_y versus e_x and e_y.

rules (see Table 1), the aggregation is necessary; therefore, the consequents of each rule have been recombined using a *maximum* (max) method. The used defuzzification method is the "centroid". So the outputs of the fuzzy system are crisp values, that is, the parameters (28) (see Figure 3).

Remark 1. The numerical outputs of the fuzzy inference system depend on the tracking errors (24); therefore, they are time varying functions (cf. (28)).

Remark 2. Since the parameters (28) depend on the tracking errors, the control system of this paper can be more robust and with faster convergence than the conventional controllers [4, 6], where the parameters of the kinematic control law are constant numbers.

Remark 3. About the memberships this remark is essential. The generalized bell functions have been chosen for the smoothness which assures continuous functions to guarantee the Lyapunov stability of the control system.

Remark 4. The parameters k_x, k_y and k_ϕ are positive numbers (see Figure 3) always to assure the stability.

Remark 5. Note that the numerical inputs of the fuzzy system (cf. Figure 2) are the absolute values of the tracking errors (the range of the errors is constituted by positive values only). In any case the sign (positive or negative) of the errors above is considered by the fuzzy control laws (27).

Now Figures 4 and 5 show the fuzzy control surfaces. In particular the plots above show the output k_y of the fuzzy inference mechanism versus two of the inputs. In other words Figures 4 and 5 show the fuzzy map, where the parameter k_y depends on the tracking errors (24) through the fuzzy inference system which has been described. So the maps of Figures 4 and 5 depend on the fuzzy inference system, that is, empirical rules and value of the rules. To assure the Lyapunov stability of the motion control system, one must investigate the input-output properties of the fuzzy system. So, from

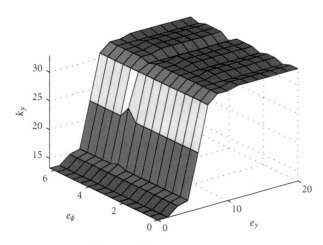

FIGURE 5: k_y versus e_ϕ and e_y.

Figures 2, 3, 4, and 5, the properties of the parameters (28) are the following.

Property 1 (a). The parameters of the kinematical control law (28) are continuous time functions.

Property 2 (a). The vector $\mathbf{k}(\mathbf{e}(t))$ (cf. (28)) is equal to zero if only if $\mathbf{e}$ is equal to zero, that is,

$$\mathbf{k}^{\mathbf{T}}\left(\mathbf{e}\left(t\right)\right) = \left[k_x\left(t\right) \ k_y\left(t\right) \ k_\phi\left(t\right)\right] = \mathbf{0} \Longleftrightarrow \mathbf{e} = \mathbf{0}. \quad (29)$$

Property 3 (a). All the outputs of the fuzzy inference system are positive numbers and are bounded, that is,

$$0 \le k_x\left(t\right) \le k_{x\,\max}; \qquad 0 \le k_y\left(t\right) \le k_{y\,\max}; \quad (30)$$
$$0 \le k_\phi\left(t\right) \le k_{\phi\,\max}.$$

Property 4 (a). Considering $j \in N$ and $M > 0$ and taking into account Property 3 (a) lead to

$$\sum_{j=0}^{M-1}\left[\int_j^{j+1} k_y\left(t\right)dt\right] > 0. \quad (31)$$

Now replacing fuzzy control law (27) into model (26) leads to

$$\dot{\mathbf{e}}^{\mathbf{T}} = \left[\dot{e}_x \ \dot{e}_y \ \dot{e}_\phi\right]$$
$$= \begin{bmatrix} \left(\omega_r + u_r\left(k_y\left(t\right)\right)e_y + k_\phi\left(t\right)\sin e_\phi\right)e_y - k_x\left(t\right)e_x \\ -\left(\omega_r + u_r\left(k_y\left(t\right)e_y + k_\phi\left(t\right)\sin e_\phi\right)e_x + u_r\sin e_\phi\right) \\ -u_r\left(k_y\left(t\right)e_y + k_\phi\left(t\right)\sin e_\phi\right) \end{bmatrix}. \quad (32)$$

3.2. Lyapunov Stability Proof Based on the Input-Output Properties of the Fuzzy System. From the fuzzy inference system, equations, and properties so far, it follows the first main result of this work.

Theorem 6. *Let the kinematical model and the fuzzy kinematical control laws be (17) and (27), respectively. Let the linear*

reference velocity u_r be positive. The Properties 1 (a)–4 (a) are verified for hypothesis. Then the equilibrium state of the nonautonomous closed loop system (32) is the origin of the state space and it is asymptotically stable.

Proof. Since the vector $\mathbf{k}(\mathbf{e})$ (cf. (28)) is equal to zero if only if $\mathbf{e}$ is equal to zero, the equilibrium state of the closed loop system (32) is the origin of the state space. The system (32) is nonautonomous. The following Lyapunov function is chosen:

$$V_0 = \frac{1}{2}\left(e_x^2 + e_y^2\right) + \left(1 - \cos e_\phi\right)\sum_{j=0}^{M-1}\left[\int_j^{j+1} k_y\left(t\right)dt\right], \quad (33)$$

where

$$j \in N, \quad M > 0. \quad (34)$$

For hypothesis it is

$$\sum_{j=0}^{M-1}\left[\int_j^{j+1} k_y\left(t\right)dt\right] > 0. \quad (35)$$

Therefore, the Lyapunov function (33) is positive definite. The time derivative of (33) is

$$\dot{V}_0 = e_x\dot{e}_x + e_y\dot{e}_y + \dot{e}_\phi\sin e_\phi\sum_{j=0}^{M-1}\left[\int_j^{j+1} k_y\left(t\right)dt\right]$$
$$+ \left(1 - \cos e_\phi\right)\frac{d}{dt}\left(\sum_{j=0}^{M-1}\left[\int_j^{j+1} k_y\left(t\right)dt\right]\right), \quad (36)$$

where

$$\frac{d}{dt}\left(\sum_{j=0}^{M-1}\left[\int_j^{j+1} k_y\left(t\right)dt\right]\right) = \sum_{j=0}^{M-1} k_y\left(j\right). \quad (37)$$

By substituting (32) into (36), it yields

$$\dot{V}_0 = -k_x\left(t\right)e_x^2 - u_r k_\phi\left(t\right)\sin^2\left(e_\phi\right)\sum_{j=0}^{M-1}\left[\int_j^{j+1} k_y\left(t\right)dt\right]$$
$$+ \left(1 - \cos e_\phi\right)\sum_{j=0}^{M-1} k_y\left(j\right). \quad (38)$$

Due to Properties 3 (a) and 4 (a) of the fuzzy map, the first and second terms of (38) are negative. Also it results

$$u_r k_\phi\left(t\right)\left(1 - \cos^2 e_\phi\right)\sum_{j=0}^{M-1}\int_j^{j+1} k_y\left(t\right)dt$$
$$> \left(1 - \cos e_\phi\right)\sum_{j=0}^{M-1} k_y\left(j\right). \quad (39)$$

Since the function (39) does not depend on e_y error, it is negative semidefinite. Therefore, vector (24) is bounded and

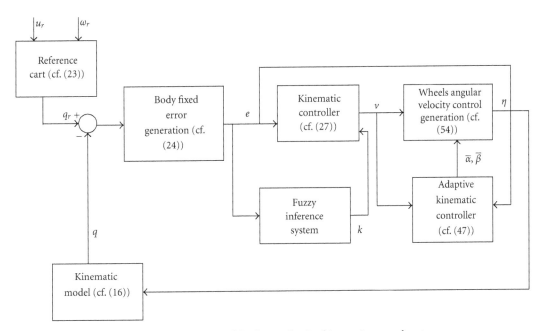

FIGURE 6: Block diagram of the fuzzy adaptive kinematic control system.

the equilibrium state of the closed loop system (32) is stable. It is also possible to calculate the second-time derivative of Lyapunov function (33). Since the second-time derivative of (33) depends on bounded variables, it is a bounded function. Therefore, the function (38) is uniformly continuous. From Barbalat's lemma [23], it yields

$$\lim_{t \to \infty} \dot{V}_0(t) = 0. \tag{40}$$

From (38) and (40), e_x and e_ϕ converge to zero. From the second equation of (32) that is

$$\dot{e}_y = -\left(\omega_r + u_r\left(k_y(t)e_y + k_\phi(t)\sin e_\phi\right)\right)e_x + u_r \sin e_\phi, \tag{41}$$

the function $\dot{e}_y$ converges to zero. Therefore, the steady state error along y-direction is constant. Examining the third equation of (32) leads to

$$\dot{e}_\phi(\infty) = -u_r k_y(\infty)\bar{e}_y, \tag{42}$$

where $\bar{e}_y$ is the steady state value of e_y. Since e_ϕ converges to zero, e_y converges to zero. Now k_y is equal to zero if $\bar{e}_y$ is equal to zero. Therefore, the equilibrium point of the closed loop system (32) is asymptotically stable. □

Remark 7. Note that the proof of Theorem 6 requires the system kinematical parameters of the vehicle to be accurately known.

3.3. Fuzzy Adaptive Kinematic Motion Control with Lyapunov Stability Proof. In this subsection the second main result of this work is explained. An adaptive controller is added to previous fuzzy control and the stability is proved. This step is necessary because the kinematical parameters as the

ray of the wheels and particularly the distance between the driving wheels and the axis of symmetry can be difficult to be determined accurately. In fact without adaptive control one must measure the parameters above manually and this can cause a measurement error perturbing the performances of the control system. Figure 6 shows the block diagram of the fuzzy adaptive control system.

Preliminarily, from (6), (16), and (26) and after simple calculations, the closed loop kinematical control system can be written in the following way

$$\frac{d}{dt}\begin{bmatrix} e_x \\ e_y \\ e_\phi \end{bmatrix} = \dot{\theta}_r \begin{bmatrix} -\dfrac{r}{2} + \dfrac{r}{2b}e_y \\ -\dfrac{r}{2b}e_x \\ -\dfrac{r}{2b} \end{bmatrix} + \dot{\theta}_l \begin{bmatrix} -\dfrac{r}{2} - \dfrac{r}{2b} \\ \dfrac{r}{2b}e_x \\ \dfrac{r}{2b} \end{bmatrix}$$

$$+ \begin{bmatrix} u_r \cos\left(e_\phi\right) \\ u_r \sin\left(e_\phi\right) \\ \omega_r \end{bmatrix}. \tag{43}$$

We set

$$\alpha = \frac{1}{r}; \qquad \beta = \frac{b}{r}. \tag{44}$$

Differential equations (43) can be exploited by considering the estimation errors of the kinematical parameters (44):

$$\widehat{\alpha} = \bar{\alpha} - \alpha; \qquad \widehat{\beta} = \bar{\beta} - \beta, \tag{45}$$

where $\overline{\alpha}$ and $\overline{\beta}$ are the estimated values. It results

$$\frac{d}{dt}\begin{bmatrix} e_x \\ e_y \\ e_\phi \end{bmatrix} = \left(1 + \frac{\widehat{\alpha}}{\alpha}\right)u_c \begin{bmatrix} -1 \\ 0 \\ 0 \end{bmatrix} + \left(1 + \frac{\widehat{\beta}}{\beta}\right)\omega_c \begin{bmatrix} e_y \\ -e_x \\ -1 \end{bmatrix} \quad (46)$$

$$+ \left[u_r \cos\left(e_\phi\right) u_r \sin\left(e_\phi\right) \omega_r\right]^{\mathbf{T}}.$$

Now it is possible to formulate the following theorem.

Theorem 8. *Let the kinematical model and the fuzzy control law be (17) and (27), respectively. If the reference linear and angular velocities are bounded functions and the reference angular velocity converges to zero, by choosing of the following adaptive kinematic control law:*

$$\dot{\widehat{\alpha}} = \gamma e_x u_c \quad \dot{\widehat{\beta}} = \delta \frac{\omega_c \sin\left(e_\phi\right)}{k_y(t)} \quad \gamma, \delta > 0, \quad (47)$$

the components of the vector $[e_x, e_y, e_\phi]^T$ of the closed loop system (46) converge to zero.

Proof. An extended state vector can be defined as

$$\overline{\mathbf{e}}^{\mathbf{T}} = \begin{bmatrix} e_x & e_y & e_\phi & \widehat{\alpha} & \widehat{\beta} \end{bmatrix}. \quad (48)$$

The Lyapunov function can be chosen as it follows

$$V_1 = V_0 + \frac{1}{2\gamma\alpha}\widehat{\alpha}^2 + \frac{1}{2\delta\beta}\widehat{\beta}^2 \quad \gamma, \delta > 0, \quad (49)$$

where V_0 is given by (33). Since V_0 is positive definite, it is obvious that V_1 is positive definite. Substituting the fuzzy control law (27) into (47) and differentiating (49) lead to

$$\dot{V}_1 = \dot{V}_0 + \frac{\widehat{\alpha}}{\gamma\alpha}\left(\dot{\widehat{\alpha}} - \gamma e_x u_c\right) + \frac{\widehat{\beta}}{\delta\beta}\left(\dot{\widehat{\beta}} - \delta\frac{\omega_c \sin\left(e_\phi\right)}{k_y(t)}\right), \quad (50)$$

where u_c and ω_c are given by (27) and $\dot{V}_0$ is given by (38). Function (50) is negative semidefinite if and only if equations (47) are verified. In this case it results

$$\dot{V}_1 = \dot{V}_0. \quad (51)$$

Since the function (51) does not depend on e_y component (cf. (38)), it is negative semidefinite. Therefore, the closed loop system (46) is stable and the components of the state vector (48) are bounded. It is also possible to calculate the second-time derivative of Lyapunov function (49). Since it depends on bounded variables, from Barbalat's lemma it results

$$\lim_{t \to \infty} \dot{V}_1(t) = 0. \quad (52)$$

Therefore, e_x and e_ϕ converge to zero. Now, by substituting (27) into (46), it results

$$\dot{e}_\phi = -\left(1 + \frac{\widehat{\beta}}{\beta}\right)$$

$$\times \left(\omega_r + u_r k_y(t) e_y + k_\phi(t) \sin\left(e_\phi\right)\right) + \omega_r. \quad (53)$$

Since the reference linear velocity u_r, the reference angular velocity ω_r, and the components of state vector (48) are bounded, $\ddot{e}_\phi$ is bounded. Therefore, $\dot{e}_\phi$ is uniformly continuous. Since e_ϕ converges to zero, from Barbalat's lemma, $\dot{e}_\phi$ converges to zero; therefore, from (53) e_y converges to zero only if ω_r converges to zero. $\qquad \square$

Remark 9. From the previous results, the adaptive fuzzy kinematic control law can be written in terms of angular velocities of left ($\dot{\theta}_{lc}$) and right ($\dot{\theta}_{rc}$) wheels as it follows

$$\eta_{\mathbf{c}} = \begin{bmatrix} \dot{\theta}_{rc} \\ \dot{\theta}_{lc} \end{bmatrix} = \begin{bmatrix} \overline{\alpha} & \overline{\beta} \\ \overline{\alpha} & -\overline{\beta} \end{bmatrix}\begin{bmatrix} u_c \\ \omega_c \end{bmatrix}, \quad (54)$$

where $\overline{\alpha}$ and $\overline{\beta}$ are the solutions of the differential equations (47), while u_c and ω_c are the fuzzy control laws given by (27). For Theorems 6 and 8, by employing the adaptive fuzzy kinematic control law (54), the closed loop motion control system of the nonholonomic vehicle is asymptotically stable.

Remark 10. Note that if the kinematical adaptive control law (54) is applied to vehicle directly, then the perfect velocity tracking is assumed and it is not true practically.

Remark 11. About tuning of the fuzzy memberships (cf. Figure 2), one considers the initial conditions of the reference and of the actual positions and orientations. So we have initial values of the motion errors (24). Due to the asymptotical stability and boundedness of the errors above (cf. Theorems 6 and 8), one choices a range of the inputs between zero and the initial values above. In this sense the fuzzy memberships are tuned manually.

4. Adaptive Dynamic Motion Control Extension

In this section a low-level adaptive controller based on *backstepping* method [4, 6] is added to previous fuzzy adaptive high level control for nonholonomic autonomous vehicles. The computed torque controller proposed in [4] requires exact knowledge of the dynamics of the vehicle in order to work properly. Since the dynamical parameters of the model (20) cannot be accurately known, an adaptive mechanism is inserted.

Preliminarily important properties of the dynamical model (20) and kinematical model (16) must be presented.

Property 5 (b). *The linearity in the parameters* $\mathbf{p}$ *of the dynamical model (20) is shown:*

$$\overline{\mathbf{M}}\dot{\eta} + \overline{\mathbf{V}}_{\mathbf{m}}(\eta)\eta = \mathbf{Y}(\eta, \dot{\eta})\mathbf{p}, \quad (55)$$

where the vector $\mathbf{p} \in \mathbb{R}^l$ and $\mathbf{Y}(\eta, \dot{\eta}) \in \mathbb{R}^{(n-m)\times l}$ are

$$\mathbf{p} = \begin{bmatrix} p_1 & p_2 & p_3 \end{bmatrix}^T = \begin{bmatrix} b^2 c^2 m + c^2 I + I_w \\ b^2 c^2 m - c^2 I \\ 2bc^3 dm_c \end{bmatrix}, \quad (56)$$

$$\mathbf{Y}(\eta, \dot{\eta}) = \begin{bmatrix} \ddot{\theta}_r & \ddot{\theta}_l & \left(\dot{\theta}_r - \dot{\theta}_l\right)\dot{\theta}_l \\ \ddot{\theta}_l & \ddot{\theta}_r & -\left(\dot{\theta}_r - \dot{\theta}_l\right)\dot{\theta}_r \end{bmatrix}. \quad (57)$$

The elements of the vector $\mathbf{p}$ consist of unknown dynamical parameters.

Property 6 (b). The kinematical model (16) appears as it follows

$$
\begin{bmatrix} \dot{x}_0 \\ \dot{y}_0 \\ \dot{\phi} \end{bmatrix} = \begin{bmatrix} \dfrac{r}{2}\cos(\phi) & \dfrac{r}{2}\cos(\phi) \\ \dfrac{r}{2}\sin(\phi) & \dfrac{r}{2}\sin(\phi) \\ \dfrac{r}{2b} & -\dfrac{r}{2b} \end{bmatrix} \begin{bmatrix} \dot{\theta}_r \\ \dot{\theta}_l \end{bmatrix}
$$

$$
= \begin{bmatrix} \dfrac{r}{2}\cos(\phi) \\ \dfrac{r}{2}\sin(\phi) \\ \dfrac{r}{2b} \end{bmatrix} \dot{\theta}_r + \begin{bmatrix} \dfrac{r}{2}\cos(\phi) \\ \dfrac{r}{2}\sin(\phi) \\ -\dfrac{r}{2b} \end{bmatrix} \dot{\theta}_l
$$

$$
= \begin{bmatrix} \cos(\phi) & 0 \\ \sin(\phi) & 0 \\ 0 & 1 \end{bmatrix} \begin{bmatrix} \dfrac{r}{2} \\ \dfrac{r}{2b} \end{bmatrix} \dot{\theta}_r + \begin{bmatrix} \cos(\phi) & 0 \\ \sin(\phi) & 0 \\ 0 & -1 \end{bmatrix} \begin{bmatrix} \dfrac{r}{2} \\ \dfrac{r}{2b} \end{bmatrix} \dot{\theta}_l
$$

$$
= \boldsymbol{\Sigma}_1 \boldsymbol{\theta}_1 \dot{\theta}_r + \boldsymbol{\Sigma}_2 \boldsymbol{\theta}_2 \dot{\theta}_l,
\tag{58}
$$

where $\boldsymbol{\theta}_1$ and $\boldsymbol{\theta}_2$ are parametric vectors while $\boldsymbol{\Sigma}_1$ and $\boldsymbol{\Sigma}_2$ are vectors whose elements consist of known functions.

Now, by inserting the new fuzzy inference system of the previous sections, the adaptive backstepping technique [6] is reformulated.

From (47) and (54) the fuzzy kinematical adaptive tracking controller model can be written as it follows

$$
\boldsymbol{\eta}_\mathbf{c} = \boldsymbol{\eta}_\mathbf{c}\left(\mathbf{e}, \overline{\alpha}, \overline{\beta}\right) = \boldsymbol{\eta}_\mathbf{c}\left(\mathbf{q}, \mathbf{q}_\mathbf{r}, \overline{\alpha}, \overline{\beta}\right),
$$

$$
\dot{\overline{\alpha}} = f_1\left(\mathbf{e}, \overline{\alpha}\right) = f_1\left(\mathbf{q}, \mathbf{q}_\mathbf{r}, \overline{\alpha}\right),
\tag{59}
$$

$$
\dot{\overline{\beta}} = f_2\left(\mathbf{e}, \overline{\beta}\right) = f_2\left(\mathbf{q}, \mathbf{q}_\mathbf{r}, \overline{\beta}\right).
$$

Also the Lyapunov function (49) appears as it follows

$$
V_1 = V_1\left(\mathbf{e}, \overline{\alpha}, \overline{\beta}\right) = V_1\left(\mathbf{q}, \mathbf{q}_\mathbf{r}, \overline{\alpha}, \overline{\beta}\right).
\tag{60}
$$

Assumption 12. The adaptive tracking controller (59) exists for the kinematical model (16). Also there is a positive-definite and radially unbounded function V_1 such that

$$
\dot{V}_1 = \frac{\partial V_1}{\partial \mathbf{q}}\dot{\mathbf{q}} + \frac{\partial V_1}{\partial \mathbf{q}_\mathbf{r}}\dot{\mathbf{q}}_\mathbf{r} + \frac{\partial V_1}{\partial \overline{\alpha}}f_1 + \frac{\partial V_1}{\partial \overline{\beta}}f_2 \leq 0,
\tag{61}
$$

where all the signals are bounded.

The following theorem can be formulated.

Theorem 13. *Let* (16) *and* (20) *be the kinematical and dynamical model, respectively. There is the fuzzy kinematical adaptive control* (59). *Properties 5 (b) and 6 (b) are verified and*

Assumption 12 is satisfied. The reference linear and angular velocities are bounded functions and the reference angular velocity converges to zero. The following adaptive dynamical control law is chosen:

$$
\boldsymbol{\tau} = \begin{bmatrix} \tau_l \\ \tau_r \end{bmatrix} = \overline{\mathbf{B}}^{-1}\left(-\mathbf{K_d}\widetilde{\boldsymbol{\eta}} + \mathbf{Y}\widehat{\mathbf{p}} - \left(\frac{\partial V_1}{\partial \mathbf{q}}\widehat{\mathbf{S}}\right)^\mathbf{T} \right)
\tag{62}
$$

$$
\dot{\widehat{\boldsymbol{\theta}}}_\mathbf{i} = \boldsymbol{\Lambda}_1\left(\frac{\partial V_1}{\partial \mathbf{q}}\boldsymbol{\Sigma}_i\right)\widetilde{\eta}_i \quad i = 1,\dots,2; \quad \dot{\widehat{\mathbf{p}}} = -\boldsymbol{\Psi}\mathbf{Y}^T\widetilde{\boldsymbol{\eta}},
$$

where τ_l is the control torque applied to the left wheel; τ_r is the control torque applied to the right wheel; $\widehat{\boldsymbol{\theta}}_i$ is the estimation of $\boldsymbol{\theta}_i$, $i = 1, 2$ (cf. (58)); $\mathbf{Y}$ and $\mathbf{p}$ are given by (56); $\widehat{\mathbf{p}}$ is the estimation of the dynamical parameters of $\mathbf{p}$ vector; $\boldsymbol{\Sigma}_i$ ($i = 1, 2$) matrices are given by (58); V_1 is given by (50) and satisfies Assumption 12; $\widehat{\mathbf{S}}$ is the Jacobian matrix (cf (16)) and it depends on estimated kinematic parameters $\widehat{\boldsymbol{\theta}}_\mathbf{i}$ for $i = 1, 2$; $\widetilde{\boldsymbol{\eta}}$ is given by

$$
\widetilde{\boldsymbol{\eta}} = \boldsymbol{\eta}_\mathbf{c} - \boldsymbol{\eta} = \left[\widetilde{\eta}_1 \widetilde{\eta}_2\right]^T,
\tag{63}
$$

where $\boldsymbol{\eta}_\mathbf{c}$ is given by (54) and $\boldsymbol{\eta}$ is the dynamical velocity vector of model (20); $\mathbf{K_d}$, $\boldsymbol{\Psi}$, and $\boldsymbol{\Lambda}_i$ are symmetric and positive definite matrices.

Then $\widetilde{\boldsymbol{\eta}}$ converges to zero.

Proof Track. The following Lyapunov function is chosen

$$
V_2 = V_1 + \frac{1}{2}\widetilde{\boldsymbol{\eta}}^\mathbf{T}\mathbf{M}\widetilde{\boldsymbol{\eta}} + \frac{1}{2}\widetilde{\mathbf{p}}^\mathbf{T}\boldsymbol{\Gamma}^{-1}\widetilde{\mathbf{p}} + \frac{1}{2}\widetilde{\boldsymbol{\theta}}_1^\mathbf{T}\boldsymbol{\Lambda}_1\widetilde{\boldsymbol{\theta}}_2 + \frac{1}{2}\widetilde{\boldsymbol{\theta}}_2^\mathbf{T}\boldsymbol{\Lambda}_2\widetilde{\boldsymbol{\theta}}_2,
\tag{64}
$$

$$
\widetilde{\mathbf{p}} = \widehat{\mathbf{p}} - \mathbf{p}; \qquad \widetilde{\boldsymbol{\theta}}_1 = \widehat{\boldsymbol{\theta}}_1 - \boldsymbol{\theta}_1; \qquad \widetilde{\boldsymbol{\theta}}_2 = \widehat{\boldsymbol{\theta}}_2 - \boldsymbol{\theta}_2.
\tag{65}
$$

By considering Assumption 12, after some calculations, the time derivative of (64) results [6]

$$
\dot{V}_2 = \frac{\partial V_1}{\partial \mathbf{q}}\mathbf{S}_1\boldsymbol{\eta}_\mathbf{c} + \frac{\partial V_1}{\partial \mathbf{q}_\mathbf{r}}\dot{\mathbf{q}}_\mathbf{r} + \frac{\partial V_1}{\partial \overline{\alpha}}f_1
$$

$$
+ \frac{\partial V_1}{\partial \overline{\beta}}f_2 - \widetilde{\boldsymbol{\eta}}^\mathbf{T}\mathbf{K_d}\widetilde{\boldsymbol{\eta}}.
\tag{66}
$$

From Assumption 12 and (66) the signals included in $\dot{V}_2$ are bounded; therefore, from Barbalat's lemma, the function (66) is uniformly continuous and it can be written as

$$
\lim_{t \to \infty}\dot{V}_2(t) = 0.
\tag{67}
$$

From (52) and (67), it yields

$$
\lim_{t \to \infty}\widetilde{\boldsymbol{\eta}}(t) = 0.
\tag{68}
$$

Remark 14. If we assume the adaptive kinematical controller of Section 3 only, the perfect tracking velocity hypothesis is considered, that is, the control velocity $\boldsymbol{\eta}_\mathbf{c}$ is instantaneously applied to nonholonomic vehicle, but it is not true. By inserting the dynamical control, instead, (68) is satisfied and the velocity of the nonholonomic vehicle converges to control signal after some time due to dynamical effects. This is shown in the next section.

Remark 15. If (68) is satisfied, then boundedness and convergence of the tracking errors (24) are assured.

5. Simulation Results

We first simulate the adaptive fuzzy controller for nonholonomic vehicles in MATLAB Simulink environment to verify the asymptotical stability and robustness performance before the experimental implementation. Also we use simulation results to compare our method with the control system proposed in [6]. In this section two simulations results are shown: the first does not consider disturbance; the second consider disturbance violating the nonholonomic constraints of the vehicle motion. Besides, two controllers have been simulated in MATLAB environment:

(1) a controller with adaptive dynamical extension assuming knowledge of the parameters (28), that is, adaptive control without fuzzy inference system [6];

(2) the new controller of this work where the parameters (28) are the outputs of the new fuzzy system of the Section 3, with the new adaptive kinematical control of the Section 3.3 (cf. (54)) and the adaptive dynamical control extension of the Section 4 (cf. (62)).

So the performances and robustness of the two motion control system are compared.

The kinematical and dynamical parameters of the electric nonholonomic vehicle are the following:

$$b = 0.75 \, \text{m}; \quad d = 0.3 \, \text{m}; \quad r = 0.15 \, \text{m}; \quad m_c = 30 \, \text{kg}$$

$$m_w = 1 \, \text{kg}; \quad I_c = 15.6; \quad I_w = 0.005; \quad I_m = 0.0025. \tag{69}$$

The parameters of the kinematic controller (27) are the outputs of the fuzzy system. The parameters of the kinematical (47) and dynamical (62) adaptive controllers are

$$\gamma = 0.005; \quad \delta = 20.75; \quad K_d = 5; \quad \psi = 5. \tag{70}$$

About the controller without fuzzy inference system, the parameters (28) are chosen as

$$k_x = k_y = k_\phi = 5 \quad \forall t. \tag{71}$$

About the two DC motors, one must consider the following model:

$$\tau_m = \mathbf{K}\mathbf{i_a},$$

$$v_a = \mathbf{L_a}\frac{d\mathbf{i_a}}{dt} + \mathbf{R_a}\mathbf{i_a},$$

$$v_a = \mathbf{G}_v v_c, \tag{72}$$

$$\tau = \overline{\mathbf{K}}\tau_m,$$

where $\mathbf{i_a} = \begin{bmatrix} i_{a1} \\ i_{a2} \end{bmatrix}$ armature currents; $v_a = \begin{bmatrix} v_{a1} \\ v_{a2} \end{bmatrix}$ armature voltages; $v_c = \begin{bmatrix} v_{c1} \\ v_{c2} \end{bmatrix}$ control voltages; $\tau = \begin{bmatrix} \tau_r \\ \tau_l \end{bmatrix}$ transmitted

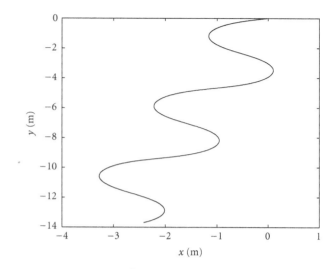

FIGURE 7: Reference trajectory x (m), y (m).

command torques to right and left wheels; $\tau_m = \begin{bmatrix} \tau_{m1} \\ \tau_{m2} \end{bmatrix}$ produced torques; $\mathbf{K} = 3.34 \times \mathbf{I}\,\text{Ncm/A}$ constant torque parameter; $\overline{\mathbf{K}} = 4 \times \mathbf{I}$ proportionality coefficient between produced and transmitted torque; $\mathbf{R_a} = 10 \times \mathbf{I}\,\Omega$ armature resistance; $\mathbf{L_a} = 0.0241 \times \mathbf{I}\,\text{H}$ armature inductance; the matrix $\mathbf{I}$ is an identity matrix with two rows and two columns.

5.1. Trajectory without Disturbance. In this test the problem of motion control for nonholonomic vehicles is simulated using a feasible, nonholonomic reference trajectory (see Figure 7).

The initial conditions for the reference position are

$$(x(0), y(0), \phi(0)) = (0, 0, 3.48 \, \text{rad}). \tag{73}$$

The initial conditions for the actual vehicle position are

$$(x(0), y(0), \phi(0)) = (-30, 20, 5.68 \, \text{rad}). \tag{74}$$

So the control laws (54) and (62) are simulated suitably.

Figures 8 and 9 show the tracking errors (24) along x- and y-directions where we compare the performances of our control system (i.e., fuzzy adaptive motion control) with the performances of the control system proposed in [6] (i.e., adaptive motion control without fuzzy).

The tracking errors resulting from the new fuzzy adaptive control of this work are bounded and converge to zero more rapidly than the tracking errors of the solution one without fuzzy mechanism [6].

Figure 10 shows the orientation error of the fuzzy adaptive kinematic and dynamic control system, while Figures 11 and 12 present the estimated kinematical parameters $\overline{\alpha}, \overline{\beta}$ (cf. (47)) and the dynamical parameters of $\widehat{\mathbf{p}}$ vector (cf. (57) and (62)), respectively.

Remark 16. From Figure 10 it is evident that the trajectory of the robot reaches the trajectory with inclination which leads to an overshoot of near −45 degrees then a posterior correction goes near 25 degrees. In fact note that the ray

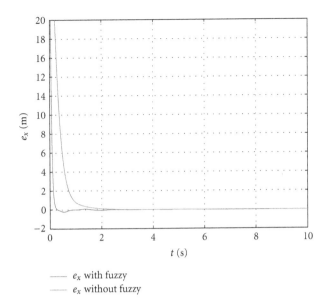

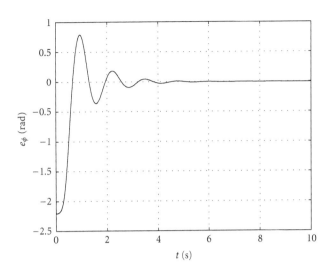

FIGURE 10: Orientation error with fuzzy system, e_ϕ (rad).

FIGURE 8: Longitudinal position error e_x (m) with (blue line) and
without (green line) fuzzy system.

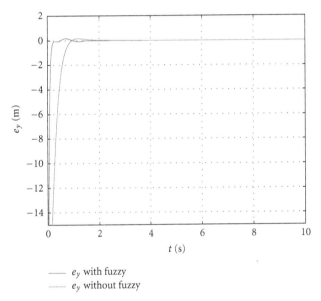

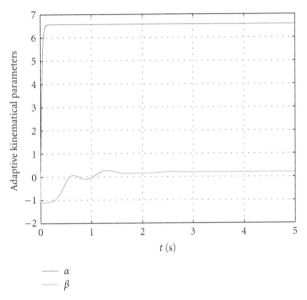

FIGURE 11: Adaptive kinematic parameters.

FIGURE 9: Lateral position error e_y (m) with (blue line) and without
(green line) fuzzy system.

of the vehicle is small, so that the vehicle is not a bigger
one. In any case the control strategy may be applied for a
variety of vehicles, by varying the input-output values of the
memberships fuzzy. In the next section the experiments have
been developed for a small nonholonomic vehicle.

From Figure 10 it is evident that the orientation error is
bounded and converges to 0 rad.

From Figures 11 and 12 we observe that the adaptive
control is direct, because the estimated parameters are not
physical values, but the steady state parameters are constant
and the tracking errors of Figures 8, 9, and 10 converge to
zero.

Remark 17. Note that all the absolute tracking errors values
of the simulation tests (see Figures 8, 9, and 10) are in the
range of the numerical inputs of the fuzzy system (see Figure
2). In fact the fuzzy map was adjusted based on the control
performance as it is explained in Remark 11.

Figure 13 shows the velocity error (63) between the
dynamic velocity of the vehicle and the fuzzy control velocity
(54). As discussed in Remarks 10 and 14, due to dynamical
effects, the physical velocity of the vehicle tracks the fuzzy
control velocity only after some time. The motion control
reacts in a good way and, after some time instants, the
velocity error (63) converges to zero. In other words the
kinematic control signals cannot affect the vehicle velocities
instantaneously.

Now the electrical vehicle has motors installed in two
wheels. The model of the motor has been shown in (72).
From our simulations, the control torques (cf. (62)) for the

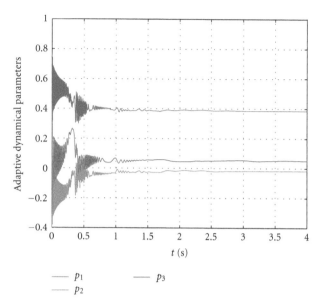

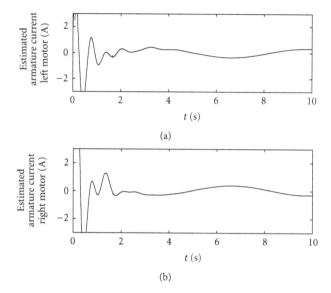

FIGURE 14: Estimated armature currents of left and right motor.

FIGURE 12: Adaptive dynamical parameters.

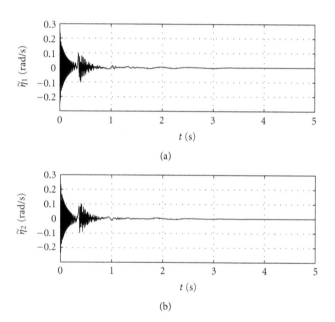

FIGURE 13: Tracking velocity error $\tilde{\eta}$ (rad/s).

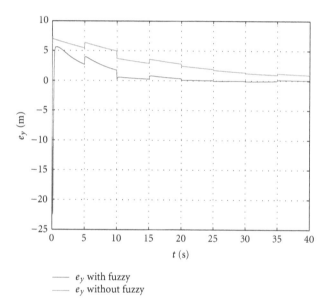

FIGURE 15: Lateral position error e_y (m) with (blue line) and without (green line) fuzzy system.

left and right wheels can be known precisely and therefore we can estimate the currents for the motors. Based on the experimental system explained in the next section, we consider an amplification between the transmitted and the produced torques equal to 4. So Figure 14 shows the estimated armature currents for right and left motors.

5.2. Trajectory with Disturbance Violating the Nonholonomic Constraints of the Vehicle Motion. This simulation test shows the robustness of the fuzzy adaptive motion control system with respect to outside disturbances violating the nonholonomic constraints (9). The disturbance above can be caused by the impact of the vehicle with the external environment,

as, for example, the road conditions and the contact between the wheels and the ground where the vehicle moves. In this sense the dynamic model (20) has a bounded unknown disturbance term τ_d including unstructured dynamics. Now effects of the disturbances above, that is, perturbations of the actual trajectory of the vehicle, are considered only. So the simulation test consists of generating the slipping of the wheels by a step disturbance of the actual lateral position y of the vehicle for every 5 s. The reference trajectory is shown in Figure 7 and it is feasible, that is, it does not violate the nonholonomic constraints. Figure 15 shows the tracking error along y-direction in case of control with and without fuzzy system. In case of control without fuzzy system, the parameters (28) are fixed as it results in (70). As discussed in

(a)

(b)

Figure 16: Nonholonomic vehicle top and rear views: PC target and independent traction axis.

Figure 17: Motor axis pulley local view.

Remark 2 it is evident that, with respect to the itself control without fuzzy inference [6], the adaptive fuzzy control system of our paper reacts to the disturbance, recovering the vehicle motion with a very good control effort.

6. Experimental System and Results

In this section a motion control experiment has been established based on the fuzzy control laws (54) and (62). Experimentation is performed on a vehicle with the same dynamical and kinematical parameters of the simulations.

6.1. Main Technical Aspects of the Nonholonomic Vehicle and of the Implemented Fuzzy Adaptive Control System. The details of our vehicle are shown in Figure 16. The vehicle above is constituted by a mechanical support of circular form, under which two independent traction axes have been installed (differential drive actuation). The information on linear and angular velocities and therefore on position and orientation of the vehicle have been obtained by two proprioceptive sensors, that is, one encoder for each wheel.

The electric motors are controlled by on-board personal computer (PC Target) with Pentium processor. The signals for the actuators are PWM type. Therefore, drivers for the motors have been installed. The motors and the drivers require a set of two on-board batteries of 12 V.

Principal components of the experimental system are

(i) two DC motors;

(ii) two encoders Baumer, BHK series;

(iii) two drivers LMD18200;

(iv) PC Target on board with Encoder Card PCL-833, Multifunctional Card PCL-1800.

We use another PC (host computer) for motion control, where the adaptive fuzzy motion controller has been implemented by using MATLAB Simulink.

About the motors, they have been chosen for the good torques and robustness performance. The parameters of the model have been shown in the simulation section. The main characteristics of the motors are

(i) nominal tension value: 24 V;

(ii) nominal current value: 2.8 A;

(iii) continuous torque: 6 Ncm;

(iv) Constant torque-current: 3.34 Ncm/A.

The employed drivers produce current for the motors to generate the torques. However, the drivers above assure maximum current of 3 A for the motors with consequential very low torque. So we do not change the driver, but we use a system of motor-axis pulley (see Figure 17) introducing an amplification between the produced and the transmitted torque. To use the driver LMD18200, the amplification above is $1:4$.

The circuit for the PWM generation has been shown in Figure 18. In our experimental system the card above is positioned upon the PC target (see Figure 16 top view). Note that the LMD18200 has three inputs: PWM, DIR, and BRAKE. The brake input can be controlled by microcontroller. In our experiments the input above is not used. So it is "ground". The input "DIR" is the direction of the motor rotation. Now

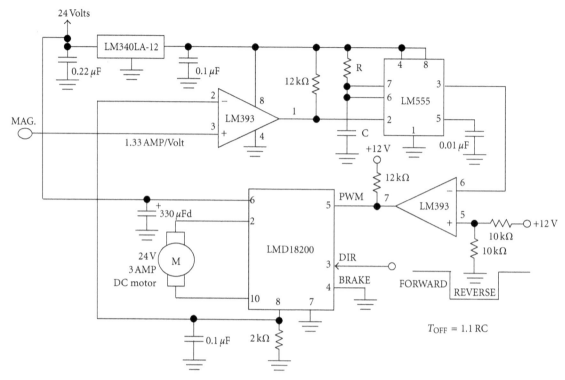

FIGURE 18: PWM generation for driver LMD18200.

the multifunctional card PCL-1800 has A/D converter, buffer FIFO of 1 Kword, two converters D/A 12 bit, 16 digital inputs, and 16 digital outputs. From the D/A of the PCL-1800, reference voltages proportional to the currents are obtained. The card above has been employed to monitor the armature currents, the reference voltages, and the current signs. So the difference between the current reference and the measure current feedback is fed into a current control block. Hence, it generates the duty ratio for the PWM converter which provides bidirectional current control of the DC motors.

The encoders have been employed to evaluate the velocity rotation of the axis. They use two pulse trains, 90 degree out of phase.

The host computer loads to the PC Target of the vehicle the program and the reference trajectory, while the PC Target communicates to it some variables, as, for example, the actual position. The host PC reads motor positions for use in graphics routines by using MATLAB software. The PC target passes latest position to the fuzzy control algorithm implemented in the host PC using MATLAB simulink. So the Fuzzy control algorithm calculates the new outputs for the DAC of the PCL-1800 generating the reference voltage and waits for the next command from the PC target.

About the software implementation of the fuzzy control laws (54) and (62), the system has been realized by using MATLAB Simulink, Real-Time Workshop, and XpcTarget toolboxes. In particular we have used MATLAB Simulink to implement the dynamical and kinematical fuzzy controllers and the blocks for the card I/O interfaces. So, by employing RealTime WorkShop toolbox, the blocks above are converted in C language suitably. The executable code is generated

by using *Visual C* compiler. Therefore, the code above is downloaded in the PC target, where there is a real-time operative system. So we monitor the parameters in the remote PC by graphical routines of MATLAB.

Figure 19 shows the block diagram for the acquisition of the encoders data, that is, angular velocities of the right and left wheels. The data above are downloaded in the host PC. So, by using MATLAB simulink blocks to implement (16), they are processed to obtain the feedback signal and the motion errors (24) of the control system.

In conclusion the control architecture has three levels:

(i) from the positions errors (24), the adaptive fuzzy kinematic control generates the speed control (cf. (54));

(ii) from the velocity error (63), the adaptive dynamic control generates the desired torque commands (cf. (62));

(iii) actuation of the torques above by the PCL-1800 with generation of error between the reference and the measured current for the PWM input generation of the driver LMD18200.

6.2. Results. In this section experimental results are shown to confirm the simulation results. In the host computer we have implemented a reference curvilinear trajectory. The trajectory above is shown in Figure 20 and it is equal to the curvilinear length of the simulation tests (see Figure 7). The initial conditions of the reference trajectory and of the vehicle position are the same of the simulation tests (cf. (73), (74)).

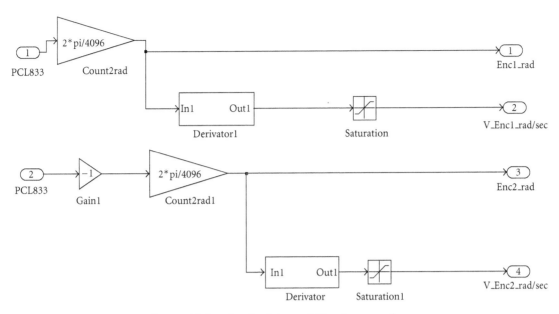

FIGURE 19: Interface for data acquisition from encoders.

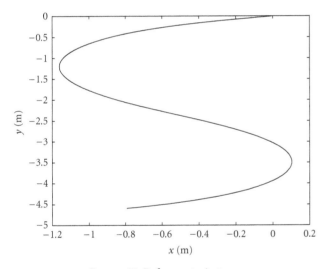

FIGURE 20: Reference trajectory.

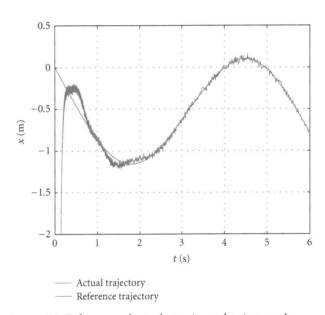

—— Actual trajectory
—— Reference trajectory

FIGURE 21: Reference and actual experimental trajectory along x-direction.

By using the fuzzy control laws (54) and (62), time after time, we have monitored the actual position of the vehicle. Figures 21 and 22 show the experimental results of the system output response to the reference trajectory of Figure 20. In particular the reference and experimental actual trajectories along x-direction versus time are shown in Figure 21, while Figure 22 shows the same functions along y-direction versus time. To compare experimental and simulation results directly, it is evident that the vertical distances between the trace of the actual and of the reference trajectories (see Figures 21 and 22) represent the longitudinal and the lateral tracking errors. The values of the distances above are similar to the values of the simulation results (see Figures 8 and 9).

Figures 23 and 24 show the reference voltages and the sign of the currents for the left and right motors, respectively.

The information above come from output DAC of PCL 1800 card.

Figure 25 shows the measured armature currents for right and left motors. Note that the driver may have done 3 A max to the motors. The measured armature currents of Figure 25 are similar to the simulation results of Figure 14.

7. Conclusions

In this paper an evolution of the adaptive control for motion control of autonomous nonholonomic vehicles by inserting a new Fuzzy inference system has been presented.

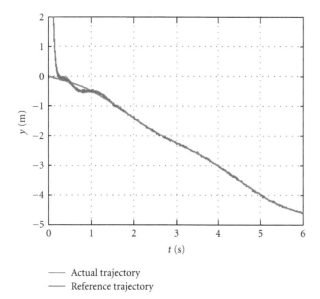

— Actual trajectory
— Reference trajectory

FIGURE 22: Reference and actual experimental trajectory along y-direction.

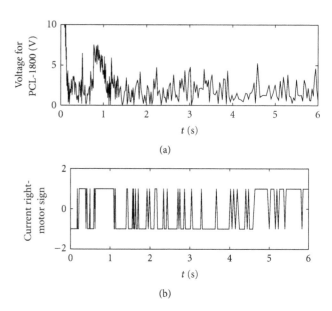

FIGURE 24: Reference voltage and current right motor sign from PCL-1800 card.

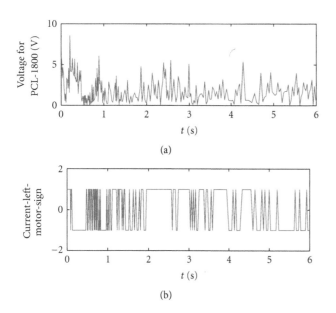

FIGURE 23: Reference voltage and current left-motor sign from PCL 1800 card.

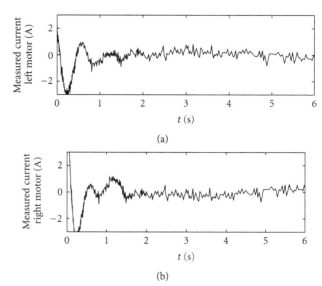

FIGURE 25: Measured armature currents.

In particular the fuzzy inference determines the parameters of the kinematic controller with better performance than the adaptive controller without fuzzy proposed in [6]. An adaptive mechanism on line estimated the unknown dynamical and kinematical parameters of the vehicle model. Also, by using the dynamical extension, it is evident that the hypothesis of perfect velocity tracking cannot be satisfied because it is not true practically. Our concepts are formulated to have the asymptotical stability of the tracking errors through Lyapunov theory and Barbalat's lemma. The stability results are based on the input-output properties of the fuzzy inference system. Based on theoretical and simulation results we conclude

(i) Lyapunov stability theory can be effectively applied to determine the properties of fuzzy system for problem of motion control of nonholonomic vehicles;

(ii) the fuzzy adaptive approach of this paper reduces the response time of the tracking errors with respect to controller without fuzzy inference mechanism [6];

(iii) the simulation results show the robustness, the asymptotical stability, and the fast convergence of the motion errors;

(iv) the experimental results confirm the validity of the proposed method.

References

[1] C. Zhu and R. Rajamani, "Global positioning system-based vehicle control for automated parking," *Journal of Automobile Engineering*, vol. 220, no. 1, pp. 37–52, 2006.

[2] M. Aicardi, G. Casalino, A. Bicchi, and A. Balestrino, "Closed loop steering of unicycle-like vehicles via Lyapunov techniques," *IEEE Robotics and Automation Magazine*, vol. 2, no. 1, pp. 27–35, 1995.

[3] M. L. Corradini, T. Leo, and G. Orlando, "Robust stabilization of a mobile robot violating the nonholonomic constraint via quasi-sliding modes," in *Proceedings of the American Control Conference (ACC '99)*, pp. 3935–3939, June 1999.

[4] R. Fierro and F. L. Lewis, "Control of a nonholonomic mobile robot: backsteppins kinematics into dynamics," *Journal of Robotic Systems*, vol. 14, no. 3, pp. 149–163, 1997.

[5] C. de Sousa, E. M. Hemerly, and R. K. Harrop Galvão, "Adaptive control for mobile robot using wavelet networks," *IEEE Transactions on Systems, Man, and Cybernetics B*, vol. 32, no. 4, pp. 493–504, 2002.

[6] T. Fukao, H. Nakagawa, and N. Adachi, "Adaptive tracking control of a nonholonomic mobile robot," *IEEE Transactions on Robotics and Automation*, vol. 16, no. 5, pp. 609–615, 2000.

[7] G. Indiveri, *An Introduction to Wheeled Mobile Robot Kinematics and Dynamics*, University of Lecce-DII, Department of Innovation Engineering, Robocamp, Paderborn, Germany, 2002.

[8] D. G. Wilson and R. D. Robinett, "Robust adaptive backstepping control for a nonholonomic mobile robot," in *Proceedings of the IEEE International Conference on Systems, Man and Cybernetics*, vol. 5, pp. 3241–3245, October 2001.

[9] T. Leo and G. Orlando, "Robust discrete time control of a nonholonomic mobile robot," in *Proceedings of the 14th IFAC World Congress*, pp. 137–142, 1999.

[10] G. Calcev, "Some remarks on the stability of Mamdani fuzzy control systems," *IEEE Transactions on Fuzzy Systems*, vol. 6, no. 3, pp. 436–442, 1998.

[11] M. Sugeno and T. Taniguchi, "On improvement of stability conditions for continuous Mamdani-like fuzzy systems," *IEEE Transactions on Systems, Man, and Cybernetics B*, vol. 34, no. 1, pp. 120–131, 2004.

[12] S. Bentalba, A. E. Hajjaji, and A. Rachid, "Fuzzy control of a mobile robot: a new approach," in *Proceedings of the IEEE International Conference on Control Applications*, pp. 69–72, October 1997.

[13] H. K. Lam, T. H. Lee, F. H. F. Leung, and P. K. S. Tam, "Fuzzy model reference control of wheeled mobile robots," in *Proceedings of the 27th Annual Conference of the IEEE Industrial Electronics Society (IECON '01)*, pp. 570–573, December 2001.

[14] T. H. Lee, H. K. Lam, F. H. F. Leung, and P. K. S. Tam, "A practical fuzzy logic controller for the path tracking of wheeled mobile robots," in *Proceedings of the 27th Annual Conference of the IEEE Industrial Electronics Society (IECON '01)*, pp. 574–579, December 2001.

[15] G. Schuster, *Simulation of Fuzzy Motion Controlled Four Wheel Steered Mobile Robot*, Institute of Instrumentation and Automation, Budapest, Hungary, 2000.

[16] P. Shahmaleki and M. Mahzoon, "Designing a hierarchical fuzzy controller for backing-up a four wheel autonomous robot," in *Proceedings of the American Control Conference (ACC '08)*, pp. 4893–4897, Seattle, Wash, USA, June 2008.

[17] F. M. Raimondi and M. Melluso, "Fuzzy control strategy for cooperative non-holonomic motion of cybercars with passengers vibration analysis," in *Motion Control*, pp. 325–350, In-Teh, 2010.

[18] M. A. Llama, R. Kelly, and V. Santibanez, "Stable computed-torque control of robot manipulators via fuzzy self-tuning," *IEEE Transactions on Systems, Man, and Cybernetics B*, vol. 30, no. 1, pp. 143–150, 2000.

[19] F. M. Raimondi and M. Melluso, "A neuro fuzzy controller for planar robot manipulators," *WSEAS Transactions on Systems*, vol. 3, no. 10, pp. 2991–2997, 2004.

[20] H. Gartner and A. Astolfi, "Stability study of a fuzzy controlled mobile robot," in *Proceedings of the 35th IEEE Conference on Decision and Control*, pp. 1121–1126, December 1996.

[21] F. M. Raimondi, M. Melluso, and L. S. Ciancimino, "A new kinematic and dynamic direct adaptive Fuzzy control of constrained mobile wheeled vehicles," in *Proceedings of the 10th IEEE International Conference on Emerging Technologies and Factory Automation (ETFA '05)*, vol. 2, pp. 181–188, September 2005.

[22] Y. Yamamoto and X. Yun, "Coordinating locomotion and manipulation of a mobile manipulator," in *Proceedings of the 31th IEEE Conference on Decision and Control*, pp. 2643–2648, 1992.

[23] G. Tao, "A simple alternative to the Barbalat lemma," *IEEE Transactions on Automatic Control*, vol. 42, no. 5, article 698, 1997.

12

Classification of Clothing Using Midlevel Layers

Bryan Willimon, Ian Walker, and Stan Birchfield

Department of Electrical and Computer Engineering, Clemson University, Clemson, SC 29634, USA

Correspondence should be addressed to Bryan Willimon; rwillim@clemson.edu

Academic Editors: K. K. Ahn, L. Asplund, and R. Safaric

We present a multilayer approach to classify articles of clothing within a pile of laundry. The classification features are composed of color, texture, shape, and edge information from 2D and 3D data within a local and global perspective. The contribution of this paper is a novel approach of classification termed L-M-H, more specifically LC-S-H for clothing classification. The multilayer approach compartmentalizes the problem into a high (H) layer, multiple midlevel (characteristics (C), selection masks (S)) layers, and a low (L) layer. This approach produces "local" solutions to solve the global classification problem. Experiments demonstrate the ability of the system to efficiently classify each article of clothing into one of seven categories (pants, shorts, shirts, socks, dresses, cloths, or jackets). The results presented in this paper show that, on average, the classification rates improve by +27.47% for three categories (Willimon et al., 2011), +17.90% for four categories, and +10.35% for seven categories over the baseline system, using SVMs (Chang and Lin, 2001).

1. Introduction

Sorting laundry is a common routine that involves classifying and labeling each piece of clothing. This particular task is not close to becoming an automated procedure. The laundry process consists of several steps: handling, washing, drying, separating/isolating, classifying, unfolding/flattening, folding, and putting it away into a predetermined drawer or storage unit. Figure 1 gives a high-level flow chart of these various steps. In the past, several bodies of work have attempted at solving the tasks of handling [1–8], separating/isolating [8–12], classifying [6, 9, 11–15], unfolding/flattening [14, 16], and folding [17] clothes. Figure 1 gives a flow chart of the various areas.

A robotic classification system is designed to accurately sort a pile of clothes in predefined categories, before and after the washing/drying process. Laundry is normally sorted by individual, then by category. Our procedure allows for clothing to be classified/sorted by category, age, gender, color (i.e., whites, colors, darks), or season of use. The problem that we address in this paper is grouping isolated articles of clothing into a specified category (e.g., shirts, pants, shorts, cloths, socks, dresses, jackets) using midlevel layers (i.e., physical characteristics and selection masks).

Previous work on classifying clothing [6, 11–14] used dual manipulators to freely hang each article of clothing at two grasp points to reveal the overall shape of each article of clothing. In contrast to previous work, our approach is tested on an unorganized, unflattened article for the purpose of classifying each individual piece of clothing. The database of clothing, that we use in this paper, consists of individual articles placed on a table by a single robotic manipulator.

Our approach uses a set of characteristics, a local/global histogram for each article, and low-level image/point cloud calculations in order to accomplish this task. The proposed method can be seen as a particular application of the paradigm of interactive perception, also known as manipulation-guided sensing, in which the manipulation is used to guide the sensing in order to gather information not obtainable through passive sensing alone [18–22]. The articles of clothing that we use in this paper have been manipulated in a predefined set of movements/operations in order to gather more information for our approach. Each article of clothing is initially placed on a flat surface and then pulled in four directions $\{\Uparrow, \Downarrow, \Leftarrow, \Rightarrow\}$ (i.e., up, down, left, right) which results in five unique configurations of each piece of laundry. In other words, deliberate actions change the state of the world in

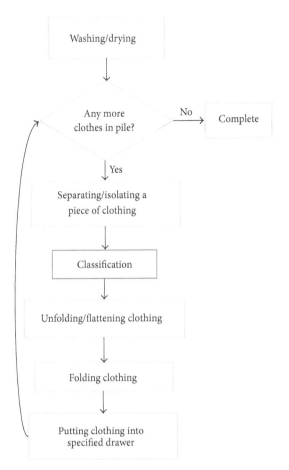

FIGURE 1: Overview of the laundry process, adapted from [10]. Green areas represent parts of the process that have already been explored in previous work, while the Red area represents the part of the process that is the focus of this paper.

a way that simplifies perception and consequently future interactions.

In this paper, we demonstrate the approach based on characteristics, which was introduced in [15], for automatically classifying and sorting laundry. We extend [15] by applying this approach to a larger database. This new database increases the number of midlevel characteristics as well as increasing the number of categories. This paper will display the results of the algorithm by increasing the complexity of the problem. Figure 2 and Table 1 illustrate examples of laundry items from several actual household hampers which form the data set that will be used in this paper. Our new approach is comprised of a multilayer classification strategy consisting of SVM [23] and bag-of-words model [24], similar to [25], that utilizes characteristics and selection masks to bridge together each calculated low-level feature to the correct category for each article of clothing.

2. Previous Work

There has been previous work in robot laundry which relates to the research in this paper. Kaneko and Kakikura [11] focused on a strategy to isolate and classify clothing. The work

in [11] is an extension of the authors' pioneering work in [10]. In these papers, the authors categorize what steps and tasks are needed for laundry (isolate, unfold, classify, fold, and put away clothes), as in Figure 1. The authors classify each object into one of three groups (shirt, pants, or towel) by deforming the article of clothing. The process of deforming the object aims to find hemlines as grasp points and the grasp points cannot be closer than a predefined threshold. Once the object is held at two grasp points, then the shape of the object is broken up into different regions and the values of the different regions are used to calculate feature values. Each of the feature values is compared against threshold values. If the features are above or below the thresholds, then the object is classified as a shirt, pant, or towel based on a decision tree. The results achieved a 90% classification rate.

Osawa et al. [12] use two manipulators to pick up/separate a piece of cloth, unfold, and classify it. The approach in [12] begins the process by picking up a piece of cloth by holding it with one manipulator. While the item is being held by the first manipulator, the second manipulator looks for the lowest point of the cloth as a second grasp point. The grasp spreads the article of clothing by the longest two corner points. The article of clothing now held by both robot arms is imaged by a camera and the image is converted into a binary image using background subtraction. This binary image is then compared with the binary template to classify the article of clothing. The approach is tested with eight different categories (male short sleeve shirt, women/child short sleeve shirt, long sleeve shirts, trousers, underwear shorts, bras, towels, and handkerchiefs). Fifty trials were conducted with clothing of the same type as the training data, achieving an average of 96% classification.

Kita et al. [6] extend their original work [4] of determining the state of clothing. The work in [6] provides a three-step process to successfully find a grasp point that the humanoid robot can grab: (1) clothing state estimation (previous work [4]); (2) calculation of the theoretically optimal position and orientation of the hand for the next action; and (3) modification of position and orientation, based on the robots limitations, so the action can be executed. The 3D model is used by calculating the orientation of the shirt model at the grasp point. The 3D model gives three vectors around the grasp point and the vectors are used in the calculation of the orientation. The authors tested their results of six scenarios and were successful on five. One scenario failed in predicting the correct clothing state, four scenarios were successful but had to use step (3) for completion, and the last scenario was successful without using step (3).

The results in [13] are another extension to Y. Kita and N. Kita's previous work [4]. The purpose is to accurately determine the shape/configuration of a piece of clothing based on the observed 3D data and the simulated 3D model. Each of the clothing states is compared against the 3D observed data based on the length of the clothing as a first step. Each of the shape states within a threshold value is selected to use in the next step of the process. Then, a correlation function is applied to the 2D plane of the observed data and simulated data to calculate which shape state model is closest to the observed data. The experimental results show that 22 out of 27 attempts were correctly classified as the correct shape state.

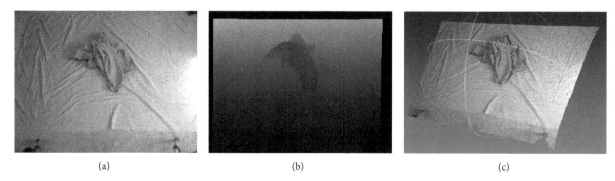

(a)   (b)   (c)

FIGURE 2: The proposed setting for classification. The system classifies the items automatically by comparing the color, texture, shape, and size of the object with those of a learned database. Sensory information is provided by a Kinect sensor. Data to be used in our approach. From left to right: color image, depth image, and a point cloud.

TABLE 1: Seven instances of clothing for each of the seven categories. From top row to bottom row: shirts, cloths, pants, shorts, dresses, socks, and jackets.

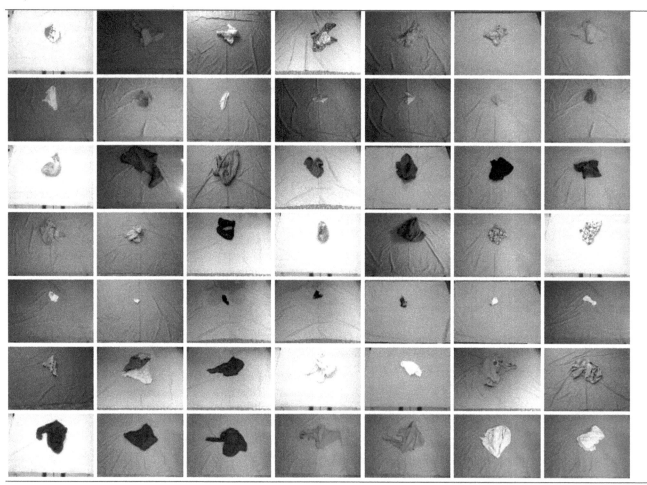

Cusumano-Towner et al. [14] present an extension of Osawa et al. [12] and Kita et al. [13] combined. The authors identified a clothing article by matching together silhouettes of the article to precomputed simulated articles of clothing. The silhouettes of each iteration were placed into a hidden markov model (HMM) to determine how well the silhouettes of the current article match against the simulated models of

all categories of clothing. The authors placed the article on a table by sliding the clothing along the edge of the table to maintain the configuration while it was hanging in the air. The authors grasped two locations on the cloth during each iteration. The planning algorithm that determines where the next set of grasp points are located was computed by using a directed grasp-ability graph that locates all possible grasp

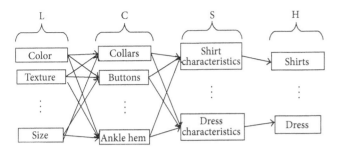

FIGURE 3: The L-C-S-H hierarchy with categories at the high level, binary vectors at the selection levels, attributes at the characteristic level, and features at the low-level.

points that can allow the system to reach. The authors tested their approach on seven articles of clothing of the end-to-end approach and were successful with 20 out of 30 trials.

Our work differs from the previous papers [6, 11–14] in that we work with a single manipulator and our results do not depend on hanging our clothing in the air by two grasp points. Our approach is independent of the type or how many manipulators that are used to collect the data. Our work also differs from that of [6, 13, 14] in that we do not require or use predefined shape models. We instead use novel characteristic features that describe each category of clothing. The characteristic features are not predefined but calculated through training the algorithm with a priori collected clothing data.

Our current work extends the problem of our previous work [15] by expanding the midlevel layer with more characteristics and incorporating more categories in the high layer. We expand the database of clothing that was used in our previous paper from 117 articles to over 200 articles of various size, color, and type. We then compare how well our algorithm improves over a baseline system of SVMs, one per category, to classify a pile of laundry into three, four, and seven groups (Tables 3 and 4).

3. Approach

3.1. Overview. We call the proposed algorithm L-C-S-H, for low-level-characteristics-selection mask-high level. Low-level refers to the features that are calculated from the images of each article (e.g., 2D shape, 2D color, 2D texture, 2D edges, and 3D shape). Characteristics refer to the attributes that are found on generic articles of clothing (e.g., pockets, collars, hems). Selection mask refers to a vector that describes what characteristics are most useful for each category (e.g., collars and buttons are most useful for classifying shirts), used as a filter. High level refers to the categories that we are attempting to classify (e.g., shirts, socks, dresses). Figure 3 illustrates the path of the L-C-S-H process. The L-C-S-H algorithm is described in detail in later sections.

3.2. Clothing Database. The database that we used consists of over 200 articles of clothing in over 1000 total configurations. The entire database is separated into seven categories and

more than three dozen subcategories. Each article of clothing is collected from real laundry hampers to better capture actual items encountered in the real world. Each one is laid flat on a table in a canonical position and dropped on the table in a crumpled position from four random grasp points for a total of five instances per article. Figure 1 illustrates seven instances of clothing for each of the seven categories that we used.

The database contains 2D color images, depth images, and 3D point clouds. For this paper, we will utilize the assortment of different types of items, such as shirts, cloths, pants, shorts, dresses, socks, and jackets, that might be encountered by a domestic robot involved in automating household laundry tasks. Figure 2 illustrates an example of a single color image, a single depth image, and a single point cloud for one article.

3.3. Low-Level Features. The L component of the approach uses the low-level features to estimate if the article does or does not have a particular characteristic. The low-level features that were used in this approach consist of color histogram (CH), histogram of line lengths (HLL), table point feature histogram (TPFH), boundary, scale-invariant feature transform (SIFT), and fast point feature histogram (FPFH). Each low-level feature will be described in detail in further subsections. The database that we used consisted of five instances of each article, see Section 3.2. In order to combine the low-level features of all five instances into a single value or histogram, we calculated each value by averaging each individual value along with its neighbors, in the case of the histogram. Equation (1) was the computation used to combine all five instances of each article

$$C_j = \frac{1}{N} \sum_{j=1}^{N} v_j + \frac{1}{2} \left(v_{j-1} + v_{j+1} \right), \tag{1}$$

where C_j is the combined score of the article, N is the number of instances of each article (we use $N = 5$), v_j is the current value within the histogram along with v_{j-1} and v_{j+1} to be the immediate neighbors to the left and right of the current value, respectively.

For the part of the algorithm that converts from low-level to characteristics, we compared the low-level features, described in the following subsections, to the various characteristics. Since the characteristics were binary values, we used libSVM [23] to solve the two-class problem. We used each low-level feature to determine if the characteristic is in class 1 or 2. Class 1 contains positive instances and class 2 contains negative instances.

For an article of clothing, we capture an RGB image and a raw depth map, from which we get a 3D point cloud. We perform background subtraction on the RGB image to yield an image of only the object. The background subtraction is performed using graph-based segmentation [26], see Section 3.3.1. Once the object is isolated within the image, multiple features are calculated from the RGB image and the 3D point cloud. These features, which are discussed in later sections, capture 2D shape, 2D color, 2D texture, 2D edges, and 3D shape for both global and local regions of the object.

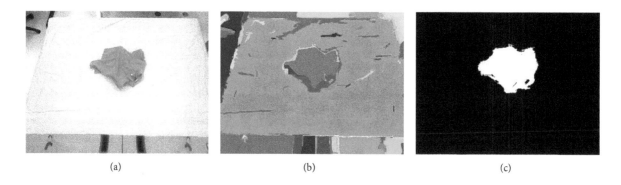

(a)   (b)   (c)

FIGURE 4: (a) An image taken by one of the overhead cameras in our setup. (b) The results of applying the graph-based segmentation algorithm to locate the foreground. (c) The binary image represents the location of the foreground object.

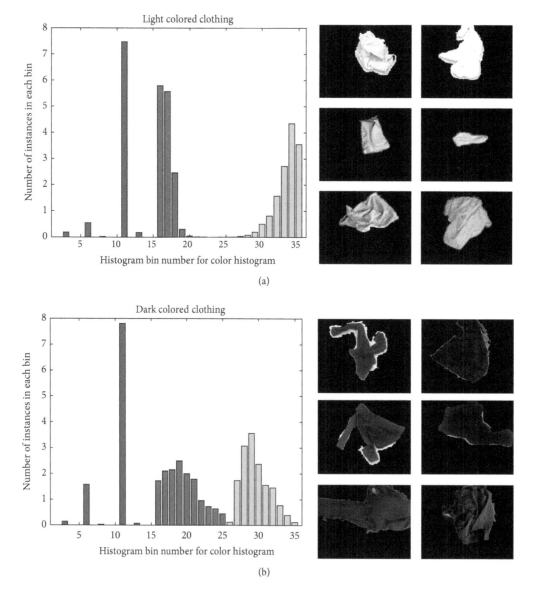

FIGURE 5: Resulting histograms of light (a) and dark (b) colored clothing. Each plot shows the histogram of the HSV color space, which consists of three parts: hue (blue), saturation (red), and value (green). For each category, the 6 examples used to compute the histogram are shown.

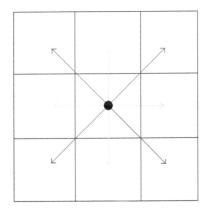

FIGURE 6: illustrative Example of diagonal movements and isothetic movements. The red arrows refer to diagonal movements and green arrows refer to isothetic movements.

3.3.1. Graph-Based Segmentation.

We use Felzenswalb and Huttenlocher's graph-based segmentation algorithm [26] because of its straightforward implementation, effective results, and efficient computation. This algorithm uses a variation of Kruskal's minimum spanning tree algorithm to iteratively cluster pixels in decreasing order of their similarity in appearance. An adaptive estimate of the internal similarity of the clusters is used to determine whether to continue clustering. Figure 4 shows the results of graph-based segmentation on an example of 640×480 RGB color image taken in our lab using the default value for the scale parameter ($k = 500$). As can be seen, the segmentation provides a reasonable representation of the layout of the items in the pile. From this result, we determine the foreground regions as those that do not touch the boundary of the image.

3.4. Global Features

3.4.1. Color Histogram (CH). A CH is a representation of the distribution of the colors in a region of an image, derived by counting the number of pixels with a given set of color values. CH are chosen in this work because they are invariant to translation and rotation about the viewing axis, and for most objects they remain stable despite changes in viewing direction, scale, and 3D rotation. CH is used to distinguish, for example, between lights and darks, as well as denim. We compute the CH of each object in HSV color space. The HSV color space is computed by converting the RGB space to hue, saturation, and value. Equations (2)–(6) display the equations needed to compute the hue of a pixel. In the case of $C = 0$, the first bin in the hue color channel is incremented to keep track of all undefined instances. Equations (7)-(8) display the equations needed to compute the value and saturations of a pixel, respectively. We use 15 bins for hue color channel and 10 bins for the saturation and value color channels, leading to 35 total bins. The hue ranges from $0 \rightarrow 360$ degrees; the saturation and the value both range from $0.0 \rightarrow 1.0$. Figure 5 illustrates the difference in an article of clothing with light colored and dark colored fabric

$$M = \max{(R, G, B)}, \tag{2}$$

$$m = \min{(R, G, B)}, \tag{3}$$

$$C = M - m, \tag{4}$$

$$H' = \begin{cases} \text{undefined}, & \text{if } C = 0, \\ \dfrac{G - B}{C} \bmod 6, & \text{if } M = R, \\ \dfrac{B - R}{C} + 2, & \text{if } M = G, \\ \dfrac{R - G}{C} + 4, & \text{if } M = B, \end{cases} \tag{5}$$

$$H = 60^{\circ} x\, H', \tag{6}$$

$$V = \max{(R, G, B)}, \tag{7}$$

$$S = \frac{C}{V}. \tag{8}$$

3.4.2. Histogram of Line Lengths (HLL). The histogram of line lengths (HLL) is a novel feature that we are introducing to help distinguish between stripes, patterns, plaid, and so forth. For this, we use the object image as before (after background subtraction) and compute the Canny edges [27], then erode with a 3×3 structuring element of ones to remove effects of the object boundary. Then we compute the length of each Canny edge using Kimura et al.'s [28] method. The Kimura et al.'s method uses diagonal movement (N_d) and isothetic movement (N_o) to accurately calculate the length of a pixelated edge within an image, see (9). Diagonal movements (N_d) refer to moving from the center pixel to one of the four corners within a 3×3 window and isothetic movements (N_o) refer to moving directly left, right, up, or down, see Figure 6. These pixel lengths are used to compute a histogram of 20 bins that range from 0 pixels to 1000 pixels, so each bin captures lengths within 50 pixels. Lengths greater than 1000 get mapped down to the last bin. Figure 7 illustrates the difference in an article of clothing with no texture, with stripes, and with plaid

$$L = \left[N_d^2 + \left(N_d + \frac{N_o}{2} \right)^2 \right]^{1/2} + \frac{N_o}{2}. \tag{9}$$

3.4.3. Table Point Feature Histogram (TPFH). The TPFH consists of a 263-dimension array of float values that result from three 45-value subdivisions, that are calculated from extended fast point feature histograms (eFPFH), and 128-value subdivision for table angle information. This feature is a variant on the viewpoint feature histogram (VFH) [29]. The eFPFH values are calculated by taking the difference of the estimated normals of each point and the estimated normal of the objects centerpoint. The estimated normals of each point and the centerpoint are calculated by projecting them on the XY, YZ, and XZ plane. The differences between the two normals are labeled β, θ, and ϕ. These three values, ranging from $-90 \rightarrow +90$ degrees (4 degrees each bin), are placed within bins in the three 45-value histograms of the eFPFH. Figure 8 illustrates the graphical representation of the normals and how they are calculated. The 128-value table

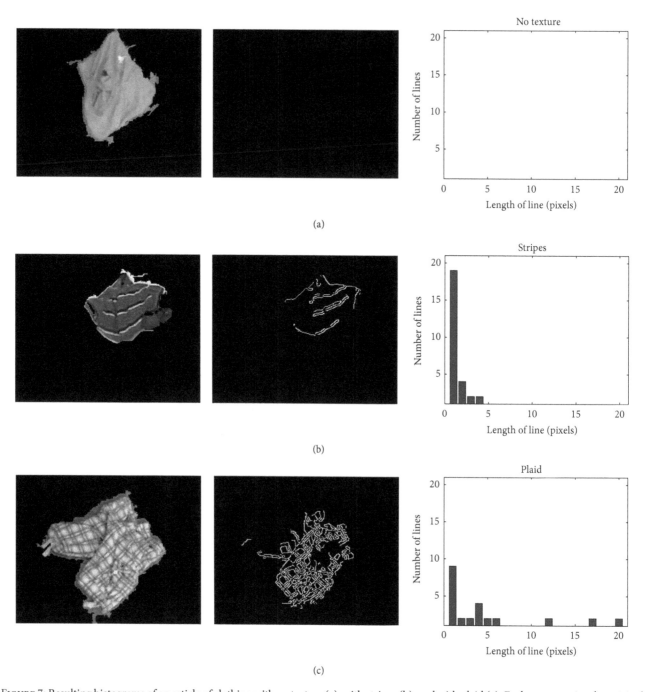

FIGURE 7: Resulting histograms of an article of clothing with no texture (a), with stripes (b), and with plaid (c). Each row contains the original image, the image after using Canny edge detector, and the histogram of line lengths.

histogram is computed by finding the angle, α, between each normal vector and the translated central table vector for each point. The central table vector is translated to the same point as the normal that is currently being computed. Figure 8 illustrates the difference in direction for each vector. In TPFH, the eFPFH component is a translation, rotation, and scale invariant, while the table component is only a scale invariant, 3D representation of the local shape. Figure 9 illustrates an example of how the TPFH values are visually different in two separate categories.

3.4.4. Boundary. The boundary feature captures 2D shape information by storing the Euclidean distances from the centroid of each article to the boundary. First, the centroid of each binary image is calculated containing the object (after background subtraction). Then, starting at the angle of the major axis found by principle components analysis, 16 angles that range from 0 to 360 (i.e., 0 to 337.5) are calculated around the object. Angles are 0, 22.5, 45, 67.5, ... , 315, 337.5. For each angle, we measure the distance from the centroid to the furthest boundary pixel, see Figure 10.

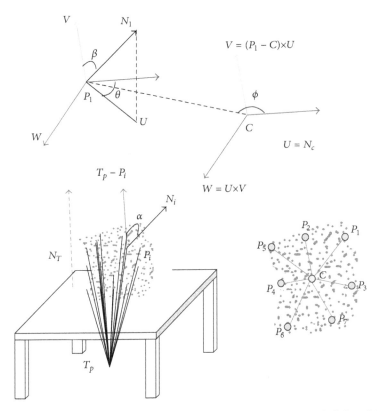

FIGURE 8: Graphical representation of the two components of TPFH. Top: eFPFH component with $\beta, \theta,$ and ϕ shown. $V, W,$ and U represent the coordinates of point C (centroid), with respect to the normal of C and the position of C and P_1. N_1 is the normal of point P_1. Bottom: Table component with α shown. T_p is the centroid of the table, while N_T is the normal of the table. N_i is the normal of point P_i and $P_1 \rightarrow P_7$ are arbitrary points in the cloud surrounding point C.

TABLE 2: List of 27 unique characteristics and the number of instances for each characteristic that were chosen to differentiate categories of clothing. The number of articles containing each characteristic is indicated in parantheses.

Collar (21)	Front pockets (39)	Back pockets (26)	Side pockets (8)	Elastic band (32)	Front zipper (28)
Top brackets (10)	Graphic pictures (47)	Graphic texts (7)	Belt loops (25)	Top buttons (30)	Shoulder hem (15)
Dark colored (70)	Colored (94)	White colored (38)	V-neck (7)	Striped (11)	Wrist hem (26)
Denim (13)	Plaid (5)	Patterns (18)	Round neck (73)	Bicep hem (59)	Shin hem (15)
Ankle hem (30)	Thigh hem (28)	Inseam (52)			

3.5. Local Features

3.5.1. SIFT Descriptor.
The SIFT, scale invariant feature transform [30], descriptor is used to gather useful 2D local texture information. The SIFT descriptor locates points on the article (after background subtraction) that provide local extremum when convolved with a Gaussian function. These points are then used to calculate a histogram of gradients (HoG) from the neighboring pixels. The descriptor consists of a 128-value feature vector that is scale and rotation invariant. Figure 11 illustrates the SIFT feature points found on an article. The arrows represent the orientation and magnitude of the feature point. After all of the feature points are found on an article, the SIFT descriptors are placed within a bag-of-words model [24] to calculate 100 codewords. These codewords provide each article with a 100-element feature vector that represents the local texture information.

3.5.2. FPFH.
The FPFH, fast point feature histogram [31], descriptor is used to gather local 3D shape information. The FPFH descriptor utilizes the 3D point cloud and background subtraction for each article and segments the article from the background of the point cloud. For each 3D point, a simple point feature histogram (SPFH) is calculated by taking the difference of the normals between the current point and its k neighboring points with a radius r. Figure 12 illustrates an example of a 3D point along with its neighbors. The radius is precomputed for each point cloud to best capture local shape information. Once all of the SPFHs are computed, the FPFH descriptor of each point is found by adding the SPFH of that point along with a weighted sum of the k neighbors, see (10). FPFH is a histogram of 33 values, that is, three sets of 11 bins for the three different orthogonal planes of $XY, YZ,$ and XZ

$$\text{FPFH}(p) = \text{SPFH}(p) + \frac{1}{k}\sum_{i=1}^{k} w_i \text{ SPFH}(i). \tag{10}$$

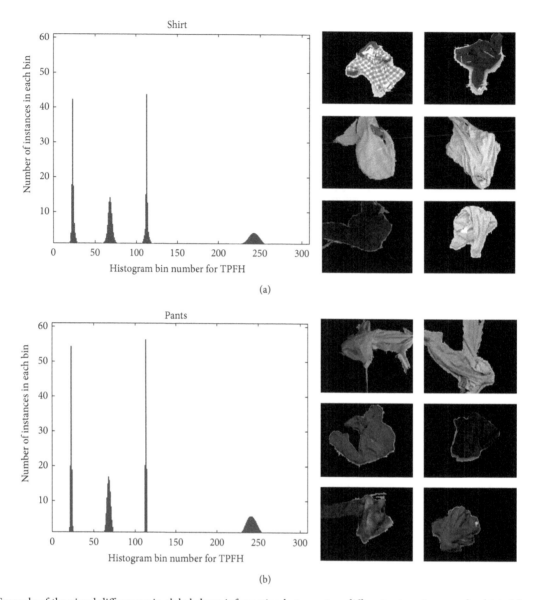

FIGURE 9: Example of the visual differences in global shape information between two different categories, namely, shirts (a) and pants (b). Each row contains the average histogram of the TPFH (left) and 6 examples of each category used to calculate the average (right). Shirts have a relatively lower number of instances in the first and third peak than pants. This example shows why the TPFH feature is useful in classifying clothing.

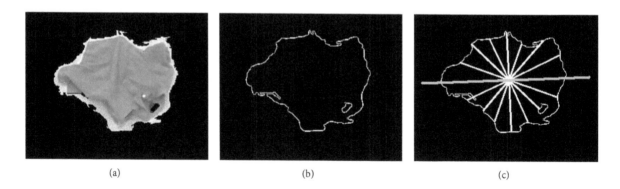

FIGURE 10: (a) Article segmented from background. (b) The binary boundary of the article. (c) The boundary of the article along with the lines connecting the centroid to the boundary, whose distances are used in the feature vector. The green line represents the major axis found by PCA.

FIGURE 11: Resulting SIFT features overlayed on the image. The arrows represent the orientation and scale (magnitude) of each SIFT descriptor.

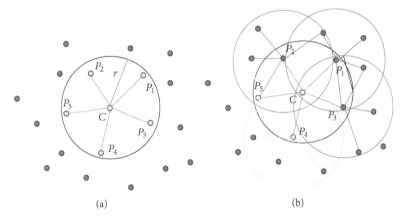

(a)   (b)

FIGURE 12: (a) Example of the SPFH of a single point. An area of radius r encircles 5 neighboring points for this example. (b) An example of the FPFH of the current point along with surrounding SPFHs used in the reweighting scheme. Each neighboring SPFH is color coded to represent the surrounding connections within the various regions.

TABLE 3: Results of baseline system in previous work.

	Shirt	Dress	Socks
Local features			
Shirt	**98.82**	1.18	0.00
Dress	100.00	**0.00**	0.00
Socks	0.00	13.64	**86.36**
Average TPR = 61.73%			
Global features			
Shirt	**57.65**	2.35	40.00
Dress	60.00	**0.00**	40.00
Socks	36.36	18.18	**45.45**
Average TPR = 34.37%			
Local and global features			
Shirt	**40.00**	0.00	60.00
Dress	40.00	**0.00**	60.00
Socks	18.18	27.27	**54.55**
Average TPR = 31.52%			

TPR stands for true positive rate.

3.5.3. Final Input Feature Vector. Once the features are computed, the global features are concatenated to create a histogram of $35 + 20 + 263 + 16 = 334$ values. For local features, SIFT and FPFH are calculated separately through bag-of-words to get two 100-element histograms of codewords.

Being concatenated, this yields 200 values for the local features. Then being concatenated with global features yields 534 values, which are then fed to the multiple one-versus-all SVMs.

3.6. Midlevel Layers

3.6.1. Characteristics. The C component of the approach uses the characteristics found on everyday clothing that is best suited for each category. We use a binary vector of 27 values that correspond to each characteristic used to learn what attributes are needed to separate the differences between shirts and dresses. The 27 characteristics that were chosen are shown in Table 2, along with the number of instances of each characteristic in the database. Figure 13 illustrates the breakdown of how much each characteristic is used per category. Light red blocks represent small percentages, dark purple blocks represent high precentages, and blank areas represent a percentage of zero. The color scheme changes from red to purple as the percentage increases.

3.6.2. Selection Mask. The S component of the approach uses the characteristics to determine which subset is best suited for each category. The selection masks are stored as a binary value; 0 or *FALSE*, means that the category does not need

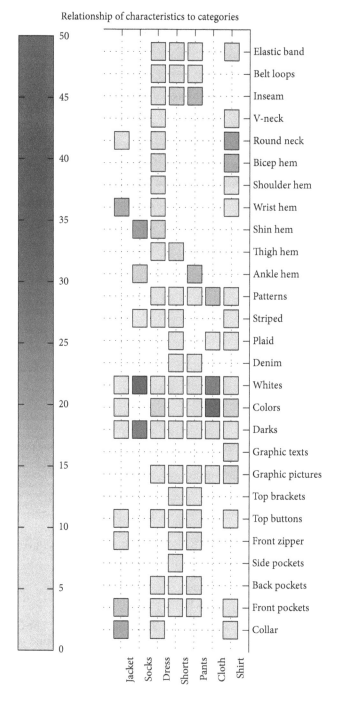

FIGURE 13: A graphical representation of the percentage of characteristics that are contained within each category. The color scheme changes from red to purple as the percentage increases. Light red colors represent small percentages. Dark purple colors represent high precentages. Blank areas represent a percentage of zero.

that particular characteristic, and 1 or *TRUE*, means that the category does need that particular characteristic.

We aimed to determine what characteristics have a higher importance and which have a lower importance for each category. Therefore, we zeroed one characteristic at a time and viewed the resulting percentage over the rest of the characteristics. The percentage was determined by comparing the characteristic vector for each article against mean vectors

for each category, which are calculated in Section 3.7. If the current percentage was higher or equal to the previously calculated percentage, then we zeroed that particular characteristic for the next iteration.

Importance values closer to 1.00 represent a positive type of instance and importance value scloser to 0.00 represent a negative type of instance. Importance values closer to 1.00 were chosen based on the fact that for one particular category,

TABLE 4: Results of baseline system using SVM to classify objects within seven categories.

	Shirt	Cloth	Pants	Shorts	Dress	Socks	Jacket
Local features							
Shirt	**98.82**	0.00	1.18	0.00	0.00	0.00	0.00
Cloth	63.33	**0.00**	20.00	10.00	0.00	6.67	0.00
Pants	100.00	0.00	**0.00**	0.00	0.00	0.00	0.00
Shorts	96.00	0.00	4.00	**0.00**	0.00	0.00	0.00
Dress	100.00	0.00	0.00	0.00	**0.00**	0.00	0.00
Socks	0.00	0.00	0.00	13.64	0.00	**86.36**	0.00
Jacket	100.00	0.00	0.00	0.00	0.00	0.00	**0.00**
Average TPR = **26.46**%							
Global features							
Shirt	**48.24**	0.00	1.18	10.59	0.00	40.00	0.00
Cloth	13.33	**50.00**	3.33	23.33	0.00	10.00	0.00
Pants	28.00	0.00	**0.00**	16.00	0.00	56.00	0.00
Shorts	44.00	0.00	4.00	**16.00**	0.00	36.00	0.00
Dress	40.00	0.00	0.00	20.00	**0.00**	40.00	0.00
Socks	18.18	9.09	0.00	27.27	0.00	**45.45**	0.00
Jacket	60.00	0.00	0.00	20.00	0.00	20.00	**0.00**
Average TPR = **22.81**%							
Local and global features							
Shirt	**1.18**	0.00	4.71	34.12	0.00	60.00	0.00
Cloth	0.00	**0.00**	13.33	43.33	0.00	43.33	0.00
Pants	0.00	0.00	**8.00**	32.00	0.00	60.00	0.00
Shorts	0.00	0.00	8.00	**32.00**	0.00	60.00	0.00
Dress	0.00	0.00	0.00	40.00	**0.00**	60.00	0.00
Socks	0.00	0.00	4.55	45.45	0.00	**50.00**	0.00
Jacket	0.00	0.00	0.00	40.00	0.00	60.00	**0.00**
Average TPR = **13.03**%							

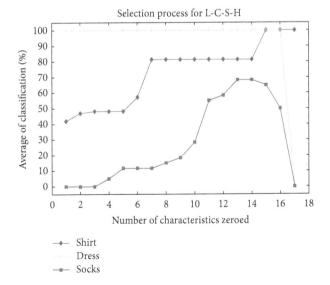

FIGURE 14: Characteristic selection process for L-C-S-H: results of removing a single redundant characteristic at each iteration. Starting from removing no characteristics and finishing with removing all characteristics.

TABLE 5: Results of L-C-H proposed system in previous work.

	Shirt	Dress	Socks
Local features			
Shirt	**41.18**	58.82	0.00
Dress	40.00	**60.00**	0.00
Socks	0.00	90.91	**9.09**
Average TPR = **36.76**%			
Global features			
Shirt	**15.29**	84.71	0.00
Dress	40.00	**60.00**	0.00
Socks	13.64	86.36	**0.00**
Average TPR = **25.10**%			
Local and global features			
Shirt	**21.18**	78.82	0.00
Dress	20.00	**80.00**	0.00
Socks	36.36	63.64	**0.00**
Average TPR = **33.73**%			

there is a likelihood that the category will contain a characteristic, more often, over the other categories. Importance

TABLE 6: Results of L-C-H proposed system to classify clothing using seven categories.

	Shirt	Cloth	Pants	Shorts	Dress	Socks	Jacket
Local features							
Shirt	**41.18**	0.00	0.00	0.00	58.82	0.00	0.00
Cloth	23.33	**0.00**	6.67	0.00	70.00	0.00	0.00
Pants	44.00	0.00	**0.00**	0.00	56.00	0.00	0.00
Shorts	36.00	0.00	0.00	**0.00**	64.00	0.00	0.00
Dress	40.00	0.00	0.00	0.00	**60.00**	0.00	0.00
Socks	0.00	0.00	54.55	13.64	31.82	**0.00**	0.00
Jacket	20.00	0.00	0.00	0.00	80.00	0.00	**0.00**
Average TPR = **14.45%**							
Global features							
Shirt	**14.12**	0.00	4.71	0.00	80.00	0.00	1.18
Cloth	16.67	**0.00**	6.67	13.33	63.33	0.00	0.00
Pants	20.00	0.00	**4.00**	0.00	76.00	0.00	0.00
Shorts	28.00	0.00	4.00	**4.00**	64.00	0.00	0.00
Dress	40.00	0.00	0.00	0.00	**60.00**	0.00	0.00
Socks	13.64	0.00	0.00	0.00	86.36	**0.00**	0.00
Jacket	20.00	0.00	0.00	0.00	80.00	0.00	**0.00**
Average TPR = **11.73%**							
Local and global features							
Shirt	**21.18**	0.00	0.00	0.00	78.82	0.00	0.00
Cloth	10.00	**0.00**	0.00	0.00	90.00	0.00	0.00
Pants	24.00	0.00	**0.00**	0.00	76.00	0.00	0.00
Shorts	28.00	0.00	0.00	**0.00**	72.00	0.00	0.00
Dress	20.00	0.00	0.00	0.00	**80.00**	0.00	0.00
Socks	36.36	0.00	0.00	4.55	59.09	**0.00**	0.00
Jacket	20.00	0.00	0.00	0.00	80.00	0.00	**0.00**
Average TPR = **14.45%**							

TABLE 7: Results of L-C-S-H proposed system in previous work.

	Shirt	Dress	Socks
Local features			
Shirt	**95.80**	4.20	0.00
Dress	13.32	**86.65**	0.02
Socks	0.60	11.67	**87.72**
Average TPR = **90.06%**			
Global features			
Shirt	**90.41**	9.51	0.08
Dress	2.80	**96.95**	0.25
Socks	30.45	69.55	**0.00**
Average TPR = **62.45%**			
Local and global features			
Shirt	**58.64**	40.64	0.72
Dress	4.32	**95.67**	0.02
Socks	37.10	44.66	**18.24**
Average TPR = **57.52%**			

will contain that characteristic. Positive importance values can be converted to +1 and negative importance values can be converted to −1 to better understand how each characteristic contributes to that one category.

The next iteration repeated the same process of removing one characteristic at a time along with having the previously chosen characteristics removed. After permanently removing several features, the resulting classification percentage began to increase to a peak and after the peak began to decrease when we removed the remaining characteristics. Next, we then created a binary vector for each category that contained a 1 or *TRUE* if the characteristic has a higher importance and a 0 or *FALSE* if the characteristic has a lower importance. Algorithm 1 steps through the process of C-S.

3.7. High-Level Categories. The H component of the approach uses the characteristic vectors that correspond to the articles within the training set to average the binary vectors of each category together to create a mean vector, as a descriptor, for each category. In other words, all shirts have averaged their characteristic vectors together, all dresses have averaged their characteristic vectors, and so on to create seven unique mean vectors, one for each category. Then the selection mask

values closer to 0.00 were chosen based on the fact that for one particular category, there is a likelihood that the category will not contain a characteristic while the other categories

TABLE 8: Results of L-C-S-H proposed system to classify objects.

	Shirt	Cloth	Pants	Shorts	Dress	Socks	Jacket
			Local Features				
Shirt	**95.80**	0.00	0.00	0.00	4.20	0.00	0.00
Cloth	28.08	**0.00**	0.00	0.00	69.45	2.48	0.00
Pants	53.33	0.00	**0.00**	0.00	46.67	0.00	0.00
Shorts	47.53	0.00	0.00	**0.00**	52.47	0.00	0.00
Dress	13.32	0.00	0.00	0.00	**86.65**	0.02	0.00
Socks	0.60	0.01	0.00	0.00	11.67	**87.72**	0.00
Jacket	33.81	0.00	0.00	0.00	66.19	0.00	**0.00**
			Average TPR = **38.60%**				
			Global Features				
Shirt	**90.41**	0.00	0.00	0.00	9.51	0.08	0.00
Cloth	23.04	**0.00**	0.00	0.00	76.90	0.06	0.00
Pants	37.04	0.00	**0.00**	0.00	62.94	0.02	0.00
Shorts	36.93	0.00	0.00	**0.00**	63.00	0.07	0.00
Dress	2.80	0.00	0.00	0.00	**96.95**	0.25	0.00
Socks	30.45	0.00	0.00	0.00	69.55	**0.00**	0.00
Jacket	23.36	0.00	0.00	0.00	76.64	0.00	**0.00**
			Average TPR = **26.77%**				
			Local and Global Features				
Shirt	**65.79**	0.00	0.00	0.89	31.49	0.04	1.79
Cloth	18.67	**0.00**	3.72	4.43	67.42	0.01	5.75
Pants	36.00	0.00	**1.93**	0.52	45.53	0.00	16.02
Shorts	32.94	0.00	1.72	**2.24**	45.62	0.05	17.43
Dress	5.48	0.00	0.00	0.07	**93.80**	0.00	0.65
Socks	37.54	0.00	1.26	3.17	50.06	**0.00**	7.97
Jacket	17.39	0.00	0.00	0.03	50.37	0.02	**32.20**
			Average TPR = **27.99%**				

Input: Characteristic vector for wth category (CC_w)
Output: Selection mask for wth category (SM_w)
$SM_w = 2^{26} - 1$;
$RM_w = 2^{27} - 1$;
foreach $Article_i \in Category_w$ **do**
    $NC_w = (CC_w \times SM_w) \cap RM$;
    If $Result(NC_w) \geq Result(CC_w)$ **then**
        $RM_w = RM_w \cap 2^{27} - 2^i - 1$;
    end
    $SM_w = SM_w \gg 1$;
end

ALGORITHM 1: The process of C-S to determine the final selection mask for each category. CC_w, NC_w, SM_w, and RM_w are binary vectors that represent if a characteristic is used (1) or removed (0), out of the 27 listed in Table 2, for each category. $\gg$ stands for a bit shift in the binary vector. Result($\cdot$) calculates the resulting classification percentage after running the new selection mask on the training set.

is multiplied by the characteristic vector to zero out any characteristics with a negative importance.

4. Experimental Results

The proposed approach was applied to a laundry scenario to test its ability to perform practical classification. In each experiment, the entire database consisted of 85 shirts, 30 cloths, 25 pants, 25 shorts, 10 dresses, 22 socks, and 5 jackets. The database was labeled using a supervised learning approach so that the corresponding category of each image was known. We provide an approach that illustrates the use of having midlevel characteristics (attributes) in grouping clothing categories that are difficult to classify. First, we consider the baseline approach that uses SVMs to directly classify each category without the use of midlevel characteristics. Then, we

TABLE 9: Overview of results for varying numbers of categories: (A) 3, (B) 4, and (C) 7. Group (A) consists of shirts, socks, and dresses. Group (B) consists of group (A) plus cloths. Group (C) consists of group (B) plus pants, shorts, and jackets.

Number of categories	Local	Global	Local + Global
Baseline			
3	61.73	34.37	31.52
4	46.3	38.28	19.22
7	26.46	22.81	13.03
L-C-S-H			
3	90.06	62.45	57.52
4	67.54	46.84	43.13
7	38.60	26.77	27.99
Increase from Baseline to L-C-S-H			
3	+28.33	+28.08	+26.00
4	+21.24	+8.56	+23.91
7	+12.14	+3.96	+14.96

introduce characteristics as an alternate mapping from low-level features to high-level categories.

4.1. Baseline Approach without Midlevel Layers. This experiment demonstrates the baseline approach using the low-level features to classify each article of clothing correctly with support vector machines (SVM). We consider various aspects of the SVM approach to better understand how the articles are categorized. This experiment uses local, global, and a combined set of low-level features as input for each SVM that is used to classify for a particular article. Since there are seven categories to choose from, then seven SVMs are trained in order to provide a probability value for each input vector from the test set. For this type of multiclass classi-fication, we chose the one-versus-all (OVA) approach for each SVM, which uses a single SVM to compare each class with all other classes combined. Previous researchers [32–35] suggest that for sparse data sets, the OVA approach provides better results over the max-wins-voting (MWV) approach, which uses a single SVM for each pair of classes resulting in a voting scheme.

Each experiment was conducted using the 5-fold cross validation (CV) [36] to completely test this stage of the algo-rithm. We used 80% of each category for training and 20% for testing, with each train and test set being mutually exclusive for each validation. To better describe the separation, we used 80% of the database that had a 1 or *TRUE* for that category 80% of the database that had a 0 or *FALSE* for that category to make the training set, and the rest of the database went to the test set. The resulting value from each SVM ranges from $-1 \rightarrow +1$, with a deciding threshold of 0.

4.2. Testing Approach with Characteristics (L-C-H). For our experiment with L-C-H, we used 5-fold CV to test this stage of the algorithm, as in the previous experiments (Tables 5–8). The goal of this experiment is to determine the increase of overall performance with the addition of characteristics. The

training set still consists of the ground truth characteristics to compute the mean vectors for each category.

4.3. L-C-H versus L-C-S-H. For our experiment with L-C-S-H, we used 5-fold CV to test this stage of the algorithm, as in the previous experiments. The goal of this experiment is to determine the increase of overall performance with the addition of a selection mask between the characteristics and the high-level categories. The training set still consists of the ground truth characteristics to compute the mean vectors for each category. Each category demonstrates an increase in percentage until a threshold has been reached. Each threshold varies based on the low-level features used and what category is being tested. At that time, the percentage then eventually decreases to 0% after reaching the threshold.

Figure 14 illustrates the resulting TPR (true positive rate) as the most negatively important characteristic removed at each iteration, using local and global features. Each category demonstrates an increase in percentage until a threshold has been reached. This threshold is decided to coincide with the least amount of remaining characteristics that produce the highest TPR. At that time, the percentage then eventually decreases to 0% when the rest of the characteristics are zeroed out. So, zeroing out a subset of negatively important chara-cteristics improves the overall TPR. Characteristic values for the mean category vector in the training set are the only values that are zeroed out. The training vectors go through this process to better describe how each category is characterized, while the testing vectors are not changed and compared to how close they are to each mean vector.

5. Conclusion

We have proposed a novel method to classify clothing (L-M-H, more specifically L-S-C-H) in which midlevel layers (i.e., physical characteristics and selection masks) are used to classify categories of clothing. The proposed system uses a database of 2D color images and 3D point clouds of clothing captured from a Kinect sensor. The paper is focused on deter-mining how well this new approach improves classification over a baseline system. The database of clothing, that we use in our experiments, contains articles of clothing whose configurations are difficult to determine their corresponding category.

The overall improvement of this new approach illustrates the critical importance of middle-level information. The addition of middle-level features, termed characteristics and selection masks for this problem, enabled the classification process to improve, on average, by +27.47% for three cate-gories, +17.90% for four categories and +10.35% for seven categories, see Table 9. Increasing the number of categories, increases the number of characteristics for the algorithm to classify. With the increase in complexity, the average true positive rate decreases due to the difficulty of the problem.

Using this approach could improve other types of clas-sification/identification problems such as object recognition, object identification, person recognition. The use of middle-level features could range from one or more layers. This approach does not have to be limited to using only two layers of features (e.g., characteristics and selection masks). The notion of adding more features in between the low and high level may increase the percentage rate. Layers of filters, that could be used to distinguish between categories, could include separating adult clothing from child clothing or male clothing from female clothing.

Future extensions of this approach include classification of subcategories (e.g., types of shirts, types of dresses), age, gender, and the season of each article of clothing. The experiments are used on a subset of characteristics that are useful for each category. Perhaps the amount of characteristics that are used in the midlevel layer correspond to the resulting classification percentages. This approach could be applied to separating clothing into three groups of darks, colors, and whites before the laundry is placed into the washing machine. This novel approach can apply to grouping and labeling other rigid and nonrigid items beyond clothing.

Acknowledgment

This research was supported by the US National Science Foundation under Grants IIS-1017007 and IIS-0904116.

References

[1] S. Hata, T. Hiroyasu, J. Hayash, H. Hojoh, and T. Hamada, "Flexible handling robot system for cloth," in *Proceedings of the IEEE International Conference on Mechatronics and Automation (ICMA '09)*, pp. 49–54, August 2009.

[2] Y. Yoshida, J. Hayashi, S. Hata, H. Hojoh, and T. Hamada, "Status estimation of cloth handling robot using force sensor," in *Proceedings of the IEEE International Symposium on Industrial Electronics (ISIE '09)*, pp. 339–343, July 2009.

[3] K. Salleh, H. Seki, Y. Kamiya, and M. Hikizu, "Tracing manipulation in clothes spreading by robot arms," *Journal of Robotics and Mechatronics*, vol. 18, no. 5, pp. 564–571, 2006.

[4] Y. Kita and N. Kita, "A model-driven method of estimating the state of clothes for manipulating it," in *Proceedings of the 6th Workshop on Applications of Computer Vision*, pp. 63–69, 2002.

[5] Y. Kita, F. Saito, and N. Kita, "A deformable model driven visual method for handling clothes," in *Proceedings of the IEEE International Conference on Robotics and Automation*, pp. 3889–3895, May 2004.

[6] Y. Kita, T. Ueshiba, E. Neo, and N. Kita, "A method for handling a specific part of clothing by dual arms," in *Proceedings of the Conference on Intelligent Robots and Systems (IROS '09)*, pp. 3403–3408, 2009.

[7] P. Gibbons, P. Culverhouse, and G. Bugmann, "Visual identification of grasp locations on clothing for a personal robot," in *Proceedings of the Conference Towards Autonomous Robotics Systems (TAROS '09)*, pp. 78–81, August 2009.

[8] H. Kobayashi, S. Hata, H. Hojoh, T. Hamada, and H. Kawai, "A study on handling system for cloth using 3-D vision sensor," in *Proceedings of the 34th Annual Conference of the IEEE Industrial Electronics Society (IECON '08)*, pp. 3403–3408, November 2008.

[9] B. Willimon, S. Birchfield, and I. Walker, "Classification of clothing using interactive perception," in *Proceedings of the IEEE International Conference on Robotics and Automation (ICRA '11)*, pp. 1862–1868, 2011.

[10] M. Kaneko and M. Kakikura, "Planning strategy for unfolding task of clothes—isolation of clothes from washed mass," in *Proceedings of the 13th annual conference of the Robotics Society of Japan (RSJ '96)*, pp. 455–456, 1996.

[11] M. Kaneko and M. Kakikura, "Planning strategy for putting away laundry—isolating and unfolding task," in *Proceedings of the IEEE International Symposium on Assembly and Task Planning (ISATP '01)*, pp. 429–434, May 2001.

[12] F. Osawa, H. Seki, and Y. Kamiya, "Unfolding of massive laundry and classification types by dual manipulator," *Journal of Advanced Computational Intelligence and Intelligent Informatics*, vol. 11, no. 5, pp. 457–463.

[13] Y. Kita, T. Ueshiba, E. S. Neo, and N. Kita, "Clothes state recognition using 3d observed data," in *Proceedings of the IEEE International Conference on Robotics and Automation (ICRA '09)*, pp. 1220–1225, May 2009.

[14] M. Cusumano-Towner, A. Singh, S. Miller, J. F. O'Brien, and P. Abbeel, "Bringing clothing into desired configurations with limited perception," in *Proceedings of the International Conference on Robotics and Automation*, May 2011.

[15] B. Willimon, I. Walker, and S. Birchfield, "A new approach to clothing classification using mid-level layers," in *Proceedings of the IEEE International Conference on Robotics and Automation (ICRA '13)*, 2013.

[16] B. Willimon, S. Birchfield, and I. Walker, "Model for unfolding laundry using interactive perception," in *Proceedings of the IEEE/RSJ International Conference on Intelligent Robots and Systems (IROS '11)*, 2011.

[17] S. Miller, M. Fritz, T. Darrell, and P. Abbeel, "Parametrized shape models for clothing," in *Proceedings of the International Conference on Robotics and Automation*, pp. 4861–4868, May 2011.

[18] D. Katz and O. Brock, "Manipulating articulated objects with interactive perception," in *Proceedings of the IEEE International Conference on Robotics and Automation (ICRA '08)*, pp. 272–277, May 2008.

[19] J. Kenney, T. Buckley, and O. Brock, "Interactive segmentation for manipulation in unstructured environments," in *Proceedings of the International Conference on Robotics and Automation (ICRA '09)*, pp. 1377–1382, 2009.

[20] P. Fitzpatrick, "First contact: an active vision approach to segmentation," in *Proceedings of the International Conference on Intelligent Robots and Systems (IROS '03)*, pp. 2161–2166, 2003.

[21] B. Willimon, S. Birchfield, and I. Walker, "Rigid and non-rigid classification using interactive perception," in *Proceedings of the 23rd IEEE/RSJ International Conference on Intelligent Robots and Systems (IROS '10)*, pp. 1728–1733, October 2010.

[22] R. B. Willimon, *Interactive perception for cluttered environments [M.S. thesis]*, Clemson University, 2009.

[23] C. C. Chang and C. J. Lin, *LIBSVM: A Library for Support Vector Machines*, 2001.

[24] H. M. Wallach, "Topic modeling: beyond bag-of-words," in *Proceedings of the 23rd International Conference on Machine Learning (ICML '06)*, pp. 977–984, June 2006.

[25] A. Ramisa, G. Alenyà, F. Moreno-Noguer, and C. Torras, "Using depth and appearance features for informed robot grasping of highly wrinkled clothes," in *Proceedings of the International Conference on Robotics and Automation*, pp. 1703–1708, 2012.

[26] P. F. Felzenszwalb and D. P. Huttenlocher, "Efficient graph-based image segmentation," *International Journal of Computer Vision*, vol. 59, no. 2, pp. 167–181, 2004.

[27] J. F. Canny, "A computational approach to edge detection," *IEEE Transactions on Pattern Analysis and Machine Intelligence*, vol. 8, no. 6, pp. 679–698, 1986.

[28] K. Kimura, S. Kikuchi, and S. Yamasaki, "Accurate root length measurement by image analysis," *Plant and Soil*, vol. 216, no. 1, pp. 117–127, 1999.

[29] R. B. Rusu, G. Bradski, R. Thibaux, and J. Hsu, "Fast 3D recognition and pose using the viewpoint feature histogram," in *Proceedings of the 23rd IEEE/RSJ International Conference on Intelligent Robots and Systems (IROS '10)*, pp. 2155–2162, October 2010.

[30] D. G. Lowe, "Distinctive image features from scale-invariant keypoints," *International Journal of Computer Vision*, vol. 60, no. 2, pp. 91–110, 2004.

[31] R. Rusu, N. Blodow, and M. Beetz, "Fast point feature histograms (FPFH) for 3D registration," in *Proceedings of the IEEE International Conference on Robotics and Automation (ICRA '09)*, Intelligent Autonomous Systems IAS, May 2009.

[32] A. Gidudu, G. Hulley, and T. Marwala, "Image classification using SVMs: one-against-one vs one-against-all," in *Proccedings of the 28th Asian Conference on Remote Sensing*, 2007.

[33] J. Milgram, M. Cheriet, and R. Sabourin, "One against one or one against all: which one is better for handwriting recognition with SVMs?" in *Proceedings of the 10th International Workshop on Frontiers in Handwriting Recognition*, October 2006.

[34] R. Rifkin and A. Klautau, "In defense of one-vs-all classification," *Journal of Machine Learning Research*, vol. 5, pp. 101–141, 2004.

[35] K. bo Duan and S. S. Keerthi, "Which is the best multiclass SVM method? an empirical study," in *Proceedings of the 6th International Workshop on Multiple Classifier Systems*, pp. 278–285, 2005.

[36] P. A. Devijver and J. Kittler, *Pattern Recognition: A Statistical Approach*, Prentice Hall, London, UK, 1982.

13

Continuous Backbone "Continuum" Robot Manipulators

Ian D. Walker

Department of Electrical and Computer Engineering, Clemson University, Clemson, SC 29634, USA

Correspondence should be addressed to Ian D. Walker; iwalker@clemson.edu

Academic Editors: J. Archibald and J. B. Koeneman

This paper describes and discusses the history and state of the art of continuous backbone robot manipulators. Also known as continuum manipulators, these robots, which resemble biological trunks and tentacles, offer capabilities beyond the scope of traditional rigid-link manipulators. They are able to adapt their shape to navigate through complex environments and grasp a wide variety of payloads using their compliant backbones. In this paper, we review the current state of knowledge in the field, focusing particularly on kinematic and dynamic models for continuum robots. We discuss the relationships of these robots and their models to their counterparts in conventional rigid-link robots. Ongoing research and future developments in the field are discussed.

1. Introduction

Robotics as a field is still in its formative stages. Designers of robots are continuing to explore the range of possibilities for robot structures which can sense and perceive, navigate and locomote, as well as grasp and manipulate. The creation of programmable manipulators can be traced to be very beginning of robotics as a discipline [1]. To date, robot manipulators remain the core product of the field, being productively and profitably deployed in industrial settings worldwide.

However, when moving outside the highly structured world of industry, especially the factory floor, traditional rigid-link manipulators have been less successful. Their rigid-link structure (while excellent for precise positioning of their end effector) tends to be the cause of unwanted collisions when not in workcell environments specially engineered to maintain open spaces for their movements. Their inability to grasp objects other than at their end effector significantly restricts their manipulation capabilities beyond those of objects preengineered to fit their end effectors. Consequently, in real-world environments and situations not prechoreographed, it is generally nontrivial, and often not possible, to deploy rigid-link manipulators.

Robot manipulators do not, however, have to be formed from rigid-links. An alternative design possibility, which we discuss in this paper, is to create a robot with a continuous form or backbone. These robots, termed *continuum robots*, can be viewed as being "invertebrate" robots, as compared with the "vertebrate" design of conventional rigid-link robots. Continuum robots can bend (and often extend/contract and sometimes twist) at any point along their structure. This provides them with capabilities beyond the scope of their rigid-link counterparts. An example (in the following paragraph) serves to illustrate this.

In Figure 1, a continuum robot gently contacts and adapts its shape to wrap around a fragile object (a glass lampshade). Subsequent to this image, the robot lifted and performed "whole arm manipulation" [2] of the object, without causing breakage or damage. This was achieved with no prior planning or knowledge of the object and without any sensing of the contact between robot and object. This would be an extremely difficult operation for a conventional rigid-link robot manipulator. Active force sensing would be required to present a sufficiently compliant interface to avoid breakage of the object. Further, note that even grasping such an object would require significant a priori specialized tooling or fixturing, as the object geometry is inherently unsuitable for grasping with a parallel jaw gripper. However, the continuum robot was able to use its compliant, actively controlled continuous structure to perform the operation easily, quickly, and without a priori knowledge or task engineering.

FIGURE 1: A continuum robot grasping and manipulating a fragile (glass) object, using its compliant backbone to adapt to the object's shape.

The above example of compliant whole arm grasping demonstrates one novel and appealing feature offered by continuum robots, compared to conventional rigid-link robots. Another key feature (and dual to the previous one above) is the potential to use the backbone to keep away from, rather than contract and grasp, complex environmental geometries. In this way, continuum backbones (note that the term backbone is used for continuum robots despite their invertebrate nature) can "twist and turn" to negotiate very tight spaces, thus penetrating areas where conventional robots would be unable to enter or would get their links stuck in. This novel potential and the attempt to realize that potential in useful hardware remain at the core of the field of continuum robots.

Historically, interest in continuous backbone robots began as early as the 1960s. As for the first continuum robot, Anderson and Horn's Tensor Arm [3] (discussed further in Section 2) appears to have been the first prototype reported in the literature. Intended for underwater applications, the prototype did not, however, progress from the laboratory stage. It was quickly realized that, while early prototypes could be made to achieve a wide range of shapes, the relationship between the shapes and inputs was highly complex—much more than for rigid-link robots and certainly challenging for implementations using the computing environments of the time.

There followed a lull in activities in the area until the late 1980s and early 1990s, when two key developments occurred. Inspired by the need to approximate hyperredundant (rigidlink) robot backbones, Chirikjian published the first works [4, 5] providing general continuous backbone kinematics and dynamics for robots. Inspired by the example of snake locomotion, Hirose [6] published innovative results on the evolution of continuous backbone shapes. (Hirose also produced continuum robot prototypes [6]). Together, the above efforts are the seminal work establishing the field.

Further efforts in continuous backbone robot hardware in the 1990s centered in two directions: (1) extension of the original tendon-driven design concepts of Anderson/Horn and Hirose aimed at practical implementation [7, 8] and applications [9–11] and (2) the new innovation of creating backbones with pneumatically actuated chambers [12–14]. Robinson and Davies, codevelopers of some of the second

group of contributions, coined the term "continuum robot" in 1999 [15].

In parallel with the above developments in hardware, the 1990s saw progress and innovation in continuum robot modeling, particularly in kinematics. In a series of papers [16–18], "bottom-up" continuum robot kinematics models were developed. These works began with the constraints of physical continuum robot backbones and formulated backbone kinematics from them. It can be seen (this is reviewed in detail in Section 3) that the models resulting from these "bottom-up" approaches can be formed from the initially published "top-down" theory of [4, 5]. The new models, being matched directly to hardware constraints, enabled modelbased implementations and thus real-time computer control of continuum robot shapes.

The late 1990s and the 2000s have seen a significant increase in the number of researchers in continuum robots and a corresponding increase in the number and breadth of published papers on the topic. In this paper, we review and discuss the current state of the art in the field of continuum robots. Summaries of early developments in the field have appeared [19, 20]. In this paper, we summarize the early work and update for the many recent developments in this rapidly emerging field. We begin in Section 2 by discussing the underlying design principles of continuum robots and classify continuum robot designs to date into three main design types. Section 3 provides an overview of the kinematics of continuum robots. The dynamics and control of continuum robots are reviewed and discussed in Section 4. Ongoing research in the field is summarized in Section 5. Conclusions follow in Section 6.

2. Design Principles

The defining feature of a continuum robot is a continuously curving core structure, or backbone, whose shape can be actuated in some way. An almost universal additional property is that the backbone is compliant; that is, it yields smoothly to externally applied loads. Together, these properties enable the physical capabilities which motivate continuum robots: to adapt the backbone shape to maneuver the robot within more complex environments and to conform to grasp a wider class of objects than feasible with rigid-link robots.

The design space available to achieve the above properties is very large. For example, the backbone core does not even have to be continuous. Snakes present the external appearance of having a continuous structure, but are vertebrates, with an internal segmented backbone comprised of (many very small) rigid-links. Robots with segmented rigidlink interior backbones presenting a continuous external form have been developed [8, 21–23]. These are sometimes termed "continuum-style" robots. However, such designs are rare, and almost all designers have sought to create truly continuous backbone structures. The most significant exceptions are the "snake-arms" [24] of OC Robotics [25], the only continuum-style robot currently commercially available. These robot arms, as the name suggests, are composed of serially connected modular rigid-link sections. While not truly continuum, with enough modules, the form resembles a continuous backbone. They have been deployed in nuclear reactors and inside airframes, among other applications [25].

Design of robot structures in the absence of rigid elements is an unfamiliar process for most robotics designers. However, several fundamental design principles can be identified by a careful study of biological "tongues, trunks, and tentacles" [26–28]. In particular, the group of structures termed "muscular hydrostats" [29], which includes octopus arms, elephant trunks, squid tentacles, and mammalian tongues, has provided a rich vein of insight for continuum robot designers. Animals do not have to be the only source of inspiration; the vines and tendrils of plants [30] are a source of inspiration also [31, 32].

Muscular hydrostats are structures comprised almost entirely of their own actuators (muscle), with some additional fluid and connective tissue. They can typically bend and twist and often extend to some extent at any point along their structure. The muscles are arranged in oriented arrays (longitudinal, transverse, and oblique) in a way that enables both the motive force and structural support for bending, extension, and torsion to be provided by the muscles [29]. Some initial work [33] aimed to mimic (albeit at a much less detailed scale) the muscular hydrostat design concept in continuum robots, using various artificial muscle technologies. However, practical continuum robots require not only significant bending but also high force generation, and the state of the art in artificial muscle technology (both at the time of publication of [33] and at the time of writing this paper) was not capable of satisfying these needs at scales suitable for continuum robots. If, at some future time, artificial muscle technologies advance sufficiently, the possibilities for design and operation of continuum robots could be revolutionized [34]. Note that issues of packaging, power consumption, wiring, and so forth would remain major challenges.

In the absence of technologies which can easily mimic the key biological inspirations, designers have followed several alternative paths. The basic requirements are to produce active bending and ideally also some extension and local torsion, of continuous backbone structure which possesses some helpful (predesigned) internal energy properties. Three alternative fundamental design strategies have emerged. Each strategy and notable continuum robots constructed to date using it are summarized in the following subsections.

2.1. Tendon-Based Designs.

Perhaps the most direct approach to bending a continuous structure is the use of remotely actuated tendons. Given a backbone which, in the absence of external loads, consistently attains a given shape (typically a straight line, though this is not strictly necessary [35]), tendons can be used to deviate it from that shape via bending. Tendons are routed along the backbone and terminated in groups at selected points down it. Forces applied to the tendons at the base produce torques at the termination points, resulting in bending. The design is quite simple and (relatively) straightforward to realize in hardware.

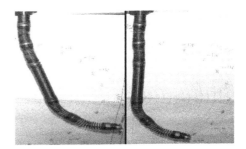

FIGURE 2: The Tendril, a tendon-driven continuum robot.

The first published example of a continuum robot, the "Tensor Arm" [3], is a good example of a tendon-based design. Tendons, routed through spacer elements, were used to effect bending of the core backbone element in several "sections." The termination points of sets of tendons along the backbone define the sections; see Figure 2.

One choice for the core backbone element is a compressible spring. An early spring-backbone-based design was produced by Hirose [6]. The more recent long thin "Tendril" continuum robot by NASA Johnson Space Center [31] is also based on a spring backbone (Figure 2). The spring backbone provides natural compliance. However, this also makes, the designs difficult to control, as control effort intended for backbone bending is lost in compression. The same is true for tendon-actuated pneumatic backbones (Figure 3).

A simple solution to the problem of uncontrolled compression is to use a flexible incompressible rod as the backbone element [7]; see Figure 4. This approach has several advantages including a slender low-profile backbone and more predictable behavior. The disadvantage of course is that this approach precludes the incorporation of backbone extension. However, the incompressible backbone concept has proved a popular and successful design, with numerous implementations based on it [36–39].

Tendon-based continuum designs share the following general features: (1) the backbone shape resolves into a finite series of "sections" whose end points are defined by the tendon termination points along the backbone; (2) the forces achievable with the device are relatively high (tendons generate relatively high forces); (3) some method must be found to prevent slack [17] and backlash [36] in the tendons; and (4) the design requires a relatively bulky actuator (motor) package at the base of the robot. With respect to (3), most implementations either actively actuate all tendons [40] or use a single actuator to actuate antagonistic tendon pairs, with a spring mechanism to take up the slack [17]. With respect to (4), the location of the actuator package outside the backbone has led to the tendon design being categorized as an "extrinsically actuated" continuum robot design [20].

Tendon-actuated continuum robots have been designed for space operations [31] and, in particular, medical procedures [40, 41]. A spring-based tendon-driven backbone continuum robot was developed for sinus surgery in [42] and another developed for ACL surgery in [43]. A system for laryngeal surgery was developed in [44]. A "robot octopus"

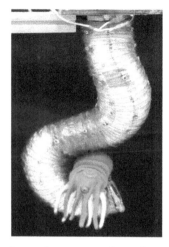

FIGURE 3: Air-Octor Continuum robot. This two-section, six-degree-of-freedom robot bends a pneumatically inflated core tube using six tendons.

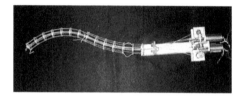

FIGURE 4: Tendon-based continuum robot with incompressible flexible rod core.

with six cable-actuated limbs has been demonstrated underwater in [45].

2.2. Concentric Tube Designs.

A second form of extrinsically actuated continuum robot (and the most recent to emerge) is based on a backbone formed by concentric compliant tubes. The tubes are free to move (translate and rotate) with respect to each other (subject to hardware limits) with the translations and rotations actuated at the base of the robot. The net effect is similar to some telescopes: the structure can extend and contract by translational sliding of the tubes longitudinally (modulo the length of the tubes, the smaller diameter tubes becoming the most distal), and the structure can achieve local rotation by rotational sliding of the tubes; see Figure 5.

The concentric tube design thus directly achieves both extension and torsion [46]. However, it does not inherently provide for backbone bending. The simplest approach to this issue is to use precurved compliant tubes [47, 48]. This, when combined with the directly controllable extension and torsion, provides some useful variation in backbone shapes. Another approach is to use tendons to bend the tubes [49, 50]. However, this significantly increases the complexity of the design [32].

Advantages of the concentric tube design include the inherently clean and thin design (assuming the design with no tendons to bend the tubes) and the fact that the actuator values (unlike with tendons) directly correspond to backbone

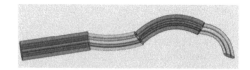

FIGURE 5: Concentric tube continuum robot concept.

shape variables. Disadvantages include the need for an external actuator package and the lack of inherent support for actively controlled bending.

Concentric tube continuum robots have found a niche application in the medical field, where their small profile and high compliance are well suited for minimally invasive procedures [49, 51, 52]. In this context, they are smaller-scale and lower-force devices than their counterparts constructed via the other two designs and are sometimes termed "active cannulas" [53]. For example, in [52], sampling-based motion planning techniques are used to design a concentric tube robot specifically for the task of navigation through the human lung. In [48], an MRI-compatible, piezoelectrically actuated concentric tube robot is designed for neurosurgery and percutaneous interventions.

2.3. Locally Actuated Backbone Designs.

The third design type differs from the previous two by including the actuators directly in the backbone. Indeed, this type of "locally actuated" continuum robot typically forms the backbone from its actuators. In this regard, the design is closest to the biological continuum structures which often motivate continuum robots. This also gives rise to the categorization of the design as "intrinsically actuated" [20].

Typical locally actuated designs form the backbone from pneumatic "McKibben" muscles [54, 55], though numerous versions using shape memory alloys [56] have also been built. The strategy is to form the backbone from independently actuated sections. Each section is constructed from (typically) three independently actuated muscles, connected together along their length. The muscles can be "extenders" (increased length as a function of increased pressure) [54, 57] or "contractors" (decreased length as a function of higher pressure) [54, 58]. See Figure 6 for an example of the "Octarm" series of locally pneumatically actuated continuum robots.

When pressure is evenly increased or decreased in all three actuators of a straight section, the section length increases or decreases. When differing pressures are applied to the actuators, the section bends into a segment with approximately constant curvature. The plane of the curve is determined by the three pressures. In general, the section extends, contracts, and changes its curvature and plane of curvature as a function of the three applied pressures. The net shape of the backbone is thus a serially connected set of approximately constant curvature segments (with the end tangents coinciding).

The locally actuated continuum robot design has been the subject of much research and numerous realizations in the recent years. In particular, the high-profile "Octarm"

FIGURE 6: Intrinsically actuated three-section, nine-degree-of-freedom pneumatic "Octarm" continuum manipulator.

[33, 57, 59, 60] and "European Octopus" [45, 54, 61, 62] projects featured continuum robots based on this design. Other realizations of the design include the "Bionic Assistant" [35, 63], which closely resembles the trunk of an elephant [28]. Shape memory alloy actuation has been used to steer an active cannula for medical procedures, and in [64, 65], dual shape memory alloy-based backbones are used in a system designed for single port access surgery. Additionally, a locally actuated system for endoscopic stitching intended for surgical obesity treatment is presented in [66], and a design for colonoscopic insertion is described in [67].

Actuator selection for intrinsically actuated continuum robots can be from any available type of artificial muscle. This could include muscles based on engineered polymers, such as elastomers, for example. An extensive study of the potential of these types of actuators is presented in [34]. However, at this time, only the pneumatic or hydraulic actuator technologies feature the combination of bending and force generation capabilities for continuum robots at the human scale or larger.

Locally actuated continuum robot designs have the key advantage of inherently providing the backbone with extension, bending, and torsion (actually, bending in two dimensions). This is a feature not directly provided by either tendons or concentric tubes, as discussed in the preceding subsections. Disadvantages of locally actuated designs include relatively low force generation capabilities (for pneumatically actuated designs at least), fairly complex tube routing/valving, and the need for external pressure regulation equipment and a compressor.

2.4. Variable Backbone Stiffness.
An interesting choice for continuum backbones is to use pneumatically actuated tubes. The KSI Tentacle Manipulator [11] and the Air-Octor robot ([68, 69] Figure 3) were each based on tendon-actuated extensible pneumatic chambers. This design allows tendon actuation of both bending and extension. Notice, however, that the pneumatically actuated tube design adds the advantage of being able to actively regulate the internal stiffness of the backbone. However, these designs, in common with spring-based backbones, suffer from the problem of uncontrolled longitudinal compliance along the backbone. Also, pneumatics offer a limited range of possible backbone stiffnesses.

Alternative approaches to variable (controllable) stiffness backbones have considered magnetorheological and electrorheological fluid-based actuation [70, 71]. In these materials, magnetic and electric fields can be used to change the properties from fluid to stiff or solid. This allows backbones built from, or strongly biased by, such materials to feature tunable stiffness.

More recently, the idea of using "jamming" of suitable media (such as sand or coffee grains) has been exploited for novel variable stiffness continuum robot design [70, 72, 73]. The underlying notion is to pack the media in a closed chamber to bring and vary the internal pressure to "loosen" the media in a fluid state, or "jam" it into a solid state. For example, in [73], granular media are used as the jamming element. Initially packed into a chamber under a vacuum, the grains jam and unjam the chamber as a function of applied pressure. It is demonstrated in [73] that, when three such chambers are combined in parallel with a McKibben air muscle, a tunable stiffness section element can be produced. A prototype tendon-driven continuum robot using granular jamming for variable stiffness is demonstrated in [72].

In [70], the jamming elements are multiple surface layers, interleaved in various ways. Negative pressure is used to bring the layers together and exploit friction to create tunable stiffness via "layer jamming." A tubular continuum backbone is built (locally actuated using shape memory alloy wires as core actuators) and shown to exhibit significant range of backbone stiffness. This approach to augmenting core continuum robot designs with new innovations to enhance performance shows significant promise for producing the next generation of continuum manipulators.

2.5. Common Property: Constant Curvature.
Notice that, independent of underlying physical structure, a common property exhibited by virtually all continuum robots ([35, 63] being notable exceptions) is that the resulting backbone approximates a serially connected set of constant curvature sections. This arises due to the following: (1) all three previous design types create a series of serially connected sections; (2) internal potential energy in each section is uniformly distributed (unactuated, each section is straight, or bent at a fixed configuration); and thus, within each section, internal forces act to drive the unactuated (passive) degrees of freedom to equalize in value along the section. This produces internal section bending of constant curvature at any given moment.

Therefore, in practice, achievable continuum backbone shapes are (fairly close approximations to) sequentially connected segments of circles in three dimensions (with the tangents to successive section end points aligned and the arc lengths of the segments corresponding to robot section lengths). While the "constant curvature" property is affected by external loading (some sag typically exists due to gravity or grasped objects), it remains a good first approximation to backbone shape and has been strongly exploited in kinematic models, as discussed in the next section.

3. Kinematics

In order to coordinate the movements available in continuum robots, kinematic models, which capture the relationship between configuration (backbone shape) variables and both task (e.g., tip) and actuator (e.g., tendon or muscle length), variables need to be established. Such models form the basis for motion planning and control algorithms and are the critical step between prototype development and practical implementation of continuum robot hardware.

Since continuum robots can change their shape at any point along their structure, their models necessarily differ significantly from those of conventional rigid-link robots, where configuration changes can occur only at a finite number of fixed locations along their structure (the joints between the rigid-links). For rigid-link robots, the well-established Denavit-Hartenberg (D-H) convention [1] provides a general underlying framework for the development of kinematic (and dynamic) models. The D-H convention establishes a local coordinate frame fixed in each of the (finite number of) links and develops the overall kinematics via a sequential series of frame-to-frame steps, as a function of the (finite) number of joint angles [1].

For continuum robots, the fact that the local shape varies continuously along the backbone needs to be reflected in kinematic models. Two alternative approaches have emerged. The first takes a "bottom-up" strategy, building a continuum model via exploiting the D-H approach to fit a "virtual" rigid-link robot to the backbone. The second uses a "top-down" philosophy, explicitly treating the backbone as a continuous curve, in order to formulate the models. We review each approach and demonstrate how ultimately they lead to the same models in the following two subsections.

3.1. Continuum Kinematics via Virtual Rigid-Link Kinematics. The first (and the most inspired by hardware) approach to continuum robot kinematics strongly exploits the constant curvature sections feature possessed by almost all continuum robots to date. This approach, which first appeared in [8], is based on the observation that the evolution from one end to the other of a constant curvature curve can be represented, in the plane of that curve, via three discrete transformations: (1) a rotation to "point" the tangent at the curve beginning to the curve end point; (2) a translation along the newly aligned direction (from curve beginning to end); and (3) a second rotation (of same amount as the first) to realign with the tangent at the curve's end; see Figure 7.

Given this observation, in the plane, a "virtual" three-joint rigid-link manipulator, with identical (i.e., coupled) rotations as its first and third joints and a prismatic joint in the middle, can be used to model the kinematic transformation along any constant curvature backbone. Consequently, it is possible to find the corresponding kinematic model,

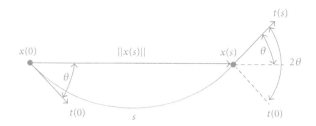

FIGURE 7: Geometry of constant curvature in the plane.

using the conventional D-H approach, for the virtual robot. This approach, first used in [8], has been used numerous times subsequently [18, 36, 39]. The details (D-H table and associated homogeneous transformation matrix) are given in Table 1 and (1).

Consider

$$
\left[H_3^0\right] = \begin{bmatrix} \cos(\theta_1 + \theta_3) & -\sin(\theta_1 + \theta_3) & 0 & -d_2 \sin\theta_1 \\ \sin(\theta_1 + \theta_3) & \cos(\theta_1 + \theta_3) & 0 & d_2 \cos\theta_1 \\ 0 & 0 & 1 & 0 \\ 0 & 0 & 0 & 1 \end{bmatrix}. \tag{1}
$$

Useful continuum robot kinematics can now be developed by noting, as well as substituting in the virtual robot kinematics, relationships between the joint variables for the virtual robot and corresponding configuration space variables for the continuous curve. Specifically (see Figure 7),

$$
\theta_1 = \theta_3 = \theta, \qquad d_2 = \|x(s)\|, \qquad k = \left(\frac{1}{\text{radius}}\right). \tag{2}
$$

We have (utilizing the underlying geometry)

$$
s = r(2\theta) = \frac{(2\theta)}{k} = \frac{(\theta_1 + \theta_3)}{k}. \tag{3}
$$

So

$$
(\theta_1 + \theta_3) = sk. \tag{4}
$$

Also

$$
\frac{\|x(s)\|}{2} = \frac{d_2}{2} = r\sin\theta = \frac{\sin\theta}{k}. \tag{5}
$$

So

$$
d_2 = \frac{2\sin\theta}{k}. \tag{6}
$$

Substituting (4) and (6) into the model (1) and simplifying gives

$$
\left[H_3^0\right] = \begin{bmatrix} \cos(sk) & -\sin(sk) & 0 & \left(\frac{1}{k}\right)\{\cos(sk) - 1\} \\ \sin(sk) & \cos(sk) & 0 & \left(\frac{1}{k}\right)\sin(sk) \\ 0 & 0 & 1 & 0 \\ 0 & 0 & 0 & 1 \end{bmatrix}. \tag{7}
$$

TABLE 1

Link	θ	d	a	α
2	*	0	0	-90
3	0	*	0	90
3	*	0	0	0

TABLE 2

Link	θ	d	a	α
1	*	0	0	90
2	*	0	0	-90
3	0	*	0	90
4	*	0	0	-90

a suitable coordinate system down the backbone. The position at σ along the backbone is found as (Φ is frame orientation)

$$^0\mathbf{p}(\sigma, t) = \int_0^\sigma {}^0\Phi(\eta, t) \begin{bmatrix} 1 \\ 0 \\ 0 \end{bmatrix} d\eta. \tag{8}$$

The above equation reflects the model developed by Mochiyama and Suzuki [75–77], wherein the x-axis of the local coordinate system is aligned with the tangent down the backbone. An equivalent formulation developed earlier—the first kinematic analysis for continuum robot backbones—was developed by Chirikjian [4, 5]. In that formulation, the y-axis was aligned with the backbone tangent.

For the planar constant curvature section in Figure 7, the orientation matrix is given by

$$^0\Phi(\sigma, t) = \left[R_z^{\text{orientation}} \right]$$

$$= \begin{bmatrix} \cos\left(\int_0^\sigma k\,d\eta\right) & -\sin\left(\int_0^\sigma k\,d\eta\right) & 0 \\ \sin\left(\int_0^\sigma k\,d\eta\right) & \cos\left(\int_0^\sigma k\,d\eta\right) & 0 \\ 0 & 0 & 1 \end{bmatrix} \tag{9}$$

(k is the curvature). Utilizing (9) in (8) and performing the integration, we obtain

$$^0\mathbf{p}(\sigma, t) = \begin{bmatrix} \left(\dfrac{1}{k}\right)\{\cos(k\sigma) - 1\} \\ \left(\dfrac{1}{k}\right)\sin(k\sigma) \\ 0 \end{bmatrix}. \tag{10}$$

Noting that

$$^0\Phi(\sigma, t) = \begin{bmatrix} \cos\left(\int_0^\sigma k\,d\eta\right) & -\sin\left(\int_0^\sigma k\,d\eta\right) & 0 \\ \sin\left(\int_0^\sigma k\,d\eta\right) & \cos\left(\int_0^\sigma k\,d\eta\right) & 0 \\ 0 & 0 & 1 \end{bmatrix} \tag{11}$$

$$= \begin{bmatrix} \cos(k\sigma) & -\sin(k\sigma) & 0 \\ \sin(k\sigma) & \cos(k\sigma) & 0 \\ 0 & 0 & 1 \end{bmatrix},$$

and recalling that

$$\left[H_3^0 \right] = \begin{bmatrix} {}^0\Phi(\sigma, t) & {}^0\mathbf{p}(\sigma, t) \\ 0 & 1 \end{bmatrix}^0. \tag{12}$$

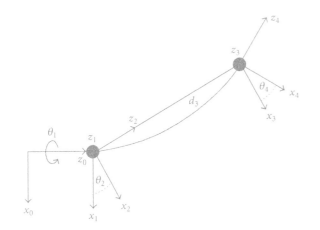

FIGURE 8: Three-dimensional constant curvature section geometry obtained via rotation about initial tangent.

The model (7) describes the forward kinematic relationship (3 by 3 orientation, top left of (7), and 3 by 1 translation, top right) between continuum curve shape (arc length and curvature) and task space. Note that the relationship is not, as for the rigid-link case, restricted to transformations from end to end of the "link" ("section" here). By making the arc length s arbitrary, the expression (7) models the transformation from curve shape to *any* task-space point along the backbone. Thus, the D-H algorithm for discrete jointed robots has been used to create a truly continuum section kinematic model in (7). Planar multisection kinematic models can be easily created by chaining together (multiplying the homogeneous transformation matrices) the models for the individual sections [17].

The kinematics of spatial constant curvature curves can similarly be modeled by the addition of an extra pair of (again identical, coupled) rotations to each end of the planar version to create a 3D virtual rigid-link robot. In a similar fashion, continuum kinematics are found by substitution of appropriate geometric relationships; see Figure 8 and Table 2. The 3D virtual robot is formally a 5-joint robot, with 2D rotational joints at each end of a prismatic joint. However, the robot has only three independent degrees of freedom, as the two 2D rotational joints are coupled. This agrees with the intuitive number of degrees of freedom of a constant curvature curve in space, that is, arc length, radius of curvature, and orientation of curve plane in space. Multisection 3D kinematic models can be created by chaining together individual section models as before [17].

3.2. *"Direct" Continuum Kinematics Approach.* An alternative (and more mathematically direct) approach explicitly treats the continuum backbone as a curve in space and "floats"

We obtain (noting the "0" in the previous equation is a 1 by 3 vector)

$$
\left[H_3^0\right] = \begin{bmatrix} \cos(sk) & -\sin(sk) & 0 & \left(\dfrac{1}{k}\right)\{\cos(sk)-1\} \\[2mm] \sin(sk) & \cos(sk) & 0 & \left(\dfrac{1}{k}\right)\sin(sk) \\[2mm] 0 & 0 & 1 & 0 \\[2mm] 0 & 0 & 0 & 1 \end{bmatrix}. \quad (13)
$$

Note that the resulting model in (13) is identical to the one obtained in (7). A similar parallel calculation can be performed to generate the 3D kinematic model. Note that the model suffers from singularities (division by zero) when the curvature is zero or when any section is straight.

Consequently, we have established a baseline kinematic model relating backbone shape to task-space variables, independent of the approach used to find it.

3.3. Modal Approaches. The previous approaches establish kinematics which directly model the nominal shapes the robots can obtain. However, they are fairly complex to formulate and manipulate. An alternative strategy is to "build" backbone shapes via a finite number of relatively simple modal functions. Originally introduced to robotics in [78] (in which the resulting shapes were used to plan movements for hyperredundant rigid-link robots), the modal approach builds the kinematics using as backbone curvature:

$$
k(s) = \sum_{i=1}^{n} \mu_i \phi_i(s), \quad (14)
$$

where μ_i are coefficients, and $\phi_i(s)$ are the modal functions. The modal functions act as "basis" functions for the backbone curvature, with the coefficients selected to tune their combination to approximate (or, in some special cases, match) the robot backbone shape [16, 78]. The coefficients become the "configuration" of the robot.

The (number and type of) modal functions can be selected from a wide range of possibilities [16, 78, 79]. For example, in [78], Chirikjian and Burdick used the following model:

$$
k(s) = \sum_{i=1}^{n} \mu_i \cos(i\pi s) + \beta_i \sin(i\pi s). \quad (15)
$$

In this model, the configuration becomes $q = [\mu_1(t), \beta_1(t), \ldots, \beta_i(t)\mu_i(t), \ldots, \mu_n(t), \beta_n(t)]$. The use of the classical trigonometric basis functions appears a natural choice. However, an infinite number of trigonometric modes are needed to model an arbitrary backbone shape. Also, this basis set provides no spatial resolution (each basis function affects the shape of the whole robot); so it is not possible to "tune" a given region of the backbone.

It is sometimes possible to select modal functions to achieve spatial resolution. In [16], (the first few elements of) two alternative sets of Wavelet basis functions are used. These use the "natural basis set" or "box functions" (left column in Figure 9):

$$
k(s) = \sum_{i=1}^{n} \mu_i \phi_i^b(s) \quad (16)
$$

and the "Haar" basis set (right column in Figure 9):

$$
k(s) = \sum_{i=1}^{n} \mu_i \phi_i^w(s). \quad (17)
$$

The natural basis set comprises "box functions," with (fixed) support, chosen to match the backbone region of (nonextensible, planar) sections, and with the box magnitudes corresponding directly to the curvature of those sections. The effect of using this basis set is illustrated in Figure 9 (column 2) to successively (top to bottom) form a specific shape for a four-section planar backbone. Note that the natural basis set features fixed spatial resolution at variable locations along the backbone.

The (first four elements of the) Haar basis set (both sets are orthogonal sets in the sense of Wavelet bases) is shown in the right hand column, top to bottom, of Figure 9. These functions feature variable spatial resolution, at variable locations. However, for this particular example, it can be seen that they can also be combined (top to bottom, third column of Figure 9) to produce the same shape as with the natural basis set.

Note that the natural basis "box" functions in Figure 9 directly synthesize the kinematics for four constant curvature sections. This is an example of exact modal function modeling. However, the box function approach is not generalized to extensible sections or to 3D backbones; so this is a (convenient) special case.

The key advantage of the modal function approach is that the robot shape can be parameterized by a finite set of user-selected functions with convenient properties. The number of "modes" used can be user-selected, for example, to constrain the computational complexity of the resulting model. Modal models can be synthesized to eliminate the singularities inherent in the models of Sections 3.1 and 3.2 (when sections straighten and curvature is zero) [79].

The main disadvantage of modal function-based approaches is that they are inherently approximations: most modal function sets which are convenient to manipulate require many (typically, infinite) numbers of them to achieve a given backbone shape. Most importantly, the set of shapes available in the model is inherently restricted by the range of (linear combinations of) the modal basis functions. For many modal function sets, even if an infinite number is used, it is not possible to model an arbitrary backbone shape. Therefore, some physically achievable backbone shapes may not be included in the modal models. This particularly is a problem for 3D backbones [16]. Therefore, the use of modal function approaches typically needs to be augmented with additional analysis of and compensation for the inherent mismatch between models and hardware.

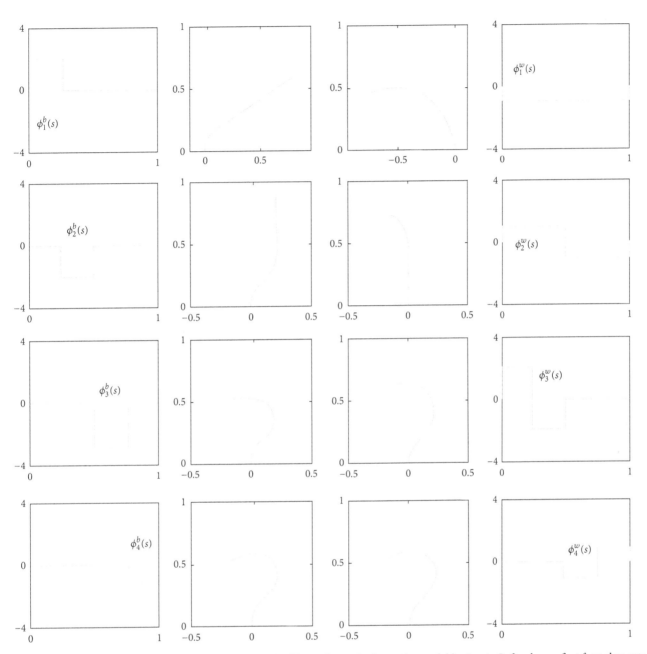

FIGURE 9: Construction of four-section planar continuum backbone shape via alternative modal basis sets. Left column: first four elements (top to bottom) of natural basis set. Right column: first four elements (top to bottom) of Haar basis set. Second column: backbone shape generation (top to bottom), adding successive natural basis functions. Third column: backbone shape generation (top to bottom), adding successive Haar basis functions.

3.4. Kinematic Transformations Incorporating Actuator Variables. Kinematic backbone models are very useful and provide key insight into the possible configurations and behavior of continuum robots. However, for practical implementation of continuum robot realizations, even at the kinematic level, further modeling is required. In the case of rigid-link robots, the variables underlying their kinematic models (joint angles and displacements) correspond closely to actuator geometry. Conversion between configuration and actuator variables (typically involving gear/belt/drive reduction ratios) is relatively straightforward [1]. However, for continuum

robots, the relationship between the key variables defining backbone configuration (extension, curvature, and torsion) and actuated variables is considerably more complex.

For example, consider tendon-based continuum robots. Here, the only actuated (and, often, sensed) variables are tendon lengths, and it is desirable in practice to be able to convert these tendon lengths to backbone configuration (extension, curvature, torsion). This issue has been addressed in [18], and in the following, we summarize the solution for the case of a single (extensible) section with circular cross-section, actuated by three tendons, spaced at 120 degrees apart around the section perimeter. A good example of such a section is the "Air-Octor" continuum robot [68, 69], illustrated in Figure 10.

For the continuum section in Figure 10 (the kinematics are similar, if not identical, for the sections of almost all tendon-driven continuum robots), the forward problem is to find the section shape from the three tendon lengths l_{1-3}. The shape is given by the three configuration space variables: section length s, curvature k_ϕ, and angle of curvature (from the x-axis, measured about the z-axis of a coordinate frame with its z-axis aligned with the base tangent of the section) (see Figure 11).

The key to developing the needed transformations is to exploit the geometric constraints of the design. The three tendons are routed through a series of $n - 1$ intermediate connection points before being terminated at the end of the section. During actuation, this causes the tendons to form n straight line segments within the section. Straightforward geometrical analysis can be used to show that the length h_c of a (imaginary) tendon running directly through the center of a single such segment of the section is given by

$$h_c = \frac{l_3 + l_2 - 2l_1}{6n},\tag{18}$$

where the shortest tendon length is l_1, and n is the number of segments in the section. This length can be used to analyze the "side-on" geometry (Figure 12).

Use of the geometric information in Figure 12 and a projection onto the (z, ϕ) plane results [18] in expressions for the curvature and angle of curvature in terms of tendon lengths

$$k_\phi = 2\frac{\sqrt{l_1^2 + l_2^2 + l_3^2 - l_1 l_2 - l_2 l_3 - l_1 l_3}}{d\,(l_1 + l_2 + l_3)},$$

$$\phi = \tan^{-1}\left(\frac{\sqrt{3}}{3}\frac{l_3 + l_2 - 2l_1}{l_2 - l_3}\right),\tag{19}$$

where d is the radius of the section cross-section, and r_1 is the inverse of its curvature. Finally, after some further geometrical analysis, it can be shown that [18]:

$$s = \frac{nd\,(l_1 + l_2 + l_3)}{\sqrt{l_1^2 + l_2^2 + l_3^2 - l_1 l_2 - l_2 l_3 - l_1 l_3}}$$

$$\cdot \sin^{-1}\left(\frac{\sqrt{l_1^2 + l_2^2 + l_3^2 - l_1 l_2 - l_2 l_3 - l_1 l_3}}{3nd}\right).\tag{20}$$

Equations (19) and (20) constitute the needed forward map between actuator and shape variables for tendon-driven extensible sections. Further work on kinematic transformations can be found in [18, 80, 81]. For example, in [80], a mechanics-based model for transforming between beam configuration and tendon displacements is formulated. Inverse maps can also be formulated [81, 82]. It is fairly straightforward to chain together multiple section models to model a multisection robot; see [18] for details.

The aforementioned in models are critical in implementation of tendon-based continuum robots. They can be easily modified for locally actuated designs, where tendon lengths are replaced by internal actuator lengths. Finally, note that the concentric tube realization of continuum robots presents a distinct advantage in the context of kinematic transformations, as the local extension and torsion (of each tube section) are directly actuated, and thus no kinematic transformation between these configuration and actuation variables is required.

3.5. Extensions, Inverse and Velocity Kinematics. The kinematics formulations in Sections 3.1–3.4 represent the core theory underlying continuum robots and have been the subject of much of the theoretical research activity in the area thus far. Extensions to this core theory have been developed and there remains active research in the area. In particular, efforts to remove the restriction to constant curvature sections have been made.

More accurate kinematic models which explicitly include the effects of external (particularly gravitational) loading have been explored in the literature. The theory of Cosserat Rods has proved particularly helpful in enabling researchers to develop "geometrically exact" nonconstant curvature kinematic models [37, 60, 83]. However, the models are computationally complex [60] and harder to implement than the constant curvature models. Consequently, the constant curvature models remain predominant in continuum robot implementations.

Inverse models (including those for both the configuration-workspace transformations of Sections 3.1–3.3 and the actuator-configuration relationships of Section 3.4) have been developed in [74] (for nonconstant curvature models), [79, 82].

Various approaches to exploiting the kinematic relationships to formulate and exploit Jacobians which reflect the velocity-level kinematic relationships have been proposed [16, 74, 84]. Conventional techniques for formulating Jacobians for rigid-link robots can be applied to the "virtual" rigid-link manipulator of Section 3.1 to derive a "continuum" Jacobian. More directly, any of the kinematic relationships (modal or direct) can be differentiated to find the appropriate Jacobian. A Jacobian (pseudo-) inverse can then be used to iteratively solve configuration space rates given desired tip rates. For example, the modal function approach for the planar four-degree-of-freedom example in Section 3.3 can be used to derive

$$\frac{d\underline{x}\,(s)}{dt} = \left[J\left(\underline{\mu}, s\right)\right]\frac{d\underline{\mu}}{dt},\tag{21}$$

thus formulating the Jacobian and its relationship in terms of the modal function coefficients and their time derivatives [16]. Inverting this relationship yields model coefficient (and hence shape) rates which can be numerically integrated to provide shape trajectories corresponding to the input tip rates. See Figure 13 for an example trajectory generated for the example robot of Section 3.3 using this approach.

Research into continuum robot kinematics continues. For example, an alternative (screw theoretic) approach to

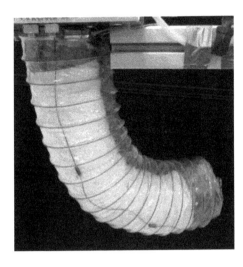

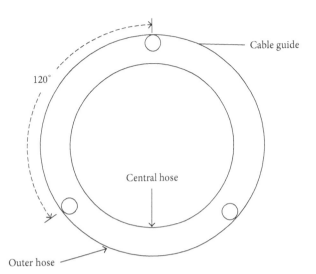

FIGURE 10: The single-section "Air-Octor." Internal hose is pressurized; external hose is actuated (two independent degrees of freedom bending, plus one of extension) by three remotely actuated tendons, terminated at the end of the section and spaced 120 degrees apart around its perimeter.

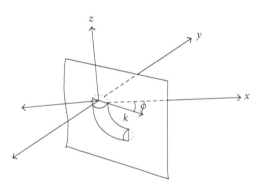

FIGURE 11: Definition of section configuration space variables for curvature and angle of curvature.

the development of both kinematics and Jacobian formulation, using the "product of exponentials" approach, is given recently in [39]. The approach is shown to produce the same results as using the models described previously.

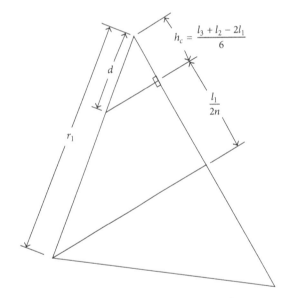

FIGURE 12: View from side of one segment of section.

4. Forces, Dynamics, and Control

4.1. Forces and Continuum Robots. The natural next step in modeling of continuum robots is to include the relationships involving forces (and moments) and backbone shape and shape changes. For conventional rigid-link robots, the kinematic variables (joint angles/displacements) completely determine the shape (configuration) of the robot. However, for continuum robots, external forces (in particular, gravity) act with the configuration variables and the internal energy of the backbone to determine the ultimate shape of each section [19, 47], even in free space. In any physically realizable system, there can be only a finite number of actuated (i.e., directly controlled) configuration degrees of freedom. The values of the remainder of the (infinite) degrees of freedom in

a continuum robot backbone will be determined by both the constraints of the controlled degrees of freedom and internal and external forces.

The kinematic models of Section 3 made no explicit assumptions of internal or external loading. Implicitly, the constant curvature assumptions in Section 3 assumed no external loading and an even distribution of internal loading within each section (to even out the uncontrolled degrees of freedom to create the constant curvature). In practice, gravitational loads cause some "section sag," resulting in section curvatures that are not truly constant. However, the deviation from constant curvature in free space is typically not large, and the constant curvature models have proved

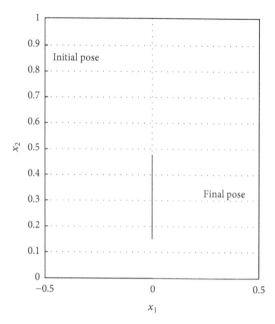

FIGURE 13: Straight line tip trajectory for four-section planar continuum robot, generated using Jacobian from modal kinematics.

a good practical approximation in many implementations [17, 59, 63].

However, as applications become more challenging, the desire for more accurate models is increasing. Internal loads can play a significant role in determining the shape of concentric tube robots in particular. In [47], a quasistatic model for predicting the shape of concentric tube robots is presented. The model in [47] takes internal forces from both bending and shear effects into account. Mechanics-based models which consider torsional interaction between the tubes of concentric tube robots are presented in [85]. Lumped-parameter models to model friction within a continuum catheter device are presented in [86].

More accurate kinematic models which explicitly include the effects of external (particularly, gravitational) loading have been explored in the literature [37, 83]. However, these models are relatively complex. Consequently, the constant curvature models remain predominant in continuum robot implementations.

External loading becomes a much more significant factor when the loads result from environmental contact, however. In this case (inevitable when using continuum elements for locomotion and actively sought when using them for grasping and manipulation), the inherent compliance of the continuum structures allows for significant deviation from constant curvature. Notice that this deviation is inevitable— the finite number of actuated degrees of freedom cannot, in general, be made to control the infinite number of other degrees of freedom in the structure, in the presence of general and significant external forces. The deviation is also a desired property, in order to allow the robot to adapt its shape to environmental constraints, both for navigation and grasping.

In order to address some of these issues, new work considers applied loading. A solution to the statics problem

for concentric tube robots is presented in [87]. An approach to continuum backbone contact detection and location of contact along the backbone is developed in [88]. Methods based on kinematics and statics are presented, supported by experimental results with a tendon-driven continuum backbone. Recent extensions [38] present algorithms (supported by experimental results) to register and locate continuum backbones under external contact conditions with respect to an a priori 3D model.

A novel alternative strategy is to explicitly use continuum robots as force sensors [37]. In [37], an Extended Kalman Filter approach is used with a tendon-driven continuum robot to provide tip force estimates given kinematic models and estimates.

4.2. Continuum Robot Dynamics.
The earliest published work on continuum robot dynamics, based on a modal model, was [5]. Subsequent efforts based on the well-understood [1] Lagrangian [75, 76, 89, 90] and Newton-Euler [61, 91, 92] methods have been established. In the following, we outline the Lagrangian dynamics approaches [75, 76, 90], which generally parallel the commonly used formulation for rigid-link robots. However, there are several steps which are both specialized to continuum robot scenario and which give good insight into the nature of continuum robots.

The key initial step [75] is to model the backbone as being comprised of circular cross-sectional "slices," of infinitesimal thickness. Each slice, at a location σ along the backbone, has mass $m(\sigma)$, inertia tensor $I(\sigma)$, and first moment of inertia $m(\sigma)r(\sigma)$, where $r(\sigma)$ is the distance from the slice geometric center to its center of mass. The overall strategy is to find the kinetic and potential energy of each slice, then the total energies K and P (via integration along the backbone), and finally substitute $L = K - P$ into Lagrange's equations ($i = 1, \ldots, n$)

$$\frac{d}{dt}\left[\frac{\partial L}{\partial \dot{\theta}_i(\sigma, t)}\right] - \frac{\partial L}{\partial \theta_i(\sigma, t)} = \tau_i(\sigma, t) \qquad (22)$$

to find the dynamic model. In the above, (θ_i, τ_i) are variables selected to correspond to the n actuated configuration space variables and the corresponding forces which change them.

The kinetic energy of a slice (assuming the center of mass is aligned with the geometric center of the slice) is most directly given by

$$K(\sigma, t) = \left(\frac{1}{2}\right)m(\sigma)\left\{\frac{\partial \mathbf{p}(\sigma, t)}{\partial t}\right\}^T \left\{\frac{\partial \mathbf{p}(\sigma, t)}{\partial t}\right\}$$

$$+ \left(\frac{1}{2}\right)\boldsymbol{\omega}(\sigma, t)^T I(\sigma)\boldsymbol{\omega}(\sigma, t) \qquad (23)$$

$$\triangleq \left(\frac{1}{2}\right)v(\sigma, t)^T M(\sigma, t)v(\sigma, t),$$

where $\{\partial \mathbf{p}(\sigma, t)/\partial t, \boldsymbol{\omega}(\sigma, t)\}$ are the linear and angular velocities of the slice center at σ.

An additional step (analogous to the process for rigid-link robot Lagrangian dynamics) is now necessary. In order to obtain the dynamics in terms of the useful variables (θ_i, τ_i), a (Jacobian) transformation must be found to convert $v(\sigma, t)$ in the above to $\partial\theta(\sigma, t)/\partial t$. This Jacobian needs to account for the phenomenon that the velocity at σ is a function of the velocities at all locations η prior to it along the backbone. To this end, intermediate Jacobians $[J_1]$, $[J_2]$ are found such that

$$\begin{bmatrix} \mathbf{v}(\sigma) \\ \boldsymbol{\omega}(\sigma) \end{bmatrix} = [J_1] \begin{bmatrix} \mathbf{v}(\eta) \\ \boldsymbol{\omega}(\eta) \end{bmatrix},$$

$$\begin{bmatrix} \mathbf{v}(\eta) \\ \boldsymbol{\omega}(\eta) \end{bmatrix} = [J_2] \frac{\partial\theta(\eta, t)}{\partial t},$$
(24)

and a desired overall Jacobian operator $[J_{(\sigma,t)}]$ is found as

$$v(\sigma, t) = [J_{(\sigma,t)}]\left\{\frac{\partial\theta}{\partial t}\right\} = \int_0^{\sigma} [J_1][J_2]\frac{\partial\theta(\eta, t)}{\partial t} d\eta. \quad (25)$$

For full details, see [75].

Thus, the kinetic energy of a slice can now be represented as

$$K(\sigma, t) = \left(\frac{1}{2}\right)\left\{\frac{\partial\theta}{\partial t}\right\}^T J_{(\sigma,t)}{}^T M(\sigma) J_{(\sigma,t)} \left\{\frac{\partial\theta}{\partial t}\right\}. \quad (26)$$

The overall kinetic energy is therefore

$$K(t) = \int_0^l K(\sigma, t) d\sigma, \quad (27)$$

where l is the length of the backbone. The potential energy of a slice is found as

$$P_g(\sigma, t) = -m(\sigma)\mathbf{g}^T(\sigma, t)\mathbf{p}(\sigma, t), \quad (28)$$

where $\mathbf{g}$ is the gravitation vector at σ. The overall potential energy given by

$$P_g(t) = \int_0^l P_g(\sigma, t) d\sigma = -\int_0^l m(\sigma)\mathbf{g}^T(\sigma, t)\mathbf{p}(\sigma, t). \quad (29)$$

After forming $L = K - P$ and substituting into Lagrange's equations (22), the resulting dynamic model takes the form

$$\mathbf{M}\ddot{\mathbf{q}} + \mathbf{V}(\mathbf{q}, \dot{\mathbf{q}})\dot{\mathbf{q}} + \mathbf{g}(\mathbf{q}) = \boldsymbol{\tau}. \quad (30)$$

The underlying structure of the dynamic model closely matches that of rigid-link robots, apart from being continuous in nature. For example, the inertia matrix M can be shown [90, 93] to be positive definite and symmetric, and it satisfies the property (useful for control)

$$\xi^T\left(\dot{M} - 2V\right)\xi = 0, \quad \forall\xi \in \mathbb{R}^n. \quad (31)$$

The original derivation of (30) [75] assumed fixed length (i.e., nonextensible) backbones and the only potential energy in the system arose from gravity. Later work [90] generalized the models to include extensible sections, and the effects of elastic internal potential energy due to both bending and extension. The corresponding energy terms are

$$P_b(t) = \left(\frac{1}{2}\right)\int_0^l k_b(\sigma)\left\{\pi - \left(\frac{1}{2}\right)\sigma\kappa(\sigma)\right\}^2 d\sigma \quad (32)$$

for bending (spring constant k_b) and

$$P_e(t) = \left(\frac{1}{2}\right)k_e(l - l^*)^2 \quad (33)$$

for extension (spring constant k_e). Details of application of the previous approach to compute the dynamics for extensible and nonextensible backbones are given in [90].

Establishing the previous closed form dynamic models for continuum robots has been significant in yielding insight into the underlying structure of these devices. The structure of the model is useful in synthesizing control strategies [93, 94], and the dynamics enables realistic physics-based simulations of continuum robots. However, the computational complexity of the resulting model is very high, and the calculations for nonplanar backbones are nontrivial. Real-time implementation of these models (even with the simplifying assumptions of simple mass distribution) is a daunting prospect.

Consequently, researchers have explored alternative approaches to dynamic modeling for continuum robots. Formulations based on the iterative Newton-Euler approach have been established [61, 91, 92]. More recently, computationally (more) efficient lumped-parameter models, based on linear mass-spring-damper elements, have appeared in the literature [95–97]. The model in [97] is tuned to octopus-inspired underwater operation and includes terms to model buoyancy and drag. These approaches approximate the dynamics of (sections of) continuum backbones by various combinations of linear elements, with a view of trading off computational complexity of the model against accuracy. Experiments have shown good correspondence between the models and hardware, for relatively a small number (less than twenty) of linear elements [95].

Dynamic models for nonconstant curvature continuum robots are beginning to appear in the literature [83]. However, at the time of this writing, there are very few examples of continuum dynamics being implemented on continuum robot hardware. It is expected that, as applications expand, particularly in areas such as medical procedures and locomotion with continuum limbs, the availability of dynamics in real time will become increasingly necessary. Research in continuum robot dynamics continues to be a very active area.

4.3. Continuum Robot Control. Controller development for robotic structures is a fundamental issue, and several of the early works [98, 99] in continuum robots concentrated on this topic. Control of continuum structures is obviously complicated by the inherently underactuated nature of the backbone. Additional problems arise from the (typical) non-collocation of actuators with configuration space variables, the complexity of the dynamic models, and the typical dearth of local sensors in the structure.

For tendon-based continuum robots particularly, the existence of kinematic transformations between configuration space and actuator space variables is critical in enabling effective control. Controllers specific to tendon-based continuum robots have been presented in [80, 81, 83]. Stiffness controllers for continuum robots are introduced in [46]. In [46], a Cosserat Rod model is used to calculate the tip deflection due to applied forces, enabling implementation of stiffness control. The approach is applied in [46] to a concentric tube robot, but the modeling strategy (combining noncontact kinematics as in Section 3 with the Cosserat Rod model to include applied forces) is applicable to other continuum robot designs as well.

Control strategies attempting to compensate for the complexity of the dynamics or for the uncertainty inherently present in implementation of dynamic models are presented in [98–100]. Inverse dynamics controllers are described in [100]. In [99, 100], variable structure controllers are proposed. A feedforward neural network approach for compensation for the dynamics is discussed in [94]. Controllers in the task space are presented in [49, 100]. A controller based on a mechanics model describing coupling between sections is presented in [81].

A key practical problem for continuum robot control is at which level to close the loop. Sensors are typically noncollocated with the backbone. Sensed quantities are usually limited to tendon lengths (sensed at the base), or pneumatic or hydraulic pressures of artificial muscles (again, sensed remotely at pressure regulators, not at the muscles themselves). Direct internal sensing of backbone shape is complicated by the limited space available and the current lack of suitable sensor technologies. Technologies based on fiber optics offer promise for low-profile, high-quality local sensing of backbone curvature. However, this has not yet been demonstrated in continuum robot hardware. Consequently, transformations between actuator and configuration space become important for controller implementation, with the loop closed (error calculated) in either space.

External sensing of continuum robot shape has also been demonstrated. Electromagnetic field sensors were used in [36] to sense the shape of tendon-driven endoscopic systems. Vision has been used to infer the shape of continuum robots in [101] (off-board cameras) and [102] (body-mounted cameras), but the effectiveness of this strategy is limited by issues of lighting conditions, occlusions, and so forth. Vision has also been used to sense backbone tip location [81]. An electromagnetic sensor is used in [49] to sense tip location and enable task-space control.

5. Ongoing Research

With the field rapidly expanding and the core underlying theory having been established over the last ten to fifteen years, a wider variety of issues and problems are now being considered by researchers. New work in motion planning for continuum robots [52, 85, 103–105] is expanding the boundaries of the possible for the field. Motion planners based on mechanics models for concentric tube robots are presented in [85, 103]. Planners have been proposed which use the structure of continuum backbones to plan trajectories which simultaneously avoid obstacles and grasp objects. These planners are proposed for both 2D [105] and 3D [103]

environments and are intended for real-time, or near real-time, implementation [103]. Extensions for moving obstacles can be handled [105]. The emergence of low-cost and readily available sensors such as the Kinect RGB-D sensor catalyzes this type of research.

The existence of practical, real-time, sensor-based motion planning algorithms will be important in moving the technology from the laboratory to numerous real applications [106]. Currently, most of the higher-level functions (including planning) are delegated to humans. Most implementations to this point require teleoperation of the device [107], typically using a joystick [108]. User interfaces for continuum robots is a relatively neglected and poorly understood topic [108]. The movements of continuum elements are often counterintuitive to human operators, much more than for rigid-link robots, leading to confusion and slow or poor decision making in many experiments. Efforts to reduce operator cognitive load via automatic motion planning and the synthesis of low degree of freedom "synergies" [109, 110] are expected to prove significant in widening the scope and effectiveness of possible operations.

Recent theoretical work has investigated the structure of the "self-motion" inherent in continuum structures [111]. This self-motion (movement of the backbone while maintaining the location of the tip), present in kinematically redundant robots, has proved useful in conventional rigid-link manipulators. Multisection continuum robots are inherently kinematically redundant, but, apart from its proposed use in task-space control strategies [100], their self-motion remains a little studied phenomenon.

The use of continuum robot structures as limbs for "legged" locomotion has recently been the subject of attention [61, 112, 113]. Demonstration of multicontinuum-limbed locomotion has been reported both underwater [33, 45], and in air [112]. Multi- (two-) continuum-limbed swimming is analyzed with feasibility demonstrated via a simple prototype in [114]. Multicontinuum-legged robots have been demonstrated to walk and trot [112]. Possible applications for this novel locomotion mode include various undersea and space applications. Other space-based applications in which continuum robots could be used effectively are as "active hooks" [113] and as long, thin "tendril-like" robots [31, 115–117]. In the latter mode, the robots could penetrate and explore within tight obstacle fields such as crevasses, lava tubes, or skylights, where key scientific questions are currently focused.

Novel applications are emerging. Continuum robots have been deployed recently as "active hoses" for ship-to-shore refueling [118]. Extension to continuum robot surfaces, with application to rehabilitation therapy for poststroke patients, has been proposed [119].

6. Conclusions

We have reviewed the state of the art in continuum manipulators, focusing particularly on hardware design, kinematics, and dynamics. The design of continuum robot hardware is seen to have evolved into three fundamentally different directions. Two of these directions feature out-of-backbone "extrinsic" actuation: one via remote actuation via tendons and the other via remotely actuated sliding of concentric tubes. The third direction forms the continuum backbone from the actuators themselves and is hence termed "intrinsically actuated." Actuator selection for intrinsically actuated continuum robots can be from any available type of artificial muscle. This could include pneumatic "McKibben" muscles, hydraulically actuated muscles, muscles based on novel polymers, or shape memory alloys, for example. However, at this time only the pneumatic or hydraulic actuator technologies feature the combination of bending and force generation capabilities for continuum robots at the human scale or larger. At a large scale, the extrinsic tendon-driven designs have the advantage of high force capability. At the small scale, the concentric tendon design has advantages and is already showing promise in numerous medical applications.

Understanding of the kinematics of continuum robots has been the subject of much research and has now reached a mature stage, with theory matching most of the corresponding results for rigid-link robots now established. Indeed, key aspects of the core theory for rigid-link robots can be used to form a baseline model for continuum robot kinematics, as has been discussed herein. Alternatively, the same models can be derived from first principles, and the results are seen to be equivalent. However, continuum robot kinematics modeling presents issues and difficulties not present for rigid-link robots, due to the inherent compliance and infinite degrees of freedom present in continuum robot backbones. Models which take into account the effects on the kinematics from external loading such as from gravity have been established. However, the additional computational complexity in these models remains to be a barrier to implementation at this time.

Computational complexity is also a significant issue in the study and application of continuum robot dynamics, and related subfields. As discussed herein, traditional methods for dynamics formulation, such as the Lagrangian and Newton-Euler approaches, can be extended and adapted to form continuum robot dynamic models. These models are seen to possess the same key structural properties as for rigid-link robots, encouraging the development of corresponding control strategies. However, the continuous nature of the continuum backbone renders these models extremely computationally complex. Some recent work has developed less computationally complex approximate dynamic models. However, at this time, few dynamics-based implementations have been reported, and continuum robot dynamics and control remain active research issues.

Taking advantage of the previous developments, research into continuum robots is actively expanding at the time of writing this paper. New work in areas such as motion planning and contact modeling is extending our underlying body of understanding and widening the scope of the field. Researchers are partnering with various industries to explore continuum robot solutions to such diverse applications such as terrain-adapting continuum-limbed vehicles, ship-to-ship refueling, and exploration of extraterrestrial surfaces. It is anticipated that the next ten years will see an explosion of research, both basic and applied, in the area of continuum robots.

Acknowledgments

This research was supported in part by NASA under NRI Contract NNX12AM01G and in part by the U.S. National Science Foundation under Grant IIS-0904116.

References

[1] M. W. Spong, S. Hutchinson, and M. Vidyasagar, *Robot Modeling and Control*, Wiley, 2006.

[2] J. K. Salisbury, "Whole arm manipulation," in *Proceedings of the 4th Symposium on Robotics Research*, MIT Press, 1987.

[3] V. C. Anderson and R. C. Horn, "Tensor arm manipulator design," *Transactions of the ASME*, vol. 67, DE-57, pp. 1–12, 1967.

[4] G. S. Chirikjian, *Theory and applications of hyperredundant robotic mechanisms [Ph.D. thesis]*, Department of Applied Mechanics, California Institute of Technology, 1992.

[5] G. S. Chirikjian, "Hyper-redundant manipulator dynamics: a continuum approximation," *Advanced Robotics*, vol. 9, no. 3, pp. 217–243, 1994.

[6] S. Hirose, *Biologically Inspired Robots*, Oxford University Press, 1993.

[7] I. A. Gravagne, C. D. Rahn, and I. D. Walker, "Large deflection dynamics and control for planar continuum robots," *IEEE/ASME Transactions on Mechatronics*, vol. 8, no. 2, pp. 299–307, 2003.

[8] M. W. Hannan and I. D. Walker, "Analysis and experiments with an elephant's trunk robot," *Advanced Robotics*, vol. 15, no. 8, pp. 847–858, 2001.

[9] R. Cieślak and A. Morecki, "Elephant trunk type elastic manipulator—a tool for bulk and liquid materials transportation," *Robotica*, vol. 17, no. 1, pp. 11–16, 1999.

[10] G. Immega, "Tentacle-like Manipulators with adjustable tension lines," U.S. Patent 5317952, 1992.

[11] G. Immega and K. Antonelli, "KSI tentacle manipulator," in *Proceedings of the 1995 IEEE International Conference on Robotics and Automation. Part 1 (of 3)*, pp. 3149–3154, Nagoya, Japan, May 1995.

[12] D. M. Lane, J. B. C. Davies, G. Robinson et al., "The AMADEUS dextrous subsea hand: design, modeling, and sensor processing," *IEEE Journal of Oceanic Engineering*, vol. 24, no. 1, pp. 96–111, 1999.

[13] K. Suzumori, S. Iikura, and H. Tanaka, "Development of flexible microactuator and its applications to robotic mechanisms," in *Proceedings of the IEEE International Conference on Robotics and Automation*, pp. 1622–1627, April 1991.

[14] J. F. Wilson, D. Li, Z. Chen, and R. T. George, "flexible robot manipulators and grippers: relatives of elephant trunks and squid tentacles," in *Robots and Biological Systems: Towards a New Bionics?* vol. 102, pp. 474–479, 1993.

[15] G. Robinson and J. B. C. Davies, "Continuum robots—a state of the art," in *Proceedings of the IEEE International Conference on Robotics and Automation (ICRA '99)*, pp. 2849–2854, May 1999.

[16] I. Gravagne and I. D. Walker, "Kinematics for constrained continuum robots using wavelet decomposition," in *Proceedings of the 4th International Conference and Exposition/Demonstration*

on *Robotics for Challenging Situations and Environments*, pp. 292–298, Albuquerque, NM, USA, March 2000.

[17] M. W. Hannan and I. D. Walker, "Kinematics and the implementation of an elephant's trunk manipulator and other continuum style robots," *Journal of Robotic Systems*, vol. 20, no. 2, pp. 45–63, 2003.

[18] B. A. Jones and I. D. Walker, "Kinematics for multisection continuum robots," *IEEE Transactions on Robotics*, vol. 22, no. 1, pp. 43–55, 2006.

[19] D. Trivedi, C. D. Rahn, W. M. Kier, and I. D. Walker, "Soft robotics: biological inspiration, state of the art, and future research," *Applied Bionics and Biomechanics*, vol. 5, no. 3, pp. 99–117, 2008.

[20] R. J. Webster III and B. A. Jones, "Design and kinematic modeling of constant curvature continuum robots: a review," *International Journal of Robotics Research*, vol. 29, no. 13, pp. 1661–1683, 2010.

[21] T. Aoki, A. Ochiai, and S. Hirose, "Study on slime robot development of the mobile robot prototype model using bridle bellows," in *Proceedings of the IEEE International Conference on Robotics and Automation*, pp. 2808–2813, New Orleans, La, USA, May 2004.

[22] H. Ohno and S. Hirose, "Design of slim slime robot and its gait of locomotion," in *Proceedings of the IEEE/RSJ International Conference on Intelligent Robots and Systems*, pp. 707–715, Maui, Hawaii, USA, November 2001.

[23] H. Tsukagoshi, A. Kitagawa, and M. Segawa, "Active hose: an artificial elephant's nose with maneuverability for rescue operation," in *Proceedings of the IEEE International Conference on Robotics and Automation*, pp. 2454–2459, Seoul, Korea, May 2001.

[24] R. Buckingham, "Snake arm robots," *Industrial Robot*, vol. 29, no. 3, pp. 242–245, 2002.

[25] R. Buckingham, OC Robotics, http://www.ocrobotics.com/.

[26] F. W. Grasso, "Octopus sucker-arm coordination in grasping and manipulation," *American Malacological Bulletin*, vol. 24, no. 1-2, pp. 13–23, 2008.

[27] J. L. Van Leeuwen and W. M. Kier, "Functional design of tentacles in squid: linking sarcomere ultrastructure to gross morphological dynamics," *Philosophical Transactions of the Royal Society B*, vol. 352, no. 1353, pp. 551–571, 1997.

[28] F. Martin and C. Niemitz, "How do African elephants (Loxodonta africana) optimize goal-directed trunk movements?" in *Jahresversammlung der Dt. Zool. Ges. und der Dt.Ges. f. Parasitologie*, vol. 96, Berlin, Germany, 2003.

[29] W. M. Kier and K. K. Smith, "Tongues, tentacles and trunks: the biomechanics of movement in muscular-hydrostats," *Zoological Journal of the Linnean Society*, vol. 83, no. 4, pp. 307–324, 1985.

[30] A. Goriely and S. Neukirch, "Mechanics of climbing and attachment in twining plants," *Physical Review Letters*, vol. 97, no. 18, Article ID 184302, 2006.

[31] J. S. Mehling, M. A. Diftler, M. Chu, and M. Valvo, "A minimally invasive tendril robot for in-space inspection," in *Proceedings of the 1st IEEE/RAS-EMBS International Conference on Biomedical Robotics and Biomechatronics (BioRob '06)*, pp. 690–695, February 2006.

[32] I. D. Walker, "Robot strings: long, thin continuum robots," in *Proceedings of the IEEE Aerospace Conference*, pp. 1–12, Big Sky, Mont, USA, 2013.

[33] I. D. Walker, D. M. Dawson, T. Flash et al., "Continuum robot arms inspired by cephalopods," in *Unmanned Ground Vehicle Technology VII*, Proceedings of SPIE, pp. 303–314, Orlando, Fla, USA, March 2005.

[34] J. Bishop-Moser, G. Krishnan, C. Kim, and S. Kota, "Design of soft robotic actuators using fluid-filler fiber-reinforced elastomeric enclosures in parallel combinations," in *Proceedings of the IEEE/RSJ International Conference on Intelligent Robot Systems (IROS '12)*, pp. 4262–4269, Vilamoura, Portugal, 2012.

[35] A. Grzesiak, R. Becker, and A. Verl, "The bionic handling assistant: a success story of additive manufacturing," *Assembly Automation*, vol. 31, no. 4, pp. 329–333, 2011.

[36] B. Bardou, P. Zanne, F. Nageotte, and M. De Mathelin, "Control of a multiple sections flexible endoscopic system," in *Proceedings of the 23rd IEEE/RSJ 2010 International Conference on Intelligent Robots and Systems (IROS '10)*, pp. 2345–2350, Taipei, Taiwan, October 2010.

[37] D. C. Rucker and R. J. Webster III, "Deflection-based force sensing for continuum robots: a probabilistic approach," in *Proceedings of the IEEE/RSJ International Conference on Intelligent Robots and Systems: Celebrating 50 Years of Robotics (IROS '11)*, pp. 3764–3769, San Francisco, Calif, USA, September 2011.

[38] S. Tully, A. Bajo, G. Kantor, H. Choset, and N. Simaan, "Constrained filtering with contact detection for the localization and registration of continuum robots in flexible environments," in *Proceedings of the IEEE International Conference on Robotics and Automation*, pp. 3388–3394, St. Paul, Minn, USA, 2012.

[39] Q. Zhao and F. Gao, "Design and analysis of a kind of biomimetic continuum robot," in *Proceedings of the IEEE International Conference on Robotics and Biomimetics (ROBIO '10)*, pp. 1316–1320, Tianjin, China, December 2010.

[40] J. Shang, C. J. Payne, J. Clark et al., "Design of a multitasking robotic platform with flexible arms and articulated hand for minimally invasive surgery," in *Proceedings IEEE/RSJ International Conference on Intelligent Robot Systems (IROS '12)*, pp. 1998–1993, Vilamoura, Portugal, 2012.

[41] G. Chen, P. M. Tu, T. R. Herve, and C. Prelle, "Design and modeling of a micro-robotic manipulator for colonoscopy," in *Proceedings of the 5th International Workshop on Research and Education in Mechatronics*, pp. 109–114, Annecy, France, 2005.

[42] H.-S. Yoon, S. M. Oh, J. H. Jeong et al., "Active bending endoscope robot system for navigation through sinus area," in *Proceedings of the IEEE/RSJ International Conference on Intelligent Robots and Systems: Celebrating 50 Years of Robotics (IROS '11)*, pp. 967–972, San Francisco, Calif, USA, September 2011.

[43] H. Watanabe, K. Kanou, Y. Kobayashi, and M. G. Fujie, "Development of a "steerable drill" for ACL reconstruction to create the arbitrary trajectory of a bone tunnel," in *Proceedings of the IEEE/RSJ International Conference on Intelligent Robots and Systems: Celebrating 50 Years of Robotics (IROS '11)*, pp. 955–960, San Francisco, Calif, USA, September 2011.

[44] N. Simaan, R. Taylor, and P. Flint, "A dexterous system for laryngeal surgery," in *Proceedings of the IEEE International Conference on Robotics and Automation*, pp. 351–357, New Orleans, La, USA, May 2004.

[45] M. Calisti, A. Arienti, F. Renda et al., "Design and development of a soft robot with crawling and grasping capabilities," in *Proceedings of the IEEE International Conference on Robotics and Automation*, pp. 4950–4955, St. Paul, Minn, USA, 2012.

[46] M. Mahvash and P. E. Dupont, "Stiffness control of a continuum manipulator in contact with a soft environment," in *Proceedings of the 23rd IEEE/RSJ 2010 International Conference on Intelligent

Robots and Systems (IROS '10), pp. 863–870, Taipei, Taiwan, October 2010.

[47] J. Lock, G. Laing, M. Mahvash, and P. E. Dupont, "Quasistatic modeling of concentric tube robots with external loads," in *Proceedings of the 23rd IEEE/RSJ 2010 International Conference on Intelligent Robots and Systems (IROS '10)*, pp. 2325–2332, Taipei, Taiwan, October 2010.

[48] H. Su, D. C. Cardona, W. Shang et al., "A MRI-guided concentric tube continuum robot with piezoelectric actuation: a feasibility study," in *Proceedings IEEE International Conference on Robotics and Automation*, pp. 1939–1945, St. Paul, Minn, USA, 2012.

[49] R. S. Penning, J. Jung, N. J. Ferrier, and M. R. Zinn, "An evaluation of closed-loop control options for continuum manipulators," in *Proceedings of the IEEE International Conference on Robotics and Automation*, pp. 5392–5397, St. Paul, Minn, USA, 2012.

[50] A. Degani, H. Choset, A. Wolf, T. Ota, and M. A. Zenati, "Percutaneous intrapericardial interventions using a highly articulated robotic probe," in *Proceedings of the 1st IEEE/RAS-EMBS International Conference on Biomedical Robotics and Biomechatronics (BioRob '06)*, pp. 7–12, Pisa, Italy, February 2006.

[51] E. J. Butler, R. Hammond-Oakley, S. Chawarski et al., "Robotic neuro-endoscope with concentric tube augmentation," in *Proceedings of the IEEE/RSJ International Conference on Intelligent Robot Systems (IROS '12)*, pp. 2941–2946, Vilamoura, Portugal, 2012.

[52] L. G. Torres, R. J. Webster III, and R. Alterovitz, "Task-oriented design of concentric tube robots using mechanics-based models," in *Proceedings of the IEEE/RSJ International Conference on Intelligent Robots and Systems (IROS '12)*, pp. 4449–4455, Vilamoura, Portugal, 2012.

[53] R. J. Webster III, J. M. Romano, and N. J. Cowan, "Kinematics and calibration of active cannulas," in *Proceedings of the IEEE International Conference on Robotics and Automation (ICRA '08)*, pp. 3888–3895, Pasadena, Calif, USA, May 2008.

[54] E. Guglielmino, N. Tsagarakis, and D. G. Caldwell, "An octopus anatomy-inspired robotic arm," in *Proceedings of the 23rd IEEE/RSJ 2010 International Conference on Intelligent Robots and Systems (IROS '10)*, pp. 3091–3096, Taipei, Taiwan, October 2010.

[55] M. B. Pritts and C. D. Rahn, "Design of an artificial muscle continuum robot," in *Proceedings of the IEEE International Conference on Robotics and Automation*, pp. 4742–4746, New Orleans, La, USA, May 2004.

[56] E. Ayvali and J. P. Desai, "Towards a discretely actuated steerable cannula," in *Proceedings of the IEEE International Conference on Robotics and Automation*, pp. 1614–1619, St. Paul, Minn, USA, 2012.

[57] B. A. Jones, M. Csencsits, W. McMahan et al., "Grasping, manipulation, and exploration tasks with the OctArm continuum manipulator," in *Proceedings of the International Conference on Robotics and Automation*, Orlando, Fla, USA, 2006.

[58] A. Bartow, A. Kapadia, and I. D. Walker, "A novel continuum trunk robot based on contractor muscles," in *Proceedings of the 12th WSEAS International Conference on Signal Processing, Robotics, and Automation*, pp. 181–186, Cambridge, UK, 2013.

[59] W. McMahan, V. Chitrakaran, M. Csencsits et al., "Field trials and testing of "OCTARM" continuum robots," in *Proceedings of the IEEE International Conference on Robotics and Automation (ICRA '06)*, pp. 2336–2341, May 2006.

[60] D. Trivedi, A. Lotfi, and C. D. Rahn, "Geometrically exact dynamic models for soft robotic manipulators," in *Proceedings of the IEEE/RSJ International Conference on Intelligent Robots and Systems (IROS '07)*, pp. 1497–1502, San Diego, Calif, USA, November 2007.

[61] R. Kang, E. Guglielmino, D. T. Branson, and D. G. Caldwell, "Bio-Inspired crawling locomotion of a multi-arm octopus-like continuum system," in *Proceedings of the IEEE/RSJ International Conference on Intelligent Robots and Systems (IROS '12)*, pp. 145–150, Vilamoura, Portugal, 2012.

[62] C. Laschi, B. Mazzolai, V. Mattoli, M. Cianchetti, and P. Dario, "Design of a biomimetic robotic octopus arm," *Bioinspiration and Biomimetics*, vol. 4, no. 1, Article ID 015006, 2009.

[63] M. Rolf and J. J. Steil, "Constant curvature continuum kinematics as fast approximate model for the bionic handling assistant," in *Proceedings of the IEEE/RSJ International Conference on Intelligent Robot Systems (IROS '12)*, pp. 3440–3446, Vilamoura, Portugal, 2012.

[64] J. Ding, K. Xu, R. E. Goldman, P. K. Allen, D. L. Fowler, and N. Simaan, "Design, simulation and evaluation of kinematic alternatives for insertable robotic effectors platforms in single port access surgery," in *Proceedings of the IEEE International Conference on Robotics and Automation (ICRA '10)*, pp. 1053–1058, Anchorage, Alaska, USA, May 2010.

[65] K. Xu, R. E. Goldman, J. Ding, P. K. Allen, D. L. Fowler, and N. Simaan, "System design of an insertable robotic effector platform for Single Port Access (SPA) surgery," in *Proceedings of the IEEE/RSJ International Conference on Intelligent Robots and Systems (IROS '09)*, pp. 5546–5552, St. Louis, MO, USA, October 2009.

[66] K. Xu, J. Zhao, J. Geiger, A. J. Shih, and M. Zheng, "Design of an endoscopic stitching device for surgical obesity treatment using a N.O.T.E.S approach," in *Proceedings of the IEEE/RSJ International Conference on Intelligent Robots and Systems: Celebrating 50 Years of Robotics (IROS '11)*, pp. 961–966, San Francisco, Calif, USA, September 2011.

[67] S. Wakimoto and K. Suzumori, "Fabrication and basic experiments of pneumatic multi-chamber rubber tube actuator for assisting colonoscope insertion," in *Proceedings of the IEEE International Conference on Robotics and Automation (ICRA '10)*, pp. 3260–3265, Anchorage, Alaska, USA, May 2010.

[68] B. A. Jones, W. McMahan, and I. D. Walker, "Design and analysis of a novel pneumatic manipulator," in *Proceedings of the 3rd IFAC Symposium on Mechatronic Systems*, pp. 745–750, Sydney, Australia, 2004.

[69] W. McMahan, B. A. Jones, and I. D. Walker, "Design and implementation of a multi-section continuum robot: air-octor," in *Proceedings of the IEEE IRS/RSJ International Conference on Intelligent Robots and Systems (IROS '05)*, pp. 3345–3352, Edmonton, Canada, August 2005.

[70] Y. J. Kim, S. Cheng, S. Kim, and K. Iagnemma, "Design of a tubular snake-like manipulator with stiffening capability by layer jamming," in *Proceedings of the IEEE/RSJ International Conference on Intelligent Robot Systems (IROS '12)*, pp. 4251–4256, Vilamoura, Portugal, 2012.

[71] A. Sadeghi, L. Beccai, and B. Mazzolai, "Innovative soft robots based on electro-rheological fluids," in *Proceedings of the IEEE/RSJ International Conference on Intelligent Robot Systems (IROS '12)*, pp. 4237–4242, Vilamoura, Portugal, 2012.

[72] N. G. Cheng, M. B. Lobovsky, S. J. Keating et al., "Design and analysis of a robust, low-cost, highly articulated manipulator enabled by jamming of granular media," in *Proceedings of the*

IEEE International Conference on Robotics and Automation, pp. 4328–4333, St. Paul, Minn, USA, 2012.

[73] A. Jiang, G. Xynogalas, P. Dasgupta, K. Althoefer, and T. Nanayakkara, "Design of a variable stiffness flexible manipulator with composite granular jamming and membrane coupling," in *Proceedings IEEE/RSJ International Conference on Intelligent Robots and Systems (IROS '12)*, pp. 2922–2927, Vilamoura, Portugal, 2012.

[74] M. Giorelli, F. Renda, M. Calisti, A. Arienti, G. Ferri, and C. Laschi, "A two dimensional inverse kinetics model of a cable-driven manipulator inspired by the octopus arm," in *Proceedings of the IEEE International Conference on Robotics and Automation*, pp. 3819–3824, St. Paul, Minn, USA, 2012.

[75] H. Mochiyama and T. Suzuki, "Dynamics modeling of a hyper-flexible manipulator," in *Proceedings of the 41st SICE Annual Conference*, pp. 1505–1510, Osaka, Japan, 2002.

[76] H. Mochiyama and T. Suzuki, "Kinematics and dynamics of a cable-like hyper-flexible manipulator," in *Proceedings of the IEEE International Conference on Robotics and Automation*, pp. 3672–3677, Taipei, Taiwan, September 2003.

[77] H. Mochiyama, "Whole-arm impedance of a serial-chain manipulator," in *Proceedings of the IEEE International Conference on Robotics and Automation*, pp. 2223–2228, Seoul, Korea, May 2001.

[78] G. S. Chirikjian and J. W. Burdick, "Modal approach to hyper-redundant manipulator kinematics," *IEEE Transactions on Robotics and Automation*, vol. 10, no. 3, pp. 343–354, 1994.

[79] I. S. Godage, E. Guglielmino, D. T. Branson, G. A. Medrano-Cerda, and D. G. Caldwell, "Novel modal approach for kinematics of multisection continuum arms," in *Proceedings of the IEEE/RSJ International Conference on Intelligent Robots and Systems: Celebrating 50 Years of Robotics (IROS '11)*, pp. 1093–1098, San Francisco, Calif, USA, September 2011.

[80] D. B. Camarillo, C. F. Milne, C. R. Carlson, M. R. Zinn, and J. K. Salisbury, "Mechanics modeling of tendon-driven continuum manipulators," *IEEE Transactions on Robotics*, vol. 24, no. 6, pp. 1262–1273, 2008.

[81] D. B. Camarillo, C. R. Carlson, and J. K. Salisbury, "Task-space control of continuum manipulators with coupled tendon drive," in *Experimental Robotics: The 11th International Symposium*, O. Khatib, V. Kumar, and G. Pappas, Eds., pp. 271–280, Springer, 2009.

[82] S. Neppalli, M. A. Csencsits, B. A. Jones, and I. D. Walker, "Closed-form inverse kinematics for continuum manipulators," *Advanced Robotics*, vol. 23, no. 15, pp. 2077–2091, 2009.

[83] F. Renda and C. Laschi, "A general mechanical model for tendon-driven continuum manipulators," in *Proceedings of the IEEE International Conference on Robotics and Automation*, pp. 3813–3818, St. Paul, Minn, USA, 2012.

[84] I. A. Gravagne and I. D. Walker, "Manipulability, force, and compliance analysis for planar continuum manipulators," *IEEE Transactions on Robotics and Automation*, vol. 18, no. 3, pp. 263–273, 2002.

[85] L. G. Torres and R. Alterovitz, "Motion planning for concentric tube robots using mechanics-based models," in *Proceedings of the IEEE/RSJ International Conference on Intelligent Robots and Systems: Celebrating 50 Years of Robotics (IROS '11)*, pp. 5153–5159, San Francisco, Calif, USA, September 2011.

[86] J. Jung, R. S. Penning, N. J. Ferrier, and M. R. Zinn, "A modeling approach for continuum robotic manipulators: effects of nonlinear internal device friction," in *Proceedings of the*

IEEE/RSJ International Conference on Intelligent Robots and Systems: Celebrating 50 Years of Robotics (IROS '11), pp. 5139–5146, San Francisco, Calif, USA, September 2011.

[87] D. C. Rucker, B. A. Jones, and R. J. Webster III, "A model for concentric tube continuum robots under applied wrenches," in *Proceedings of the IEEE International Conference on Robotics and Automation (ICRA '10)*, pp. 1047–1052, Anchorage, Alaska, USA, May 2010.

[88] A. Bajo and N. Simaan, "Finding lost wrenches: using continuum robots for contact detection and estimation of contact location," in *Proceedings of the IEEE International Conference on Robotics and Automation (ICRA '10)*, pp. 3666–3673, Anchorage, Alaska, USA, May 2010.

[89] I. S. Godage, D. T. Branson, E. Guglielmino, G. A. Medrano-Cerda, and D. G. Caldwell, "Shape function-based kinematics and dynamics for variable-length continuum robotic arms," in *Proceedings of the IEEE International Conference on Robotics and Automation*, pp. 452–457, Shanghai, China, September 2011.

[90] E. Tatlicioglu, I. D. Walker, and D. M. Dawson, "New dynamic models for planar extensible continuum robot manipulators," in *Proceedings of the IEEE/RSJ International Conference on Intelligent Robots and Systems (IROS '07)*, pp. 1485–1490, San Diego, Calif, USA, November 2007.

[91] R. Kang, A. Kazakidi, E. Guglielmino et al., "Dynamic model of a hyper-redundant, octopus-like manipulator for underwater applications," in *Proceedings of the IEEE/RSJ International Conference on Intelligent Robots and Systems: Celebrating 50 Years of Robotics (IROS '11)*, pp. 4054–4059, San Francisco, Calif, USA, September 2011.

[92] W. Khalil, G. Gallot, O. Ibrahim, and F. Boyer, "Dynamic modeling of a 3-D serial eel-like robot," in *Proceedings of the IEEE International Conference on Robotics and Automation*, pp. 1270–1275, Barcelona, Spain, April 2005.

[93] A. Kapadia, E. Tatlicioglu, D. Dawson, and I. D. Walker, "A new approach to extensible continuum robot control using the sliding-mode," *Computer Technology and Application*, vol. 2, no. 4, pp. 293–300, 2011.

[94] D. Braganza, D. M. Dawson, I. D. Walker, and N. Nath, "Neural network grasping controller for continuum robots," in *Proceedings of the 45th IEEE Conference on Decision and Control (CDC '06)*, pp. 6445–6449, San Diego, Calif, USA, December 2006.

[95] N. Giri and I. D. Walker, "Three module lumped element model of a continuum arm section," in *Proceedings of the IEEE/RSJ International Conference on Intelligent Robots and Systems: Celebrating 50 Years of Robotics (IROS '11)*, pp. 4060–4065, San Francisco, Calif, USA, September 2011.

[96] R. S. Penning, J. Jung, J. A. Borgstadt, N. J. Ferrier, and M. R. Zinn, "Towards closed loop control of a continuum robotic manipulator for medical applications," in *Proceedings IEEE International Conference on Robotics and Automation*, pp. 4822–4827, 2011.

[97] T. Zheng, D. T. Branson III, R. Kang et al., "Dynamic continuum arm model for use with underwater robotic manipulators inspired by Octopus vulgaris," in *Proceedings of the IEEE International Conference on Robotics and Automation*, pp. 5289–5294, St. Paul, Minn, USA, 2012.

[98] M. Ivanescu, N. Bizdoaca, and D. Pana, "Dynamic control for a tentacle manipulator with SMA actuators," in *Proceedings of the IEEE International Conference on Robotics and Automation*, pp. 2079–2084, Taipei, Taiwan, September 2003.

[99] M. Ivanescu and V. Stoian, "A Variable structure controller for a tentacle manipulator," in *Proceedings of the 1995 IEEE International Conference on Robotics and Automation. Part 1 (of 3)*, pp. 3155–3160, May 1995.

[100] A. Kapadia and I. D. Walker, "Task-space control of extensible continuum manipulators," in *Proceedings of the IEEE/RSJ International Conference on Intelligent Robots and Systems: Celebrating 50 Years of Robotics (IROS '11)*, pp. 1087–1092, San Francisco, Calif, USA, September 2011.

[101] M. W. Hannan and I. D. Walker, "Real-time shape estimation for continuum robots using vision," *Robotica*, vol. 23, no. 5, pp. 645–651, 2005.

[102] B. Weber, P. Zeller, and K. Kuhnlenz, "Multi-camera based real-time configuration estimation of continuum robots," in *Proceedings IEEE/RSJ International Conference on Intelligent Robot Systems (IROS '12)*, pp. 3550–3555, Vilamoura, Portugal, 2012.

[103] J. Li and J. Xiao, "Determining "grasping" configurations for a spatial continuum manipulator," in *Proceedings of the IEEE/RSJ International Conference on Intelligent Robots and Systems: Celebrating 50 Years of Robotics (IROS '11)*, pp. 4207–4214, San Francisco, Calif, USA, September 2011.

[104] L. A. Lyons, R. J. Webster III, and R. Alterovitz, "Planning active cannula configurations through tubular anatomy," in *Proceedings of the IEEE International Conference on Robotics and Automation (ICRA '10)*, pp. 2082–2087, Anchorage, Alaska, USA, May 2010.

[105] J. Xiao and R. Vatcha, "Real-time adaptive motion planning for a continuum manipulator," in *Proceedings of the 23rd IEEE/RSJ 2010 International Conference on Intelligent Robots and Systems (IROS '10)*, pp. 5919–5926, Taipei, Taiwan, October 2010.

[106] M. Saha and P. Isto, "Motion planning for robotic manipulation of deformable linear objects," in *Proceedings of the IEEE International Conference on Robotics and Automation (ICRA '06)*, pp. 2478–2484, Orlando, Fla, USA, May 2006.

[107] A. Kapadia, E. Tatlicioglu, and I. D. Walker, "Teleoperation control of a redundant continuum manipulator using a non-redundant rigid-link master," in *Proceedings of the IEEE/RSJ International Conference on Intelligent Robots and Systems (IROS '12)*, pp. 3105–3110, Vilamoura, Portugal, 2012.

[108] M. Csencsits, B. A. Jones, W. McMahan, V. Iyengar, and I. D. Walker, "User interfaces for continuum robot arms," in *Proceedings of the IEEE IRS/RSJ International Conference on Intelligent Robots and Systems, IROS 2005*, pp. 3011–3018, Edmonton, Canada, August 2005.

[109] W. McMahan and I. D. Walker, "Octopus-inspired grasp synergies for continuum manipulators," in *Proceedings of the IEEE International Conference on Robotics and Biomimetics*, pp. 945–950, Bangkok, Thailand, 2009.

[110] Y. Yekutieli, R. Sagiv-Zohar, B. Hochner, and T. Flash, "Dynamic model of the octopus arm. II: control of reaching movements," *Journal of Neurophysiology*, vol. 94, no. 2, pp. 1459–1468, 2005.

[111] A. Kapadia and I. D. Walker, "Self-Motion analysis of extensible continuum manipulators," in *Proceedings of the IEEE International Conference on Robotics and Automation*, Karlsruhe, Germany, May 2013.

[112] I. S. Godage, T. Nanayakkara, and D. G. Caldwell, "Locomotion with continuum limbs," in *Proceedings IEEE/RSJ International Conference on Intelligent Robot Systems (IROS '12)*, pp. 293–298, Vilamoura, Portugal, 2012.

[113] I. D. Walker, "Continuum robot appendages for traversal of uneven terrain in in situ exploration," in *Proceedings of the IEEE Aerospace Conference (AERO '11)*, Big Sky, Mont, USA, March 2011.

[114] M. Sfakiotakis, A. Kazakidi, N. Pateromichelakis, J. A. Ekaterinaris, and D. P. Tsakiris, "Robotic underwater propulsion inspired by the octopus multi-arm swimming," in *Proceedings of the IEEE International Conference on Robotics and Automation*, pp. 3833–3839, St. Paul, Minn, USA, 2012.

[115] L. Cowan and I. D. Walker, "The importance of continuous and discrete elements in continuum robots," *International Journal of Advanced Robot Systems*, vol. 10, pp. 1–13, 2013.

[116] A. Kapoor, N. Simaan, and R. H. Taylor, "Suturing in confined spaces: constrained motion control of a hybrid 8-DoF robot," in *Proceedings of the 12th International Conference on Advanced Robotics (ICAR '05)*, pp. 452–459, Seattle, Wash, USA, July 2005.

[117] A. Kapoor, K. Xu, W. Wei, N. Simaan, and R. H. Taylor, "Telemanipulation of snake-like robots for minimally invasive surgery of the upper airway," in *Proceedings of the 9th International Conference on Medical Image Computing and Computer-Assisted Intervention (MICCAI) Medical Robotics Workshop*, 2006.

[118] G. P. Scott, C. G. Henshaw, D. Walker, and B. Willimon, "Autonomous robotic refueling of an unmanned surface vehicle in varying sea states," submitted to *Journal of Field Robotics*.

[119] J. Merino, A. L. Threatt, I. D. Walker, and K. E. Green, "Kinematic models for continuum robotic surfaces," in *Proceedings of the IEEE/RSJ International Conference on Intelligent Robots and Systems (IROS '12)*, pp. 3453–3460, Vilamoura, Portugal, 2012.

14

Biologically Inspired Perimeter Detection for Whole-Arm Grasping

David Devereux,[1] Robert Richardson,[2] Arjun Nagendran,[3] and Paul Nutter[1]

[1] *Department of Computer Science, University of Manchester, M13 9PL, UK*
[2] *School of Mechanical Engineering, University of Leeds, LS2 9JT, UK*
[3] *Institute for Simulation and Training, University of Central Florida, 32826, USA*

Correspondence should be addressed to Robert Richardson; r.c.richardson@leeds.ac.uk

Academic Editors: J. Archibald, A. Hamzaoui, and J.-S. Liu

Grasping is a useful ability that allows manipulators to constrain objects to a desired location or trajectory. Whole-arm grasping is a specific method of grasping an object that uses the entire surface of the manipulator to apply contact forces. Elephant trunks and snakes and octopus arms are illustrative of these methods. One of the greatest challenges of whole-arm grasping in poorly defined environments is accurately identifying the perimeter of an object. Existing algorithms for this task use restrictive assumptions or place unrealistic demands on the required hardware. Here, a new algorithm (termed Octograsp) has been developed as a method of gaining information on the shape of the grasped object through tactile information alone. The contact information is processed using an inverse convex hull algorithm to build a model of the object's shape and position. The performance of the algorithm is examined using both simulated and experimental hardware. Methods of increasing the level of contact information through repeated contact attempts are presented. It is demonstrated that experimentally obtained, coarsely spaced, contact information can result in an accurate model of an object's shape and position.

1. Introduction

To grasp an object is to seize or hold it, thereby constraining it to a desired position or trajectory. Industrial robots implement finger-tip grasping (based around biological inspiration from humans) to perform tasks on objects that are normally well defined, often rigid, and always considerably smaller than the robotic manipulator. Robotic systems are increasingly being considered for new application areas where the operating requirements are more complex and less well defined; consider the use of robotic end-effectors for the assembly of complex machines with components of varying size and consistency. For applications such as these, an alternative approach to robotic grasping is required. Whole-arm grasping is an alternative to finger-tip grasping [1, 2] that is used by animals such as elephants, snakes and octopuses. Whole-arm grasping uses the entire surface of the manipulator to provide contacts between the object and manipulator. This allows the distribution of grasp forces and an increased surface area to aid the grasping of smooth

objects. For example, consider the scenario of Figure 1 where a 10-link multiple section robot arm has encircled an object and is applying grasping forces. Each link has the capability of exerting forces at various points along the objects body. The grasping control aim is to exert the minimum forces whilst grasping the object.

At each of the contacts between an object and manipulator there is a force applied to the object f_i. This force causes a torque τ_i around the centre of mass. The torque and force can be combined into a single vector called a wrench, as shown in

$$\mathbf{w}_i = \begin{pmatrix} f_i \\ \tau_i \end{pmatrix} = \begin{pmatrix} f_i \\ r_i \times f_i \end{pmatrix}, \tag{1}$$

where r_i is a vector from the centre of mass of the object to the contact point i. The set of all wrenches forms the wrench space.

The quality of a grasp is a measure of its ability to reject all possible external wrenches acting on the object, one measure

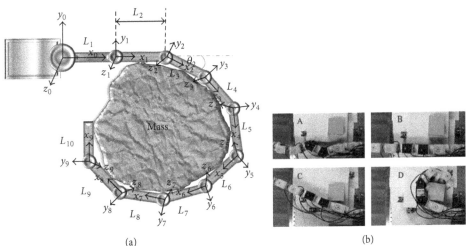

FIGURE 1: (a) Coordinate frames are assigned to a 10-link serial link manipulator, with "z" in all frames pointing out of the page. Link lengths can vary and are measured between joint centers as shown for L_2. Counter-clockwise rotation about the z-axis is positive. Controlling the manipulator so that it encircles an object and applies the necessary forces at all contact points to ensure a stable grasp is referred to as whole-arm grasping. (b) Experimental hardware demonstrating whole-arm grasping. Stages of the whole-arm grasping include (A) starting from an initial random position, (B) straightening out prior to a "sweep-phase", (C) proximal joints sweeping prior to contact, and (D) distal joints sweeping to complete the encirclement.

often used being the wrench ball measure [3]. The unfortunate drawback of wrench ball method is that it does not give any indication of stability. If a method simply attempts to maximise the measure, then points on extremes of facets are chosen. This risks the possibility of unstable grasps due to positioning errors, which may place contacts past edges thereby drastically changing the grasp. This problem is mitigated using whole-arm grasping as the idea is to apply lots of contact, which provides more redundancy in the grasp.

An accurate definition of the perimeter of an object is required so that the locations and magnitude of constraining forces can be identified. Existing approaches make additional demands in terms of equipment and processing power in order to be effective. In general, they require additional equipment, such as cameras, graphics cards, or force sensitive skins, and/or are computationally expensive. Current methods assume the availability of a tactile sensor skin that stretches over the surface of the manipulator; an example method is by Asano et al. [4] who use the contact location and force information to dynamically manipulate an object. Unfortunately, the fully force sensitive skin has yet to be developed, and so these methods remain simulations. This may yet change due to new material research. One such material is ionic electroactive polymers as used by Shahinpoor [5] and, more recently, Biddiss and Chau [6] who both describe using IPMCs as touch sensors. The tactile information can be processed to obtain a model of the shape and position of the unknown object. Methods for discovering the shape and location of an object through contact information alone must be able to intentionally, systematically, and reactively contact the object. The control algorithms must react to the contacts such that the positional disturbance of the object is minimised. These reactive methods can be used to fully encircle an object and gain information about the surface of that object.

Busch [7] describes three reactive methods that could be employed to grasp an object by using whole-arm grasping. The first method is the same method of grasping as McMahan et al. [8], Walker et al. [9], and Desai et al. [10]; Busch calls this method *Zorro*. The method contains two competing controllers, one of which attempts to make the end-effector of the robot circle around the object, while the other attempts to keep the body of the robot away from the object. The combination of these two controllers causes the arm to tighten around the object as the end-effector circles the object. The second method is the *Follow-the-Leader* method. This method operates by initially making the end-effector contact and follow the surface of the object, while the remaining links follow the path the end-effector took along the surface of the object. This approach is based on the work by Reznik and Lumelsky [11]. Both approaches require the availability of a force sensitive skin to detect contacts, contours, and forces. The last method is called *Lasso* and requires the use of sensors covering the entirety of the arm that can detect the distance to any object normal to the sensor. The *Lasso* method encircles the object without making contact with it, meanwhile, the object's structure is analysed for grasp planning purposes with the hypothetical sensors. All three of these methods analyse the structure of the object on the fly and reactively move to adapt the grasp to the object. Unfortunately the *Lasso* and *Follow-the-Leader* methods require additional complex sensors, whilst the *Zorro* method requires the knowledge of the object's position and shape.

A new method that does not require additional sensors other than those needed for actuation in a closed-loop system and also does not require excessive assumptions/prior knowledge may therefore be beneficial. The contributions of this paper are in demonstrating how to interpret and combine the coarse contact information provided by such a

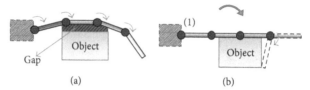

FIGURE 2: (a) All joints move simultaneously resulting in contact at link 3 and leaving a gap between object and manipulator. (b) Only base joint moves until contact is made—the result is multiple points of contact at link 2 and link 3. Link 4 then moves inward until contact is made, resulting in wraparound.

method, through a novel and systematic object exploration algorithm. The approach taken here is as follows. A snake-like serial-link manipulator is first controlled to encircle a free-moving object. This is performed using a joint-based impedance control scheme that stops the links from moving as soon as contact is detected. Multiple attempts at encircling the object are made that include placing the manipulator in a different reference position relative to the object. The contact information obtained from these attempts is preserved and added to the gathered data. This data is then passed to an algorithm called the *inverse convex hull*. The algorithm filters the contact information from the innermost links and forms a continuous shape that is representative of the object being grasped from them.

The rest of this paper is organised as follows. Section 2 details a newly proposed novel method for gathering contact information. Section 3 describes a method for analysing that contact information to model the shape and position of the object to be grasped. Section 4 describes the experimental equipment used to examine the performance of algorithms, which is demonstrated and discussed in Section 5.

2. Gathering the Contact Information

A new method inspired by the motion of an octopus's arm has been developed that can reactively and systematically interact with the object to gain the required contact information to determine its shape for grasping. An octopus has an amazing amount of flexibility, but it only uses relatively simplistic and planar movements [12]. One method the octopus has for grasping an object begins by bringing the arm into contact with the object a small distance down from the tip of the arm. Progressively more links of the arm are then brought into contact with the object until the object is entirely encircled [9]. This method can be thought of as a combination of the *Zorro* and *Follow-the-Leader* methods. The method does not use the object's shape information but instead relies on its octopus-like movements that can result in a partial envelopment of the object. This in turn will provide the required contact information to analyse the object's shape, although multiple attempts at contacting the object may be required to gain enough information to accurately model the object completely. The method proposed here mimics this process and has been termed an *Octograsp* in homage to its inspiration.

In the following work, a fixed base serial link manipulator with rigid links is used to demonstrate the *Octograsp* algorithm. The algorithm initializes the serial link manipulator

by aligning all the joints to a straight line. During the wraparound stage, only one joint of the serial link manipulator is moved at a time, until the object is completely encircled. Moving only one joint at a time may improve efficiency in terms of the amount of contacts being made, while also preventing the arm from displacing the object during the motion. This is illustrated in Figure 2(a) where all of the links have been moved simultaneously, and a gap results between the object and arm. In Figure 2(b) only the base joint has been moved causing the rest of the arm to sweep across the environment. This method results in a flat contact between the object and arm.

A feed-forward computed torque controller using the Recursive Newton Euler dynamics with a secondary PID controller for disturbance rejection is used to decouple the joints and achieve the desired torques. The manipulator itself is controlled using a joint-based impedance controller that is described in detail in Section 5. It has been shown in previous work [13] that the same methods outlined in this work operate well without the additional torque sensors; they are used here to improve the performance of the impedance controller.

2.1. Detecting the Contacts. The joint angles can provide valuable information on the perimeter of an object. At each instant in time, the desired and actual positions of the joints are known. If the error between them breaches a normal operating error threshold, then it can be assumed that a contact has occurred and react accordingly. This type of process is called a model reference controller [14].

The initial experiments using the *Octograsp* algorithm showed that although the object can be encircled with a snake-like arm, very limited information regarding the contacts is available with one attempt. This is especially the case when using the highly simplified experimental robot described in Section 4. To compensate for this, and to gain more information, multiple attempts at grasping can be made. Two methods are proposed towards this. (i) The first involves moving the base of the arm to a different initial position relative to the object, resulting in new contact information. There may, however, be errors in the global movement or measurement of the base. (ii) The second alters the contact positions of the links by limiting the rotation of the baselink during encirclement; a reduction in the base link rotation restricts the reach of the arm and thereby repositions the links. The amount the baselink which is restricted is referred to as a *back amount* in the remainder of the paper (e.g., a back amount of 0.5 radians means the base link stopped rotating 0.5 radians from an unrestricted encirclement). The

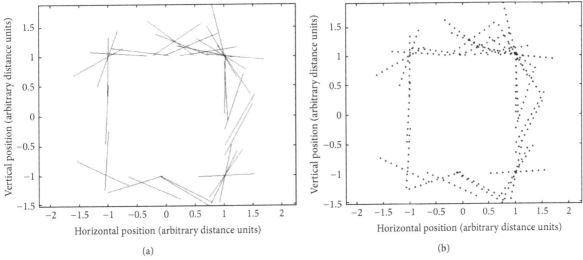

FIGURE 3: (a) Known link positions during the grasp. (b) Result of discretising link positions.

technique of restricting the baselink will be referred to from now on as the *multiple orientations* method. Once contact information has been obtained, a method is required to process this information to gain a model of the shape and location of the object.

3. Interpreting the Contact Information

A numerical simulation was created to develop algorithms to process contact information into object perimeter information. Thirty rigid independent links were randomly placed on the perimeter of a simulated square. It can be seen from Figure 3(a) that the absence of links passing through the central part of the figure suggests that the shape is square. A method will now be described that can model the shape of an object by inferring it from this absence of links.

3.1. Inverse Convex Hull. The innermost parts of the links represent the object circumference. An algorithm is required to indentify the contact points and convert them into an object perimeter. The commonly used convex hull algorithm produces a perimeter that encloses a set of points. The problem described here is the opposite to a convex hull, as a perimeter that contains no points (links) is required. This problem can be solved using the inverse convex hull algorithm [15], which selects a set of points that forms a shape that contains no points. The inverse convex hull algorithm first inverts the distance of discrete points from an origin, following which the convex hull of that set is found. The origin point needs to be located within the object, ideally as close to the centre as possible. In this work, the mean of the contact locations gives the origin, since the mean returns a position within the object as long as the arm contacts the object evenly across its entire surface. The corresponding points from the original set are the inverse convex hull set. Since the inverse convex hull processes discrete points, it requires discrete link positions. This involves converting the continuous links into a set of individual points. The number

of points that each link is converted into, that is, the level of discretisation, is a user-controlled parameter. Figure 3(b) shows the discretisation of the links, using 10 points per line.

Each of the i points is represented as an n-dimensional vector ($\mathbf{P}_i$) that specifies its position relative to an origin; the origin needs to be located within the object. In the 3D case, $\mathbf{P}_i$ would be represented as

$$\mathbf{P}_i = \begin{bmatrix} x & y & z \end{bmatrix}^{\mathrm{T}}. \tag{2}$$

The distance of each of the points from the origin (r_i) is

$$r_i = \sqrt{\mathbf{P}_i \cdot \mathbf{P}_i}. \tag{3}$$

To invert that distance, such that the distant points are now the closest and vice versa, the distance is raised to a negative power ($-A_{\mathrm{exp}}$) which is another user-controlled parameter. The inverted scalar distance (d_i) is calculated as

$$d_i = r_i^{-A_{\mathrm{exp}}}. \tag{4}$$

Finally, the direction of each point needs to be preserved such that only the distance is inverted. The convex hull is then generated from those inverted data points $\mathbf{P}_i^{\mathrm{inv}}$, where

$$\mathbf{P}_i^{\mathrm{inv}} = d_i \frac{\mathbf{P}_i}{|\mathbf{P}_i|}. \tag{5}$$

This process has been applied to all of the points in Figure 3(b) with the result shown in Figure 4. Each of the points are at the same angle as they originally were, but the points that were the closest to the origin are now the furthest and vice versa. The shape that this conversion forms depends upon the value of A_{exp}. Low values, such as 0.05 as used in this example, tend to squeeze the points together forming a circular shape (as seen in Figure 4).

The final step involves finding the convex hull of the inverted points and matching them to the corresponding points within the original set. Figure 5 shows the original

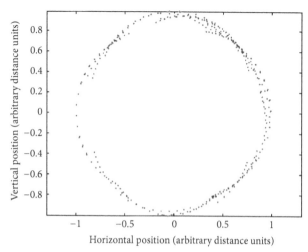

FIGURE 4: The discretised points after their distance from a centre point has been inverted.

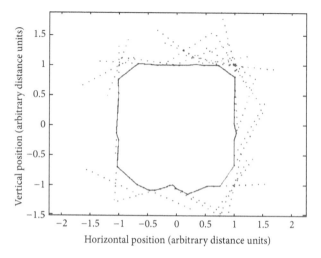

    ·   Discretised link positions
   —— Generated object

FIGURE 5: The points making up the object's shape are determined by finding the corresponding points making-up the convex hull of the points in Figure 4.

discretised points and the polygon that is the inferred shape of the object. It can be seen that the inferred object, which is a square, is not 100% accurate, due to the lack of contacts at certain points along the length of the square. Therefore, the aim of the algorithm is to gain as much surface contact over the object as possible. However, even with full contact, the algorithm has two problems. Firstly, even with perfect information, an amount of rounding at corners will occur, the precise amount depends on the value of A_{exp}. Secondly, modelling of concave objects will be troublesome as the inverse convex hull algorithm tends to smooth over them. Further discussion of these problems and their consequences are presented later in this section.

3.2. Inverse Convex Hull Parameters. The two user-controlled parameters of the inverse convex hull algorithm, level of discretisation and A_{exp}, will each have an effect on the quality of the resulting object shape generated. Investigations were conducted to examine the effects of each parameter and to determine their optimal values. Three shapes were used in each of the investigations: an equilateral triangle, a square, and a regular pentagon. A circle of diameter 2 units encloses the shapes and therefore lengths of their sides were 1.7321, 1.4142, and 1.1756 arbitrary distance units, respectively. Equation (6) is used to measure the accuracy by returning a percentage error (Err) with zero being the best and lowest possible outcome as follows:

$$Err = 100 * \frac{A_{gen} + A_{orig} - 2A_{int}}{A_{orig}}, \qquad (6)$$

where A_{orig} is the area of the actual shape, and A_{gen} is the area of the generated shape, A_{int} is the area of the intersection between the actual and generated shapes. The area of intersection between two shapes is difficult to calculate for the case where the two shapes can be any size and shape. Therefore, an algorithm [16] was used that breaks the objects into very small discrete elements that are analysed for whether the shapes overlap, intersect, or do not overlap in that

element. The sum total of the area of those that overlap and intersect approximates the area of overlap. Decreasing the size of the discrete elements increases the accuracy of the resulting intersection calculation.

3.2.1. Investigating the Discretization Parameter. The set of previously mentioned shapes was analysed with the inverse convex hull algorithm several times with varying levels of discretisation. To isolate the discretization parameter from errors in measured input data, the shapes themselves were used as the input to the algorithm instead of the data obtained from robot contact in simulation. A_{exp} was held at a constant value of 0.05 for the duration of this experiment.

The percentage area error for the three shapes when the level of discretisation varies between 10 and 1000 points per segment of the shape is shown in Figure 6. The area error is very low for all shapes and discretisation levels since perfect information is being fed to the inverse convex hull algorithm. It can be seen that the error is quite variable in the region between 10 and 200 points but settles down to a consistent low value beyond that region. A value of more than 100 and less than 300 points per segment is therefore recommended since lower values are not consistent, whilst higher values increase the amount of data that needs to be processed. Figure 7 shows an approximately linear correlation between the level of discretisation and the computation time. This is confirmed by the fact that the objects with fewer sides consume lesser time during computation.

3.2.2. Investigating the A_{exp} Parameter. The effect of varying A_{exp} (see (4)) while keeping discretization level constant at 100 was investigated, with the same three objects serving as input to the inverse convex hull algorithm. Figure 8 shows this effect on the area error for values between 0.05 and 1. The graph's trend in general shows an increase in error as A_{exp} is

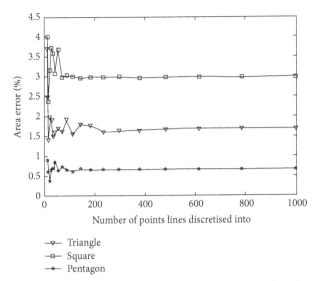

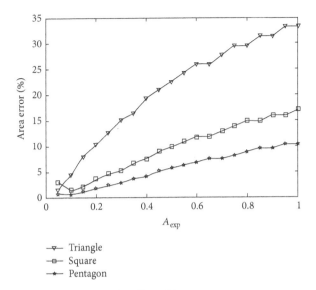

FIGURE 6: The effect of discretisation level on area error when A_{exp} is fixed at 0.05.

FIGURE 8: The effect of A_{exp} on area error.

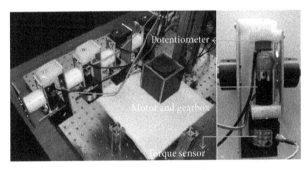

FIGURE 9: The experimental setup.

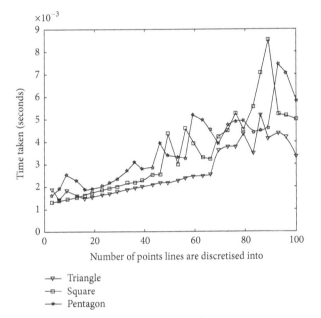

FIGURE 7: The effect of discretisation level on computation time.

increased. This is due to an increased amount of rounding at corners.

4. Experimental Platform

The proposed algorithm was evaluated using experimental equipment. This stage is crucial as a large proportion of work in the area of multilink snake-like robots for manipulation is restricted to simulations due to ideal assumptions and technology demands. The experimental equipment is designed to demonstrate whole-arm grasping with coarse contact information. The manipulator consists of four links and contains minimal sensors. The hardware has been designed to be modular such that it can be reconfigured with a minimal

effort and allows for the possibility of correction if a particular configuration is found to be lacking. The experimental manipulator (shown in Figure 9) consists of four identical modules with each module consisting of a motor, gearbox, potentiometer, and torque sensor. The control of the arm and the acquisition and processing of contact data are performed using LabView on a standard desktop PC.

The results obtained from the experiments are 2D, although the algorithm can process 3D information by exploring multiple planes using one of the two methods explained in Section 2. 2D information may be sufficient for grasping purposes; the only disadvantage is that potentially stronger grasps in alternative planes will not be discovered. However, there is generally little difference between the strength of good and optimal grasps [17].

5. Joint-Based Impedance Control

Individual joints are controlled by an impedance controller. Impedance control attempts to implement a dynamic relationship between manipulator variables such as force and end point position, rather than controlling each of these variables alone [18]. A conventional impedance controller [19] defines a relationship between the position and velocity

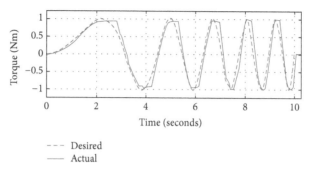

FIGURE 10: Closed-loop torque control.

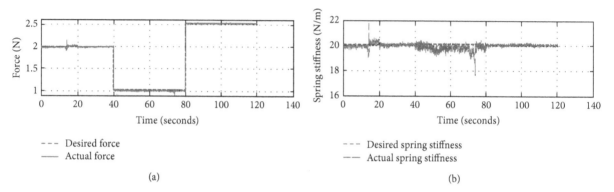

FIGURE 11: Experimental verification of the target impedance with spring constant of 20 N/m.

error of the end-effector and the force the end-effector applies (and therefore the torques at each joint). The joint-based impedance controller operates instead in the joint space allowing for a dependable contact behaviour at the cost of having to manually calculate a trajectory. This is a biologically inspired scheme that is capable of mimicking muscular compliance. As the error in tracking a certain response deviates from the expected behaviour, the impedance scheme reduces the amount of torque applied, resulting in reduction of overall torque of the joint. Hence less force is exerted by the link tip, and this reduces the risk of displacing the object. Furthermore, having such a scheme in place allows for smooth transition between the contact and not contact states and enables smoother actuator loads with minimum jerk.

Under ideal conditions, the computed torque controller enables joint space trajectories to be tracked very closely. Closed-loop torque control response of one of the joints to a chirp signal of magnitude 1 Nm, varying in normalized frequency between 0 and 0.05 Hz, is shown in Figure 10. The desired torque is accurately tracked with some phase lag and friction effects.

A closed-loop torque controller for a spring constant of 20 N/m was implemented at the joint tip. End-effector force for a single link was measured using a sensor and compared to the desired force generated by the impedance scheme. The corresponding stiffness from the relationship of force and position was computed. The results show a good agreement between the theoretical and experimental responses as seen in Figure 11.

6. Evaluation of Performance

The performance of the *Octograsp* algorithm at analysing the shape of an object was examined by varying the algorithm parameters and comparing the generated model of the object to the actual object. It must be noted that due to the limited number and size of the links, the objects being examined could not be fully encircled and touched. As a result, the evaluation of modeling will only focus on the sides being contacted. The accuracy of the generated model when multiple attempts at contacting the object are made from the same relative position (method 2 from Section 2.1(ii)) was examined. The parameters that were controlled were (i) the number of attempts at encircling and (ii) the amount the base joint of the robot moves back after each attempt (back amount). A square object was positioned and orientated the same for each run of the experiment with camera-based tracking used to verify the exact location. The inverse convex hull algorithm was used to generate a model of the object from the obtained contact information and compared to the known location and shape of the object to find the accuracy error.

An example of the contact information provided by a typical *Octograsp* is shown in Figure 12(a). The example shows four attempts at grasping the object with a back amount of 0.1 radians. The four-end configurations of the arm (one sequence of lines with dots for each attempt) are shown in relation to the actual object (dashed lines). The path of the centre of the free-moving square object (obtained from camera-based tracking) shows the displacement of the object

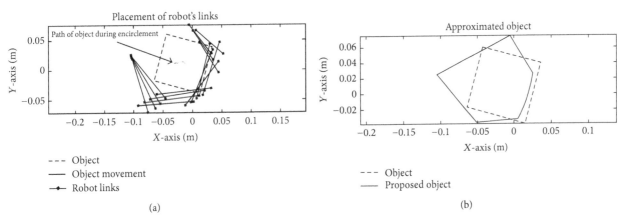

(a)

(b)

FIGURE 12: Example result from a run where 4 attempts were made with back amount of 0.1 radians.

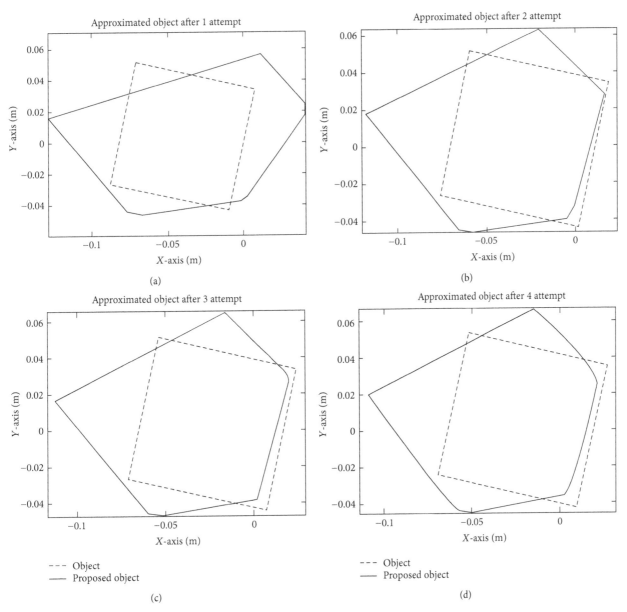

(a)

(b)

(c)

(d)

FIGURE 13: The shape being more accurately represented as more attempts are made.

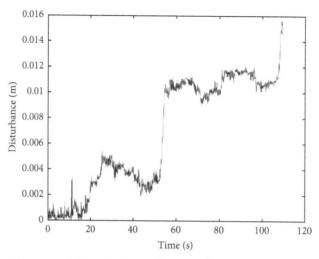

FIGURE 14: Displacement of object during first four encircling attempts from the first position.

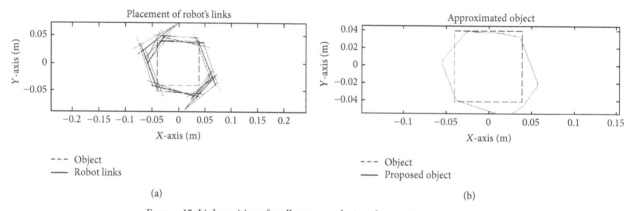

FIGURE 15: Link positions for all attempts during the grasping experiment.

over time due to contact. The major disturbance to the object is caused when the link of the arm fully coincides with a face of the square. As a result, later attempts by link 4 pass through where the square shape should be positioned, since the square is no longer present having been pushed by previous attempts. The resulting model generated by the inverse convex hull algorithm is shown in Figure 12(b).

Figures 13(a)–13(d) show how the shape is progressively builtup and improved upon after each successive attempt. The displacement of the object causes the right hand side to be underestimated while the lack of contacts on the other sides causes those sides to be overestimated in size; the overestimation arises from a lack of information that could be readily corrected through a longer snake arm or multiple robot positions. The important result is that the side of the square encircled accurately represents the objects original shape.

The object was encircled from two different base positions, with the second position rotated by π radians from the first position. There were four attempts per position with a back amount of 0.1 radians. It was found that the accuracy error reduced significantly after each position change attempt, dropping by about 30%. Analysing the object from

the second position greatly improves upon the accuracy and compensates for the displacement of the object.

The object disturbance over time for the first four encircling attempts is shown in Figure 14. Each contact produces a small but noticeable increase in object disturbance. At roughly 55 seconds, there is a prominent spike that is the cause of the increase in model error. The overall disturbance is however less than 16 mm after four encircling attempts. This is a significant result for the proposed joint-based impedance control scheme given that the robot weighs 1.672 Kg and the object only weighs 200 g.

The information provided by the eight attempts at contacting the object and the resulting model produced by that contact information are shown in Figure 15. This result illustrates that the accuracy of the produced model can be increased (in comparison to results from Figure 12) by contacting the object multiple times from different positions and orientations. Object displacement can be limited by making the manipulator lightweight in comparison with the object and also by reducing the manipulator's speed of operation. The amount of contact information gathered can be improved by increasing the number of links and reducing their size.

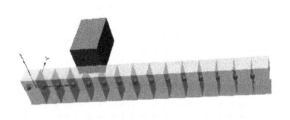

FIGURE 16: Simulation setup of manipulator with several small links grasping an object.

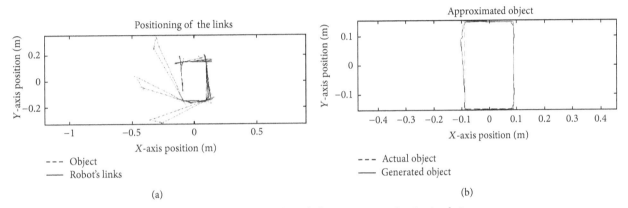

(a)

(b)

FIGURE 17: Placement of links and object representation in simulation.

6.1. Improvements through Increased Number of Links. To demonstrate the effectiveness of the algorithms under representative conditions, a simulated robot that consists of greater number of smaller links was analysed. The simulation setup is shown in Figure 16. The dynamic simulation environment was created in *MSC Visual Nastran 4D* and controlled using *Matlab-Simulink*.

The *Octograsp* algorithm was used to encircle the cuboid object from three positions, each rotated by $(\pi/4)$ degrees from each other. Two attempts at encircling the object with a back amount of 0.7 radians were made in each position for a total of 6 attempts. As before, the resulting contact information was processed using the inverse convex hull algorithm to determine the object's shape and compared with the known shape, position, and orientation of the object. The results were similar to that of the experimental situation in that there is a significant decrease in representation accuracy error when encircling from the second position (reduced from 19.9% to 9% on the third attempt). The final error for this experiment is only 4% and demonstrates that an increased number of links of reduced size provides for higher resolution data.

Figure 17 shows the contact information provided by each encircling attempt and the resulting object representation from the simulation. Having several small links in comparison to the length of the side of the object allows the arm to contact much more of the straight sides of the object in parallel, which in turn provides a large amount of useful contact information that can produce an accurate representation of the object.

7. Conclusion

In this paper, methods for building a model of an object from tactile information have been presented. The *Octograsp* algorithm allows snake-like robots to gain contact information regarding the shape of an object. The inverse convex hull algorithm can then process that contact information in order to determine the object's shape and position. Both of the methods require no external sensors, such as touch sensors, but also do not preclude their use. The method is generic enough to work on any kinematic serial chain (snake-like) robot. In general, the *Octograsp* and inverse convex hull algorithm can generate accurate models of objects without the need for sophisticated sensors. The algorithms were implemented experimentally as well as in simulation, with the experimental kit providing coarse information and demonstrating the feasibility of the method for real-world application, while the simulation was used to demonstrate the accuracy of the method based on drawbacks identified with the experimental equipment.

It was found that the best approach was to select as many positions around the object as possible but only make two attempts in each position, one where direct contact is made and another with as large a shift in the base joint as possible.

This ensured that the largest amount of different surface contact is made, with minimal object disturbance.

A drawback of the proposed approach is that concave objects cannot be accurately represented with these methods. However, these concave elements are often not required to obtain a good grasp and may in some cases be too small in comparison to the robot's size to fully utilise. The second issue is that of object disturbance; a minor disturbance has a negative effect on the resulting accuracy of the object representation.

References

[1] J. R. Napier, "The prehensile movements of the human hand," *The Journal of Bone & Joint Surgery—British Volume*, vol. 38, no. 4, pp. 902–913, 1956.

[2] K. Salisbury, "Whole arm manipulation," in *Proceedings of the 4th Symposium on Robotics Research*, pp. 183–189, 1988.

[3] D. Kirkpatrick, B. Mishra, and C.-K. Yap, "Quantitative Steinitz's theorems with applications to multifingered grasping," *Discrete & Computational Geometry*, vol. 7, no. 1, pp. 295–318, 1992.

[4] F. Asano, Z.-W. Luo, M. Yamakita, and S. Hosoe, "Dynamic modeling and control for whole body manipulation," in *Proceedings of the IEEE/RSJ International Conference on Intelligent Robots and Systems (IROS '03)*, vol. 4, pp. 3162–3167, October 2003.

[5] M. Shahinpoor, "Ionic polymer-conductor composites as biomimetic sensors, robotic actuators and artificial muscles—a review," *Electrochimica Acta*, vol. 48, no. 14–16, pp. 2343–2353, 2003.

[6] E. Biddiss and T. Chau, "Electroactive polymeric sensors in hand prostheses: bending response of an ionic polymer metal composite," *Medical Engineering & Physics*, vol. 28, no. 6, pp. 568–578, 2006.

[7] C. Busch, *Whole-arm grasping with hyper-redundant planar manipulators using neural networks [Ph.D. dissertation]*, Vorarlberg University of Applied Sciences, 2002.

[8] W. McMahan, B. Jones, I. Walker, V. Chitrakaran, A. Seshadri, and D. Dawson, "Robotic manipulators inspired by cephalopod limbs," in *Proceedings of the CDEN Design Conference*, Montreal, Canada, July 2004.

[9] I. D. Walker, D. M. Dawson, T. Flash et al., "Continuum robot arms inspired by cephalopods," in *Unmanned Ground Vehicle Technology VII*, vol. 5804 of *Proceedings of SPIE*, pp. 303–314, March 2005.

[10] R. Desai, C. Rosenberg, and J. Jones, "Kaa: an autonomous serpentine robot utilizes behavior control," in *Proceedings of the IEEE/RSJ International Conference on Intelligent Robots and Systems: Human Robot Interaction and Cooperative Robots*, vol. 3, pp. 250–255, August 1995.

[11] D. Reznik and V. Lumelsky, "Multi-finger "hugging": a robust approach to sensor-based grasp planning," in *Proceedings of IEEE International Conference on Robotics and Automation*, vol. 1, pp. 754–759, May 1994.

[12] Y. Y. Yekutieli, S. G. German, F. T. Tamar, and H. B. Binyamin, "How to move with no rigid skeleton? The octopus has the answers," *Biologist*, vol. 49, no. 6, pp. 250–254, 2002.

[13] D. Devereux, P. Nutter, and R. Richardson, "Reactive and pre-planned encirclement for whole arm grasping," in *Proceedings of the 7th IEEE International Conference on Industrial Informatics (INDIN '09)*, pp. 668–673, June 2009.

[14] P. J. McKerrow, *Introduction To Robotics*, Addison Wesley, 4th edition, 1998.

[15] F. D. Snyder, D. D. Morris, P. H. Haley, R. T. Collins, and A. M. Okerholm, "Autonomous river navigation," in *Mobile Robots XVII*, vol. 5609 of *Proceedings of SPIE*, pp. 221–232, October 2004.

[16] P. Koprowski, "areaintersection.m," http://www.mathworks.cn/matlabcentral/fileexchange/15557-areaintersection-m, 2007.

[17] D. Devereux, *Control strategies for whole arm grasping [Ph.D. thesis]*, The University of Manchester, Manchester, UK, 2010.

[18] N. Hogan, "Impedance control: an approach to manipulation," in *Proceedings of IEEE American Control Conference*, pp. 304–313, 1984.

[19] J. K. Salisbury and B. Roth, "Kinematic and force analysis of articulated hands," *ASME Journal of Mechanisms, Transmissions, and Automation in Design*, vol. 105, no. 1, pp. 33–41, 1982.

Permissions

The contributors of this book come from diverse backgrounds, making this book a truly international effort. This book will bring forth new frontiers with its revolutionizing research information and detailed analysis of the nascent developments around the world.

We would like to thank all the contributing authors for lending their expertise to make the book truly unique. They have played a crucial role in the development of this book. Without their invaluable contributions this book wouldn't have been possible. They have made vital efforts to compile up to date information on the varied aspects of this subject to make this book a valuable addition to the collection of many professionals and students.

This book was conceptualized with the vision of imparting up-to-date information and advanced data in this field. To ensure the same, a matchless editorial board was set up. Every individual on the board went through rigorous rounds of assessment to prove their worth. After which they invested a large part of their time researching and compiling the most relevant data for our readers. Conferences and sessions were held from time to time between the editorial board and the contributing authors to present the data in the most comprehensible form. The editorial team has worked tirelessly to provide valuable and valid information to help people across the globe.

Every chapter published in this book has been scrutinized by our experts. Their significance has been extensively debated. The topics covered herein carry significant findings which will fuel the growth of the discipline. They may even be implemented as practical applications or may be referred to as a beginning point for another development. Chapters in this book were first published by Hindawi Publishing Corporation; hereby published with permission under the Creative Commons Attribution License or equivalent.

The editorial board has been involved in producing this book since its inception. They have spent rigorous hours researching and exploring the diverse topics which have resulted in the successful publishing of this book. They have passed on their knowledge of decades through this book. To expedite this challenging task, the publisher supported the team at every step. A small team of assistant editors was also appointed to further simplify the editing procedure and attain best results for the readers.

Our editorial team has been hand-picked from every corner of the world. Their multi-ethnicity adds dynamic inputs to the discussions which result in innovative outcomes. These outcomes are then further discussed with the researchers and contributors who give their valuable feedback and opinion regarding the same. The feedback is then collaborated with the researches and they are edited in a comprehensive manner to aid the understanding of the subject.

Apart from the editorial board, the designing team has also invested a significant amount of their time in understanding the subject and creating the most relevant covers. They scrutinized every image to scout for the most suitable representation of the subject and create an appropriate cover for the book.

The publishing team has been involved in this book since its early stages. They were actively engaged in every process, be it collecting the data, connecting with the contributors or procuring relevant information. The team has been an ardent support to the editorial, designing and production team. Their endless efforts to recruit the best for this project, has resulted in the accomplishment of this book. They are a veteran in the field of academics and their pool of knowledge is as vast as their experience in printing. Their expertise and guidance has proved useful at every step. Their uncompromising quality standards have made this book an exceptional effort. Their encouragement from time to time has been an inspiration for everyone.

The publisher and the editorial board hope that this book will prove to be a valuable piece of knowledge for researchers, students, practitioners and scholars across the globe.

List of Contributors

Guillermo Enriquez and Shuji Hashimoto
Department of Advanced Science and Engineering,Waseda University, 3-4-1 Okubo, Shinjuku, Tokyo 169-8555, Japan

Sunhong Park
Korea Automotive Technology Institute, 303 Pungse-ro, 303 Pungse-ro, Pungse-Myeon, Dongnam-gu, Cheonan-si, Chungnam 330-912, Republic of Korea

H. F. Yu, E. H. K. Fung, and X. J. Jing
Department of Mechanical Engineering, Hong Kong Polytechnic University, Hung Hom, Kowloon, Hong Kong

Nadya Ghrab
National Institute of Applied Science and Technology (INSAT), Northern Urban Center Mailbox 676, 1080 Tunis, Tunisia

Hichem Kallel
Department of Physics and Electrical Engineering, National Institute of Applied Science and Technology (INSAT), Tunisia

Faridoon Shabani, Bijan Ranjbar and Ali Ghadamyari
School of Electrical Engineering, Shiraz University, Shiraz, Iran

M. H. Korayem, A. M. Shafei and F. Absalan
Mechanical Engineering Department, Iran University of Science and Technology, Narmak, Tehran 13114-16846, Iran

Evgeny Lazarenko, Satoshi Kitano, Shigeo Hirose and Gen Endo
Fukushima Laboratory Department of Mechanical and Aerospace Engineering, Tokyo Institute of Technology, Ishikawadai 1st Building, 2-12-1 I1-52 Ookayama, Meguro-ku, Tokyo 152-8552, Japan

K. D. Do
Department of Mechanical Engineering, Curtin University of Technology, Perth, WA 6845, Australia

Pong-in Pipatpaibul and P. R. Ouyang
Department of Aerospace Engineering, Ryerson University, Toronto, ON, Canada

A. Al-Asasfeh
Department of Mechanical Engineering,The University of Jordan, P.O. Box 962069, Sport City, Amman 11196, Jordan

N. Hamdan
Mechanical Engineering Department, King Faisal University, Al Hofuf, Saudi Arabia

Z. Abo-Hammour
Department of Mechatronics Engineering,The University of Jordan, Amman, Jordan

Iñaki Navarro and Fernando Matía
ETSI Industriales, Universidad Politécnica de Madrid, c/José Gutiérrez Abascal, 2, 28006 Madrid, Spain

Maurizio Melluso
CIRIAS-C.I. di Ricerca dell'Automazione e dei Sistemi, University of Palermo, Palermo 90128, Italy

Bryan Willimon, Ian Walker and Stan Birchfield
Department of Electrical and Computer Engineering, Clemson University, Clemson, SC 29634, USA

Ian D. Walker
Department of Electrical and Computer Engineering, Clemson University, Clemson, SC 29634, USA

David Devereux and Paul Nutter
Department of Computer Science, University of Manchester, M13 9PL, UK

Robert Richardson
School of Mechanical Engineering, University of Leeds, LS2 9JT, UK

Arjun Nagendran
Institute for Simulation and Training, University of Central Florida, 32826, USA

Printed in the USA
CPSIA information can be obtained
at www.ICGtesting.com
JSHW051442221024
72173JS00006B/1556